Where Happiness Dwells

Where Happiness Dwells
A History of the Dane-zaa First Nations

ROBIN RIDINGTON AND JILLIAN RIDINGTON
in collaboration with
ELDERS OF THE DANE-ZAA FIRST NATIONS

UBC Press • Vancouver • Toronto

© UBC Press 2013

All rights reserved. No part of this publication may be reproduced, stored in a retrieval system, or transmitted, in any form or by any means, without prior written permission of the publisher, or, in Canada, in the case of photocopying or other reprographic copying, a licence from Access Copyright, www. accesscopyright. ca.

21 20 19 18 17 16 15 14 13   5 4 3 2

Printed in Canada on FSC-certified ancient-forest-free paper (100% post-consumer recycled) that is processed chlorine- and acid-free.

Library and Archives Canada Cataloguing in Publication

Ridington, Robin
   Where happiness dwells : a history of the Dane-zaa First Nations / Robin Ridington and Jillian Ridington ; in collaboration with elders of the Dane-zaa First Nations.

Includes bibliographical references and index.
Also issued in electronic format.
ISBN 978-0-7748-2295-4 (bound); ISBN 978-0-7748-2296-1 (pbk.)

   1. Tsattine Indians – Peace River Region (B.C. and Alta.) – History. 2. Tsattine Indians – Peace River Region (B.C. and Alta.) – Interviews. 3. Oral tradition – Peace River Region (B.C. and Alta.). 4. Oral history – Peace River Region (B.C. and Alta.). 5. Doig River First Nation. 6. Blueberry River First Nation. I. Ridington, Jillian II. Blueberry River First Nation III. Doig River First Nation IV. Title.

E99.T77R54 2013   971.1'87004972   C2012-907099-8

Canadä

UBC Press gratefully acknowledges the financial support for our publishing program of the Government of Canada (through the Canada Book Fund), the Canada Council for the Arts, and the British Columbia Arts Council.

This book has been published with the help of a grant from the Canadian Federation for the Humanities and Social Sciences, through the Awards to Scholarly Publications Program, using funds provided by the Social Sciences and Humanities Research Council of Canada, and with the help of the K.D. Srivastava Fund.

Printed and bound in Canada by Friesens
Set in New Baskerville and Charis SIL by Artegraphica Design Co. Ltd.
Copy editor: Lesley Erickson
Proofreader: Helen Godolphin

UBC Press
The University of British Columbia
2029 West Mall
Vancouver, BC V6T 1Z2
www.ubcpress.ca

Contents

Illustrations / vii

Preface, with Linguistic Note and Pronunciation Guide / xi

Introduction: Trails of Time / 1

1 The Dane-zaa Creation Story / 10

2 Tsááyaa, the Culture Hero / 25

3 Shin kaa, the Vision Quest / 45

4 Archaeology, Prehistory, and Oral History / 67

5 The Early Fur Trade / 97

6 The Later Fur Trade and the Hudson's Bay Company Killings / 113

7 Priests and Dreamers / 136

8 The First and Last Dreamers / 156

9 Kinship and Community / 197

10 The 1899 North West Mounted Police Census and Treaty 8 / 219

11 Seasonal Rounds in British Columbia and Alberta / 234

12 The 1918 Flu Epidemic / 253

13 Losing Suu Na chii k'chige, the Great Fire, and Petersen's Crossing / 277

14 The Place Where Happiness Dwells, Indian Reserve 172 / 302

15 Today and Tomorrow / 341

16 Dane-zaa Stories and the Anthropological Literature / 359

Appendices / 371

Works Cited / 382

Acknowledgments / 390

Index / 392

Illustrations

Maps

Areas referred to in the text / 4

Rupert's Land / 98

Sweeney Creek area / 250

Wildlife units within proposed Site C reservoir / 348

K'ih tsaaʔdze Tribal Park / 356

Figures

Billy Attachie, ca. 1968 / xii

Howard Broomfield, Jillian Ridington, and Robin Ridington, 1978 / 7

Charlie Yahey with Dreamer's drum, 1968 / 23

A sacred rock in Dane-zaa territory / 48

Elder May Apsassin with granddaughter, 2010 / 56

Charlie Dominic on horseback, ca. 1960 / 60

Eskama at Doig, 1968 / 71

Tommy Attachie at Beaver Camp, 2002 / 93

The confluence of the Halfway and Peace rivers / 103

Charlie Yahey and Aku, 1966 / 105

Chief Sagónáá? at Doig, 1920s / 108

A reconstruction of Rocky Mountain Fort / 111

Ts'ibiisaa, 1964 / 123

Traders at Fort St. John, 1902 / 132

Dane-zaa at Fort St. John, 1906 / 135

Image of bird at the gate to heaven / 149

Charlie Yahey and Aanaatswęą at Doig, 1968 / 159

Marguerite Yahey (Mrs. Pete) Davis, 2003 / 169

Amaa (Mrs. Skookum) and Marguerite Jumbie, Halfway, 1968 / 186

Alice Askoty, Alice Attachie, Charlie Yahey, Aanaatswęą, Murray Attachie, and Albert Askoty, 1968 / 199

Moccasins by Margaret Dominic Davis / 201

Aku, Charlie Yahey, and Aanaatswęą, 1968 / 203

Nachę, 1966 / 209

Dane-zaa at Fort St. John, 1914 / 231

Old Village on the Blueberry Reserve, 1966 / 232

Nachę at Doig, 1966 / 235

Tommy Attachie at Moose Creek cabin, 1981 / 243

Tommy Davis driving Jack Acko's team of horses and wagon, 1966 / 249

Johnny Chipesia with Robin's truck, 1966 / 254

Ts'ibiisaa (George Chipesia), 1929 / 256

Khatakose Harvey in 1929 / 257

Ano Davis (Dedama) on horseback, 1950s / 269

Jebís (Old Davis) and son John Davis, 1929 / 272

Atluke, 1929 / 275

Chief Attachie, 1915 / 276

Slim Byrnes, 1982 / 279

Winnis Baker, 1982 / 280

Sally Makadahay, 1979 / 285

Gerry Attachie at Petersen's Crossing, 2009 / 291

Rene Dominic and Gerry Attachie, Doig River Reserve, 1966 / 296

Roundup at Doig, 1979 / 298

Chief Norman Davis with his great-grandfather Chief Sagónáá?'s coat, 2010 / 304

Albert Askoty and Alice Moccasin, 1960s / 318

Elder John Davis, 1995 / 325

Doig River First Nation Band Hall and Cultural Complex, May 2010 / 342

Sam Acko teaching boys to drum, 2010 / 342

Gathering for a meal at Nenan Youth and Elders Camp, 2009 / 343

Old Blueberry Reserve, 1966 / 345

Garry Oker teaching a training session for environmental assessment team, 2009 / 345

Tommy and Billy Attachie at their grandfather's grave, 2010 / 347

Jack Askoty demonstrating snowshoe making at Doig Days, 2010 / 351

Brian Jungen, *The Men of My Family* / 353

Artwork by Garry Oker / 354

Sam Acko performing a story for schoolchildren, 2010 / 368

Preface, with Linguistic Note and Pronunciation Guide

Where Happiness Dwells, a history of the Dane-zaa First Nations, focuses on the people who were known as the Fort St. John Beaver Band until they divided into the Doig River and Blueberry River First Nations in 1977. A large part of the book takes the form of stories told by Dane-zaa elders and recorded on tape, minidisc, and video. The citations refer to recordings in the Ridington/Dane-zaa Archive, which is in our possession. Many of the stories have been digitized and are available online.* Although we recorded a few stories in English, most were told in Dane-zaa Záágé? (Beaver), an Athapaskan language. We owe a great deal to Doig linguistic expert Billy Attachie as well as to Madeline Oker, Eddie Apsassin, Margaret Davis, Maryann Adekat, Lana Wolf, and Liza Wolf for their translations of Dane-zaa texts. We also owe a debt of gratitude to linguists Marshall and Jean Holdstock, Patrick Moore, and Julia Miller for providing a proper orthography of Dane-zaa words.

To help readers understand these stories, we include the pronunciation guide used in *Dane Wajich: Dane-zaa Stories and Songs – Dreamers and the Land,* a National Museum of Canada virtual website developed by Amber Ridington and Kate Hennessy in collaboration with members of the Doig community and participating linguists. Previous scholars

---

* Search online for "Ridington/Dane-zaa Digital Archive" for further information on accessing the archive.

Billy Attachie, a Doig linguistic expert, ca. 1968. Photo by Robin Ridington

used the terms *Dunne-za* or *Beaver Indians,* but following Billy Attachie's direction, we use *Dane-zaa* throughout the book.*

Dane-zaa Záágé? (Beaver Language) Pronunciation Guide †

This guide, based on the *Doig River Dictionary* by Marshall Holdstock and Jean Holdstock, is intended as an introduction to pronouncing and writing the sounds used in Dane-zaa Záágé?. Since Dane-zaa Záágé? has sounds not found in English, these descriptions in English are only close approximations.

To begin learning the language, go to the virtual website,‡ where you can hear Billy Attachie pronouncing the alphabet. Click on each letter and then practise the pronunciation.

---

* We have chosen to retain the simple and most common orthography of *Dane-zaa,* with no underline under the z.
† © Doig River First Nation, 2006. Prepared by Billy Attachie, Patrick Moore, and Julia Miller, July 2006. Funded in part by a grant from the Volkswagen Foundation and titled "Beaver Knowledge Systems: Documentation of a Canadian First Nation Language from a Place Name Perspective."
‡ See http://www.museevirtuel-virtualmuseum.ca/sgc-cms/expositions-exhibitions/danewajich/.

PREFACE, WITH LINGUISTIC NOTE AND PRONUNCIATION GUIDE xiii

Beaver Letter	Beaver Word	English meaning	English equivalent (or near equivalent) of the sound
a	gat	"tree"	Sounds like the vowel in the English word *cut*.
aa	saa	"sun"	Sounds like the sound at the beginning of the English word *ah*.
ąą	aháą	"yes"	Sounds like Beaver *aa*, but pronounced through the nose.
ae	egae	"spoon"	Sounds like the two vowels *a* and *e* pronounced as a single vowel, with the *a* brief and the *e* longer.
ai	hak'ai	"cow"	Sounds like the two vowels *a* and *ii* pronounced as a single vowel.
b	bes	"knife"	Sounds like the consonant at the beginning of *ball*.
ch	aché?	"tail"	Sounds like the consonant at the beginning of *chain*.
ch'	ch'ǫnê	"coyote"	Sounds like the consonant at the beginning of *chain*, except the sound is glottalized so there is a "popping" sound.
d	dane	"person"	Sounds like the consonant at the beginning of *dog*.
dl	dlezhe	"grizzly"	Sounds like a sequence of *d* followed by *l* as in *toddler*.
dz	adzě?	"heart"	Sounds like a sequence of *d* followed by *z* as in the English word *lids*.
d̲z̲	d̲z̲eníi	"calendar"	Sounds like a sequence of *d* followed by *z* as in the English word *lids*, except with the tongue just behind or between the teeth.
e	s̲e	"belt"	Sounds like the vowel in *face* but without the glide to *i* at the end of the vowel.
ę	ębaa	"weasel"	Sounds like the Beaver vowel *e* said through the nose.
ea	dabea	"sheep"	Sounds like the vowel in the English word *hat*.
ęą	kulęą	"old man"	Sounds like the Beaver vowel *ea* said through the nose.
g	gaah	"rabbit"	Sounds like the consonant at the beginning of the English word *goat*.

▶

Beaver Letter	Beaver Word	English meaning	English equivalent (or near equivalent) of the sound
gh	ghaje	"goose"	This sound is different than any English sound, although in rapid speech many English speakers change the *g* sound of *ragged* to a sound that is close to the *gh* sound of Beaver.
h	aháą	"yes"	Sounds like the consonant at the beginning of *hen*.
	hadaa	"moose"	In many words *h* has a stronger sound at the beginning of syllables.
i	shin	"song"	Sounds like the vowel in *stick*.
ii	jiih	"grouse"	Sounds like the vowel in *seat*.
j	jéyǫʔ	"bull moose"	Sounds like the consonant at the beginning of *job*.
k	ke	"shoes"	Sounds like the sound at the beginning of *kite*.
k'	k'at	"willow"	Sounds like the consonant at the beginning of *kite*, except the sound is glottalized so there is a "popping" sound.
l	alááʔ	"boat"	Sounds like the consonant at the beginning of *leaf*.
lh	lhuuge	"fish"	This sound is different than any English sound. It has the sibilant quality of *s,* but the air comes around the sides of the tongue.
m	męlh	"snare"	Sounds like the consonant at the beginning of *me*.
n	nódaa	"lynx"	Sounds like the consonant at the beginning of *net*.
o	gogosh	"pig"	Sounds like the vowel at the beginning of *only*.
ǫ	at'ǫʔ	"leaf"	Sounds like the vowel at the beginning of *only,* but pronounced through the nose.
s	sas	"bear"	Sounds like the consonant at the beginning of *son*.
s̲	s̲án	"star"	Sounds like the consonant at the beginning of *son,* except with the tongue just behind or between the teeth.
sh	shin	"song"	Sounds like the sound at the beginning of *she*.

Beaver Letter	Beaver Word	English meaning	English equivalent (or near equivalent) of the sound
t	tís	"crutch"	Sounds like the consonant at the beginning of *tea*.
t'	at'ǫ?	"leaf"	Sounds like the consonant at the beginning of *tea*, except the sound is glottalized so there is a "popping" sound.
tl	tle̱zaa	"dog"	Sounds like a sequence of *t* followed by Beaver *lh*. There is no similar sound in English.
tl'	tl'uulh	"rope"	Sounds like a sequence of *t* followed by Beaver *lh*, except the sound is glottalized so there is a "popping" sound. There is no similar sound in English.
ts	tsáá?	"beaver"	Sounds like a sequence of *t* followed by *s* as at the end of *lets*.
t̲s̲	t̲s̲e	"pipe"	Sounds like a sequence of *t* followed by *s* as at the end of *lets*, except with the tongue just behind or between the teeth.
ts'	ts'ádé?	"blanket"	Sounds like a sequence of *t* followed by *s* as at the end of *lets*, except the sound is glottalized so there is a "popping" sound.
t̲s̲'	t̲s̲'iih	"mosquito"	Sounds like a sequence of *t* followed by *s* as at the end of *lets*, except the sound is glottalized so there is a "popping" sound and the tongue is just behind or between the teeth.
u	chush	"down feather"	Sounds like the vowel in *book*.
uu	chuu	"water"	Sounds like the vowel in *food*.
w	wa̱lále	"butterfly"	Sounds like the consonant at the beginning of *worm*.
y	ya̱s̲	"snow"	Sounds like the consonant at the beginning of *yes*.
z	mazíí?	"his/her body"	Sounds like the consonant at the beginning of *zigzag*.
zh	dézhaa	"she/he has started to go"	Sounds like the second consonant in *measure*.

Accents used			English equivalent (or near equivalent) of the sound
Beaver	Beaver	English	
ʔ	ma'aahé?	"his/her snowshoes"	Sounds like the consonant sound that comes between the two parts of *Oh-Oh!* It is heard as a break between vowels.
á	táádézhaa	"he is going up"	The acute accent (high tone) indicates that the vowel has a relatively higher pitch.
ě	maděʔ	"his/her eye"	The hachek over the vowel indicates a rising pitch.
ê	ch'ǫnê	"coyote"	The circumflex over the vowel indicates a falling pitch.

Where Happiness Dwells

Introduction: Trails of Time

"Those stories I remember, that's what I live by now." When Billy Attachie told us this, he was talking about the stories his grandmother Nachę had told him and her other grandchildren, but he was also talking about stories that had been told for centuries by the Dane-zaa people. *Dane-zaa* means "real people" in Dane-zaa Záágé? or Beaver, an Athapaskan language. Nachę had learned the stories from her first husband, Apąa, in the early years of the twentieth century. She told them to Billy and his siblings when they were children, many years ago. This is the nature of oral history, and all history, for history is a series of stories. Nachę, and many of the other elders whose stories make this book possible, have followed their relatives along *yaak'ihts'ę? atanii,* the trail to heaven. The elders say that heaven is like Su Na chii k'chige, the summer gathering place where people from different bands met to sing and dance and renew their relationships. Lana Wolf translates *Su Na chii k'chige* as "the place where happiness dwells." Former chief Gerry Attachie suggested that *Where Happiness Dwells* would be a suitable title for this book.

When the chief and council of the Doig River First Nation of the Dane-zaa asked us to create a history of their people based on oral histories, we knew that our work would be to put together and explain all the wise stories the Dane-zaa had told us over the past half century. We wrote this book in collaboration with Dane-zaa people who have kept their stories alive for millennia. Whenever possible, Dane-zaa people tell their own stories. We add information from historical documents only when necessary to help non-Dane-zaa understand the context. We wrote this book so future generations of Dane-zaa can know and understand their heritage and so interested lay readers and other First Nations can have access to Dane-zaa knowledge. Consequently, we have kept the language accessible. Readers who want to learn more about the academic literature pertaining to northern First Nations will find a discussion of relevant sources in Chapter 16, "Dane-zaa Stories and the Anthropological Literature."

The history of the people who are members of the Doig River and Blueberry First Nations is a trail of time, a trail of braided stories. We recorded most of the stories in this book in Dane-zaa Záágéʔ. Robin recorded some of them from elders in the 1960s. We recorded others specifically for this book. In both cases, we relied on the expertise of bilingual translators to convey the meaning of Dane-zaa Záágéʔ words in English. In the 1960s, Robin used two tape recorders. He played the original story as told in Beaver on one recorder and recorded the translation on the other. We now use a computer to play digital audio files and transcribe the translations directly into a word-processing program. We take careful note of the time code of the original recording. Recordings and translations were on reel-to-reel tape before Robin developed a system for cataloguing them. Recordings and translations from the 1960s are catalogued according to the name of the speaker and the translator. Some are included in an unpublished collection of the translations called Beaver Tales; others appear in our later publications (see Works Cited). For those recordings that were transferred to or recorded as digital audio files and then catalogued, we note the catalogue references. Many people contributed to the translation process and are listed in the Preface, but much of our recent work has been in collaboration with Billy Attachie, who obtained training in linguistic transcription during his work with Marshall and Jean Holdstock. They taught him well, and his work has been invaluable.

To understand Dane-zaa history and culture, one must understand Dane-zaa storytelling. As in all small communities where people share a common history, Dane-zaa tell stories without direct references to shared experiences. Storytellers do not begin a story with a full description of the context. Billy Attachie told us that people in the old days got together each evening to tell and listen to stories. The storyteller knew that each member of the audience had heard some version of the story in the past and understood the system of kin terms that guided Dane-zaa in their relationships with one another. Because everyone understood the references, the storyteller used pronouns rather than the names of characters, much the same way one would use a kin term to talk about a relative. In other publications (e.g., Ridington and Ridington 2006), we describe this type of discourse as highly contexted. To facilitate and enrich understanding of these stories, we present most of them in a poetic form that does justice to the rhythms of Dane-zaa storytelling.

Some of the stories describe people and events that occurred before the arrival of white explorers and settlers. Fur traders first recorded Dane-zaa names in a North West Company post journal in 1799, but Dane-zaa families had lived in the land east of the Rocky Mountains, where the Peace River flows through what is now northeastern BC and northwestern Alberta, for millennia. Some oral stories record the names of people who lived in the region before there were white people in the country. Others describe the fur trade, the Dreamers, and events in the recent past.

In 1977, the former Fort St. John band split into the Doig River and Blueberry River First Nations. The English names *Doig* and *Blueberry* reflect recent events and are derived from the white place names for the rivers that run through Dane-zaa land. Tommy Attachie told us that white people named the Doig River for a Scottish trapper named Fred Doig. The Dane-zaa name for the river is Hanás̱ Saahgé? (Raft River, also spelled *Saahgii*). The name reflects a time during the fur trade when Dane-zaa trappers loaded their furs onto rafts and floated down the Raft River and the Pine (Beatton) River to trade. White people named the river *Doig*, however, and the Scottish surname is now used by those Dane-zaa people who were once called Ts'ibe Dané? (Muskeg people, also spelled *Ts'ibii*) because some of the land where they hunted and camped was in the muskeg north of the Peace River and east into present-day Alberta. This muskeg country is good for hunting and trapping. Those Dane-zaa people who sometimes camped near Charlie Lake were called Lhuuge Lęą (suckerfish people; literally "fish penis") because suckerfish were once abundant there. Elders from Doig remember fishing in the area as part of their seasonal rounds (see Chapter 11).

Dane-zaa nané? (the people's land) is ideal habitat for moose, beaver, and other fur-bearing animals whose boss is *Nôwe* (the wolverine). Bison were also abundant in the territory until demand for meat and furs by white traders caused the animals to be hunted to near extinction in the late nineteenth century. When Alexander Mackenzie visited Dane-zaa country in 1793, he described the prairie near the place later named for Chief Attachie as "so crowded with animals as to have

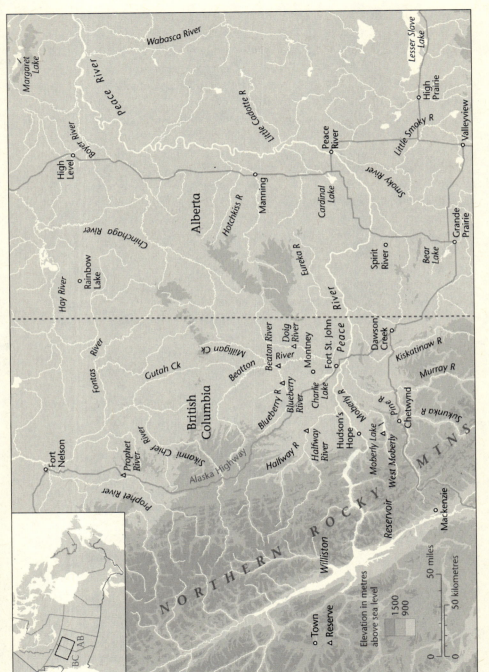

Areas referred to in the text. Map by Eric Leinberger

the appearance, in some places, of a stall-yard, from the state of the ground, and the quantity of dung which is scattered over it" (Mackenzie and Lamb 1970, 264).

For the Ts'ibe Dané?, Lhuuge Lęą, and all other Dane-zaa people, history is a trail that begins in a time before measured time. It is a trail defined by the Dreamers, people who have shown the way when the trail ahead seemed to be unclear. The trail's branches follow all of the creeks, rivers, and valleys that lead from Lake Athabasca to the Arctic-Pacific Divide. Within that territory, the Dane-zaa's trails intersected with those of animals who shared their land and who, when needed, gave their lives to Dane-zaa hunters. Their trails intersected with those of people from other bands who were related by blood or by marriage and with those of neighbouring tribes such as the Slavey who also spoke an Athapaskan language. Their trails began to intersect with those of the Cree, who belong to the Algonkian language family, when the Cree became middlemen in the fur trade in the eighteenth century and began to move west. The Dane-zaa met no Europeans until just over two centuries ago, when Peter Pond established Fort Vermilion in 1788 and when Mackenzie passed through their land on his epic journey to the Coast, "from Canada by land," in 1793.

In some ways, Dane-zaa history is like the history of all First Nations in Canada. Yet it differs in one critical way. At the time when the Cree, the Iroquoian nations of Quebec and Ontario, and many other First Nations were adapting to newcomers (or, in the case of Beothuk in Newfoundland, were exterminated by them), the Dane-zaa were still following the trails of their ancestors. They first learned of the changes to come in the late eighteenth century, when the Dreamers prophesied the coming of the white men. Loss of land and traditional culture, developments that began to affect the indigenous people of eastern Canada three and a half centuries ago, have challenged the Dane-zaa for little more than a hundred years. Pond built his forts on the eastern side of Dane-zaa territory, and Mackenzie passed through the area but did not stay. Fur traders came to the area in 1794, and Catholic priests arrived in 1859, but neither lived with the people. Fur traders stayed at the post, and priests came through about once a year to perform baptisms and marriages. As we discuss in Chapter 7, the Dane-zaa successfully integrated the new teachings into their traditional beliefs.

Fort St. John, now the centre of British Columbia's oil and gas industry as well as a hub city for the thousands of farmers in the region, is near the site of Rocky Mountain Fort, the earliest fur trade post in British Columbia, established in 1794. So-called pioneers began settling in Dane-zaa territory early in the twentieth century, but they were too few to have a heavy impact on the Dane-zaa's traditional way of life. Many Dane-zaa, especially the women, had little contact with the fur traders and rarely encountered white people until the building of the Alaska Highway in 1942. The fathers and mothers of contemporary Doig elders spoke little or no English, had no driver's licences, and lived most of their lives without a telephone, electricity, or indoor plumbing. No Dane-zaa children attended school until 1950.

Today, the Dane-zaa language is written by tribal linguists but not spoken by most Dane-zaa children, and the trails of the people are invisible beneath roads, highways, and seismic lines that bring opportunity but also threaten to extinguish the traditional ways of the Dane-zaa. Members of the Doig River and Blueberry River First Nations run energy companies, negotiate land claims, and meet to decide how to allocate trust funds. In only six decades, a traditional hunting-and-gathering people have learned to succeed in a modern world that would have been incomprehensible only one or two generations ago. Despite these changes, the Dane-zaa remain strong in their sense of kinship, community, and culture. They still think of themselves as being related to one another, even though younger people may not know the proper Dane-zaa Zááge̱? terms for these relationships.

Robin first visited the Dane-zaa in 1959. He returned for a year in 1965-66 and for shorter visits throughout the late 1960s with his first wife, Antonia (now Antonia Mills), and their small son, Eric, who was called Aballi by the Dane-zaa. Their daughter, Amber, was born in Dane-zaa territory in 1969. She relates her own experiences with the Dane-zaa in her biography on the website she created with Kate Hennessy and Dane-Zaa youth and elders, *Dane Wajich: Dane-za̱a Stories and Songs – Dreamers and the Land* (Doig River First Nation 2008).

We (Jillian and Robin) married in 1976 and made our first trip to Doig in June and July 1978. Eric, Amber, and the late "soundman" Howard Broomfield accompanied us. We have visited "Beaverland" on a regular basis since then. Howard was part of those journeys until his death in 1986, and our children and grandchildren often travelled with us. More recently, we have worked with Amber and our former student Kate Hennessy. We watched as new houses replaced the government-issued plywood buildings that once lined Doig's main street. We recorded preachers who came through the area with a

Howard Broomfield, Jillian Ridington, and Robin Ridington at Doig, 1978.
Photo by Amber Ridington

newer, more inspiring message, and we watched as the Catholic church, no longer used, came down. We were there when the new band hall and cultural centre opened with drumming and song, replacing a small, worn, and dark old building. Our contemporaries have grown old, as have we, and the children whose voices we recorded as they played in the 1970s are now parents. We have shared in Dane-zaa celebrations and memorials and in times of sorrow. Jillian has observed and documented everyday and unusual happenings and tried to learn traditional women skills. She relates some of these interactions in *When You Sing It Now, Just Like New* (Ridington and Ridington 2006). Her experiences also formed the basis for radio documentaries for the CBC (Canadian Broadcasting Corporation) and Vancouver's CFRO (see Works Cited). Robin continued to learn from the elders and to document traditional stories. He began to add video documentaries to the archive in 2002.

In the late 1970s, the Dane-zaa communicated with relatives on other reserves via "Message Time," a radio program that was broadcast at noon every day on CKNL Fort St. John. Now, almost everyone, from teenagers to pensioners, has his or her own cellphone or Blackberry and uses them frequently. Communication is constant and immediate. When we met with the Doig council and elders to discuss this book, Chief Norman Davis sent Robin, who was sitting across the table, a message from his Blackberry. It arrived in Robin's in-box seconds later.

Throughout the years, we have used cassettes, cameras, microphones, reel-to-reel tape, minidiscs, and video recorders to document images, songs, stories, and conversations. The Ridington/Dane-zaa Archive includes photographs, tape recordings, and videos, along with radio programs produced by Jillian Ridington and Howard Broomfield in the 1960s and broadcast on the CBC or local stations. It also contains an extensive genealogy based on Robin's fieldwork in the 1980s. The chief and council of the Doig First Nation asked Jillian to update the genealogy in 1990. The request turned into a five-year project. Both of us worked closely with Patrick Cleary and Mitchell Goodjohn, researchers for Blueberry River First Nation, to include government and church records and many more interviews. Our work resulted in a comprehensive genealogy of the former Fort St. John Band. The Doig and Blueberry First Nations used this genealogy in treaty land entitlement negotiations with the federal government. The genealogy is also a resource for Dane-zaa seeking to know more about their ancestors.

The archive also includes many hours of stories, some told in Dane-zaa Záágé?, some in English. Elders shared with us their rich oral history of events. They documented key events; they explained the very nature of the universe and how people and animals developed ways of living together. *Where Happiness Dwells* is very much their book. We bring their stories together with historical documents to create a portrait of life as it has evolved and changed in the territory of the Ts'ibe Dané? and Lhuuge Lęą and beyond to all the people of Dane-zaa nané?. We have tried to facilitate understanding of their stories and, where necessary, contextualize them for a non-Dane-zaa audience and younger Dane-zaa who do not speak the Beaver language and are not familiar with their oral history. Younger people continue to create history and tell about it in new electronic media. Some of them worked with Amber Ridington and Kate Hennessy to create the Virtual Museum of Canada's exhibition *Dane Wajich: Dane-zaa Stories and Songs* (Doig River First Nation 2008).

We are now elders ourselves, and the Dane-zaa elders we record are our contemporaries. These elders include Tommy Attachie, Billy Attachie, Gerry Attachie, May Dominic Apsassin, Sam Acko, Margaret Dominic Davis, Madeline Sagónáá? Davis, and Jack Askoty.

Others who taught us a great deal have gone on the trail to heaven. Margaret Attachie, Albert Askoty, Alice Askoty, Sally Takola Makadahay, John Davis, Mary (Daeda) Davis Dominic, Margie Wolf, and Marguerite Yahey Davis were among them. These elders listened to their own elders. Some of them also studied the recordings we made of people from their parents' and grandparents' generations; Aku, Charlie Yahey, Jumbie, Sam St. Pierre, Charlie Dominic, Johnny Chipesia, and Nachę (Mary Pouce Coupe). Those of us who are now elders feel a responsibility to the people we knew when we were young to bring their words forward to a new generation. As the Dreamer Charlie Yahey said on one of Robin's recordings, "I am talking to this white man and his tape recorder, but through this the world will listen to my voice" (Ridington/Dane-zaa Archive [RDA] CMC 8-1).

Charlie Yahey was the last of the Dreamers. The Dreamers have been essential to Dane-zaa life since before white people came to their land. Dreamers are men, and sometimes women, who can follow a trail of song to a place beyond the sky where they come into contact with the spirits of the people who have gone before. Prior to contact, they were hunt chiefs who visualized the plans for communal hunts. Since the white people came, Dreamers have dreamed about the future and told their people how to cope with the pressures of living in a changing world. This book would not have been possible without Charlie Yahey's wise words and the encouragement he gave Robin to document his knowledge.

For us, this book is more than a collaborative ethnography. It is a celebration and fulfillment of fifty years of friendship, and it expresses our appreciation of the Dane-zaa. Any wisdom that it contains comes from the wise stories we have been privileged to learn. Any errors are our own. If this book informs and enriches the lives of future generations, we will have achieved the purpose set out for us by the Doig River First Nation. The Dane-zaa oral history that follows goes back more than two hundred years. Many of the stories are no doubt much older than that. We hope that two hundred years from now the descendants of today's Dane-zaa will continue to learn from the wise stories the elders remembered.

1
The Dane-zaa Creation Story

Every culture has a story that takes us back to the beginning of time. The Dane-zaa creation story has many parallels with explanations of the universe found in Western science. It describes the unfolding of time and space, but unlike the creation story told by physicists, the Dane-zaa creation story is also about people, animals, and other living things. It also bears similarities to the biblical story of creation, but creation unfolds in the Dane-zaa universe as a result of conversations between the creator and conscious and sentient animal persons, rather than through the actions of a solitary creator. As in the Bible, the Dane-zaa creation story begins with an enormous body of water and a creator, but it then takes a different direction. The creator, Yaak'ih Sadę (Sky Keeper), draws a cross on the water as a way of establishing the four directions. He or she (Dane-zaa Záágé? has gender neutral pronouns, and we follow that usage in our commentaries) then sends animals down beneath the water's surface to bring back earth, from which Yaak'ih Sadę creates land. Muskrat dives way down and brings a bit of earth up under his or her fingernails. The creator tells this earth to grow, and it eventually becomes large enough to support people and the animals whose bodies give the people life. Instead of giving man dominion over other beings, the creator enters into a conversation with the animal people, who already existed in the creator's mind. Indeed, humans do not play an important part in the Dane-zaa creation story. Sky Keeper made men and women, just as he or she made him- or herself. The late Dreamer Charlie Yahey told Robin two versions of the Dane-zaa creation story. At the end of the second version, the Dreamer says, "At that time, there was starting to be people" (Ridington/Dane-zaa Archive [RDA], CY 8).

This creation story is the basis on which the Dane-zaa First Nations' understanding of the past, present, and future has been built. The creation story is so familiar to those brought up speaking Dane-z̲aa Záágé? that it is seldom told from beginning to end. Every Dane-zaa person recognizes elements of the story that form part of other stories. References to the cross on the water and to the Muskrat come up frequently in ordinary conversation, much the same way that a literate Christian can bring up a Bible story, knowing that his or her audience of believers will understand the references. Similarly, when Dane-zaa storytellers talk about Chehk'aa, the Muskrat, listeners already know that this animal played a central role in creation. The late Sally Makadahay was called Chehk'aa. For those who knew her, she was both a unique human being and the embodiment of the brave little muskrat who long ago brought up from the primordial ocean a speck of dirt that became the world.

When Dane-zaa children listen to elders telling stories, they hear bits and pieces of the creation story. When Robin heard segments in the mid-1960s, he realized that there was a bigger story, and he wanted to hear the whole thing from beginning to end. Only someone from outside the culture would have thought to ask for the whole story in one sitting. The obvious person to give such a special telling was the last Dreamer, Charlie Yahey. Charlie Yahey was a Dreamer for everyone in the former Fort St. John Band as well as for Dane-zaa of the Halfway River and Prophet River bands. Robin recorded him speaking to people at both Doig River and Halfway River as well as at his own Blueberry River Reserve. Charlie insisted that his real home was Charlie Lake, the lake near Fort St. John that was named for his stepfather, Usulets (Big Charlie), and perhaps also for his grandfather Charlie Aluulah. The Fort St. John Band was divided into the Doig River and Blueberry River bands one year after the Dreamer's death in 1976. His relatives and descendants are now members of both these First Nations.

Robin first recorded the Dreamer telling the creation story in August 1965, when he visited the Halfway River Reserve with people from Prophet River. One of Charlie Yahey's daughters, Jihgenahshihle (pronounced "Chikenesia"), lived at Halfway with her husband, Bob Achla, and their children. Back then, vehicles such as Robin's 1965 Chevy panel truck were rare at Halfway River. People still used horses and wagons as their main means of transportation. Jihgenahshihle asked Robin to drive her son Amos Achla to the Blueberry Reserve to pick up Charlie Yahey. When they arrived, Charlie was out hunting, but on his return, he and his wife, Aanaatswęą (Bella Attachie), were glad to visit relatives from another community. On the drive to Blueberry River, Robin had the car radio tuned to CKNL, the Fort St. John radio station. On the way back, he turned the radio on again. Without a word, Amos turned it off. When Robin asked Amos why he had done that, Amos replied, "Old man don't like that kind music." He provided no further information. Robin later learned that Charlie Yahey's power meant that he could not listen to the sound produced by a stretched string without becoming "too strong." Country and western music is full of guitars and fiddles. Any Dane-zaa knows that the medicine power of another Dane-zaa must be respected. To wilfully ignore that knowledge is to disrespect the other person's power and to risk turning that power into a destructive force.

For a few days, Charlie visited with his daughter and with elders from Halfway River and Prophet River. He sang with the drummers and spent many hours talking with Mrs. Skookum (Amaa), one of the few women Dreamers. Finally, he was ready to make a recording of the creation story Robin had requested. Robin quickly set up his reel-to-reel Uher tape recorder. Charlie told the creation story and several others. His contemporaries Augustine Jumbie, Sawe (Jumbie's wife), Thomas Hunter, and Mrs. Skookum served as an audience.

Charlie Yahey wanted Robin to record his words so that, as he said, "the world will listen to my voice." As a Dreamer, Charlie could see ahead to a time when his words and songs would become an important resource for future generations. By speaking into the tape recorder, he sent a message to the people who would come after him.

Robin got a quick translation of the story. Many years later, in 2006, he sat down with Doig linguist Billy Attachie and recorded a closer translation of part of the story. Billy explained that Dane-zaa Záágé? speakers often use fewer words to describe something than do English speakers. Robin and Billy agreed on ways to fill in words to make Billy's literal translation meaningful in English. This contextualization appears in brackets in the oral stories or as lengthier footnotes. Dane-zaa storytelling is full of references to knowledge that the storyteller assumes the listener already has, knowledge that requires no further explanation. For instance, storytellers assume that listeners understand that dreaming is an important way to obtain knowledge. At one point in the creation story, Charlie Yahey says:

> When this world began, it was all covered with water.
> There were no people. There was only him [Sky Keeper].
> He made a big cross. He floated that cross on the water.
> (RDA, CY 8)

Charlie simply refers to the creator with a personal pronoun, which in English is usually translated as *him* but in Dane-zaa Záágé? can mean *him, her,* or *it.* In his translation, Billy Attachie substitutes *God* for the pronoun. To a modern Western reader, the term *God* almost inevitably suggests an image from the Judeo-Christian Biblical tradition. Charlie Yahey specifically distinguishes between the Western way of knowing through books and the Dane-zaa way of knowing through dreaming. The Dane-zaa have had contact with the Catholic Church for a hundred and fifty years. Many now embrace evangelical Christianity, yet knowledge through dreaming continues to be an important way of making contact with the spirits of animals and human ancestors. Charlie Yahey and other storytellers often refer to the creator as Yaak'ih Sadę, which literally means "Heaven He's Sitting" but in a more abstract sense could be translated as "motionless at the centre of the heavens." *Yaak'ih* in Dane-zaa Záágé? means "beyond the sky, heaven, or the heavens." *Sadę* is more complex but expresses the concept of sitting or being motionless. Garry Oker gives *Yaak'ih Sadę* a more poetic translation – "Sky Keeper." Garry's version tells us that Yaak'ih Sadę is the keeper of the heavens, in the same way that each animal species has its own keeper. We have chosen to use *Sky Keeper*. When referring to God rather than the creator, Dane-zaa commonly use the more Christianized term *Ahatáá?* (Our Father).

Charlie Yahey's Creation Story: Version 1

> These people, the white people, must have known
> about how Sky Keeper created the world.
> They knew it because they read it in a book.
> I myself am not old enough to remember what happened.
> I don't know what was in their book. I don't remember that
> far back.
> I only know with my dream.
>
> With my dream, I know about everything that has gone before.
> I drew a picture of the trail to heaven.

I drew a picture of what I saw in my dream.
The ancestors of the white people must have had a history
about what happened long ago.
They have a history about how he made it for them to live.
That history is in their book.

This land, this whole world, was created many times.
This story is about two or three of the worlds that he made.
A long time ago, someone stayed in a boat.
I don't know much, but with my dream, I can find the trail.
I can find the right way.
I can remember when the Dreamers made new songs.
I didn't say anything. I just listened to them singing.
They sang new songs from their dreams.

Ever since I can remember, I have been singing.
Then I started to make songs from my own dreams.
The Dreamers' songs are the music of the Dane-zaa.
They are our music.
The white people have their own music,
but the Dreamers' songs are the Dane-zaa way, our way.
The drum and the Dreamers' songs, those are our music.

You must have good ears to listen.
If you don't, you won't understand.
Those who have good ears, those who are good listeners,
will put their ears toward the storytellers.
They will hang onto what they hear. They will listen to the stories.
They will remember what they heard. They will hold onto all of it.
I thought this man himself [Robin] knows everything about the creator
because he is a white man,
but he wants to hear it from me. He wants to know.

When this world began, it was all covered with water.
There were no people. There was only him [Sky Keeper].
He made a big cross. He floated that cross on the water.
From the centre of that cross,
he sent all the water animals down to find earth.

Many tried but couldn't make it.
Then Chehk'aa, the little muskrat, tried.
He went way far down. He dove down deep into the water
and came up with a little bit of dirt [beneath his nails].
He just made it back up. He came back.
Sky Keeper put that earth at the centre of the cross.
"You are going to grow," he told it.
"You are going to grow into bigger and bigger ground.
You are just going to keep on growing."
Sky Keeper made man, and he made woman
to stay with him and work with him.

Sky Keeper wrote down everything that happened in a book.*
What he wrote about came to pass.
He wrote about water, and it came into being again.
He wrote about the rivers and creeks.
He made the water flow into the ocean.
He made these mountains, too.
He said that if there were no mountains,
the ground would break away from the force of the water.
He made the mountains big so the water wouldn't run out.
In wintertime, too, the snow falls, and then it melts,
and there is lots of water on the land.
There is lots of water, but it goes into the big water, the ocean.
He made it like that.

After he finished with making the mountains and waters of
this world,
he made the rest of the animals. He made moose.
He made black bear. He made mountain sheep and fish.
He knew that this world was becoming big.
He thought about how the people were going to live.
The people need animals. He made the spruce grouse.
He made everything from the mountain.
He made mountain sheep, mountain goat, caribou, deer.
He wrote them down in his book. He wrote them down
on paper.†

---

* Like the way the white people wrote their creation story in a book.
† The Dane-zaa Z̲áágé? word for paper is *adíshtl'íshe* (birchbark).

He wanted all the animals to multiply.
He wanted all of them to grow up.

The creator made a world
where all the different birds could find a place to live.
How could they live if it was winter all year long?
He made a place to the south,
where the birds could go during the winter.
They could stay warm there when it is winter and cold
over here.
All the birds that stay down south
know when the time has come to fly back north.
When winter is over, they come back.
Some people don't even know about these things.
They don't know that he made everything for the people.
They don't know this is how it is supposed to be.

When Sky Keeper made this country for us
he gave us the ability to live from the land.
We cut our own wood. We had a hard time,
but he accepted us into his world.
We don't know how to read and write,
but we know what is happening.
Sky Keeper knows that we don't read and write,
but he chose us.
He chose every one of us in this world.
He gave us the ability to dream to heaven.
That is a place where Dreamers talk to one another.
We talk about how to know him.
This is the way he gave us the ability to dream to heaven.
All the different tribes have ways to dream.
That is how it was. That is how he made it.

Someone [Billy says Satan] tried to imitate Sky Keeper,
but his creations were all the bad things.
He created the bad things when he tried to copy Sky Keeper.
That was the way it was, when Tsááyaa [the Transformer]
began to follow the trails of the giant animals.
Tsááyaa made all the world nice and quiet for us.
He killed one of the big animals. He followed its trail.
When he caught up with that big animal, he killed it.

He cut its body up into pieces and threw the meat away.
Every time a piece of that meat landed on the ground,
it turned into a different animal, like fisher and marten.
Even wolverine, the boss of all the fur animals,
came from a piece of meat he threw down. That is how it is.

When Sky Keeper created the world,
the other one did the same thing, too.
But Sky Keeper made all the different trees – poplar, willow, spruce.
He made all the different trees for the animals.
The animals started to eat those leaves.
Each different animal found the one it liked to eat.
They ate more of the ones they liked,
and those trees became more abundant.
Sky Keeper made beaver to live in the creek
and live from the poplar trees.
As there became many beavers all over the country,
they spread out to live in all the rivers and creeks.
There came to be many beavers. That is how it was.
He made all the different animals.
He made caribou and the rest of the animals
that live in the mountains. He made the big whistlers [marmots], too.

The animals remember that Sky Keeper provided for them.
When the winter is very hard, they start talking to him.
They start praying. When they can't survive on their own,
they begin to talk and pray to him.
Sky Keeper hears their voices. He answers them
and makes warmer weather return.
People are not the only ones who call out to him.
All the animals do the same thing.

Each animal has a different song.
The Dreamers sing songs about the different animals.
Swan, without dying, went straight through to heaven.*
There is a song about this.

---

* Like the Dreamer, Swan is able to fly through to heaven without dying.

If there are not enough swans on Earth,
they stop flying through and let the population grow up again.*

Even prairie chickens multiply in this world.
Sometimes there will be no prairie chickens and no rabbits.
Then, sometime after, they will come back.
After that, there sure are lots of them.
When they eat up all the little trees that are their food,
the trees are all gone. They disappear.
Then everything grows back, and they come back again.

Sky Keeper made himself.
He made everything else in the same way he made himself.
He made the water, everything.
He even made those big stars in the sky.
He made the big kettle [the Big Dipper] in the sky.
He made all the different stars. He made the moon.
He thought, "If there are no stars, no North Star,
when it's dark, it's going to be really dark."
He made the stars and moon so that it will not get really
dark at night.
He must have written everything down, how to make it.
If the big kettle goes wrong, it is going to be the end of
the world.
Just watch the big kettle every night. It stays in the same place.
When it's coming toward daylight,
it goes way up and turns right around.
When it turns around, that means that daylight is ready to
return.
He made the big kettle. He made how it goes around in the sky.

This is what I am thinking. I am thinking about the way it is.
Everything started happening.
Some people must have known, but they didn't do anything
about it.
I am the last one of the Dreamers. I am the only one left here.
This man [Robin] is recording my voice.

---

* The implication is that, although Charlie is the last living Dreamer, there may be more Dreamers in the future.

> This whole big world will listen to my voice.
> Through this tape recorder, the world will listen to my voice.
> (RDA, CMC 8-1)

Charlie Yahey's Creation Story: Version 2

In 1968, Robin was eager to record more of Charlie Yahey's words. He wanted to ask how Dreamers get their songs and have Charlie tell the creation story again. In July, Charlie Yahey visited his relatives at the Doig River Reserve. He sent word to Robin that he was ready to make a recording. He chose to do this in the house of Jack Acko and his wife, Eskama. Eskama was the daughter of Charlie's cousin sister (his father's brother's daughter) Tl'ok'ih Náázat. Jack was the grandson of another cousin. At that time, kinship ties were far more important than administrative details such as which reserve a person was officially registered to, and the people at both the Doig and Blueberry reserves shared membership in the Fort St. John Band. Jack Askoty interpreted the questions Robin put to Charlie. Charlie began by explaining how Dreamers get their songs. Eddie Apsassin provided this translation. (See Appendix 1 for a line-by-line phonetic transcription of the translation by Patrick Moore and Eddie Apsassin.)

> That is the way it is. *Háwǫ́ch'e*.
> Over here, they [Dreamers] are singing.
> Over here, they [Dreamers] are singing,
> and they bring the song out, just like in this tape recorder.
> That is the way they bring out the song.
> That is how they grab it. That is how they grab it there.
> They wake up with that song over there.
> They grab one song over there and then another one.
> Over here when the dream is moving.
> They wake up holding that song.
> The people over there [in heaven] are singing,
> and they sing it exactly like that.
> They do it exactly like that. They wake up with it.
> Over here, when they grab it. They know it really well.
> Sometimes, when they are going to lose it,
> it seems like it's covered, and then they don't grab it.
> But when they wake in the morning, they grab it really well.
> It looks like this. It's just there. There are many songs like this.

People [Dreamers] are singing like this.
And that is how the people listen to it.
(RDA, CY 8)

When he paused, waiting for another question, Robin asked him to tell the creation story. He laughed and said, "I guess you heard that story before, but you want to hear it twice to see which one is better."

That is how it was.
Even though he [Robin] knows everything, he wants to know it twice.
When he [Sky Keeper] first made this world, there was not much on the earth.
There was only water. He made that land, and from there,
all this land started to grow and grow.
All of it, until all this land became big. That is what people say.
There was only water. What will be on Earth? he thought.
There must be something on it.
He must have had a boat. He would make things by himself.
What he thought about appeared for him.
He made a big raft in the form of a cross.
He floated that raft. He floated that raft, at that time.
He must have done that. Something was looking for this land.
"Go into the water!" he told them, but there was nothing.
Just like that, then, they [animals] crawled out of the water like that.
It was like that.
"Wait, Chehk'áa (Muskrat). You go in the water,"
he said. And Chehk'aa was gone.
Chehk'aa pushed up a little bit of land,
and he put it on the cross raft.
Sky Keeper placed it there carefully and said, [speaking to the land], "You will grow!"
What he said was written [according to Eddie Apsassin, as commandments].
From then on, the land was growing, growing, growing.
Then finally, finally, then finally,
it must have been then, it must have been, that it was growing.
That's what people say.

His dog changed itself into a *tlęchuk* [big dog, like a wolf].*
He changed an ordinary dog into a big dog.
That's how it was.
"The earth is so big. Run around it!" he told him
[to find out how large it was].
After that, it disappeared. It was gone a long time,
and it must have travelled to a different land.
And when it returned, it brought back a person's arm.
"That is not what I made you for," he told it.
Then he sent it away. "This dog will sit behind us people.
You will only eat behind us now!
Now you will stay where you belong" [as a camp dog].
There was nothing. There was nothing at all.
People know about it. "They will run on this land," he said.
And then the wolf changed back into a camp dog,
and from there it disappeared for a long time like that
[travelling around the world].

Then, finally, finally, it was gone.
"Ah, what happened to the dog I love?"
He knew how things would be.
"Wait, he shall live by his legs," he thought [so it could catch game].
As he thought these things, they were written [as commandments].
He made its teeth out of metal. They are still like that today.
When it grabs something, its teeth are just like a knife.
And then, back then, he must have made this earth big.
Even though the dog ran away, it could not hide.
The dog heard him, but did not do what he was told.
That's what the people said.

Then something was coming onto the land, coming together onto it.
It was just like the birds landing in flocks, there were so many.
He [the dog] went where people stayed different places,

---

* Eddie translated *tlęchuk* as "horse," the modern meaning of the word, but in the context of this story it makes more sense to translate it literally as "big dog."

but not just to visit people [the dog showed the people where the Creator was staying].
At that time, there were starting to be people.
(RDA, CY 8)

Understanding the Creation Story

Each telling of a story in Dane-zaa tradition is a new experience. As Tommy Attachie told us when he was identifying Dreamers' songs that Robin had recorded, "When you sing it now, just like new." Charlie Yahey, like his contemporary elders at Doig, told a particular version of a story to fit the audience and the occasion. Telling the creation story is not like reading from the Bible. It is a re-creation, not a recitation. Essential elements of the story are the same in both versions, but the storyteller puts together particular elements differently with each telling. The storyteller may choose to emphasize different elements in different settings, but the essential meanings remain the same. In this case, the common and essential element is the story's description of how the physical world as we know it came into being as a product of the creator's thought and communication with the animal people.

The images in Charlies Yahey's stories are similar to those in the Biblical creation story. First there was water. Even the four directions had not yet come into being. Into the creator's mind, his dream, came the idea, the image, of a place where north, south, east, and west came together. He wanted the world to grow from that centre, so he floated a raft in the form of a cross on the water.

Every Dane-zaa singer's drum offers a visual retelling of the creation story. Each drum is round and has a cross of babiche (cord made of rawhide or sinew) to hold onto. Charlie Yahey's double-sided Dreamer's drum pictures the cross at the centre of creation, and each side of the drum tells the story in a slightly different way. Charlie asked Robin to photograph him holding the drum and told Robin that it had been made by Gayęą, his teacher.

The image of a place where trails intersect is central to Dane-zaa hunting. Hunters say that it is impossible to kill an animal without first having dreamed of a place where the animal's trail and that of the hunter come together. An image of the creation story, a centre where two trails come together, exists within every hunt dream. When

Charlie Yahey with Dreamer's drum, 1968. Photos by Robin Ridington

a hunter encounters an animal in his dream, he shares an image of creation with that animal. An animal will not give itself to a hunter unless it trusts that the hunter will respect its body and use it generously for the benefit of his people. When an animal gives itself to the hunter and its body is used with respect, the animal's spirit is born again in the body of another animal. Each hunt makes the world "just like new."

Charlie Yahey's creation story is similar to that of many other First Nations and to stories told by aboriginal peoples in many other places throughout the world. The story sets out the fundamental qualities of time and space within which human activity takes place. As the story begins, there is only water and no directions. The water's surface is flat and without contour. The creator wants to extend the dimension of vertical space, so he sends Chehk'aa, the Muskrat, down to discover earth. As Chehk'aa dives down, he explores the vertical dimension and discovers earth at the ocean's bottom. At the story's end, the land is created, complete with mountains, ridges, valleys, and rivers. The Dreamer tells us that swans, like Dreamers, can fly through to heaven without dying and return in the same body. The flight of swans and Dreamers completes a three-dimensional world. Muskrat dives down from the centre. Swan flies up from the same place. All of this complex symbolism is inherent and understood in Charlie Yahey's creation story.

2
Tsááyaa, the Culture Hero

Tsááyaa was the first person to go on a vision quest and seek power from the animals. *Tsááyaa* means "Sun in the Sky," and Dane-zaa stories describe Tsááyaa flying around the world like the sun, putting leaves on the trees in the spring, and helping the geese, ducks, and swans return from the warm country far to the south where they have spent the winter. In Charlie Yahey's creation story, Tsááyaa makes the world right for the Dane-zaa. Charlie explains that after Sky Keeper commanded the world to grow, he told each of the animals to choose its food from the resources he had made available and gave each animal a purpose and a place to live on the earth.

> He told the animals to choose the ones they wanted to eat.
> The animals then started to eat the bark of the trees they liked.
> They started to live by the rivers. They started to eat the bark.
> From there, they started to grow and grow.
> Now, every river always has beaver in it, even the little creeks.
> Some place you can cross a river where there is a big dam.
> That is right.
> He made all the animals in the mountain – sheep, caribou.
> He made the whistlers [marmots], all those for people to live on.
> When it is really cold, those animals pray to God in their
> own way.
> When it is cold and they start to get hungry,
> they sing their songs to God.

> Some of the songs we sing are those animal prayers.
> One from chicken [spruce hen], horse, moose, goats.
> Not only humans pray to God.
>
> All the animals pray to God, too,
> when they have hard luck.
> When they start to starve they have lots of songs, too.
> (Ridington/Dane-zaa Archive [RDA], CMC 8-1)

Many of the Dreamers' songs are also the songs that animals sing when they are having a hard time. Because the Dane-zaa regard animals as sentient people like themselves, it makes sense that the animals have prayer songs. Charlie continues and describes the songs particular to swans:

> Not only us pray to God –
> even swans [do], when they have hard luck in the fall time
> and start to starve.
> They can just go right through the sky to heaven without
> dying.
> Swans are the only big animals that God made
> that can go to heaven without dying.
> Swans are hard to get for food.
> They go right through the sky.
> Tsááyaa wanted big groups of swans in heaven
> so there would be lots up there.
> Sky Keeper made them go in big groups
> so there will be lots again. There are many swans in heaven.
> That is why there are only a few that he kept on Earth.
> Most of them are up in heaven. Only a few down here.
> (RDA, CMC 8-1)

Swans are like Dreamers. They can fly to heaven and return in the same body. Dreamers follow a trail of song, *yaak'ihts'ę̂? atanii* (the trail to heaven). Like swans, Dreamers leave this world, fly to another one, and return with songs and stories for the people they left behind on Earth. When swans fly, their wings and bodies make the sign of a cross in the sky. They remind people of the cross that Sky Keeper drew on the water when he made the world. In the fall, they fly to an unknown land where life continues during the winter months, when the water in Dane-zaa nané? is frozen solid. In spring, they return.

Dreamers die in this world and fly to another one where their relatives who have passed on are still alive. They return with stories and songs from their relatives in heaven.

Charlie continues:

> In fall time, the swans always go late.
> When they have a hard time in fall,
> they pray to God in their own way
> and go to heaven without dying.
> When it starts to get warm in the spring,
> all the chickens begin to lay eggs and grow up into big ones.
> Even if people kill lots, there will still be lots of them.
> But there are only a few swans.
> Only when the swans have a really hard time from the cold,
> they go up to heaven.
> When the rabbits eat the bark from the trees
> until there is very little left for them to eat, they disappear.
> Then, when the trees start to grow again,
> they begin to come back, and there are lots of them.
> Chickens do that, too. They go away when there is not enough food
> and come back when the food returns.
> They stay somewhere south.
> (RDA, CMC 8-1)

Charlie Yahey describes Tsááyaa as part of his creation story. As in many of Charlie's stories, instead of naming Tsááyaa directly, he refers to him simply as "one man." Dane-zaa hearing the story would know immediately that he was talking about Tsááyaa. Similarly, Charlie refers to the giant animals as *wǫlii nachii,* literally "something big."

Tsááyaa and the Giant Animals

> There must have been one person [Tsááyaa],
> there was one person that Sky Keeper chose to use.
> That one walked around,
> and wherever he found bad people,
> wherever he found bad animals,
> he would kill them.
> Those bad ones ran away from him, ran away from him.
> They ran away from him.
> He walked around following those [animal] people.

When he saw them, he killed them.
He killed them.
He killed the giant animals.
Those, too, he killed;
He killed them as well.
He cut them up like that, like that.
He cut them into small pieces and threw them.
"That's how you will be named," he said to them.
When he threw one piece, there was a weasel running along.
When he threw another, there was a marten running.
Every type of animal came from there.
At that time, Wolverine was the boss of all the fur-bearing animals.
That's what people said. Wolverine kept all of the furs.
That guy, Tsááyaa, started to work on the world
so everything would be straight for today.
Some of the animals he didn't kill.
He just chased them under that place.
That's why the ground goes high.
He also sent giant fish underneath,
and that is why even today white men
drill a hole to them to get their fat.
The oil that they get is the fat of the giant animals.
Tsááyaa made everything straight for this world of ours.
He knew it before [like a Dreamer].
That is why they get gas from down under the ground.
They look all over for it and then find it underneath.
God made that for the white people.
That is what the person and I know.
I tell the story – true story.
Tsááyaa made everything straight here.

When Sky Keeper had finished making the land,
there were still many bad and dangerous animals left in this world.
Some of them were really mean. Some of them were wǫlii nachii.
The people were powerless against their strength.
There was one man. He took a good look at all the bad animals.
This one man went around the world to kill all the bad animals.
The ones he couldn't kill, he sent them

under the big ridges and mountains. He sent them under.
The ridges are the backs of these giant animals.
He killed some of them. Others he couldn't kill.
Sky Keeper knew that there were going to be vehicles
for people to run around with.
He knew where the white people were going to get oil and gas.
The man who killed all the bad animals sent them under the
ground. Those are the ones the white people drill for now.
They get oil from their bodies underground.
Us Dane-zaa, he made us to live in the bush.
He made us to stay in the bush. We live poorly all the time.
We are not rich like the white people.
We are able to survive in the bush.
But the white people started growing grain,
growing vegetables, everything.
(RDA, CMC 8-1)

Tsááyaa was a model for the first Dreamers. He was the first hunter and the first person to follow the tracks of animals rather than running away from them. Tsááyaa began life as a boy named Swan. In his vision quest, the swans gave him power. The story suggests that a person's power is already within him and only awaits the quest, *Shin kaa,* to make itself known. The late Johnny Chipesia told Robin (in English) the story of the boy named Swan in 1965 (RDA, Beaver Tales).

This story is about a boy called Swan.
Swan lived with his mother and father.
His mother was a good woman.
She was a good woman, and she loved her boy.
When Swan was still young, his mother died,
and his father raised him.
Before his mother died, she told Swan's father,
"I like my son.
I want you to find a good woman to look after him.
You should look for a woman from where the sun
is highest in the sky. Sun up women [women from where the
sun comes up] are no good.
Where the sun goes down is no good.
You should just find a woman
from where the sun is at dinner time.
I like my son."

Like most Dane-zaa stories, this one makes subtle references to information the listener already knows. As the story begins, we learn that Swan's family has a special relationship to the sun and its position in the sky. Tsááyaa's name means "sun in the sky" because he flies across the heavens each day and is responsible for the sun's movements north and south with the seasons. All Dane-zaa know that swans fly through the heavens, south to a warmer land in the winter and north to Dane-zaa nané? in the summer. The story then goes on to explain that Swan's father was unable to find a woman from where the sun is at its highest:

> Swan began to get older.
> His father wanted to find a new woman to look after him.
> He looked for one where the sun was at its highest,
> but he could not find one.
> Swan's father went to look for a woman where the sun sets.
> He took Swan with him and travelled toward the setting sun
> until he came to the ocean.
> In that country, he found a nice-looking woman.
> He told that woman's father, "I need a woman for my boy.
> I want to take your daughter back with me."
> The woman's father said,
> "I've raised lots of daughters to be good women.
> I'll give you this one if you look after her well.
> That's what I've raised them for."

Dane-zaa generally associate the rising sun with being born, the setting sun with dying, and the sun at its highest with living. The place where the sun is highest in the sky is a point of balance and a centre, like the centre of the cross that Sky Keeper drew on the water. The choice of a woman from the place of the setting sun is an ominous sign.

> Then Swan and his father went back to their own country.
> They took that woman with them.
> When they got back, Swan's father made a bow and arrow
> for his son to use in shooting rabbits. Swan was a good shot.
> He couldn't miss anything. He got everything he shot at.
> When Swan and his father got back to their country
> with that woman, Swan's father went hunting.
> That woman was wild. She told Swan,

> "I'll go out hunting with you." Swan said,
> "All right, Sǫge [Stepmother]." They went out.
> She told him, "Every time you see rabbits, shoot them in the head. You're a good shot. You can shoot anything you want."
> That boy, Swan, tried to shoot a rabbit in the head.
> He got it in the head. The rabbit went down.
> That woman picked up the rabbit while it was still kicking.

When Johnny told Robin the story, he explained that if you shoot an animal in the head, it will kick wildly as it dies. Because of this, Johnny said, a hunter whose wife is pregnant must never shoot an animal in the head. If he does, his wife will kick and thrash around when the baby is born.

> Then that woman put the rabbit Swan had shot under her dress.
> She killed it between her legs.
> As it died, the rabbit kicked and scratched her legs.
> It spattered blood between her legs. Swan said,
> "Sǫge, why did you do that? We eat that."
> His stepmother told Swan,
> "Well, I hold him that way with my legs
> so that he will die quickly."
> When Swan's father got back to camp,
> he went to sleep with that woman.
> He saw that she was all scratched up
> and covered with dried blood.
> "What happened?" he asked. "You were not like that before."
> Then that woman lied to Swan's father. She told him,
> "Well, your boy did that. He threw me down and did that.
> He's a big boy now. He is stronger than me."
> Swan's father believed what she told him.

Here, the story takes a strange and upsetting turn. The woman from the west kills animals between her legs rather than bearing children from that place, as Swan's mother had done. Swan's father believes the woman rather than his son. Somebody from a European tradition would probably interpret this part of the story in Freudian terms, but in Dane-zaa symbolism, the main point is the contrast between killing and giving birth. The Dane-zaa would interpret the woman's act as a sign of disrespect for the animal's spirit.

Swan's father got mad at his own boy.
He knew he could not kill his own son, so he told Swan,
"Let's go hunting out where the sun goes down in the ocean."
He was planning to leave Swan on an island in the ocean.
He couldn't kill him, but he planned to leave him there to die.
Swan and his father got to the ocean.
"Swan," his father said, "let's look for country out there."
Swan looked. "Yes," he said,
"I see something black way far out."
"OK," his father said, "we go now.
We make a canoe and go out there."
Swan and his father made a canoe.
They paddled far out into the ocean
until they were almost out of sight of land.

In the story, Swan's father takes him to an island where the sun sets below the horizon, a place of death and transformation. Like every other child sent by his or her elders on the vision quest, Swan must experience the death of the world in which he grew up to be reborn as a person of power. Going to the extreme west makes it possible, even necessary, for Swan to become Tsááyaa, the transformer who brings new life to the plants and animals as the sun returns in the spring.

Then they came close to the island. Swan's father said,
"Swan, you go around one side of the island.
I'll go around the other.
We'll find out how big this ground is."
As soon as Swan was out of sight,
the old man turned around and went back to the canoe.
He got into the canoe and went out into the ocean.
He waited for Swan there.
Swan went all the way around the island,
but he didn't meet his father.
When he got back to where they had left the canoe,
he saw his father way out in the water.
His father shouted to Swan, "I am leaving you here.
We have both shared the same hole.
We can't both go in the same place.
Now, I am leaving you here."

Swan shouted back to his father,
"Daddy, Daddy. I never did that.
We just went hunting, and when I shot a rabbit in the head,
she put it under her dress."
But Swan's father didn't listen.
"Don't lie too much. I'm going back now."
Then he paddled back to the shore
and went back to his own country.

The island in this story is like the world soon after Muskrat brought up earth from beneath the water. It is small enough for a person to circle around it and return to the place where the journey began. In the creation story, Sky Keeper sends his dog around the world to see if it is large enough to sustain all the animals. When the dog returns with a person's arm in his mouth, Sky Keeper sends him beneath the earth. He then sends a wolf into the world. When the wolf does not return, he knows that the world is now big enough to sustain the animals. Swan's father asked his son to meet him on the other side, but instead of completing the circle, he turned back on his own tracks and left the island.

Swan lay down by the water and cried.
He didn't know what to do.
Pretty soon, he cried himself to sleep.
Then he heard someone talking to him, but he saw no one there.
It must be a spirit power helping him.
The voice said, "Why do you cry? Don't cry.
You're going to live." It told him,
"Do you see all those geese and ducks flying over there,
going to a different place?"
It was fall time, and the geese and ducks were flying south.
"You get lots of pitch. Put it on the rocks of this island
wherever the sun strikes. The ducks and geese will get stuck
there. You can live like that."
His friend told him this, and Swan got up and felt better.
Swan put lots of pitch on the flat rocks of the island.
It was a hot day, and the pitch melted when the sun struck it.

The next morning, Swan began to make a house
on the highest part of the island.

All he had was a stone knife,
but he cut a stick and dug into the ground
to make a hole for his house.

The next morning,
he went out to check the pitch,
just the way you go out to check a trap.
When he got to the place, he found forty ducks and geese
stuck in the pitch wherever the sun had made it soft.
He just hit them with a stick.
After that, he was happy and thought, "Maybe I'll live."

Swan took the feathers from the ducks and geese
and put them in the hole he had dug.
That way he made a good house lined with down.
Then he cut up the birds into fine pieces with his stone knife
and dried the meat.
He kept on doing this for a month
while the birds were flying south.
By then, he had caught hundreds and hundreds
and made lots of dry meat. He fixed his house
with down and feathers inside,
and he put a flat rock for the door.
He made a toilet, found a place to get water,
and began to live in his new house.
All this he did with only a stone knife.

Like children on the vision quest, who leave the world of their people and enter the world of their animal friends, Swan enters the world of his namesake. The geese and ducks, who are flying south to a land that can sustain life during the harsh winter, give themselves to him. With the help of spirit power from Swan, the keeper of all migratory birds, the boy named Swan lives from one season to another. Even though he is on an island at the western end of the world, he survives to face a new dawn with the guidance of his spirit helper. At the end of his quest, he is ready to be born again as a person with power.

Swan lived in his house, and the cold of winter did not
bother him.
Soon, it was March time, but he still had lots of dry meat.

Swan did not go back to the place where his father had left him.
He didn't want to leave any tracks there
in case his father came back.
Springtime came, and he began to see the first bluebirds.
He knew that summer was coming soon.
By then, he did not have very many bundles of dry meat,
but he still had some dry fat and guts.
After the summer birds,
the geese and ducks, began to come back from the south,
Swan tried to catch them, but this time
the pitch wouldn't melt on the rocks.
It was cold, and he couldn't get anything.
Soon he had only one bundle of dry meat left.
He thought, "Maybe my father will come back."

One day, he heard somebody singing way out in the water
and hitting a canoe like a drum. It was his father,
singing as he paddled his canoe toward the island.
"Swan," he sang, "I want to see your head bone.
We shared the same woman,
and now I come to see your bones."
Swan hid himself and watched his father
take the canoe up on the shore. He kept on singing.
"Now, Swan, you're smart enough.
You fooled around with my woman,
and now I want to see how your head bone sets.
Is it in the water or in the bush? I want to see where it is."
The old man went around one side of the island.
As soon as he was gone from sight, Swan jumped in the boat
and paddled away from the shore.
The old man kept walking around the island.
Soon, the sun came out, and he saw fresh tracks.
Swan had been smart.
He had not left tracks where his father landed the canoe.

When Swan's father returns, he completes the circle that he interrupted in the fall when he abandoned Swan on the island. Completing the circle marks the end of his life and the beginning of Swan's life as a man of power. As Tsááyaa, Swan circles the entire world each day, and he circles from one season to another like the swans.

> The man ran back to his canoe when he saw the fresh tracks,
> but it was too late. He shouted to his son in the canoe.
> "Swan, my son! I just wanted to see how tough you were.
> That's why I left you here."
> But Swan shouted back to him, "Now you are going to live
> the way I lived."
> He paddled his canoe back to the mainland.
> Swan thought to himself,
> My dad is crazy, so I will just leave him there for ten days.
> He can't die in ten days. Look how long I stayed there.
> But when Swan came back in ten days, he found his father
> dead with a little bit of feathers in his mouth.
> He had starved to death and tried to eat feathers.

The father's generation passes on, like the day that passes into night, and Swan completes his circle, like the sun that moves through the sky each day and through the seasons each year to become new again.

> Then Swan got mad. "It's that bad woman who did this.
> Now, I'm going to kill her."
> He went back to his country and saw that woman.
> "Swan," she said, "where's your dad?"
> Swan didn't say anything. He got mad.
> He took an arrow and shot it in the ground by her feet.
> The arrow caught fire when it hit the ground.
> The woman started to run away,
> and every time Swan shot an arrow at her feet, it caught fire.
> Finally, she ran into the water.
> Swan shot his arrow into the water after her.
> The arrow was so hot the water boiled.
> When the woman came out of the water, she was just bones.
> That is how Swan killed that bad woman.

In Dane-zaa thought, people who allow themselves to become angry release their power for good or evil. Swan is angry, but he still does not know how to direct that anger in a positive direction.

> After that, Swan became a man,
> but he stayed with a big animal,
> Wǫlii Nachii, that ate people.

After he killed that bad woman,
Swan met that monster, Wǫlii Nachii.

The monster said to him,
"I can't make babies anymore. You stay with me."
So Swan lived with her.
After a while, Swan told Wǫlii Nachii his story.
She told him she lived by eating people.
"You try it, too," she said. But Swan said, "No, I can't do that.
I only eat ducks and geese and chickens.
I can't eat people like myself."
Pretty soon Wǫlii Nachii saw tracks of game.
"Look," she said, "a bull, a cow, and two calves."
Swan didn't see any game tracks.
There were only people tracks. Swan couldn't follow them.
Wǫlii Nachii ran after the tracks.
"That's good game.
I hope there's lots of fat," she said.

At this point in the story, Swan begins to learn that his loyalties lie with his own people.

Pretty soon Wǫlii Nachii came to a little camp in the bush.
There was a man, a woman, and two children.
Wǫlii Nachii started to go after them. Swan tried to stop her.
"Mommy, Mommy, don't go after them. They're my people."
"That's your people yourself," she said. "That's my game."
She started after them again.
They tried to run away,
but she hit the man, and he fell down flat.
Then she hit the woman, and she fell down, too.
Swan got mad. "Mommy, Mommy! You leave them alone.
You've killed two. You leave the others alone."
Still, Wǫlii Nachii kept on after the two children.
They were smart and rolled themselves fast down a hill.
Wǫlii Nachii was too big to catch up with them.
Swan ran down the hill and put the children behind him
to hide them from the monster.
Wǫlii Nachii came down. She said,

> "My son, do you want to die, too? That's my food.
> If you don't let me have it, I can eat you, too."

With the two defenceless children behind him, Swan finally knows how to direct the power of his anger.

> Then Swan took an arrow and shot Wǫlii Nachii in the breast.
> "Swan, my son," she cried, "I should have listened."
> But Swan shot her again and killed her.
> After that, Swan changed his name and took the name of
> Tsááyaa. Since that time, he became just like a soldier
> looking for bad things that ate people.
> He cleaned up all the monsters that used to live in the world.
> If he didn't do that, maybe those things
> would still make trouble for people.
> When Tsááyaa finished killing all the monsters, he turned to
> stone. He said that he would come back
> when the world comes to an end.
> He will come back to fix it up.
> Sometime, when Jesus comes back,
> Tsááyaa will come back, too.

Johnny Chipesia's story of Tsááyaa's vision quest ends with the introduction of the Christian culture hero Jesus, who, according to the priests, is the redeemer of the world. To Dane-zaa Dreamers and storytellers, Christ the redeemer is a version of Tsááyaa, the culture hero who brings new life into the world with the turn of the seasons. Dane-zaa today often refer to Tsááyaa as Santa Claus, who flies through the heavens bringing gifts to people. Santa Claus flies at the time of winter solstice, when the sun finally turns from its southward path back to the north. Charlie Yahey told people that they should sing and dance together to the Dreamers' songs at the winter solstice to encourage the sun to return and the days to get longer. Tsááyaa was the first hunter, the first person to go on a vision quest, and a model for the first Dreamer.

Johnny Chipesia also told Robin a story about Tsááyaa's encounter with two giant people, Big Man and Big Woman (RDA, Beaver Tales).

> Tsááyaa once saw big track.
> Gee, big track, six foot wide, he said to himself.

He walked three hundred yards.
Gee, I don't know how come I see only one side,
but for sure it's a person's track I see.
He walked round and round. Finally, [he] saw the next track.
Gee. Must be Big Man.
He tracked him through snow. Finally, he saw him sitting down.
It was Yaae<u>ts</u>ííghadah [He Who Touches the Sky].
That Big Man says,
"How do you live, you little kid, you little thing?
How do you kill anything?"
"Asea [Grandfather]," Tsáayaa said. "I live just like you."
"You gonna be with me?" that Big Man asked Tsáayaa.
"I'll carry you," he said.
He put Tsáayaa inside one of his mitts in his belt.
Pretty soon, before he shot a cow and calf moose,
he broke a big tree and put his mitts on it with Tsáayaa inside.
"Now, I'm gonna kill rabbits," he said. He killed two moose.
He camped and cooked a cow moose and a little one.
"Little kid," he told Tsáayaa, "you eat that little rabbit."
He skinned them just like rabbits.
"Aseah," Tsáayaa said, "I can't eat that. It's too big."
He ate some ribs. "Gee, I'm full," he said.
And that big man said, "I don't know how you live."
He ate the rest of the little moose.

"I can't eat rabbits any more," he said.
"I have to find big game up north."
That was Wǫlii Nachii he wanted to hunt.
Tsáayaa just stayed in Yaae<u>ts</u>ííghadah's glove.
"You watch out," the Big Man said.
"That moose [Wǫlii Nachi] is pretty mean. You stay with me."
Pretty soon, Tsáayaa saw what looked like a big hill.
"That's my moose," Yaae<u>ts</u>ííghadah said.
That was Wǫlii Nachii. Tsáayaa said, "I'm scared."
So Yaae<u>ts</u>ííghadah tied his mitts on top of the big timber.
Yaae<u>ts</u>ííghadah took a big arrow and tried to kill Wǫlii Nachii.
For a long time he tried, but the giant animal was too big.
He came back to where Tsáayaa was hiding in his mitts.
"Now, I am going to kill him. We'll eat good."
Finally, he killed the giant animal.

He skinned him, and the animal was really fat.
When he opened the giant animal's guts,
there was a man inside, with his pack still on his back.
Tsááyaa didn't like that. Yaaetsííghadah told Tsááyaa,
"I live on this thing. That's good. Look how fat he is.
He ate lots of people. Others eat even more people.
They get even fatter." Tsááyaa got mad at that Big Man,
but Yaaetsííghadah started to put him back in his mitts.
"No, I don't want that anymore," Tsááyaa told him.
"What's the matter?" asked the big man.
If I leave you, you'll be food for Wǫlii Nachii, my baby."
Then Yaaetsííghadah started to talk rough.
"You're a louse," he said. "You just live on me."

Tsááyaa said, "I can live by myself.
How many years have I hunted for myself. I can make fire."
Big Man got mad. "I travel more than you," he said.
"I go across the ocean and hunt different animals."
He was talking too close to Tsááyaa. Tsááyaa walked backwards.
"What you kill with that little arrow?" he asked.
"Oh, I just carry that for fun," Tsááyaa replied.
Tsááyaa walked back.
Big man said, "You make me mad. Now, I'm going to finish you."
Tsááyaa said, "Oh. Oh. You can't kill your own shit."
Yaaetsííghadah began to chase Tsááyaa.
Tsááyaa ran up to a big hill,
and Yaaetsííghadah couldn't follow him up.
He tried to follow fast, but Tsááyaa got way high up the hill.
Yaaetsííghadah ran up near to where he was.
Tsááyaa shot down the hill and hit him in throat.
"Hey, hey," the big man cried,
"I shouldn't have tried to chase you.
Now, you finish me. My friends will go after you yet."
"OK," said Tsááyaa, "I'll meet your friends."
Yaaetsííghadah went down. Pretty soon lay down.
He was finished. Just one shot.
"What kind of person is his friend?" thought Tsááyaa.
His friend was the same kind as Yaaetsííghadah.
Tsááyaa started walking. I've got to watch myself, he thought.
What's his friend that he said was tough?

He came to a big river. I walk too much, he thought.
I'll make raft. He cut four sticks and went downriver.
Finally, way down, he decided to camp. He slept.
When he woke up, somebody was calling across the hill.
"Tsááyaa, you have a bad name. You went into bad corner.
You killed the big boss of all people. Down the river not too far,
you'll go to a bad corner."
He heard somebody say that in the night.
Next morning, he went again. There was a big flat.
No trees for ten miles, with something like a beaver dam across.
That was Big Woman, with legs that went up like two hills.
Something looks funny, Tsááyaa thought. It looks like a person.
I gotta watch myself. People can't be that big.
He saw lots of trails, people trails. He walked on.

Chickadee landed on his shoulder.
"What's the matter with you?" Chickadee asked.
"Friend, friend," he told Tsááyaa, "you came to a bad place.
Every day, five or six people killed here."
"How are they killed here?" Tsááyaa asked.
"You see these legs that look like hills?
There's a trail here. Her legs are just like two hills,
and between there's a valley where people have to go.
People come in there. Just like wind comes.
She closes her legs and kills the people.
My friend, you go back."
"No, I can't go back," Tsááyaa told him.
Chickadee said, "Big Woman is lying on her back.
When the wind comes, it knocks you down,
and she puts you between her legs."
"OK, I fix her," Tsááyaa said.
Tsááyaa took a big rock in his hand.
Chickadee warned him, "Don't get close.
This is the last time I'll tell you. You're gonna die."
Then Chickadee flew back to tell the story.
Tsááyaa got close up between Big Woman's legs
before the wind came. Then the wind blew.
Tsááyaa yelled "Hey," and the wind stopped.
When it stopped, he threw a big rock between her legs,
and a big lightning bolt came out of her.

> That was her power.
> Tsááyaa killed the lightning that lived in the ground.
> He sent it into sky. After that, people saw the lightning up in the sky.
> Because Tsááyaa killed her, that's why lightning is in sky.
> Still, today, sometimes, lightning kills people, horses, even big trees.

Tsááyaa is a trickster as well as the person who makes everything right for the people. Sometimes, when he gets carried away with how clever he is, his tricks backfire. Johnny Chipesia told Robin another story, this time about one of Tsááyaa's less glorious adventures (RDA, Beaver Tales).

> Tsááyaa made himself just like God.
> He didn't die. Tsááyaa made himself, changed himself, three times.
> He was really old, and he made himself young again three times.
> The fourth time, he tried it again, and he can't make it.
> He ran out of power.

The story begins when Tsááyaa fails to complete a circle of the four seasons to make himself new again. He is desperate to make himself young for a fourth time and calls on his animal friends, the birds that fly south for the winter. But this time, instead of accepting power from them, he tries to become a bird by borrowing their feathers.

> Every fall, all those little birds, the little ducks move to the south.
> He said to the ducks, "Give me one feather like that. Just one each." "I want to fly with you," he said.
> And they gave them, every one of them, one apiece, and he started to fly away up in the air.
> One place in the south, one place where bad people live, he flew over there. They saw him flying in the air with those birds,
> and everybody was hollering at him, and so he fell down.
> He tried, but he can't make it.

All those ducks flew under him, but he just can't make it.
He fell right in front of all those people,
right in the middle of camp.
Just easy, just easy, he hit the ground.
They put him in the bush and tied him up to use for a toilet.
Later on, they toilet on him. They use him for a toilet.
Every one of them, they take their pants down,
and they do what they like with him.
One old lady, she said, "Why do you guys toilet all over Tsááyaa?"
And she went up there to the toilet.
She start to toilet over Tsááyaa, but Tsááyaa told her,
"You untie me first. Then you toilet over me."
So she untied him. The old lady had a stick to walk with.
Tsááyaa killed her with that, and he started to run away.

In many of the Tsááyaa stories, Tsááyaa overcomes the giant animals by fooling them. But sometimes the Trickster is dominant, and Tsááyaa? manages to trick himself. The stories teach Dane-zaa children (and whoever listens to the stories) that, no matter how powerful they are, they must not be arrogant. Today, white people drill into the earth and pump up the grease of the giant animals that Tsááyaa put there in a different era. By doing so, they release the energy of a time when relations between people and animals were out of balance. When Charlie Yahey talked about this, he said that white people make the world too small. He implied that the world is reverting to the way it was when Sky Keeper sent his first dog out to measure the earth's sustainability. The dog came back with a human arm in its mouth. By exhuming energy from the time of the giant animals, the white people have created a new form of monster that upsets the very balance of nature.

The Dane-zaa deal with modern technology capably. They enjoy driving in four-by-four pickup trucks, just as do other people in northeastern BC. Members of the Doig and Blueberry First Nations participate in the oil-based economy (see Chapter 15 for a discussion of current projects), but the image of giant animals who consume humans is still alive in the memory of elders and in the stories that they tell their younger relatives. One ancestor who lived three generations back from today's generation was named Duuk'ihsachę (He Who

Sleeps with Giant Animals) (see Chapter 4). The power of these beings is literally just beneath the surface of the earth. Garry Oker, former chief and a great-great-grandson of Duuk'ihsachę, told us that he believes that Tsááyaa will have to return to Earth at some point to make things straight again.

3
Shin kaa, the Vision Quest

The word for *vision quest* in Dane-zaa Záágé? is *Shin kaa,* which means "to seek a song or power from an animal friend." Traditional hunters such as the Dane-zaa view animals as people with whom they must be friends to survive. Before a hunt, a hunter dreams to make contact with the spirit of the animal person that he wishes to bring home to his people. In his dream, he visualizes a place where his trail and that of the animal will come together. That place is like the centre of the cross the creator drew on the water, a place where two trails merge into a single point. Like the centre of the cross, it is a place of transformation. The animal's body becomes food for the people as its spirit rises, only to return in a new body. Muskrat dove down from the centre of the cross to discover earth. The hunter dives into his dream to discover an animal who is willing to give himself to the people. The hunter cannot take an animal's life without its consent. Animals do not consent unless they know the hunter has a good and generous spirit.

The Dane-zaa know animals as independent beings with their own wills and intelligence. Animals know when their bodies will be treated with respect and shared generously. The hunter and the animal accept each other's gifts when their trails come together in the hunt dream. The hunter promises to respect the animal's body and to share the meat generously. The animal promises to show up at the place where their trails come together, although the hunter must still use his skill and knowledge of the animal's nature to complete their agreement.

If the hunter fulfills his obligation, the animal's spirit will ascend to heaven and return in another body.

To the Dane-zaa, there is no such thing as luck in the hunt. A hunter is successful because the animal recognizes him as a good person. People say that a hunter who is unsuccessful must have treated animals and his fellow humans with disrespect. Dane-zaa attitudes toward animals are very different from those of farmers and herders whose animals are bred in captivity and slaughtered at the convenience of their owners. Some elders, such as May Apsassin and her father, Charlie Dominic, report having obtained power from domestic animals. To them and other Dane-zaa, even domestic animals must be treated with the respect due sentient and powerful beings.

Herders and farmers generally do not think of domestic animals as sentient beings with independent wills. Domesticated animals are like slaves. The owner controls the animal's reproduction, its care and feeding, and the moment of its death. Animal breeders select animals from their herds to sacrifice. The Bible tells the story of the good shepherd who looks after his flock as well as the man who leads his sheep to slaughter. The story of Abraham being willing to sacrifice his own son on God's command would not make much sense to a traditional Dane-zaa hunter. Unlike a game animal, Isaac had no choice about being sacrificed. The decision was entirely in the hands of his father and his father's God.

The superb training that young Dane-zaa receive from their elders and during their vision quests gives them a deep understanding of the ways of the animal people. They can read signs in tracks, in evidence left where animals have browsed, and in the places where animals have bedded down. They can read the environment with as much skill as the animal people themselves. Elders teach the younger generations by telling them what Billy Attachie calls wise stories. In 1968, Charlie Yahey visited Doig and told stories to the people there. He described to Robin how he had learned to listen and how stories were passed from one generation to another. Margaret Dominic Davis translated the story shortly after the recording was made.

> It used to be that all the old people
> would sit together in one place, make some tea,
> and one person would begin telling a story.
> Then another would tell one and another, and so on like that.
> They would keep on telling one after another
> sometimes for five or ten days.

When they would tell the stories the people would have to behave
and just hear the story really well. I listened really well.
When the old people died, the younger ones
would take all their stories and pass them on.
That is why they had to listen and get them just right.
Some people didn't behave themselves and would forget everything.
That is what all the old timers said.
That is how I got these stories.
(Ridington 1988, 101)

As Charlie Yahey explains, elders taught children to listen to the stories carefully. They did this by making the stories interesting. In a culture without radio, TV, books, or computers, oral performance was not only educational but also a form of entertainment. The stories about the giant animals from ancient times explain the power that a child can receive from each animal and teach them to recognize and respect the signs of power in others. When boys and girls have learned what they need to know to go out into the bush alone, their elders send them to Shin kaa. The song they seek comes from the power of an animal friend or the spirit of a rock, a tree, the wind, or some other natural phenomenon. Anthropologists call Shin kaa the vision quest because during the child's time alone in the bush, he or she enters into an altered or visionary state of consciousness. Sometimes, the animal friend comes to a child in a dream.

Elders know that even though there are no adults physically present during the vision quest, their children will not be entirely alone. Using their own powers, they monitor the child's experience through their dreams. They also know that wise stories will accompany the children and give them direction as they need it. Billy told us, "Those stories I remember, that's what I live by now." Many of these stories tell about the *anáághaleh* (game keepers) and the special places, such as moose licks and sacred rocks, where they may be found. The children also know stories about the dangerous giant animals of long ago and about Tsááyaa, the first hunter, who made the world safe for people to live in. When the spirit of a particular animal comes to a child during the vision quest, he or she already knows the stories that explain the animal's power. In a moment of transformation, the child enters a visionary state in which he or she becomes the central character of the story. He or she enters into the animal's world. Each

A sacred rock in Dane-zaa territory. Photo by Jillian Ridington

animal has a song that is emblematic of its power. As the animal sings its song to the child, the animal's way of being becomes the child's way of being.

When a child receives his or her song in the vision quest, he takes on the spirit of the animal friend. When a hunter meets his game in a dream and later in the bush, he and his people take the animal's body into their bodies as food. Shin kaa empowers a young person to become an adult member of Dane-zaa society. The visionary moment of Shin kaa seems like a time out of time to the children who experience it, but elders are watching over them in their dreams. They know when it is time to call the child back to the world of humans. As the child approaches the place where his or her relatives are camped, he or she is cautious and wary and experiences the sights and smells of the camp as something strange, the way an animal would experience them. Sometimes, the elders go out and physically lead the children back. Sometimes, they sing their own songs over them.

In 1999, Billy Attachie discussed Shin kaa in relation to particular spiritual places. Some of these places were made sacred by their association with anáághaleh, the game keepers. One such place is a distinctive large rock formation near Moig Flat. Billy Attachie told us about that rock.

> And there's one at Moig Flat. You know that big one.
> You ever see that rock? They – long time ago,
> they all got power from each, each animal, those things.
> And there were no doctor. No hospital.
> And if Indians sick, they going to die.
> So whoever got those kind of power,
> lay hand on them or give them water,
> or put water on their head.
> And they recover. They get healed.
> (Ridington/Dane-zaa Archive [RDA], DZ99-18)

What Billy told us reflects the Dane-zaa's deep belief in the importance of power from the vision quest. The Oblate priest Henri Faraud commented on this adherence to what he called medicine power following his conversations with the Dane-zaa in 1859 (see Chapter 7).

Billy continued:

> You gotta be really clean, and when you're ready,
> they take you in the bush and leave you up there.
> They run. They know you receive it.
> You get the power from the spiritual power of those animals.
> And then, when the time to come home,
> your grandpa who sent you over there
> will meet you and pick you up.
> But first you got to make fire. Walk you over back and forth
> on top of that spruce branch fire.
> And you get back to normal again.
> (RDA, DZ99-18)

Walking back and forth over the spruce branch fire is a ritual of transformation that allows the child to make the transition from the world of animals back into the world of humans. Other storytellers describe a child fearful of the smell of smoke and wary of humans, just like an animal. The ritual reverses that condition and brings the child back to the people. Throughout the child's life, though, the experience of the animal world remains part of his or her identity.

In the 1960s, Robin recorded a vision quest story told by Billy Attachie's grandmother Nachę (Mary Pouce Coupe, 1890-1977). The story describes the way things were years before her time. She probably learned it from her first husband, Apąą (Joseph Apąą, 1854-1917).

As was common in her time, Nachę married when she was a teenager (we discuss Nachę and her relations in Chapter 9). Apąą had been married to an older member of the Ts'ibe Dané? (Muskeg people) band, one of Chief Yehlhézęh's daughters. When his wife died, Apąą turned to other women in the band and soon married Nachę. The couple spent long winter nights on the trapline, and Apąą shared his wealth of stories with his young wife. Sadly, their marriage ended in a tragedy. A tree blew down on their tent and killed Apąą. Charlie Yahey's youngest daughter, Marguerite Yahey Davis (1924-2003), remembered the story of Apąą's death when we interviewed her in 2002, a year before she died. This translation was provided by Maryann Adekat and Lana Wolf.

> Jimmy Appaw's grandfather, his name was Apąą.
> I didn't see him. They were camping around Goodlow.
> My sǫge [mother's sister] told me.
> There was a teepee just like the one outside by the river.
> There's a place there where the river floods
> and there are no big trees. There was a big storm coming,
> big hail falling. Right behind their teepee,
> there was a big tree standing,
> and from the other side there was another tree leaning on it.
> Apąą, his wife – you know, Tommy Attachie's grandmother –
> she was my sǫge. They said, "Run away!
> There's a big storm coming.
> Grab your blankets and run."
> All the people ran away to where a dip in the ground,
> and they lay down. His wife told him, "Let's go follow them."
> He got up, and he jumped from where he was lying to the opening.
> He told his wife, "I'll do that as soon as I hear a noise."
> And sǫge was lying down, too. By now, you could hardly see.
> There was big hail. That big tree fell right in the middle of the teepee.
> And Apąą? There was nothing left of his head.
> And my sǫge? A big branch hit her on her arm.
> She got a broken arm, and after that the storm stopped.
> Sǫge told me these stories.
> All the people came back, and that tree was really big.
> They chopped it in half,
> and they brought him out from underneath the tree.

There was nothing left of his head.
Those are the stories from way back.
(RDA, DZDV02-14)

Nachę survived, but her shoulder was broken. Her daughter, Cheole (Helen), suffered a broken pelvis, but Nachę was able to use her knowledge as a healer to bring herself and her daughter back to health. Cheole married Chief Sagónáá? and became the mother of Doig elder Madeline Sagónáá? Davis.

One of the stories Nachę told Robin in the 1960s also begins with a cross-generation marriage. In this case, a teenage boy marries an older woman. Liza Wolf translated the story.

One time, there was a boy who married young.
Maybe he was ten or twelve.
Then his wife and children all died, and he was very lonely.
I will go in the bush, he decided.
Maybe some monster will kill me there. He went out.
Every night, he would sleep on some animal's trail without fire.
He wanted to get killed. "If I had been a medicine man,
my wife and children wouldn't have died," he said.
For ten years, he stayed out in the bush.
The people all thought he was dead, so they didn't look for him.
But no animals would kill him,
so he decided to try to be a medicine man after all.
But still no animals would talk to him.
(RDA, Beaver Tales)

Nachę's story explains that it's sometimes hard to find an animal friend. In this case, the animals avoid the boy because he wants an animal to kill him rather than give him life. A Dane-zaa person hearing this story would know that the boy is suffering from a sickness caused by another person's use of medicine power against him. To gain power from an animal, the boy would have to be cured.

One night, he went to sleep in a moose lick.
While he was asleep, something woke him up.
He looked up, and there was a big fat man.
"What are you doing here?" he asked.
"My wife died. My children all died.
For ten years, I have been in the bush,

> hoping some animal would kill me.
> For ten years, I haven't seen people."
> The big fat man leaned down and put his lips to the boy's
> forehead.
> He sucked and drew out blood.
> He did the same thing on the back of his head,
> and again he drew out blood.
> "That's why no animals like you," he said.
> "Now, you can make friends."
> (RDA, Beaver Tales)

The big fat man who came to the boy had the power of healing. One of the ancient marks of healers is their ability to identify the source of an illness within a person and remove it by sucking out bad blood. Following his first meeting with the Dane-zaa in 1859, Henri Faraud described this kind of shamanic healing (Faraud 1870, 225). No doubt the practice goes back much further than that. As the healer in the story explains, animals had not come to the boy because of the sickness within him.

> The big fat man took him with him.
> He opened a doorway in the lick, and they went inside.
> The next day, he told the boy to hunt,
> and he went out hunting. He got a moose,
> and he packed back some of the meat. The big fat man said,
> "You just killed a rabbit. You didn't kill a moose.
> Tomorrow, you go out and kill a moose.
> Don't skin it. Carry back the whole thing."
> He did. He carried the whole moose back.
> The big man said,
> "Another rabbit. I'll show you what kind of moose I mean."

Inside the moose lick, the guardian of that place appeared to the man as a giant. To the giant, a whole moose was like a rabbit, and a normal human being was like a doll.

> That big man had a daughter.
> She would sometimes play with the boy who had been cured
> like he was a doll – pack him around in her arms, on her back.
> That's how big they were!
> The next day, the big fat guy killed a moose,

what he called a moose.
He came back and got his daughter and the boy,
and they went to the moose.
He had never seen anything like it before.
It was the size of a mountain. They told him to eat,
and they cut off a bone for him and cracked it open
so he could eat the marrow.
He started eating and eating and eating,
and after awhile he came out the other side of the bone.
He went right through it – it was so big.
They were going to pack back the moose.
The boy could only pack back a little piece,
but the other two could pack back as much as they liked.
They went back. Soon, the big fat man said,
"It's time for you to go back and find your people now."
So the boy left him.
(RDA, Beaver Tales)

Nachę's story describes the game keeper who lives inside the moose licks. When a child who has heard this story visits one of these places, he already knows something about the power of the place. Stories like this are among the wise stories described by Billy Attachie. When Charlie Yahey visited people at Doig River, he gave Robin a similar description of the giant moose that lives inside certain moose springs. As a Dreamer, he knew that the giant moose resides there because Tsááyaa, the first hunter and the first Dreamer, sent moose beneath the earth in ancient times. Before Tsááyaa, giant moose roamed the earth, but they now live only beneath the places where moose come to lick the salty water.

Under the springs, there is a great big moose, a giant moose.
That is why all the moose on this world stay near those places.
Before Tsááyaa made everything right on this world,
there were giant moose on this world, too,
but he sent them down to the world beneath this one.
Where he sent them down there are now springs
coming up from that world still. The moose like it there
because they know the giant moose are underneath.
There is just like a house under there.
(RDA, CY 11)

Charlie explains that small moose stay beneath the earth with the game keeper, but they are special and different from ordinary moose. If a child encounters one of them on his or her vision quest, he will receive power from the boss of the moose.

> Small moose stay under there, too, in that house.
> In wintertime, they will come out from the spring or lick.
> Even if there is thick ice and frozen dirt,
> they will break through the crust, go a little ways,
> shake themselves, and all the dirt will come off.
> These moose are regular-sized,
> but they have just a single set of horns like a cow,
> just small ones with a single point.
> They shake themselves until all the dirt is gone,
> and they rub themselves against the trees.
> The boss for all the moose (the game keeper)
> stays under the spring in the other land.
> God made it like that.
> God made everything good for the world
> until the end of the world.
> (RDA, CY 11)

The Dane-zaa have always been particular about their source of drinking water. Before they lived in modern villages on reserves, they knew that water collected in the muskeg was good but that some spring water was dangerous. In the story, Charlie explains that the moose are the same way and go only to the springs they know are good.

> Some springs are for the moose, and others are no good.
> God didn't make those ones – some bad ones.
> Not all the springs are good ones.
> Sometimes, all the moose will go to one spring.
> That is his spring there. Some other places seem like good springs,
> but moose seldom go there. Those ones are different springs.
> Those are bad ones. That is what the old people said.
> I heard that.

May Dominic Apsassin also told us about Shin kaa and the meaning of spiritual power in her own life and in the life of her father, Charlie Dominic, who was raised by his stepfather, Charlie Yahey. She told us of her experience as a Dane-zaa child in the English that she had learned to speak after growing up in an entirely Dane-zaa Záágé?-speaking environment. In our transcription, we try to capture May's way of speaking, her second language, a beautiful and evocative form of "Indian English." She opens the story by telling us that children used to be sent out to "get a song" after preparing themselves by abstaining from food and water.

> *Dahghaazhiné?, Dane zhiné?.* Their songs, people's songs.
> They are looking for power.
> *Shin kaa dǫje. Dane ejidah.* They tell them to look
> for power from songs.
> *Ii la ge.* Just over there, they send the young kids out.
> Little kids, without eat, wash their face,
> without even touch water, a drink of water.
> Like that, they send them out. No wash face, like that.
> They send them out.
> *Guyághajih nazhiné? wǫlęh nááwǫtsat.*
> They said to them, "You will have songs and power. Go and
> have songs to be strong."
> They go there to get it, to find a song, to find their power.
> They say that.
> (RDA, DZDV08-11)

When May says "They say that," she is giving a literal translation of the Dane-zaa word *éhji,* which is the storyteller's way of ensuring that the story is true and comes down from past generations. She's not making it up. She is reporting what the elders said from generation to generation.

> See, that's what my dad tried to do to us. But I don't know.
> I get scared sometime. I don't want to go too far.
> But after that, I remember, and I sleep.
> I always dream of a bull or a cow.
> And that time, I don't see cow in Doig.
> We never know there's cows.
> We just stay in Doig, and from there we move to other place,
> and we see farmer, but I don't know how.
> I never know cows for a long time.
> One time, we come to Pine, I grow a little bigger,
> and from there I know there's a cow.

May Apsassin with granddaughter Winona, May 2010.
Photo by Robin Ridington

> But when I used to live in Doig, I dream of cows.
> And every time I see cow, I just smile, like that,
> but I never tell nobody.
> I just keep it to myself, and like that,
> but way after, I remember.
> That's why they tell us to do that.
> And I don't tell Tommy nothing.
> And I say, "Let's go do that. Let's go up there."
> But I never see nothing.
> No, nothing funny or nothing or anything to do.
> (RDA, DZDV08-11)

Here, May does not make an exaggerated claim to power, nor does she brag about having dreamed of an animal she had not yet known. Other people are supposed to discover a person's power by observing him or her in daily life. Rather than bragging or telling about their power directly, people are supposed to live life in such a way that others will be able to figure it out.

A few years before Doig elder Margie Wolf died, in May 2009, she told us a story about what happens if people brag about power they do not have. It is a tale of two brothers. One has real power. The other has none but brags and shows off animal hides, which he claims are signs of his power. Here is the story as Billy Attachie translated it.

> *Wawajich.* The people are telling this story.
> There were two brothers.
> The older brother was no good for nothing,
> but he thought he had power from the animals.
> The older brother kept lots of animal hides at his place.
>
> The younger brother had a lot of power. The younger brother knew lots of things, but he didn't show off.
> The younger brother told his wife,
> "I don't feel good when I'm going away with my older brother. I'm worried about you. Just look after these kids when I'm gone."
>
> After that, the two brothers slept two nights on the trail.
> The younger brother felt really bad. He told his brother,
> "I feel pretty rough. I don't know what's happening at home."
> The older brother said, "I didn't feel anything."
> He told his older brother, "You can stay here. I know there's a problem at home. I'm going home."
> The younger brother gathered all his stuff and went home,
> and the older brother just followed him really fast.
>
> When they got close to their camp, the younger brother's wife was hollering way high up. "Where have you been?"
> she said to him, hollering. He threw all his stuff away
> and ran back to his camp
> when he heard her hollering.
> His older brother was right behind.
> When he ran back to his wife and kids,
> his older brother just followed him really close.

The younger brother's wife and his kids were way up in a
spruce tree.
That big giant animal kept coming back to them.
He wrecked everything in the older brother's camp.

"That giant animal went back to the bush,
and then he came back to where we were," his wife told him.
"We had nothing to drink for many days," she said.
She told him, "The giant animal came back in the evening.
He's coming back again."
The younger brother met that giant animal.
The animal said to him,
"Your brother lied about me, and I wanted to kill him."
The older brother said to the giant animal,
"Please, I want to give you one of my younger kids."
The older brother was just shaking he was so scared.
He just held onto his younger brother.
The younger brother told him,
"You're just like an old lady. Follow those kids up in the tree."
The youngest child of the older brother was crying,
"Uncle, please don't let the giant animal eat me."
The younger brother was pretty mad,
and he told his older brother,
"Old lady. Go up in the tree."
He was mad when he heard his nephew crying.
The little boy was climbing up the tree,
but he just kept falling down.

The younger brother talked to the giant animal really well.
He knew he would have to kill him to save his nephew.
He kept two powerful arrows for bigger animals.
He used one on him,
but the animal kept on going after the kid in the tree.
Then he killed the giant animal with the second arrow.
He told his older brother, "Don't lie about the animals.
I had to kill my power for you."
He showed his brother the blood on his hand.
(RDA, DZDV09-31)

Margie's story is a warning to anyone who might want to make a false claim. Power is real. The giant animals are real. The elders who send a child out for Shin kaa know what will happen. They know about the child's animal friend from their dreams. Dreamers themselves sometimes sent children out into the bush.

One of these Dreamers was Margie Wolf's grandfather Matsíí?dak'alę (White Head, Jack Atsukwa), the son of the Dreamer Mak'íhts'ęwéswąą. He sent his sister's daughter – May Apsassin's mother-in-law, Julie Oldman Apsassin (Wanaii) – to get power. In the following story, May Apsassin refers to Julie as grandma, because that is what her children called Julie. May describes how Julie became a person who "little bit knows something" when Matsíí?dak'alę sends her out to where he had set a lynx snare, and she encounters a grizzly bear spirit.

> Like long time, the way my grandma, my granny Julie,
> she's a really strong *mazhiné?*.
> *Mazhiné? wǫlę* [she little bit knows something].
> Matsíí?dak'ale [White Head, a Dreamer] put lynx snare there
> for her.
> He want her to be mazhiné?.
> And she say she can't even lift nothing like that.
> She go put up snare for lynx, and in a couple of days
> she go back and check her snare.
> She see this grizzly bear. Is a big man sit under the tree.
> He say, "Come, I'm not going to hurt you."
> She say, "I want to run away home." But he say,
> "No, don't. Come. I want to help you."
> So she say, "I'm just shaking like that.
> I walk up to that grizzly bear." And she say,
> "He hold my hand and talk to me."
> He say, "You got two lynx.
> I'm going to take them home for you.
> But where people live in wood, far as there I go,
> and from there you're going to go home, and don't tell nobody."
> And from there, my granny said, "It happened to me."
> (RDA, DZDV08-11)

In May's story, the grizzly bear appears to Julie as a man. He becomes her friend, and she stays with him. He then takes her home. In order for the power to be contained, he tells her not to tell anybody about her experience. Only during the course of the rest of her life did the story of what happened to her become known. Now that Julie has gone along the trail to heaven, May is free to tell other people (especially

Charlie Dominic, ca. 1960. Courtesy Charlie Dominic

elders like ourselves) what Julie told her. In this way, stories of the vision quest become part of the wise stories that people live by.

May also told us about the vision quest of her father, Charlie Dominic, who was around ninety years old when he died in 1994. Charlie's mother, Atahin Yehlhézęh, married Charlie Yahey after Charlie's father died. Charlie Dominic always prided himself on having fine horses, and he particularly liked to be seen riding a beautiful white horse. The story of his vision quest helps explain this part of his personality. He had horse medicine, and his particular friend was a beautiful mare who appeared to him in the form of a big woman. Like many other vision quest stories, this one reveals that animals are persons who can transform themselves from animal to human form.

> And my dad, too, he say he see same thing.
> Horses take him away for one week.
> He say, "*Ts'ege Naachę?* [big woman]."
> He call that one mare. "Sure, big lady."

"Her arm is so big for a lady, and me, I'm just small,
and they call me Ts'ídaa [child]," he say.
"Little kid. They just carry me like that. I got no clothes on.
They carry me." He say, "Before that horse take me
down the river here, somewhere," he say,
"I went down. I wear moccasins.
It's raining, and all my clothes was sitting there,
and just me, they take me like that. And they repeat that.
And they say, "It was raining out there. Don't get wet."
And they just carry me all the way, like that, one week.
He say, "Someone want you. Your family want you,
wonder where you are. We're going to take you back soon."
(RDA, DZDV08-11)

Like many other vision quest stories, May's account of Charlie meeting with Mare Woman describes a child being taken from the spirit world, a world where animals appear in their human form, to the physical world, the world where the Dane-zaa live their day-to-day lives. Charlie leaves camp as a child and returns with the skills of an adult. He can tie his own laces and ride a horse. As he grows into manhood, Charlie becomes a skilled hunter and an accomplished horseman, using the gifts that Mare Woman gave him sometime in the early years of the twentieth century.

And they bring me back where my clothes were.
And this time ... before that I can't tie my laces ...
and there I go back and put my moccasins.
I tie my laces, and I ride one horse.
And I went back to my mom.
But she never say nothing. And I just tie horse in there.
I go round, and I go to some old guy. He say,
"I want go see him." That old guy, look at me and say,
"I know where you go. Keep it. Whatever you do, keep it.
That's for way ahead. You going to use it."
"You going to be a man," he tell me.
He say, "From there, I'm not scared.
I do anything. I go alone. I go do lot of things."
And that's how I say to my grandkids. And today, I said,
"I don't know if you kids know something like that."
(RDA, DZDV08-11)

Young Charlie's elders knew about his power from their own dreaming. One of them reassured him, "I know where you go. Keep it. Whatever you do, keep it. That's for way ahead." We spent a good deal of time with Charlie Dominic in the 1970s and 1980s, and he told us many stories. Charlie always dressed in cowboy attire and spent a lot of time with his horses. He was a gifted singer and an important influence on song keeper Tommy Attachie.

May's stories of the vision quest tell us about some of the responsibilities that a person with power must accept. Each power brings with it certain things that the person must refrain from doing, for instance, eating a certain animal or plant. Others must know and respect a person's power. As children mature and take on adult responsibilities, they will begin to give hints about the nature of their power.

If another person intentionally violates or disrespects someone's medicine, the power will spin out of control, and the person will become "too strong." He or she will begin to change into the human form of the medicine animal. Although this form is empowering in the spirit world, it is dangerous and terrifying if it appears suddenly in the world of daily life. The Dane-zaa word for this terrible being is *wehch'uuge*. When the taboo has been violated, those with power lose control. They begin to eat their own lips. The flesh of the lips enters the body and turns to ice. The wehch'uuge becomes a cannibal monster who craves human flesh, much like the giant animals who lived long ago. As May explains, the person becomes like a giant, and the world reverts to a time before Tsááyaa made it right.

> You know, they say you grow strong, *náátsat*.
> In the morning, *hatlęt'ǫʔ,* you grow strong, and your mouth –
> you start to eat your mouth.
> And you just grow big like this, really big. Giant.
> 'Cause something you're not supposed to eat, or something.
> My dad say, "Some people know horse. You can't ...
> You ride them. OK. You use them. OK.
> But you cannot touch their hair.
> If you drink with their hair or eat with their hair,
> you're going to grow strong, really strong,
> and nobody can kill you."
> (RDA, DZDV08-11)

As Charlie told May, no ordinary person can kill the monster. Only someone with greater power can restore balance to the world. When a person becomes wehch'uuge, someone with greater power must step in to fulfill the role that Tsááyaa played when he killed the giant animals that hunted people and changed them into their present form. A person who becomes wehch'uuge literally becomes one of the dangerous and destructive giant animals and must either be killed or changed back into proper human form.

Aku, a Doig elder who lived from 1879 to 1973, told Robin an amazing story about a man who had become transformed into one of the giant fish and became wehch'uuge. He lived by eating people for a long time until someone with greater power was able to overcome him. The wehch'uuge lived by a lake, the traditional place that Danezaa people went to for emergency supplies in the winter when game resources were hard to obtain.

Here is the story as Aku told it, translated by Billy Attachie.

> I don't know this story well. There's someone I don't know.
> The people knew that one lake always had lots of fish.
> Whenever they were hungry or starving in the wintertime,
> they would go to that lake.
> There was one man who was eating people. He was wehch'uuge.
> He knew that all the people would be coming to that lake,
> so he went there and made himself a great wooden teepee.
> He put holes through the logs
> so he could see when people were coming.
> He was a very tough man, big and tough.
> He didn't kill those people with a gun or bow.
> He would dream about dirty stuff.
> (RDA, Aku 1966)

The wehch'uuge's dreams are the exact opposite of normal hunt dreams. Instead of making contact with an animal who will agree to give itself if the people respect its body, this man dreams of dirty stuff. He conjures power to kill people and eat them. He carves images of his power on eating utensils, which he forces his victims to use. Unlike the images of game keepers that Dreamers write on birchbark, the wehch'uuge carves evil images that empower him to kill and eat people. Aku says *mazhiné? náátsat,* "his power was very strong."

> Then he would take green logs
> and carve plates and spoons and cups from them.
> Then he would carve something on them,

> monsters and things like that, with a stone knife.
> When people came, he would ask them if they would like to eat.
> The people were hungry, so they would say yes.
> He caught lots of fish for them,
> and he fed them from those plates.
> The people ate what he gave them.
> In not more than a minute, they would be dead.
> That man was a strong medicine man,
> really strong, *mazhiné? náátsat*. He went on like that,
> killing those people and eating them for a long time.
> He ate lots of people.
> (RDA, Aku 1966)

Aku's story takes a turn when a boy and his grandmother visit the lake. Like Tsááyaa, the man who overcame the giant animals, this boy receives instruction from his wise grandmother and from his own medicine power, which he had obtained from bison. As Aku puts it, "That boy knew something." To know something is to receive power from a vision quest. In this case, the boy had been raised by the bison people. He was half animal, half man, *ach'uu dane,* literally a different person.

> One summer, one boy and his grandmother were really hungry.
> They had heard about the man who was eating people,
> but the only way they could eat was to go to that lake.
> They decided to stay at a different place on the lake from the cannibal.
> The boy wanted to visit him all the same.
> "I think I'll go see that man," he told his grandmother.
> She told him, "Don't go."
> But he said, "I'm just going to visit him."
> Twice more she told him not to go.
>
> That boy knew something.
> Since he was a baby, the buffalo raised him.
> Finally, his grandmother agreed,
> and the boy went to the cannibal's camp.
> The boy sat down,
> and the cannibal offered him fish on a plate he had carved.
> The boy took the plate and finished it off. He didn't die.
> That boy was not really a man. He was from the buffalos.

> He was half animal, half man,
> an animal person, a different person *[ghadii dane, ach'uu dane]*.
> The cannibal told his wife, "You'd better give him another plate."
> So, they gave him another plate filled with fish.
> The boy finished all the fish on his plate, but still he didn't die.
> "How come you don't die?" the cannibal said.
> "All the other people have died."
> The boy said, "Why, I'm not filled up yet."
> (RDA, Aku 1966)

At this point in the story, Aku explains that the boy's grandmother had found him in buffalo hair scraped from a hide. He is like the boy, Aghęhtusdane (the moosehide-scrapings boy), in another well-known story. Despite the adversarial relationship between the boy and the wehch'uuge, the boy addresses the cannibal with respect, as grandfather. A remarkable conversation about exchange and reciprocity follows. When the cannibal realizes he cannot kill the boy, he asks the boy to return the food he has given him and holds out his hand. This gesture is the opposite of the generosity expected of a good hunter. The good hunter respects his game and uses the meat to give life to the people. The cannibal, unable to kill the medicine boy by feeding him, demands that the food be returned. The boy obliges, but instead of throwing up the food he has eaten, he disgorges a little green frog. Because the cannibal had requested the boy's food, he is obliged to eat it. The story ends with the boy's power overcoming that of the cannibal.

> That old lady had found the boy in the buffalo hair.
> He was like Aghęhtusdane [the moosehide-scrapings boy].
> "Grandfather," he said to the wehch'uuge.
> "I thought you were just feeding me.
> I didn't know you were trying to kill me."
> The cannibal got his arrows.
> He couldn't kill him with the plates,
> so he was going to kill him with arrows.
> The boy was still licking his plate. He told the boy,
> "You'd better throw up the food I fed you. I want to eat it."
>
> The boy made ready to throw up in the cannibal's hands.
> The only thing that came out in his hands was a little green frog.

The cannibal swallowed that frog and sat down.
The little boy sat down, too. He looked at the man.
He was sitting still, just looking at one spot on his foot.
The cannibal didn't feel very well.

The boy knew that was going to happen, so he went back.
Not long after that, the cannibal's wife came after him.
"Your grandfather tells you to come and fix him up.
Something's the matter with him. I don't know what."
"I don't know, either," the boy said. But the woman said,
"Just come and take a look." So, they went back.
When they got to the cannibal, he was lying still.
He didn't know anything.
The boy took some black sticks from the fire
and put them on his neck.
The black went right through him, and he died.
"I can't fix this man up. He's already dead," the boy said.
That's how he killed Fish Man.
(RDA, Aku 1966)

Although the giant animals lived in ancient and mythic times, they were a real presence in the traditional life of the Dane-zaa people. Each animal in the ordinary world was represented by a spirit animal who retained the power of the original giant animals. When a child went on a vision quest, he or she received the blessing of that power. If someone disrespected that power later on, the giant form crossed over into the Dane-zaa world and threatened the people, just as the giant animals had threatened people in ancient times. The vision quest was familiar to every child who grew up in a Dane-zaa community. Children learned about it by observing elders, and they experienced it directly. They also knew the creation story and the stories of Tsááyaa, who went around the world making things right. As Charlie Yahey told Robin in August 1968, "The people who lived a long time ago all knew about how the world was first made."

4
Archaeology, Prehistory, and Oral History

The Dane-zaa creation story explains the essential nature of time and space in relation to the lives of human and animal persons. Sky Keeper is the creative force that brings earth and sky into relationship with each other. When Muskrat dives down to bring back earth, he helped to create the world that humans and animals share with one another. Archaeologists and geologists use physical evidence to tell another kind of story. Their story reveals how people lived in Dane-zaa territory for the last ten or eleven thousand years. Many Dane-zaa today have received training in archaeological techniques and have used their knowledge of their land to assist archaeological investigations, including those that focus on the remains of animals from long ago. The Dane-zaa view these bones as artifacts of a time when giant animals roamed the earth. The stories that describe these animals might have been passed on from generation to generation for thousands of years.

Oil and gas companies and highway contractors are now disturbing the Dane-zaa's traditional territory. British Columbia's Heritage Conservation Act requires the companies to conduct surveys to identify significant sites. They must avoid areas of high archaeological and cultural significance where possible and conduct excavations in areas that will be disturbed. As a result of work by both contract and academic archaeologists, a picture is emerging of how people have lived in the Peace River area since the end of the last ice age.

About 10,500 years ago, hunters butchered a bison in a cave on the shore of Charlie Lake. They enjoyed their meal, and left the bison bones and a few other artifacts behind. The scene would have been a familiar one to the Dane-zaa, who hunted bison in the area until the twentieth century.* These bones and artifacts are the earliest evidence of human life in Dane-zaa territory. One of the artifacts, a small fluted projectile point shaped from stone, known as a Clovis point, resembles other points found in Canada and the United States in the same time period – from about 10,000 to 12,000 years ago – and as far south as Mexico. Scientists estimate that massive sheets of ice covered most of Canada and the northern United States until about 15,000 years ago. During a period of global warming that began 13,000 years ago, the ice began to melt, and large lakes formed from the meltwater. One of these lakes was Glacial Lake Peace, which formed when a huge ice dam kept meltwater from flowing directly into the Peace River. The lake covered much of the plateau north of the Peace, and it deposited the thick layers of clay and silt that form the greasy, thick mud for which the area is famous. When the glaciers began to melt and the ice dam broke between 11,000 and 10,000 years ago, Glacial Lake Peace drained, leaving smaller lakes as remnants. Charlie Lake is one of these remnants.

The deposits at the bottom of the glacial lake became part of Dane-zaa nané?. The word *nané?* means "the territory on which people live." It also means "the very earth from which it is made." When the waters receded, the land emerged, and the plants and animals appeared soon after. Archaeologists who worked at Charlie Lake cave found that the banks of the Peace River went through a period of deep cutting, which halted about 2,000 years ago when the river reached its current height (Burley, Hamilton, and Fladmark 1996, 5). The area around Charlie Lake became, and remains, a rich habitat for animals, large and small. The prairie lands adjacent to the Peace River are ideal for bison. The muskeg lands to the north and east can support moose, elk, deer, beaver, and a variety of fur-bearing animals. Mountain sheep, goats, and whistlers (marmots) live in the mountains to the west. Lakes and rivers provide fish.

Archaeologists believe that hunting people first entered the Peace country from the south, rather than from an earlier ice-free corridor to the north (Burley, Hamilton, and Fladmark 1996). Once the ice had gone, plants and animals colonized the newly created lands, and hunting people quickly followed. Although they hunted with stone-tipped

---

* Although no commercial bison hunting was done after the early nineteenth century, a few bison remained, and the Dane-zaa hunted them to feed their own families.

spears rather than bows and arrows, they must have possessed the same basic hunting skills that the Dane-zaa have today. As hunting and gathering people, the Dane-zaa took advantage of the land's rich and varied resources by moving seasonally to areas with abundant animals and plant life. Knowing how to use these seasonal rounds has been at the heart of the Dane-zaa way of life for thousands of years. Before the introduction of firearms, hunters used drives and surrounds to capture game. The first people would have used spears tipped with Clovis points to kill animals once they were surrounded or driven over cliffs. The hunters who enjoyed a meal at Charlie Lake passed down knowledge of the land and its resources through wise stories. As guns and the fur trade changed the ecology of the land, the Dane-zaa adapted.

In 2008 and 2009, archaeologist Aidan Burford and his colleagues at Archer CRM (Cultural Resource Management) excavated a site at the southern end of Charlie Lake. Farmers whose families had cleared the land in that area had reported finding bison skulls everywhere. The excavation began when the province was widening the highway between Fort St. John and Charlie Lake. As it progressed, the team made major discoveries. The site is immense – five kilometres by five kilometres. According to Remi Farvacque, a member of the team, the site "has all the types of tools that one would find for the last ten or twelve thousand years ... tools from the paleo-Indian period right up to the fur trade, with gunflints and everything in between ... It's been a very stable landscape for the last ten thousand years." Farvacque concluded that the area is "one of the oldest continually occupied sites in Canada" (Ridington/Dane-zaa Archive [RDA], DZHD09-20).

Archaeologists also found evidence of long-range trade networks: stone materials from the Northwest Territories, obsidian (volcanic glass) from Mount Edziza in the Tahltan Highlands of northwestern BC, and ground slate tools from the Coast. One of the stone items, an atlatl weight, was used to give thrust to a spear before the introduction of bows and arrows. Atlatls are well suited to hunting in open terrain but are not as effective as bows and arrows in forested areas. According to Farvacque, "An atlatl is very accurate for a longer distance than a bow and arrow, so you can actually puncture through thicker skin and get right to the bone and right to the organs. You can actually use an atlatl up to a hundred metres. You can sneak up on game and don't have to get too close to it." To date, the atlatl weight remains the only one found outside of southwestern BC. Based on stylistic evidence, Farvacque estimates that it "probably dates from about 2,000 to 3,000 years ago" (RDA, DZHD09-20).

The Charlie Lake site contains both bison bones and fish bones, indicating that it was (and remains) a rich and productive area where people could rely on both fish and game for food. Farvacque concludes that the earliest paleo-Indian people came to the Charlie Lake area from the south and that people with microblade stone technology came in later from the north. Although archaeologists cannot know the language spoken by the people whose tools they unearth, the appearance of microblades in the Northwest Territories and later at Charlie Lake points to the presence of people who spoke a language related to Dane-zaa Záágéʔ.

Archaeologists also found evidence of extensive burning, which indicates that the Dane-zaa and their ancestors intentionally managed the grassland habitat to support a stable bison population. According to Patricia McCormack, First Nations of the Peace River area "practiced regular controlled burning as part of a regime of environmental management and cultural construction of landscape, producing extensive grasslands throughout this Subarctic region" (McCormack 2007, 1). Archaeological evidence suggests that the Dane-zaa and their ancestors must have maintained bison habitat in the upper Peace River area for thousands of years. Even when the bison became extinct in the area because of overhunting to supply the fur trade, the Dane-zaa continued to use fire to maintain the prairie habitat as a range area for their horses.

Dane-zaa storytellers remember elders describing a time when countless bison perished from some natural cause, either a disease or flooding. McCormack explained that "bison can die off in deep snow, in snow covered by a thick layer of ice, or in floods. They swim but not like caribou; they can drown easily" (email correspondence with R. Ridington, 10 March 2010). Sam Acko heard the following story from Eskama, his brother Jack's wife. He told it to us in English.

> This boy, Eskama's great-great-grandpa, or somebody like that, when he was a little boy,
> I guess he went to one flat where there were lots of buffalo,
> but he saw one buffalo sleeping alone.
> Just like a golden one, like albino or yellow buffalo, white buffalo,
> that's sleeping really good on the sand on a hot day.
> He told that boy,
> "This is the last time I'm sleeping good. That's why I'm here.

Eskama at Doig, 1968. Photo by Robin Ridington

From west side, I think there's a sickness coming to this area
that will kill everything.
You go home and tell your parents what I told you,
and the rest of the people, your people. Warn them."
"Before the sickness come to this area, they should go to
that highest spot and live up there until everything is over,"
he told that boy.
So, that boy went home and told all his family.

And then his family told everybody, everybody, that his son
say that.
And he's going to move to that high hill,
then even two, three years up there until everything is over.
There's some families, they just laugh at him.
"There's no sickness coming. We're not going anywhere.
We'll be here."

Then those people who believed moved with him to that high
place.
That buffalo told him,

> "Some of my people will go up there, too. And different kind of
> animals will go up there, too. They will survive."
> I guess after they did that, that sickness came to this area.
> Kill everything. And then, I guess, the next year,
> when it's all over,
> the sickness came right through all the big rivers,
> rivers like Doig, Pine, and all the rivers like that.
> Just like beaver dam, those buffalo, they go in the water and die.
> They are just like a beaver dam along those rivers, too.
>
> Many years after that,
> they don't drink the water from the creeks or the rivers.
> They just live on the muskeg water
> or somewhere the water in the high places,
> high place where there's fresh water and creeks and ponds.
> Before, they live on water and lower spots like up here.
> Even trees all died, all the plants – everything died.
> I wonder what is that.
> I don't know what it is. And those people that don't believe,
> they're all gone. They are all dead.
> (RDA, DZ00-18)

This story tells us that the Dane-zaa in precontact times enjoyed large numbers of bison in their territory. From Alexander Mackenzie's journal of 1793, we also know that bison were numerous along the Peace River at the time of first contact (Mackenzie and Lamb 1970). Eskama's story explains that whatever killed the bison also killed trees and other living things. In other words, the catastrophe was environmental rather than an illness specific to bison. Whatever the cause of death, the population had recovered by the time of first contact.

One of the stories that Dane-zaa tell about the time before first contact is called "Dog Piss on Arrow War" or "Aht'uutlętahsalats" (literally "arrow, dog he piss on it"). The Dane-zaa elders also tell this story to explain the dispersal of Athapaskan languages. Doig story keepers Sam Acko and Tommy Attachie told us this version on 8 May 2010. Billy Attachie translated.

> This is the story of Aht'uutlętahsalats, dog pee on arrow,
> way before *Moniyaas* [whitemen] came to this land.
> Now, we're going to tell you a story.
> This is the story about dog pee on arrow.

People all gathered together, from down south,
all over the place,
and some of the Dane-zaa there, too. All different tribes.
They wanted to make peace. They all wanted to make peace.
People from all over the place,
they gathered together to make peace.
They wanted no more war. After they gathered together there,
they wanted to go far north from where they gathered
to meet with some other people from the north.
They wanted to tell those people to make peace.
They all wanted to be one big family, friends.
That's why they gathered together.
There was one man that told everybody,
"There's something going to happen here.
Let's try to go around it.
I think you guys are going to have a war among yourselves."
That's where it started from.

People were all happy gathered together there on a big prairie.
This is what I heard, what the people said.
That morning, people were all gathered together.
In the morning, they were all happy. They were going to
go hunt.
They told each other which way they were going to go hunt,
and still today it's like that.
Even today, we tell each other where we're going to hunt.
We really watch out for gun safety.
People tell each other where they are going, still today.
They all gathered together where they were going to go hunt.
They talked about it.
They laid out their bows and arrows outside,
and then one of the dogs peed on the arrows.
That was a good hunting dog,
but he walked around there and peed on one of the arrows.

One woman saw that dog. She said, "What happened to you guys?
Why is it a dog peed on the arrow?"
She said it, but nobody heard her yet.
At the same time, all the other women told her,
"Shut up. Don't say anything." She just said that louder.
"I told you guys, that dog peed on the arrow."

They all looked at their arrows,
and one of those guys found out that the dog
had peed on his arrow.
The owner of the arrow picked up his bow and arrow,
and he shot that dog.
The arrow went right through that dog, and it fell and died.

Then the owner of the dog shot that woman who told on the dog.
The owner of the dog shot that woman, and she died.
That's when they started fighting each other.
When they started that war, some of them ran away.
Some of them jumped in the lake.
They were holding each other from fighting for a long time.
They said, "That woman died but that's OK. Let's not fight."
But finally, they started fighting anyway.
They just wiped each other out
until there were only two people left.
They couldn't kill each other.

There was one old guy who tried to stop the war.
He just kept pushing people back, "No war. No war."
But one of the more powerful guys
threw the old man down and killed him.
From there on, they just kept fighting.
They tried to stop the fight for a long time, but it didn't work.
If that old man hadn't gotten killed,
they could have made peace.
After that, they wiped all the people out
until there were only two men left to fight.
These men tried to pick up all the bows and arrows,
but they couldn't kill each other.

People split up and went all over the place.
Some went where the sun comes up.
Some went where the sun goes down.
There wasn't any border, that time.
Way long time after, one of the really old woman told people,
"I'm the one who survived dog pee on arrow."
That old lady remembered from a long time ago.
The survivors all split off. That's the woman who survived.

> She went into the water and came out
> until her breasts were on the water. That's how she survived.
> One of the men who survived told her,
> "Go underneath my arm," and that's how she survived.
> K'e che mege, Saskatoon Lake north of Beaverlodge, Alberta,
> that's where Aht'uutlętahsalats happened.
> (RDA, DZHD10-15)

In precontact times, people who spoke Dane-zaa Záágé? and related Athapaskan languages occupied territory from Lake Athabasca to the Rocky Mountains. The story of Aht'uutlętahsalats probably explains the actual dispersal of these people sometime before the influx of white people. Even before they had any direct contact with Europeans, the Dane-zaa felt the effects of their presence. The Cree, displaced by the white people coming into the Prairies, began to move into the Peace River country in the eighteenth century. The Cree served as middlemen in the fur trade before the formation of the North West Company and charged high prices for items the traders brought from eastern Canada and Europe (see Chapter 5). In 1793, Alexander Mackenzie encountered Cree as far west as the Parsnip River, well into Sekani territory. The Cree already had firearms, which had presumably been obtained in trade from people farther east. The late Doig elder Albert Askoty told us and Howard a story in which encroaching Cree challenge the Dane-zaa along the Peace River while their fellow Athapaskans the Tsegenuu* (Sekani) challenge them in the mountains. In Albert's story, both the Dane-zaa and the Tsegenuu are named as individuals while the Cree remain nameless. Billy Attachie translated the story.

> The Cree and Dane-zaa met on the Peace River.
> There was a Dane-zaa leader named Ahatáa.
> There were no trees there, that time, along the Peace River.
> They met each other straight on.
> The Cree people were on the other side of the river.
> The Dane-zaa were on this side.
> They were ready to fight, but the chiefs said,
> "Let's send two guys each to the middle of the river

---

* This is the Dane-zaa's preferred pronunciation. Elsewhere, it is spelled *Tsekene*.

> and see who will beat. We're going to send these two guys,
> and whoever wins will take the other guy back to their side.
> Whoever they bring back, they will cut his body up with a knife
> and throw his body in the river."
> On the Dane-zaa side, this older brother said, "I'm going to do it,"
> but his younger brother said, "I will do it."
> (RDA, HB-12a&b)

The name of the Dane-zaa chief in Albert's story is particularly interesting. *Ahatáa* means "our father" and suggests that this man was thought of as a protector of his people. In later years, *Ahatáá* came to be used as a name for God, in keeping with Catholic liturgy. At the time of this story, however, there is no indication that the Dane-zaa had met any white people, and they had certainly not had any contact with the Catholic Church. Ahatáa in this story may have been an early Dreamer.

> On the Cree side, one went in the water to meet the Dane-zaa.
> They met right in the middle and started wrestling.
> The Dane-zaa brought the Cree back almost to their side.
> Then the Cree took the Dane-zaa to his side.
> The older brother said, "I was going to do it.
> Why did you take my place?"
> The Cree just about got the Dane-zaa close to the edge
> on his side,
> but the Dane-zaa made a sound like a swan.
> He just bit the water like a swan and started swimming
> back toward his side with the Cree.
> The Cree was trying to use Beaver power,
> but the Swan took him back toward the Dane-zaa side.
> The Dane-zaa man carried him up in the air
> and brought him back right on the land.
> After he brought him back on the Dane-zaa side,
> they cut him all up and threw his meat in the water.
> (RDA, HB-12a&b)

The story does not mention the use of physical weapons. Rather, the contest pits one person's power against another's. The Cree fighter used Dane-zaa medicine that would have given him power over the water, but the Dane-zaa called upon the power of Swan. First, he bit the water to disable the Cree's power, and then he carried him into the air. Gerry Attachie, commenting on this period in history, stated, "Beaver Indians beat them just like nothing, no problem. They have more power" (Broomfield and Ridington 1983).

Albert's story continues:

> The Dane-zaa said,
> "Let's all go across, and they aren't going to hurt us in the water.
> Let's swim across and fight them on the ground."
> They swam across, and they killed all the Crees.
> They killed them all.
> The chief on this side, Ahatáa, got all the people together to go over with him. His name was Ahatáa.
> Ahatáa travelled with his people
> and climbed up the highest mountain on this side.
> His mom was married over there.
> Maybe that's where he came from, Tsegenuu [Sekani, or Rocky Mountain People]. In wintertime, the people there said,
> "Let's all have a feast."
> (RDA, HB-12a&b)

The story describes a time when the Beaver and Sekani often intermarried. Ahatáa's mother was a Dane-zaa who had married a Sekani man, which gave him ties to both communities. The two groups speak closely related dialects of the same language. They both think of themselves as Dane-zaa, as opposed to Cree, who the Dane-zaa called "Dahshíne." But, as Mackenzie reported in 1793, the Beaver and Sekani were often in conflict with each other as the Cree pressed into their territories. The first part of Albert's story ends with an agreement between Ahatáa and the Sekani to get together and feast. Albert then describes the treachery and conflict that follows.

> There was one young guy named Matsíí?dáásasádlę, Curly Hair.
> He was Tsegenuu.
> This young Dane-zaa guy was visiting the Tsegenuu.
> His mother was Beaver, but she had married a Tsegenuu man.
> The Tsegenuu people told him to sit right at the corner by the door.
> They put him at the corner.

> Matsíí?dáásasádlę was outside with a knife in his jacket.
> They passed all the food among everybody,
> but the Dane-zaa guy didn't eat. They asked each other,
> "Why isn't this young guy eating the meat?"
> Those young Tsegenuu kids were going around with bow and arrow.
> They were trying to trick this young guy sitting in the corner.
> They shot with arrows, and they all jumped him
> because he didn't want to eat what they wanted to feed him.
> But he just jumped straight out of the teepee and escaped.
> He came out and had his snowshoes ready outside.
> He got his snowshoes on. Matsíí?dáásasádlę chased him with his knife, but he couldn't catch up with him.
> The young Beaver guy got away from Matsíí?dáásasádlę,
> but the Tsegenuu tried throwing spears at him.
> (RDA, HB-12a&b)

The conflicts between closely related people were different than those with the Cree, who were not named as individuals. Skirmishes between relatives had, no doubt, always been a part of precontact life, but pressure from the Cree intensified the amount of conflict in the eighteenth century. According to the Dreamers who came along later, one of the Dreamers' main aims had been to stop the fighting, which had become unsustainably destructive.

> This young Beaver guy on snowshoes went back to his people.
> The Tsegenuu were trying to trick his people.
> They all went back up to the mountain.
> Tsegenu were tired of getting beat up all the time.
> They were tired of the wars.
> They went up to the highest mountain
> and used a rope to pull themselves up to the top.
> Four Beaver guys followed them all the way up in the mountain
> to try to catch Matsíí?dáásasádlę.
> They went to where they couldn't see any more tracks.
> They don't know where the Tsegenuu went.
> That's where the Tsegenuu had lifted each other up with a rope.
> They knew they would be in trouble if he escaped.
> These four Beaver guys had power and used that
> to go up on top of the mountain.

It was wet, and they were soaking wet.
They went to sleep under a big Jack pine.
When they went to sleep, they saw some big bird
land right on top of the big Jack pine.
When it landed, the Jack pine just waved.
It must have been a big bird.
When it flew away, not too far down it landed.
Those four people were there. Matsíí?dáásasádlę was Tsegenuu.
The four guys were Beaver.

Matsíí?dáásasádlę was wearing a coat of whistler skin.
He told his people, "You guys are making too much noise."
One woman said, "Something was bothering me,"
but Matsíí?dáásasádlę said,
"Yesterday, I was sitting on top of the tree,
and I didn't see anything."
He was that big bird who made the Jack pine sway back
and forth.
"Last night, I sat in the big Jack pine, but I didn't see
anything."
He didn't see them because the four guys had power.
He didn't see them sleeping under the tree.
In the morning, they sneaked up on him.
One Tsegenuu elder said, "Something bad is going to happen.
My body is moving."
Daylight started to come, enough light so the four guys
could see their arrows, where they shoot.
The young Beaver guy said, "Leave Matsíí?dáásasádlę to me.
He just about got me with a knife. I know where he is."
Ahatáa was with them, too.
The young guy poked a knife in Matsíí?dáásasádlę's leg
through the whistler blanket.
He was still half-asleep, but he tried to run away.
The young guy said, "You're the one who chased me with
a knife."
Matsíí?dáásasádlę said, "I'm the one."
The young guy pretended that he couldn't catch up with him.
When he really wanted him, he caught up with
Matsíí?dáásasádlę.
He caught him by the hair. He pulled him down.

"You're the one who chased me all the way with a knife."
He killed him there.

He looked back, and all the Tsegenu houses were upside down.
When they are in a war like that, they hide until the morning.
They make a dawn raid.
They came out and got them fast,
like when the fastest dog runs out.
This is how much power they have.
(RDA, HB-12a&b)

Matsíí?dáásasádlę was able to transform himself into a giant bird, but the four Dane-zaa men had more power and could make themselves invisible. Fights between the Tsegenuu and Dane-zaa were different than those with the Cree, because the combatants were closely related to each other through intermarriage. The fight described above happened because of treachery during a feast that was supposed to bring people together. The underlying cause was undoubtedly the pressure both people were feeling as the Cree moved into their territories in the years before first contact with Europeans.

The story of Duuk'ihsachę Matáá? provides insight into the role of Dreamers before the arrival of white people. Duuk'ihsachę was the ancestor of many people among the Ts'ibe Dané?. His name means "he who sleeps with giant animals." He was the father of Yehlhézęh and Dechezhę, men described, respectively, as "Chief of the Muskeg Indians" and "the Great Man" in the North West Mounted Police 1899 census of Indians in the Fort St. John area.* Duuk'ihsachę was probably a young adult when the North West Company established its first trading post in Dane-zaa territory in 1794.† His father was also named Duuk'ihsachę and had power from the giant animals. The father was a Dreamer who could predict the future and protect his people from harm. For clarity, we refer to him as Duuk'ihsachę Matáá? or Duuk'ihsachę's father. He lived before the Dane-zaa had any direct contact with Europeans. In 1966, Robin recorded Aku's story about Duuk'ihsachę Matáá?.

---

* See Chapter 9 for more information about the Doig and Blueberry descendants of these men.
† See Chapter 6 for stories about Duuk'ihsachę's interactions with early traders.

Aku begins by saying that the story took place "not very long ago." By this, he means that the story describes a known ancestor rather than a mythic or legendary character but that the events happened sometime before the Dane-zaa had contact with Europeans. The story begins in early spring when the snow has thawed and frozen again, and the crust on top of the snow makes it easy for people to walk without snowshoes. The events Aku relates continue throughout the summer. The protagonist is an elder (we later learn it is Duuk'ihsache Matáá?) whose power has given him a premonition about something dangerous approaching his people. He is possessed by *náághadah*. His entire body begins to shake. At first, the people do not believe him. The feeling continues until the people come together at a summer gathering place. Billy Attachie provided the translation that follows.*

> This guy's story is not very long ago.
> It's an old story, but it's not from way back.
> These people lived by the mountain.
> It was toward the springtime,
> when the snow is hard with a crust, so you can walk on top.
> This one old guy, his body was just moving, really uncomfortable, *náághadah*. He knew something was going to happen.
> His body was moving pretty bad. He was shaking all over.
>
> *Yííchę?*, from way back, Wǫlii Nachii was coming.
> That elder, he knew about the giant animals.
> That old guy, his body was all moving when the snow was crisp.
> By their power, they know something is going to happen.
> They feel it in their body. He kept saying,
> "My body is moving. It's pretty hard, *ęhdaadedlaah*."
> Pretty soon, the snow was gone.
> Even with the snow gone, sometimes he can't sit one place.
> *Haatindon*, pretty soon, it's summertime.
> Pretty soon, the moose are all fat again, maybe in August.
> Close to the mountain there's one big river.
> There's where they have a traditional camping area.
>
> They were moving camp up the river.
> This big river is right by the mountain.

---

* Billy Attachie's translation, with subtitles cued to the original audio, is available at http://sites.google.com/site/plumeofcockatoopress/dane-zaa-videos.

It's very long and straight there.
Three camps away, the river turns.
After the moose got fat, they kept going up the river,
moving camp.
He was still feeling náághadah.
His body was still moving since last winter.
They didn't eat well either that time.
They killed a bull by that river.
After they killed that moose, they started eating well again,
and they moved camp again. Some of the people said,
"Since last winter, that guy's body has been moving,
but nothing has happened. We didn't see anything."
This was the second moose they killed.
"They're going to move camp to that moose today.
It's hard," they said.

That old man didn't eat for six days.
He knew the mind of that giant animal is really strong.
When they got to where they killed the moose,
they made a big fire and they all ate.
Where they killed that moose by the river, they all ate.
That elder told them,
"Today, you're going to see something.
That mountain is straight up.
Go up there, but don't make just one track.
Spread out and just go way up to the top.
When you get to the top, you look out from over there.
It's going to happen today."
(RDA, Aku 1966)

Duuk'ihsache Matáá? could see into the future because of the power from Wolii Nachii, the giant animal. This prophetic power was like that held by the Dreamers who came after him. It was different, however, in that it was specific to his own personal *Shin kaa* (to seek a song) power. He knew the power of Wolii Nachii from his personal dream encounter, but he did not dream about heaven.

The story continues, setting the scene for the threat that approaches.

That river is straight for three camp lengths.
After they all ate by the river, they went up to the mountain.

When they got to the top,
there were lots of people camped over there.
That river is straight for three camp lengths.
After that, it turns.
That elder is pretty troubled. Where they got up to the mountain,
not too far away, he was sitting there.
He looked down the river where they moved camp from.
He looked back where they had been.
Where the river bends three camps away,
they saw something moving over there.
You can't see anything normal moving from that far away.
It was a giant animal. You won't see horses or moose that far.
They saw some big animal coming out into the open.
He's coming fast just like a bullet. He already passed one camp.
(RDA, Aku 1966)

Finally, the people believe the old man. They can see the giant animal following their tracks. Suddenly, they find themselves transported back to the time before Tsááyaa sent the giant animals beneath the earth. Wǫlii Nachii is tracking them. Finding fresh tracks is important in Dane-zaa hunting, but in this case the roles of hunter and hunted are reversed. The giant animal has discovered their tracks and is quickly catching up with them.

The elder went back to his people. He told the people,
"Look at that giant animal coming. Some of you guys doubted.
I want you to look at it now."
They watched this big animal follow them.
When he's coming sideways, right in the middle he's white.
When he turns sideways, the people thought there were two
of them.
Those people said, "Two of them following us."
The elder told them, "That's only one."

When they first saw him three camps away, it was evening.
He's already at the second camp,
and the sun's still in one place, he's that fast.
Where they killed that moose and made fire, there's still smoke.
When he saw the smoke and smelled it,
just like he disappeared. Maybe he snuck up to that place.
When he saw that smoke, he just went down out of sight.

> When he got to where they left the fire, he showed up again,
> but there was nobody there.
> (RDA, Aku 1966)

The giant animal had already reached their last camp. The people try to confuse Wǫlii Nachii by spreading out so that there will be many trails rather than one, but by this time he is so close he can easily cover the distance between them.

> From there, the giant animal looked all over. People all
> spread out.
> They all went up the hill, but he knew what they were doing.
> He went straight up to where the people were.
> The giant animal went straight up.
> (RDA, Aku 1966)

The people realize that it will be impossible to run away. Only a person who has power from the giant animal can save them. They watch as Duuk'ihsachę Matááʔ goes out to meet the giant animal.

> That elder knew the giant animal was coming.
> He went ahead to meet him.
> That elder kept a moosehide, a really white one.
> He kept it all the time for his power.
> The elder took all his clothes off
> and covered himself with that white moosehide.
> He went to meet the giant animal.
> People were just crying for their kids.
> He kept going up after them. The elder went to meet him.
> When they got close, the elder talked to the giant animal.

> His name was Duuk'ihsachę. Duuk'ihsachę Matááʔ was the
> elder who was moving with náághadah
> ever since early spring. That's Duuk'ihsachę Matááʔ.
> He talked really loud to the giant animal.
> Duuk'ihsachę Matááʔ was yelling at that giant animal,
> but Wǫlii Nachii pretended he was looking back where he
> came from.
> The elder kept yelling at him and finally
> Wǫlii Nachii looked at him and went to meet him.
> (RDA, Aku 1966)

Duuk'ihsache Matáá? knew the giant animal from his Shin kaa. He asked Wolii Nachii why he had come to his camp and frightened his kids. The giant animal said he wanted Duuk'ihsache Matáá? to stay with him again. Even a giant animal can feel lonely.

> That giant animal looked at Duuk'ihsache Matáá?.
> Then he started coming toward him. The old man said,
> "Why did you come here? Are you going to eat Duuk'ihsache?"
> He said that. He went to meet him.
> When he met him, he pushed the giant animal back with
> his hand.
> Duuk'ihsache Matáá? asked the giant animal,
> "Why did you come here? My kids are scared of you."
> Duuk'ihsache Matáá? said that.
> The giant animal said, "I want to see you again."
> The giant animal told him,
> "Where you are moving, I'm going that way, too.
> Not too far from here, I'm going to wait for you.
> You keep me happy till I leave."
> The giant animal went back down the hill, just fast.
> "I'll be waiting for you there," he told Duuk'ihsache Matáá?.

> That giant animal is really fast. He moves fast,
> like something small that goes fast.
> He backed down, and when he got to the bottom,
> he walked through the big spruce trees.
> When he stepped on the roots, the trees bent over,
> just like when you walk on muskeg with a horse
> and step on the roots of small trees.
> Those big spruce trees were just moving like that.
> He went to where the people were going to move.
> Duuk'ihsache Matáá? stayed with him two more days.
> The animal wanted him to stay with him.
> Finally, he told Duuk'ihsache Matáá? to go back to his
> people.

> After Duuk'ihsache Matáá? came back to his camp,
> he told his people,
> "Wolii Nachii told me to follow him and keep him happy for
> a while,
> so I'm going to go follow him now."

> The old guy went to follow the giant animal
> and caught up with him where the animal waited for him.
> That animal kept going places with him slowly.
> The old guy slept with him quite a few nights.
> The giant animal told Duuk'ihsache,
> "I'm lonesome for you. What happened to you?"
> (RDA, Aku 1966)

This story reveals a lot about Dane-zaa traditional thought. Personal medicine power could be used for more than just hunting. A person with power from a giant animal could protect his or her community from danger. In this respect, Duuk'ihsache Matáá? was like Tsááyaa. From this story we learn that although Tsááyaa placed the giant animals beneath the earth in ancient times, their power was still available to people who sought it. The giant animals were like forces of nature. A person such as Duuk'ihsache Matáá?, who slept with them, could establish a relationship that he could use to protect his people from harm. Rather than being dangerous and antisocial, personal medicine power could be used for the good of all. Duuk'ihsache Matáá? belonged to the last generation of Dane-zaa before they were challenged first by contact with Europeans and their trade goods and then by European religion. His son grew up in his father's world but lived most of his life in the fur trade era. He knew Wolii Nachii from his own Shin kaa, but he also knew the ways of the traders.

Augustine Jumbie (1895-1988) told a story that connects Aht'uutletahsalats with first contact (RDA, Beaver Tales). Although the story compresses events that happened over a longer period of time, it tells us how the Dane-zaa dealt with radical challenges to their way of life. Jumbie's first contact story begins with a small group of people who fled into the mountains following the war and lost touch with their relatives. It begins, as does Sammy Acko's story, with people camping together in peace and harmony. Liza Wolf, who translated Jumbie's story, uses the familiar term *Hudson's Bay* when referring to the traders, but given the context of Jumbie's story, this first encounter must have been with North West Company traders.

> There weren't any Slavey or Cree or any Sekani there.
> All the Beaver Indians were there. They were the only people.
> There weren't any different people. No one was sick.
> No one had died.

Jumbie then blames the woman who first made a fuss about the dog for the cascade of events that followed. He calls "Aht'uutlętahsalats" "a story about how one woman made trouble." Without going into the story itself – he presumes the audience is familiar with it – he launches into an account of the war's consequences.

> One woman, maybe thirty-nine years old,
> ran away from the war with her three younger brothers
> and her three daughters. They ran far away into the mountains.
> The woman's brothers hunted, and they got lots of game,
> so they lived pretty well.
> They lived like that for two or three years.
> Then the woman told her brothers
> she wanted them to marry her daughters
> and start up more people.
> So they did.

Although this may sound strange to a modern audience, the arrangement is perfectly correct within the terms of Dane-zaa kinship. The marriage of a woman to a man her mother calls brother, a cross-generation marriage, was allowed and sometimes took place (see Chapter 9 for a discussion of Dane-zaa kinship and community).

Jumbie then describes events that took place during the time when European influences were being felt, but before direct contact.

> Before that time, Indians had never seen white men.
> The white men had sent out Cree to bring the Indians to them,
> but the Cree always killed the people instead of telling them.
> Finally, the white men found a real Indian [i.e., a Dane-zaa].
> They gave him clothes and told him to go out and find his Indians.
> He [the Dane-zaa] knew that [the white] man wouldn't kill them.
> He set out walking.
> Finally, he came to the camp of those three women who
> married their _sı́ızes_ [mother's brothers]. They had lots of kids.

As time passes, the small band of refugees from the war begins to grow.

There were lots of people there by that time,
but those people were just like bush people.
They hadn't seen any other people
since they ran away from Aht'uutlętahsalats.
They watched their camps like dogs.
That man couldn't go into their camp. In daytime, he hid.
At nighttime, he sneaked around outside of their camp.
He couldn't go to them because he knew
they would either run away or else kill him.
He waited around there for a month.
Finally, all the people left camp, packing dry meat.
They were going to make a cache where nobody would
find it.
There were lots of them, lots of teenage boys and girls,
girls younger than that, lots of babies, lots of toddlers.
They all went up except for *asǫ*, the old grandmother,
and the babies and little children too young to walk fast
and keep up.

The man who had been sent out to find new people understands that his best option was to talk to the old woman who had experienced the war directly.

The man sneaked behind the old lady's camp.
She had a tent made out of hide with branches,
poplar and spruce boughs thick all around the sides.
The man went through those quietly
and sat down behind the old lady.
"Asǫ," he said, "don't be frightened.
There's no war anymore.
There's a Hudson's Bay.
The trading man sent me to find all the people.
He wants to see all the people."
That old lady turned around slowly.
Her eyes were big. She was scared. She was surprised.
The man got up and shook hands with the old lady
and with every one of the kids.
"There is no more war now.
The traders stopped the wars.
You don't need to be afraid," the man said.
The old lady was still surprised.

The old woman had never seen clothes made of cloth before. She asks the visitor about them, and he explains they are from the white men.

> "What kind of animal hide are your clothes made from?" she asked.
> The man was wearing clothes the Hudson [sic] Bay gave him.
> "This isn't from animals," he said.
> "The Hudson Bay man [who likely worked for the North West Company] gave these to me.
> You bring him all kinds of furs –
> marten, beaver, lynx, even bear hides –
> and he gives you clothes like these and other things.
> He wants me to tell all the Indians about that.
> He sent me out to tell all the Indians and bring them back.
> He doesn't want fights. There aren't any more fights."
> "That's right?" the woman asked. "Yes, that's right, that's true," the man answered. "I'm right."

The visitor and the old woman exchange information about their families and discover that there is a kinship connection. For traditional Dane-zaa, these bonds are important. Kinship ties had been broken by the war, and it was necessary to re-establish them. In this case, the visitor turns out to be someone the old woman would call by the same term she uses for her son. Through this exchange, the kinship connections broken by the war are restored.

> The woman was quiet for awhile.
> "What people do you come from?" she asked him.
> "My father's name is Achestastlin."
> "Heeeeey!" the old lady said,
> "that's my brother-in-law [ashe].
> He's married to my sister! He's still alive?"
> "Yes," the man said. The woman was really happy.
> She started cooking whistler for her saazę [sister's son].*
> "Wait till the rest come back," she said.
> "They went to take some dry meat to our hiding place."
> While he was eating, the rest of the people came back.

---

* In Dane-zaa kinship, a woman's sister's son is like her own son.

> The old lady ran out and yelled, she was so happy.
> "White man has come to our country.
> The white man has skin the colour of snow.
> They have stopped the wars. There are no more wars," she said.
> "My *saaze̜* says so." She took the people in.

The remainder of Jumbie's story describes the remarkable experience of meeting Europeans and learning about the new tools and weapons they would make available.

> The Hudson Bay man had given the man
> quite a few knives and some axes,
> and he showed the people how to use them,
> how to chop trees with the axes and how to cut meat with the knives.
> They sure liked them. They are called "white man."
> We call them *moniyaas* [the Cree term for white man].
> The man told them, "He trades these things, and matches
> and guns, for furs – marten, lynx, bear skins, everything."
> In the late afternoon, a chicken flew into the tree near the camp.
> The man took out his gun and shot it, and it fell down.
> They all got surprised. They never saw the shot.
> "How did you do that?" they asked.
> "When we shoot with an arrow at something in the brush,
> the arrow just hits the branches."
> "Can we look at that thing?" "Sure," the man said,
> "it doesn't have any bullets or powder in it. It can't hurt you."
> so all the people looked and looked at it every which way.
> Then he showed them how to shoot with a gun.
> "Gee, that's easy to handle. That's easy to use."
> The man said, "The Hudson Bay man has this kind of stuff
> in a house he made way down the Peace River,
> where it is big and broad. You can go down there.
> Nothing will hurt you."

Jumbie's story about the traders sending out Dane-zaa men to contact new people matches an account in a North West Company journal of 1799-1800. In the journal, a trader reports on 8 January 1800 that he had sent a Dane-zaa man named Jimathush (Chimarouche) to "discover more Indians" who would be willing to trade. Although

Jumbie didn't name the man, his story documents a common fur trade practice (see Chapter 5 for further discussion of the North West Company journal.)

Jumbie then describes how the man showed his new recruits how to snare and prepare furs. He concludes with the woman asking the man's father to keep in touch through dreaming.

> "Be sure to tell your father to dream about where we are next spring.
> This winter, we'll stay here and try to trap lots of furs.
> Then, before the ice breaks and the snow melts,
> we'll try to dream about where your father is.
> That's my *tlaasé* (brother-in-law, cross-cousin).
> I sure want to see him. You tell him to find out
> where we are, too, so we can meet him."
> The man said, "Sure, I'll be certain to tell him first thing."
> The next day, the man went back.
> The others stayed behind
> and trapped furs the way he had told them.

Jumbie's story tells of first contact. In the spring of 2009, Tommy Attachie told us another story from that time. It relates how Duuk'ihsachę Matááʔ's son, who was born before first contact but lived well into the fur trade era, got his name and his power, as had his father, from the giant animal. Tommy begins by describing how stories like this one passed from person to person, from generation to generation. Tommy heard this story from his grandmother Nachę. Billy Attachie and Madeline Oker Benson provided this translation.

> This is the story of Duuk'ihsachę. People from all over –
> Doig, Blueberry, Prophet River – have told this story.
> Makenachę [Bigfoot], Old Man Aku, Jack Aku,
> Charlie Yahey, Albert Askoty, Grandma Nachę –
> each one told the story a little differently,
> but nobody said it was wrong.
> They didn't tell it exactly the same way,
> but by the meaning, they were all the same.
> My grandma's story is true.
> How do they know these stories?
> Grandma told me about how she learned her stories.

She never knew her mom. Other people raised her.
When she was a girl, somebody else raised her.
When she was young, she married old Apąą.
She said, "Apąą showed me everything in the bush.
How to trap. He knew about everything, stories too,
Apąą's stories." Grandma learned from that.
That's why Grandma said,
"I know all these stories, good stories, from my husband."
My grandma told me, "My mom never raised me,
but I learned from other people," whoever raised her.

Duuk'ih<u>s</u>achę. He knows the giant animals.
He's a Dreamer and a strong man.
He knows the power of the giant animals.
Wǫlii Nachii spread out his fingers.
He counted ten fingers.
He told Duuk'ih<u>s</u>achę to walk on them, one to ten.
He ran across all Wǫlii Nachii's fingers,
and then Wǫlii Nachii took one finger back.
So, there were nine left.
Wǫlii Nachii told Duuk'ih<u>s</u>achę, "Old age is going to kill you.
I gave you nine years. You will live to be ninety years old.
I could have given you ten. Only old age will ever beat you.
Old age is going to beat you someday."

Duuk'ih<u>s</u>achę was his name – "He Slept with Giant Animals."
Wǫlii Nachii told him, "Duuk'ih<u>s</u>achę.
That is what your name will be."
That is why people called him Duuk'ih<u>s</u>achę.
His dad knew the giant animals, too.
That is how the story is.
People don't make a short story. Don't add anything to it.
Tell it exactly the way it was told.
We don't tell more than we know.
(RDA, DZHD09-1, DZHD09-23)

Being sent on a vision quest can be frightening for a young person, especially if, as in this case, the boy knows that his father is sending him to sleep with a giant animal. At first, Duuk'ih<u>s</u>achę tries to hide in the bush, but his father finds him and sends him out again. Part of

Tommy Attachie at Beaver Camp, 2002. Photo by Robin Ridington

the Shin kaa is learning to overcome fear and discovering that the giant animal knows you come to bring it joy.

>Duuk'ihsachę Matáá?, his dad, told him,
>"You, too, will know Wǫlii Nachii after I'm gone."
>Duuk'ihsachę went to follow the tracks of Wǫlii Nachii.
>"Follow him from here," his dad told him.
>Duuk'ihsachę was still young
>when his dad sent him after Wǫlii Nachii.
>Duuk'ihsachę hid in the bush instead of finding Wǫlii Nachii,
>but his dad found him.
>His dad went after him and told him,
>"If you're scared of Wǫlii Nachii, I'm going to kill you myself."
>So, Duuk'ihsachę followed the tracks of Wǫlii Nachii.
>Wǫlii Nachii made a fire and sat beside it.
>Duuk'ihsachę was hiding, but he could see Wǫlii Nachii.
>Wǫlii Nachii knew that he was there, and he called to him,
>"Duuk'ihsachę, come out here." He called him by his name.

That's when he got his name, Duuk'ihsachę.
Wǫlii Nachii told him, "You come here to bring me joy."
His dad sent him to where Wǫlii Nachii was.
Finally, he caught up with the giant animal.
He kept on sleeping with Wǫlii Nachii.

Wǫlii Nachii took beavers from their houses.
He gave Duuk'ihsachę the tails.
Wǫlii Nachii ate beaver, but he used to throw away the tail.
He gave Duuk'ihsachę the tail. Then he said, "Let me taste it."
After he tasted the beaver tail, Wǫlii Nachi told Duuk'ihsachę,
"You're not going to eat it any more." He told Duuk'ihsachę,
"The tail is good. You're never going to eat it again."
Many nights he spent with Wǫlii Nachii.
Then the giant animal told him,
"Your dad is worried about you. Go back this way, not
too far.
Your dad will meet you."

Duuk'ihsachę went home, and his dad met him.
Long time ago it was like that. When you were young,
you were just pure and clean.
You can't get power if you're not like that.
When you live with an animal like that for a long time,
your dad or some other relative will meet you
and help you get back to your normal self.
Duuk'ihsachę came back to his dad's camp.
He went in the direction
where his dad lay his head when he slept.
When he came back from Shin kaa,
he couldn't come in the doorway,
because that is where the women come into camp.
He came in where his dad laid his head.
Then he transformed back into his normal self again.
(RDA, DZHD09-1, DZHD09-23)

Leaving camp to find power and returning to camp with a new name and identity are points of transformation in a child's life. A man with power traditionally slept with his head facing east. In the story, Duuk'ihsachę is a boy when he leaves camp for Shin kaa. He returns a man. To complete the transformation, he enters the teepee from the direction in which his father sleeps. Both Duuk'ihsachę and his father are people of the mountains, the Dane-zaa also known as Sekani, but when Duuk'ihsachę marries a woman from the Ts'ibe Dané?, the Muskeg people, he becomes an ancestor of people at Doig River.

> Duuk'ihsachę was a strong person,
> but he didn't use his power to kill.
> He straightened out people to live right.
> He straightened out everything for people.
> He put people together.
> He was originally from the mountains, Tsegenuu.
> He was Tsegenuu, but the Ts'ibe Dané? gave him a wife.
> He joined the Muskeg people. He joined their families.
> He was a strong man, a powerful man.
> He went all over the world. He walked all around the land,
> and he knew everything about the land.
> He knows about the land from his power.
> Duuk'ihsachę was buried somewhere north of Hanás Saahgé?,
> somewhere around Chinchaga Lake.
> Those old people must have known where he was buried,
> long time ago, but us today, we don't know.
> "When moss grows over my grave,
> Wǫlii Nachii will come there."
> That's the story of Duuk'ihsachę.
> (RDA, DZHD09-23)

Duuk'ihsachę and his father were like the Dreamers who came after them in that they used their power to "straighten out people to live right." But unlike the Dreamers, they dreamed of the time when giant animals roamed the earth and hunted people rather than of heaven. They made friends with the giant animals and "gave them joy." In exchange, the giant animals gave them power, and in the case of Duuk'ihsachę, a long life. His sons, Yehlhézęh and Dechezhę, were probably born in the 1840s and were alive at the time of treaty in 1900. Given that Duuk'ihsachę was a young adult in the early years of the fur trade, he must have been born before the first contact with Europeans. If, as often happened, he married a younger woman later in life, he could have been in his fifties or sixties when Yehlhézęh and Dechezhę were born. Wǫlii Nachii promised that Duuk'ihsache would live to be ninety years old. If he did, he would have been alive in the 1860s. Duuk'ihsachę is important because his life spans the prehistoric and historic phases of Dane-zaa life. He played an important role in negotiating Dane-zaa relations with the early fur traders.

5
The Early Fur Trade

The late eighteenth century was a time of great change throughout North America. At about the same time that the American colonies were declaring themselves independent of Great Britain and Captain Cook was anchoring off Nootka Sound, the first Europeans began exploring the Peace River country. Dane-zaa Dreamers had already alerted the people that non-Indian strangers were coming. They did come in search of furs they could sell at a profit in their European homelands. The outsiders quickly realized that the upper Peace River country was rich in beaver and other fur-bearing animals, as well as in game to provision the traders.

The first Europeans came to the "New World" from a culture marked by divisions. In Europe at that time, people held to be superior because of class, aristocratic rank, or skin colour had status that others could never attain. The men who first came to the New World carried these prejudices. People of wealth and nobility demonstrated their status and privilege by wearing elaborate and expensive clothing, often trimmed with furs of sable (marten) or ermine (weasel). During the Renaissance, these furs came from Scandinavia and Russia, but as demand increased, too many fur-bearing animals were trapped, and their populations declined. By the seventeenth century, French and English businessmen saw a chance to become wealthy by trading for furs with the First Nations of North America.

In 1659, the Frenchmen Radisson and des Groseilliers explored lands adjacent to Lake Superior and established trade relations with the Wendat and Odawa nations. When French colonial officials

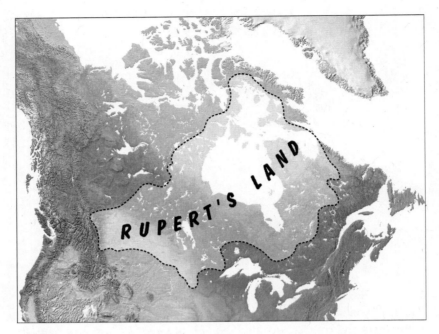

Rupert's Land. Adapted from a colour map of Rupert's Land based on Natural Earth imagery, by Weldon Hiebert

confiscated their furs because they had failed to obtain a permit, Radisson and des Groseilliers decided to ally themselves with the English, who were rivals of the French. They persuaded Prince Rupert, the cousin of the English King Charles II, to support their enterprise. On 2 May 1670, the king granted them a royal charter. The charter granted control over all lands that drained into Hudson Bay Watershed to "the Governor and Company of Adventurers of England trading into Hudson Bay." Because Prince Rupert had been the company's chief benefactor, the vast territory came to be known as "Rupert's Land." It covered roughly one and a half million square miles – almost half of modern Canada – as well as parts of Minnesota and North Dakota.

For over a century, the Hudson's Bay Company (HBC) enjoyed a monopoly on the fur trade. It established extensive trade networks with a number of First Nations and maintained a fleet of ships to transport furs from its port at Churchill, Manitoba. But in 1779 a new company based in Montreal began challenging the HBC's monopoly and looking for furs in areas that had not yet been exploited. Because of the new traders' interest in lands north and west of Rupert's Land, they called their company the North West Company (NWC). The Peace

River country of the Dane-zaa became a prime target for exploration. A desire for furs, together with competition for colonies in the New World, led to changes that transformed the lives of the Dane-zaa forever. By the eighteenth century, marten and weasel had become less important than beaver. A middle class was emerging in Europe. Men began wearing hats made of felt manufactured from the inner fur of the beaver, and beaver were abundant in the Peace River country.

The beaver hats that graced the heads of European gentlemen were the end result of an amazingly long and convoluted journey that began on a Canadian trapline. Aboriginal hunters took the beaver pelts to trading posts, where they were exchanged for guns, tools, and other goods. From there, company employees transported them by canoe and larger vessels until they ended up in some European hatter's workshop. Transforming a beaver pelt into a top hat was a labour-intensive and dangerous job because the hatters used nitrate of mercury to roughen the fibre and increase its matting ability. Long-term exposure to mercury vapour eventually caused neurological damage, thus the phrase "mad as a hatter."

Dane-zaa stories about wars with the Cree are reflected in written historical accounts. The Dane-zaa first felt the impact of the fur trade when the Cree, forced out of their own territories by strangers, pushed westward into Dane-zaa territory. Historian Harold Innis (1930, 205) notes that the Cree "crossed over by the Saskatchewan to Lesser Slave Lake and the Peace River Trail to war on the Beavers and the Indians along the Peace." The Cree had already acquired guns from the Europeans, but the Dane-zaa had only bows and arrows. The Dane-zaa eventually acquired guns, the Cree were undermined by a smallpox epidemic, and the two groups made what the Europeans called a "peace agreement."

Under the direction of Peter Pond, the NWC established a trading post in Dane-zaa territory on the Peace River near Fort Vermilion (Alberta) in 1786 (Innis 1930, 204). By 1792, the post had been replaced by a fort near Carcajou. Pond left no written record of these events, but Dane-zaa oral histories describe trading activity in Fort Vermilion in the early days of the fur trade. The Dane-zaa's name for the post was Tsiih Kwąh (tree fungus camp; literally "ochre houses or buildings"). According to Billy Attachie, the Dane-zaa used tree fungus to make a red dye, hence the name Fort Vermilion. Alexander Mackenzie, the first European to write about his encounters with the Dane-zaa, referred to them as Beaver Indians. Mackenzie, a Scot, joined the NWC in 1787 and began exploring rivers of the Arctic drainage. In the fall of 1792, he left the NWC post at Fort Chipewyan on Lake Athabasca. On 13 October, he came to a place known as Peace Point, where Lake Athabasca joins the Peace River. His interpreter told him that it was the place where the Cree and Dane-zaa had made their peace agreement. The Peace River, Mackenzie reported, took its name from that historic event.

Mackenzie proceeded up the Peace River until freeze-up made canoe travel impossible. The Dane-zaa of the Fort St. John area call the river Wǫchiigii or sometimes simply Chuu Nachii (the big water) and don't have a story about the peace between themselves and the Cree. Rather, Dane-zaa stories focus on war and conflict (see Chapter 4) and an intense battle between the Cree and a powerful Dane-zaa man named Naataazhiih, who used his medicine power to cover his arms with sharp flints. After the battle, they say, Naataazhiih turned himself to stone and continues to move from place to place in his new form. In 2009, Tommy Attachie took us to a place called Tse saǫ (stone lying there, where the rock sits) and showed us a rock that was once part of Naataazhiih.

By the end of October 1792, Mackenzie had established a NWC post at the forks of the Peace and Smoky rivers, northeast of where Grande Prairie stands today. He stopped there for the winter. In his journal, Mackenzie reports that about 150 "Beaver" and "Rocky Mountain" (Sekani) Indian men were trading into the fort and that these Dane-zaa men had adopted many Cree customs and spoke Cree as well as Dane-zaa Záágéʔ. He notes that before the forts had been established, the Dane-zaa had obtained European goods through Cree middlemen, who charged an extravagant price. Although the Dane-zaa had made peace with the Cree, hostilities occasionally broke out between the various Dane-zaa bands and between the Dane-zaa and the Sekani. Mackenzie's descriptions of the Dane-zaa reveal more about his European bias than they do about the Dane-zaa and reflect the limited time he spent with the Dane-zaa:

> The men are in general of a comely appearance, and fond of personal decoration. The women are of a contrary disposition, and the slaves of the men: in common with all the Indian tribes, polygamy is allowed among them. They are very subject to jealousy, and fatal consequences frequently result from the indulgence of that passion. But notwithstanding the vigilance and severity which is exercised by the husband, it seldom happens that a woman is without her favourite, who, in the

absence of the husband, exacts the same submission, and practices the same tyranny. And so premature is the tender passion, that it is sometimes known to invigorate so early a period of life as the age of eleven or twelve years. The women are not very prolific; a circumstance which may be attributed, in great measure, to the hardships that they suffer, for except for a few small dogs, they alone perform that labour which is allotted to beasts of burthen in other countries.

It is not uncommon, while the men carry nothing but a gun, that their wives and daughters follow with such weighty burdens, that if they lay them down they cannot replace them, and that is a kindness which the men will not deign to perform; so that during their journeys they are frequently obliged to lean against a tree for a small portion of temporary relief. When they arrive at the place which their tyrants have chosen for their encampment, they arrange the whole in a few minutes, by forming a curve of poles, meeting at the top, and expanding into circles of twelve or fifteen feet diameter at the bottom, covered with dressed skins of the moose sewed together. During these preparations, the men sit down quietly to the enjoyment of their pipes, if they happen to have any tobacco. But notwithstanding this abject state of slavery and submission, the women have a considerable influence on the opinion of the men in every thing except their own domestic situation. They are, however, remarkable for their honesty, for in the whole tribe there were only two women and a man who had been known to have swerved from that virtue, and they were considered as objects of disregard and reprobation. (Mackenzie and Lamb 1970, 253)

What Mackenzie perceived as the enslavement of women reflected a division of labour necessary to the hunting way of life. Mackenzie visited the forts, where he met male hunters, but he did not spend time in the camps, the women's domain. Women had responsibility for organizing camp life, and they had considerable authority in the camps. Dane-zaa women could, and did, go on vision quests and occasionally became Dreamers. Women who had passed menopause could hunt in Mackenzie's time, and older women still hunt today. These women are regarded as respected elders. Women serve as chiefs, band councillors, and band managers, and they have done so for decades.

Mackenzie also failed to notice that older men often took a younger, second wife to help with the work of keeping camp and processing meat and hides. Nor did he notice that these younger wives usually outlived their first husbands and then married younger men, bringing to the new relationship experience, skills, and property. Overall, the division of labour between the sexes and the generations formed a vital part of the Dane-zaa's life as nomadic hunting people.

When he continued his voyage in the spring of 1793, Mackenzie described the beauty of the Peace River country:

> The West side of the river displayed a succession of the most beautiful scenery I had ever beheld. The ground rises at intervals to a considerable height, and stretching inwards to a considerable distance: at every interval or pause in the rise, there is a very gently-ascending space or lawn, which is alternate with abrupt precipices to the summit of the whole, or, at least as far as the eye could distinguish. The magnificent theatre of nature has all the decorations which the trees and animals of the country can afford it; groves of poplars in every shape vary the scene; and their intervals are enlivened with vast herds of elks and buffaloes; the former choosing the steeps and uplands, and the latter preferring the plains. At this time the buffaloes were attended with their young ones who were frisking about them; and it appeared that the elks would soon exhibit the same enlivening circumstance. The whole country displayed an exuberant verdure, the trees that bear a blossom were advancing fast to that delightful appearance, and the velvet rind of their branches reflecting the oblique rays of a rising or setting sun, added a splendid gaiety to the scene, which no expressions of mine are qualified to describe. (Mackenzie and Lamb 1970, 258-59)

Mackenzie was particularly impressed by the abundance of game along the banks of the river. He described a large plain at a location he reckoned to be at latitude 56°16′54″ N. If accurate, the plain was either Bear Flats or Attachie, named for Chief Attachie, who signed Treaty 8 in 1900. Attachie is the grandfather of several contemporary Doig elders and the ancestor of many members of the Doig River and Blueberry River First Nations. Among his many children were Anachuaen, the last wife of Charlie Yahey, and Murray Attachie, the

The confluence of the Halfway and Peace rivers near where Mackenzie landed, May 2010. Most of this area will be flooded if the Site-C Dam is built. Photo by Jillian Ridington

father of the Attachie families living at Doig today. Mackenzie continued his description:

> The land above where we encamped, spreads into an extensive plain, and stretches on to a very high ridge, which, in some parts, presents a face of rock, but is principally covered with verdure, and varied with the poplar and white birch tree ... The soil is black and light. We this day saw two grisly and hideous bears. (Mackenzie and Lamb 1970, 264)

One year after Mackenzie passed through the area, traders for the NWC built Rocky Mountain Fort on the south side of the Peace near the mouth of the Moberly River, a few miles upstream from present-day Taylor. The company men were encouraged by Mackenzie's description of abundant game and the region's untapped fur resources. They actively sought out the Dane-zaa and enticed them into trade by offering guns, ammunition, knives, tobacco, and alcohol. They knew that the thickest, most desirable pelts were found on animals caught in northern climates such as that of the Peace River area (Innis 1930, 3-4). Every trade item the NWC men offered had been transported from Montreal by canoe and portaged across various heights of land. These new tools made it easier to destroy beaver houses and kill the beaver (ibid., 14). In return, the traders expected to be given both furs and meat, since they brought very little in the way of food supplies with them. The Dane-zaa who entered the trade had the benefit of more than ten thousand years of experience living in the Peace River area. They were the experts, the ones who knew the country. The traders, outsiders, bought their way into the territory and gained access to the riches of Dane-z̲aa nané? by offering goods from far away.

Dane-zaa oral tradition has preserved some remarkable stories about events from around the time of first contact. Doig elder Aku told Robin a story that reveals that the traders depended almost entirely on Dane-zaa hunters to supply them with meat. In the story, Aku describes conditions in the late eighteenth and early nineteenth centuries, when traders relied on hunters and the abundance of bison on the Peace River's prairie. Aku's story tells of first contact from a Dane-zaa perspective. The elders Aku had known when he was young remembered stories their parents had told them about their first meetings with the white people. Margaret Dominic Davis translated this story.

> There used to be a white man
> with a store at Gattah Kwậh.*
> The Indians didn't know anything about sugar, about tea.
> The white men didn't have any flour, tea, soup, or anything.
> They didn't know about those things. They had bison.
> They made dry meat out of the bison. They acted like Indians.
> They made atsés [pemmican],
> and they put the hide around the atsés.
> They made lard, too. That's the only stuff they knew to eat.
> They were eating that all winter.
> They didn't have much of that,
> and they don't know how to live,
> so the Indians had to hunt for them
> so they would have enough to get through the winter.

---

* Literally "white spruce tree among houses," the Dane-zaa name for the Fort St. John area.

Charlie Yahey and Aku, 1966. Photo by Robin Ridington

> We made lots and lots of dry meat and moose tallow
> for them in springtime.
> They had a great big store and we filled it up with dry meat.
> In the winter, we did the same thing.
> We got fresh meat for them to eat.
>
> All winter, whenever any Indians got fresh meat,
> two young boys would go to the store and tell the white men.
> Then they would set out for the place where the moose was
> with two big dog teams – and they would take lots of meat.
> That's the way the traders lived off the Indians all winter.
>
> And now the company should pay back the Indians.
> Today, they have a big store,
> and they won't give anything free to the Indians.
> You have to pay for everything with money.
> They should pay us back.
> If it hadn't been for us, those fur traders would have starved
> like the rest of the poor Indians.
> That's good enough I talk.
>
> (Ridington/Dane-zaa Archive [RDA], Aku 1966)

Little information has come down from written sources about the operations of Rocky Mountain Fort. Only a fragment of a journal written by the trader during winter 1799-1800 has been preserved. Unlike many other fur traders, this man, whose name was not recorded, wrote down the names of the Dane-zaa men with whom he sought to establish trading relations. He also made it clear that he did not hesitate to use alcohol and tobacco as an inducement to trade. The first entry in the journal, for 5 October 1799, states, "Gave all the men each a Dram and mixed a keg Rum – and gave all the Indians that are here each a Dram and a [piece] of [tobacco] and they brought a little meat to the Fort." Ten days later, he writes, "[Received] 66 [skins] [Beaver] and 70 [skins] [meat] [credits] and they begun to Drink" (Burley, Hamilton, and Fladmark 1996, 140). The next day, he reported that the Dane-zaa were still drinking.

Once the trader cut off the supply of rum, however, the Dane-zaa accepted trade goods on credit to be paid back with future fur and meat. They then left the fort for their hunting and trapping territories. This pattern of drinking followed by trading is described throughout the journal, although the Dane-zaa did not accept the trader's terms without complaint. On 18 December 1799, the trader reported that, "[t]he Indians complain very much of the prices of the Goods here" (Burley, Hamilton, and Fladmark 1996, 144). In a note written on 8 January 1800, he states that he had sent a Dane-zaa man, Jimathush (whom we identified as Chimarouche), to "discover more Indians" who would be willing to trade. This seems to have been a common practice in the early days of the fur trade. According to a story Aku told Robin in 1966, the trader sent out a man named Naazute on a similar mission. He located a band of people called Tsǫ́kwą̂hne. They trapped lots of furs and then followed Naazute to the trading post.

> They went there, and they got lots of ammunition and guns.
> The trader put a bullet and powder in a gun,
> and he gave it to one of the men.
> He told him to shoot at that stick.
> The man bumped the end of the gun,
> but the trader told him to pull the trigger.
> The man did, and the gun fired, and he dropped the gun.
> Then the trader showed them how to shoot, and he told them,
> "Guns are lots better than bows and arrows.
> You can kill lots more with this."

That man went back to where his daughter and husband
were living.
He showed them a knife. He just cut a big piece of meat in two.
He said, "See, really sharp. You make lots of furs,
and you follow me. There is a trading post.
You can get lots of stuff there, guns, knives, ammunition.
You follow after me."
When those people went to the trading post,
they got lots of things.
The trader gave one man chewing tobacco.
That man put it in his mouth and ate it.
Then he tried to throw up. "It's killing me.
It's killing me," he said.
The people said, "No, it's not killing you.
You're not supposed to eat it.
Just spread a little around in your mouth."
(RDA, Aku 1966)

The leader of the band trading into Rocky Mountain Fort was called "the Cigne," the trader's version of the French for "the Swan." Since swans symbolize the Dreamers, it is likely that the Cigne was a Dreamer, maybe even the Dreamer who warned his people of the strangers who would be entering their country. The trader reported that the Cigne's band consisted of nine lodges and was located about two days from the fort (Burley, Hamilton, and Fladmark 1996, 148). Although he does not give the direction from the fort, it must have been within the territory of the former Fort St. John Band and could very well have been Su Na chii k'chige, the place where happiness dwells.

The traders commonly presented the chief of a band with clothing of European manufacture to symbolize his status as a trading chief. On 1 April 1800 (a century before Attachie and others signed a treaty), the trader spoke to the Cigne and his parents and offered to clothe the Cigne, that is, set him up as a trading chief. In his journal, the trader reports that "when I offered it to him he refused and told me to give it to L'Homme Seul for that he was the most proper in the Band but when I told them that since they refused the Cigne that they should not have any Chief till next winter" (Burley, Hamilton, and Fladmark 1996, 149-50). The trader's offer to L'Homme Seul indicates that he considered this man an important and powerful leader. The Cigne's refusal to accept the role of trading chief suggests he felt it was more important to retain his role as Dreamer.

Chief Sagónáá? in his chief's coat. The blue serge jacket with brass buttons is on display in the Doig River First Nation Museum. Image D-00822 courtesy of Royal BC Museum, BC Archives

Fur trade journals tell us a lot about the relationship that developed between the Dane-zaa and traders, at least from the traders' point of view. Many of the people named can be linked directly to Dane-zaa alive today. *L'Homme Seul* (Man Alone) in Dane-zaa Záágé? is *Mazǫ*, Tommy Attachie's Dane-zaa Záágé? name. According to Tommy's brother Billy, their uncle Frank Attachie gave him the name in honour of a man named Mazǫ who lived in the early fur trade era. L'Homme Seul is mentioned in a 1806 NWC journal from Dunvegan and in the 1823 HBC journal from St. John, where he is referred to as "old L'homme Seul" (Burley, Hamilton, and Fladmark 1996, 153). It appears that old L'Homme Seul had a son by the same name, who was more of an outsider than the trading chief. Dane-zaa oral tradition describes a person named Mazǫ, one of the men implicated in the killing of HBC men in 1823 (see Chapter 6).

We know that many Dane-zaa names were passed on from generation to generation. The name of one of the men recorded by the trader in 1799, Jimathush, reappears in the HBC journal of 1823 as "Old Chimarouche." The man who carried the name died on 14 January of that year. The trader, Hugh Faries, wrote:

> This morning an old Indian (Chimarouche) was found dead in the lodge, he has been a cripple for these several years past, he remained for these three years past at the Fort, his son is generally a Fort Hunter, poor old creature had been complaining for these two or three days past, he was severely scorched, seemingly struggling in his last moments he rolled into the fire his hands and arm was very much scorched, there was no person in the lodge, but another old Indian that was both blind and lame, could give him very little assistance. I got him buried very well, as well as the weather would permit. (Burley, Hamilton, and Fladmark 1996, 164)

In Chapter 9, "Kinship and Community," we identify a man named Chimarouche as an ancestor of people alive today. He is frequently mentioned in HBC journals from the final years of the nineteenth century. In the journals, the area just west of the Doig River Reserve is known as Chimarouche's Prairie. Chimarouche (also called Samaloose in oral tradition) is well known as the father of Chief Montney (Madaayęą) and of Apąą, who signed the treaty in 1900.

In the 1799 NWC journal, the trader refers to another man only as "the hunter" employed to provide meat for the post. The game the hunter most often brought back was bison, but the trader also mentions other animals such as beaver, rabbits, deer, caribou, mountain goat, and moose. The hunter must have been Dane-zaa, for the trader mentions that his parents live nearby. The trader makes it clear that his men stay close to the fort and do not visit the Dane-zaa in their camps. In the early years of the trade, hunters who worked for the traders enjoyed the abundance of game described by Mackenzie. A single hunter armed with a musket could accomplish what had previously required an organized communal hunt. Aku's story about the white man's store offers a good picture of the way things were during the early years of the fur trade.

In 1975, Knut Fladmark, an archaeologist at Simon Fraser University, rediscovered the site of Rocky Mountain Fort near the confluence of the Moberly and Peace rivers. A decade later, Fladmark and his colleagues David Burley and Scott Hamilton began excavations at the site and continued the work for two years. When they analyzed animal bones found at the site, they found that 21 percent were from bison, 78 percent from elk, and 1 percent from moose. Because the Dane-zaa broke up bison bones to render the marrow into grease, only small fragments of the bison bones remained (Burley, Hamilton, and Fladmark 1996, 134). Bison, the largest of these three animals, are mentioned more than any other species in the 1799 NWC journal. Burley, Hamilton, and Fladmark concluded that "[i]t was the presence of bison that gave Rocky Mountain Fort its great potential" (ibid., 135). As Alexander Mackenzie wrote in his journal in 1793, the upper Peace River valley was ideal habitat for bison. It therefore became a major source of provisions for local trade and traders going into new territories. Grease from bison bones was an essential ingredient in pemmican, a staple of the fur trader's diet. Burley, Hamilton, and Fladmark (ibid., 57) report that the

> [b]one grease rendered from bison was considered far superior to that rendered from any other species. Consequently, with the Peace River area being one of the few in the Athabasca District where hunters could secure bison on a regular basis, posts such as Rocky Mountain Fort enjoyed great importance. The dominance of provisioning and grease production at Rocky Mountain Fort is not only evident in its archaeological record, it is also noted in various journal entries. After having weighed provisions on 30 October, 1799, the officer reports the amount of grease on hand at 2,100 pounds. Additional

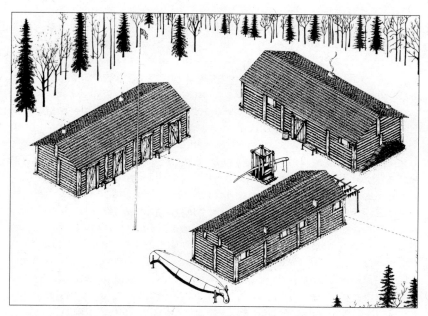

A reconstruction of Rocky Mountain Fort. From David V. Burley, J. Scott Hamilton, and Knut R. Fladmark, *Prophecy of the Swan: The Upper Peace River Fur Trade of 1794-1823* (Vancouver: UBC Press, 1996). Reprinted with permission

quantities of grease were secured later in the year both by processing at the site and by trade.

Aku supports this observation when he states:

> They made dry meat out of the bison. They act like Indians.
> They made *atsę́s* [pemmican],
> and they put the hide around the atsę́s.
> They made lard, too. That's the only stuff they know to eat.

The quantity of grease the traders accumulated is truly astonishing and proved to be unsustainable. Although bison were abundant in the area at the time of first contact, the populations could not support concentrated hunting using firearms for more than a few years. Rocky Mountain Fort was closed in 1805 when game populations, particularly bison, declined because of overhunting (Burley, Hamilton, and Fladmark 1996, 65). In addition to the rum and other spirits with which the traders usually began their trading, the fort offered access to tobacco, guns, gun parts, bullets, shot, powder, clothing, bells, beads, buttons, rings and pendants, fish hooks, and rolled copper "tinkling cones," which were used as ornaments. Traders exchanged these items for the furs and meat the hunters brought to the fort.

Before the traders came with manufactured goods, the Dane-zaa had made whatever they needed from locally available materials. Each plant, animal, geographical feature, and product of their labour was embedded in a web of stories, some of which probably extended back to the time when people lived near the cave at Charlie Lake. Just as Muskrat brought up earth to place at the centre of the creator's idea, the Dane-zaa used wise stories and knowledge they held in their minds to produce everything they required. The traders introduced something entirely new in the form of material goods for which the Dane-zaa had no stories and which could not be made from the resources of their land. Guns and knives and powder and shot were manufactured thousands of miles away. Alcohol and tobacco produced dramatic changes in the state of mind of the hunters. In some ways, they mimicked the mystical experience of the vision quest.

Hunting for the early fur trade was intensive and ultimately unsustainable. Rocky Mountain Fort operated for only twelve years. By the time it closed in 1806, the reduced yield of furs and meat had made the trade uneconomical from the trader's point of view. For the Dane-zaa, though, closing the fort caused considerable hardship. By then, they had become dependent on European manufactured goods.

6

The Later Fur Trade and the Hudson's Bay Company Killings

After Rocky Mountain Fort closed, the North West Company established a new fort east of the Peace River Portage, near the present town of Hudson's Hope. This fort, called Rocky Mountain Portage House, operated sporadically from 1804 until 1814 (Burley, Hamilton, and Fladmark 1996, 68). It supplied trading parties going on to McLeod Lake and to the Pacific drainage areas the traders called New Caledonia. The company later built posts in the Hudson's Hope area. Rocky Mountain Portage House was not well located for the Dane-zaa, who had to choose between going into the territory of the sometimes hostile Sekani at Hudson's Hope or going to Dunvegan or Fort Vermilion, located much farther to the east. In the spring of 1806, the year after Rocky Mountain Fort closed, L'Homme Seul, by then the leader of his band, requested that the North West Company open another fort in Dane-zaa territory at the mouth of the Pine (now Beatton) River. Once established, the new fort was known as both St. John and Fort d'Epinette. The trader at Dunvegan described the request as follows: "We settled with L'Homme Seul and band, and they set off. They are to be on the borders of the river, opposite to la Riviere d'Pinette on 20th October [1806], at which place they asked to have a fort this fall" (Burley, Hamilton, and Fladmark 1996, 82).

L'Homme Seul was an important man during the first three decades of the fur trade, and he was clearly respected. Tommy Attachie describes Duuk'ihsachę making the same request as the one made by

L'Homme Seul to the traders at Fort Vermilion. It is possible that L'Homme Seul and Duuk'ihsachę were in fact the same person, as the Dane-zaa frequently call one another by more than one name. If that is the case, the following story, told by Tommy Attachie, places L'Homme Seul in Fort Vermilion rather than Dunvegan. Both L'Homme Seul and Duuk'ihsachę were respected for their power and for the restraint with which they applied it. They (or he) used personal power to protect themselves and their people during a time when bands sometimes fought with one another. Powerful men such as Duuk'ihsachę could use their power to avoid fights by confronting the leaders of other bands and forcing them to back down. Tommy's story begins with a description of such an encounter. Billy Attachie and Madeline Oker Benson provided this translation.

> Duuk'ihsachę was from somewhere up in the mountains,
> near where the Halfway River people live,
> but he went to Milligan Creek
> and married into the Ts'ibe Dané? band.
> He was there when people from High Level
> [west of Fort Vermilion]
> came to attack the Ts'ibe Dané?,
> but Duuk'ihsachę never had to kill them.
> He just stopped them with his power.
>
> Those people from High Level
> wanted to go and fight the Muskeg people [Ts'ibe Dané?].
> One of them told lies about Duuk'ihsachę.
> The person who told those lies was his nephew Wayaaze.
> His name was Wayaaze.
> He was from over there, High Level people.
> They wanted to kill these Milligan Creek (Muskeg) people.
>
> Wayaaze came over to where the Muskeg people were.
> Duuk'ihsachę was sleeping up there.
> From his dream, he knew they were coming to his country.
> He dreamed they were coming. Duuk'ihsachę told his wife,
> "I am going to meet them. Let's go."
> His power told him, "You go meet them."
>
> So he went right straight toward where they were coming from.
> Some guys went with him. He met them over there.

He came back to his wife and said, "I saw their snowshoe tracks."
They went back to their camp.
Duuk'ihsachę told his wife, "Make a fire here. Cook something."

"Tomorrow, we are going to go to their next camp," he told her.
In the morning, after they ate, they went over
to where he saw the snowshoe tracks turn.
They saw a whole bunch of teepees.

He kept going, and he saw big snowshoe tracks in there.
He turned around and went back. That was Wayaaze.
His name was Wayaaze. He was Duuk'ihsachę's nephew.
He wanted to kill all the Muskeg people.
A whole bunch of his people came with him, too.
He was going to kill the Muskeg people.
(Ridington/Dane-zaa Archive [RDA], DZHD09-1, DZHD09-23)

After introducing the characters and their relationship to one another, Tommy describes a classic contest between medicine powers. In this case, a face-to-face confrontation is a way of avoiding what otherwise may have escalated into a bloody and drawn-out feud between related bands. As Tommy says at the beginning of the story, "Duuk'ihsachę never had to kill them. He just stopped them with his power."

"One time, I camped there with Wayaaze, my nephew," he said.
He met him at that place. Wayaaze came out from his camp.
He shook hands with Duuk'ihsachę.
Duuk'ihsachę shook his hand really hard.
He squeezed his hand like this. Wayaaze asked him,
"How come you squeeze my hand like that? Pretty mean."

Duuk'ihsachę told him, "You come here with all those guys.
Maybe you're going to kill me.
That's why you brought all those guys.
Do you think I'm going to shake hands with you easy?"
They stood face to face together, right there, and talked to
each other.

Duuk'ihsachę said, "There are lots of people over there in High
Level, Fort Vermilion. You just came up here with all your guys.

You're not a man. You came up here like a lady.
You think you're tough over there,
but when you come up here, you come like a lady."
"You talk like that to me," Duuk'ihsachę told him.

After that, Wayaaze quieted down. The next morning,
he and his people wanted to go back to High Level.
Duuk'ihsachę was too powerful. Lots of guys knew about him.
They knew about his power, so they wanted to go back.
They started to move back there. They went with Wayaaze.
Duuk'ihsachę told him, "You're going to go
where you said there are lots of people.
You can talk big up there."

Then Duuk'ihsachę told him, "I can go back with you."
Wayaazi said, "You see my snowshoe tracks? Big snowshoe
tracks. I wonder what you think.
You must have got scared."
Duuk'ihsachę answered,
"Oh, those snowshoes, your wife braided them for you.
You think I'm going to get scared of those?
I slept with Wǫlii Nachii.
Every night I sleep with that one. I'm never scared."
He told Wayaaze's people that.

Those guys were scared of that power,
so they started to move back with Wayaaze, to go home.
Some of them, they talked to each other about beating him.
"If we let him go back with us over there,
something might happen.
If people try to do something to him, he's going to clean us out.
He's too powerful. What can we do?
He's not going to go up there with us," they told each other.

That one guy from High Level thought he had a lot of power.
Duuk'ihsachę told him, "Sit down." He sat down.
Duuk'ihsachę said, "I can eat this kind of rock,
the special rock we use to make fire."
"I just bite it, you know, I chew it," he said.
He had his own power rock, and that guy had one, too.

> Duuk'ihsache gave his own rock to that guy.
> "Here," he said, "I'm looking right at you.
> Try this while I am looking at you."
> Duuk'ihsache said, "If you bite that rock,
> it will go inside and kill you."
> But that guy was scared to try it.
>
> So Wayaaze sent three guys to Fort Vermilion where the store is.
> They got tobacco and all that other stuff, bullets, you know,
> everything, powder. They brought back lots of stuff.
> Three people went up there. When they got back at night,
> they called Duuk'ihsache,
> "Come up here. See what we got for you.
> Tobacco, lots, everything stuff, here.
> From here you can go home, you know, then we will go home."
> So he believed in what they told him, too.
> "OK, but I'm going to go over there soon as ice has broken up.
> I'm going to go down to check fur prices, over there," he told
> them.
> (RDA, DZHD09-1, DZHD09-23)

When Wayaaze gets back to Fort Vermilion, he tells lies about Duuk'ihsache. After the ice breaks up, Duuk'ihsache carries out his plan to visit Fort Vermilion. He finds the people, armed with guns, waiting for him on the riverbank. Again, he is tested; again, he uses his power to prevent violence.

> But when they got back up to the trading post,
> they made a different story.
> They told people at Fort Vermilion that
> Duuk'ihsache had told them,
> "Wait till I get up there. I'm going to finish you guys."
> Those people made up a story about him.
>
> When the ice started to break up,
> Duuk'ihsache headed to the trading post.
> When he got to Fort Vermilion, the people there had set up
> their guns on the top of the hills on both sides.
> Wayaaze had told them lies about him.
> That's why they had their guns pointed at him.

> Duuk'ihsache came into their area anyway.
> He just looked at all those guns, and their powder all got wet.
> They couldn't fire. He was so powerful,
> all those guns never went off. The bullets never left their guns.
> So, he got out safely.
> He had an axe and a knife at his side.
> When he went in there, people just ran away.
> He got to the trading post at Fort Vermilion.
> (RDA, DZHD09-1, DZHD09-23)

At this point, the story confirms what the North West Company trader at Dunvegan wrote about L'Homme Seul's request. Duuk'ihsache tells the trader it is difficult for the Dane-zaa to access the old post on the south side of the river. He suggests a new location at Gattah Kwą̂h (Fort St. John area).

> Duuk'ihsache talked to the traders. He told them,
> "Those guys told lies. I just want to sell my furs
> up there in my own country."
> He was heading back up to his country. He told them,
> "I want my store to be at Gattah Kwą̂h,
> my side of the river this time."
> The trader said, "Everything you say is going to happen."
>
> So, next time, they put the store on this side, not across.
> Before that, they made the first post on the south side
> of the river.
> Indians had a hard time to go across.
> "This time," he told them, "I want the store on my side."
> That's what Duuk'ihsache told them, and that's what happened.
> He didn't want to kill the people there.
> He just did everything right.
> That's why their guns wouldn't fire. That's Duuk'ihsache's story.
> (RDA, DZHD09-1, DZHD09-23)

Rocky Mountain Fort was undefended, but St. John, the new post requested by Duuk'ihsache, was surrounded by a three-metre high stockade of posts set into a trench. The archaeologists who excavated the site in the mid-1970s, David Burley, Scott Hamilton, and Knut Fladmark (1996, 92), could not determine when the stockade had been built. It might have been constructed when it was a NWC fort or after the HBC took it over in 1821. They suggest that the fortifications might have been built to defend the fort from the HBC rather than from the Dane-zaa. They note that "[d]uring its seventeen years of occupation, this post witnessed substantial change in the regional environment, in relations with the Beaver, and in fur-trade economics, policy, and history. In early November, 1823, its end came swiftly" (ibid., 97).

The "end" that Burley, Hamilton, and Fladmark refer to has come to be known in written history as the "Fort St. John massacre." Hugh Faries, the last chief trader at St. John, kept a journal from October 1822 to May 1823. In contrast to the Rocky Mountain Fort journal of 1799-1800, in which the trader notes an abundance of bison, Faries makes no mention of bison. The stockyard described by Alexander Mackenzie in 1793 appears to have been effectively eliminated by almost thirty years of hunting to supply fur trade brigades. Burley, Hamilton, and Fladmark (1996, 136) conclude that

> [r]esource depletions were a fact of life in the vicinity of St Johns, and they may have begun to occur as early as the first few years of its establishment. By its final summer of operation, we suspect that this problem extended to the region as a whole, with the Beaver finding it increasingly difficult to meet even their own subsistence needs, let alone those of St Johns. Fur-bearer scarcities, a Native economy in part reliant on European goods, and the insensitivities of a company concerned with maximizing profit strained relations between the Europeans and the Beaver and propelled them inescapably toward the events of 2 and 3 November 1823.

By the time the HBC replaced the North West Company, St. John could no longer supply provisions for traders at Rocky Mountain Portage House and Fort McLeod. The latter dealt with traders who voyaged into the huge Pacific drainage area then called "New Caledonia." At times, St. John could not even sustain its own residents with local game. Faries reports that both Sekani (whom he called Slaves) and Dane-zaa (Beaver) were trading into the fort but that Sekani did most of the meat hunting. Game animals near the fort were in short supply, and the Dane-zaa were reluctant to hunt there to supply the traders, as the company requested. They made feeding their families their first priority. The following journal entries give an indication of conditions in 1822 and 1823:

> Tue., 22nd Oct. 1822. The Beaver Indians of this place are worthless, Vagabonds, their fur hunt, seldom or ever exceeds from five to seven Packs throughout the Year, what furs are procured here are chiefly got from the Slaves. (Burley, Hamilton, and Fladmark 1996, 153)

> Mon., 16th Dec. 1822. Sancho and family off, gave them about 50 lbs fresh meat, run the risk of starving very much as there is not a track of an animal to be found within a considerable distance from this place, the Beaver Indians having hunted all summer and fall about the place or country he must pass through. (Ibid., 160)

> Thur., 9th Jan. 1823. Owing to the great distance we cart our meat – can accumulate no stock. (Ibid., 163)

"Beavers" seem to have done better at trapping than hunting for the fort. In February, Faries reported: "Sun., 22nd Feb. 1823. The Beavers altho' not quite fulfilled the promises they made me in the fall, have done pretty well, much better than they have done for these several years back" (ibid., 168). Yet the meat situation remained critical. In early March, the trader reported: "Thur., 6th Mar. 1823. The hunters cannot kill owing to a scarcity of animals they say none" (ibid., 169).

In entries from late March, Faries makes it clear that the post is no longer able to supply provisions for traders going to New Caledonia:

> Mon., 31st Mar. 1823. I am really apprehensive I will have some trouble procuring the stock of provisions necessary at the Portage for the New Caledonia People as the season is coming on so rapidly and having only one Hunter for that purpose, and being entirely destitute of any kind of dry provisions. The Beaver Indians are averse to hunting in that quarter and this year unfortunately no Slaves have made their appearance there, last year it was the Slaves gave me the quantity required and done in a very short time. (Burley, Hamilton, and Fladmark 1996, 174)

> Wed., 9th Apr. 1823. I am really at a loss to procure the quantity of Provisions required for the Portage, the season is advanced and a difficult thing to procure Beaver Indians to hunt for that Quarter and unfortunately having no dry provisions. (Ibid., 176)

Finally, in late April, Faries reported that the Beavers want the HBC to move the fort back near the site of Rocky Mountain Fort, a move that did not take place until almost forty years later: "Mon., 21st. Apr. 1823. The Indians wish the Establishment to be removed to or near the Old Fort of Beaver River (Moberly River). In my opinion it is the best place, owing to the scarcity of animals about here at present and a more centrical place for the Slave Indians exclusive of the Conveniency of a lake in the vicinity where plenty of fish may be taken they tell me" (ibid.).

When Faries wrote his last entry on Sunday, 18 May 1823, he already knew that the new HBC governor, Sir George Simpson, planned to close Fort St. John after the 1823 trading season. Chief trader Francis Heron was given the task of closing the post. He arrived at the fort on 28 October to meet with the Dane-zaa. They were disappointed not to hear any comforting news from him. Heron departed for Rocky Mountain Portage shortly thereafter, leaving the clerk, Guy Hughes, in charge. On 2 November 1823, Hughes was ambushed and shot by "a Slave who had been raised by the Beavers" (Burley, Hamilton, and Fladmark 1996, 127).

Hughes had never managed to establish a good relationship with the Dane-zaa. According to Heron's report to his superiors, on 1 November 1823, Hughes tried to get some of the hunters to act as guides to lead him to the provision caches. All but one man refused to go. Dane-zaa who did not take part in the murders gave Heron the following account:

> [o]n the first of Novr., Mr. Hughes had tried to engage one from among them to act as guide to some caches of provisions, but that all of them, except one young man had refused to go. Upon this young man's consenting to guide people as required, Mr. Hughes it is said taped [sic] him on the Shoulder, saying that he should pay him well for his ready compliance – The Indian young man shortly after retired to his tent, apparently in good health, but in a few hours suddenly took ill, and died that night, which the Indians, attributed to Mr. Hughes having thrown some destructive medicine upon him when he taped him on the Shoulder, and under this plea, determined, next day to assassinate Mr. Hughes himself, which was no difficult matter to accomplish, he being entirely alone and not aware of the danger that threatened him. (Burley, Hamilton, and Fladmark 1996, 129)

Heron reported on the killings as follows:

> On the 2nd of November as he [Hughes] was returning to the house from the River side where he had been conversing with an Indian, a young Slave who had been brought up by the Indians of St. John's, discharged a pistol at him the contents of which passed through his head, but did not cause instant death; Perceiving which his accomplice shot him through the body, which put a period to his existence – They were going to cast his body into the River, but were prevailed upon by an old Indian, to allow it to remain at the house for interment – On the following day as these two assassins, and two of the brothers of one of them (the St. John's Indian) were about to transport some of the property that still remained in the store across the River to their huts, the poor unfortunate four men sent by Mr. Black from the Portage to Dunvegan, arrived and just as they were in the act of debarking, were fired upon by the four Indians I have just mention[ed], who lay in ambush for that purpose at the landing-place – Those of the men who did not immediately expire, the Murderers dispatched with their dags and cast their bodies into the river. (Ibid., 127-28)

According to Heron, the man who killed Hughes was a "Slave" (Sekani) who had been raised with the Dane-zaa, and it was his brothers who were responsible for the next day's killings. Following the second killings, another canoe bound from the Portage to Dunvegan (the canoe had been delayed to make repairs) arrived after dark. "Friendly Indians" informed the traders of the killings, and all but one, a man named Maranda, departed immediately. As had been planned, the HBC post at St. Johns was closed, and the company did not open a post in the area again until 1857 (Finley 1993, 4).

Dane-zaa oral history also records what happened in 1823. In 1965, Johnny Chipesia told Robin (in English) about the incident from a Dane-zaa perspective. He had heard the story from his father, Ts'ibiisaa or Japasa (pictured below in 1964) and other relatives. Ts'ibiisaa said that his wife's grandfather "Samaloose" (Chimarouche) had witnessed the event. Johnny told Robin that the HBC men had wanted the hunters to leave the bush and work only for the company. Since the game resources of the upper Peace River were running low, the hunters had to think about supplying their own families before fulfilling their obligations to the traders. One hunter who had worked for the company

Ts'ibiisaa (George Chipesia, Japasa), 1964. Photo by Robin Ridington

for several years decided to go back to the bush with his people for the winter.

In 1965, Robin wrote in his field notes,

> Johnny said that at that time the HB wanted the Indians to leave the bush and work for the HB. The Bay didn't sell grub

at that time and in fact didn't have any of its own. It did sell guns, axes, knives, or rather traded these goods for furs. The factor wanted the Indians to stay near The Bay and hunt and farm for him. One Indian who had worked for him for several years decided to go back with his people to the bush for the winter. The factor didn't want to let the Indian go, but he decided to go anyway. Before he left he ate a meal at the post. After the meal he took off, but he just made it to a hill on the river bank. There he died of poison that the factor had put in his food. At this, the man's father was angry and went to the factor demanding that he make a coffin and bury his son properly. The factor said, "No," and the father said, "OK, then I'll have to kill you."

The father waited several days and watched the post. When the chance came, he killed the factor and all his men. Then he took off into the bush. Shortly after the killing, a French-Canadian from Hudson's Hope came to the post looking for food and saw what had happened. He would have been killed too, except that Samaloose was across the river at the time and came over to warn him. The next year, "redcoated soldiers" came to look for the father, whose name was Khata, but they could not live off the land and so gave up the search before very long. The father was never caught by the white men for killing the Hudson's Bay man. (RDA, field notes, 1965-66)

Tommy Attachie recently told Robin about events leading up to and immediately following the killings. Billy Attachie and Madeline Oker Benson provided this translation.

> Where the Beatton meets the Peace,
> there was a trading post there.
> Nedoęslhiine, French [Metis] people, worked for the trader.
> In that trading post, there must have been powder and bullets.
> There must have been something there, food.
> There was some food, clothing, and ammunition.
> Dane-zaa came to trade with them there.
> The Dane-zaa were there to trade
> and get something from the store.
> That time, people were really bad to each other.
> People did bad things to each other.
> They were always ready to fight.

After that time, there were lots of Dreamers to make peace.
When the Dreamers came, things were straightened out.
People were really against each other before that.
Even after the Dreamers made peace,
some people wanted to fight.
There was hostility among the people,
even though the Dreamers were there.
People didn't make peace then.
They wanted to start something all the time.
People came from all over the place, High Level,
people from the north.
They doubted each other's thinking.
People respect each other today.

Dane-zaa went to that trading post.
After they traded, they moved way back in the bush
on the north side of the Peace River.
There was one boy, pretty young. He worked for the traders.
The traders told him to stay working at the post,
but he saw his people moving away up north.
That boy slipped away to go with them.
Not long after his people had moved quite a ways out,
that boy died. His people had lots of power.
They didn't like what had happened.
They went back to get some clothing to bury that boy,
but the trader said, "If he had stayed here, he would have lived."
(RDA, DZHD09-24)

Tommy then skips over the part about the boy's people coming back and killing the trader and four of his men. He expects the listener to be familiar with that part of the story, in the same way that Homer expected ancient Greeks to know about the Trojan horse and didn't include it in *The Iliad*. The "French guy" is Maranda.

Madaayęą's father [Samaloose or Chimarouche],
camped behind the store. He and his wife were camping there.
After what the boy's relatives did, they moved across the river.
More traders were coming down the river.
Nedǫeslhiine [French voyageurs] were coming in a boat.
Madaayęą's father saw them coming.
One French guy stopped the boat and ran up to the trading post.

The relatives of the boy who had died were
waiting and watching.

Madaayęa's dad told the French guys what had happened.
Madaayęa's dad told them,
"They won't bother you while I'm here."
The French guy was splitting wood.
The relatives of the boy said, "Who is splitting wood?"
Madaayęa's dad said, "It's me."
He helped that guy who came off the boat.

The relatives of that boy said, "I wiped my ass with them."
"Who was chopping wood?" they asked.
"It's only me," Madaayęa's dad said.
"This is not the people you wiped out."
He told them, "I'm the one splitting wood."
Madaayęa's dad packed up lots of food for that French guy
and told him to leave early in the morning.

That French guy took the message back to his people.
He floated back to his people and told them what had happened.
Every year, the company people came back
looking for the killers.
Every year, they came back to go after those people,
but they couldn't find them. Those people had lots of power.
They couldn't find who did it.
(RDA, DZHD09-24)

Tommy tells the story from a Dane-zaa perspective, but it corresponds to events described in the company factor's written account. The Frenchman he mentioned, Maranda, provided Heron with an account of the incident. Heron explained that after the killings, "The Indians immediately took him [Maranda] under their protection." Both Johnny Chipesia and Tommy Attachie identify the man who protected Maranda as Madaayęa's father, Samaloose.

Gerry Attachie recorded another version of the story by Dane-zaa elder John Andre in the 1980s. Billy Attachie provided this translation in 2009.

Long time ago, the people say they killed the Nedǫęslhiine.
Those people were related to Duuk'ihsachę.

There was no groceries that time,
but they gave people ammunition, tobacco.
Dahshíne [Cree or, in this case, Cree-Metis voyageurs]
were coming up the river from the east.
They came there to the post,
and then they went up the river again.
After those guys went up the river,
that's when they killed the HB [Hudson's Bay man].
Some of the traders, they went up the river.
There was one old lady who stayed there.
After trouble happened at the post, she went up the river
to wait for them and give them a message.
She wanted them to know what happened.
That's why she was waiting over there.
That old lady knew the Dane-zaa were waiting.
Duuk'ihsachę's relatives were waiting for those guys
coming down the river.
She saw them just turn the corner on the boat.
When they were coming down, they were just singing.
She yelled at them, "Nedǫęslhiine got killed,"
and they took off even faster.
She waved and yelled at them, "Nedǫęslhiine got killed,"
and she told them to go faster. They even speeded up more.
They even sang louder and faster. When they came to the ground,
there were people waiting for them with guns.
The Beavers started shooting, and they all jumped into the river,
their boss, too. Their boss was hard to kill. He kept diving down.
(RDA, JA 1b)

At this point the story gets interesting but also confusing. John Andre identifies the man who did the shooting as Mazǫ, which translates into English as "man alone" and into French as "l'homme seul." This Mazǫ is probably not the same L'Homme Seul who was made chief in 1800 and asked that a new post be established at Gattah Kwậh. Hugh Faries refers to him as "old L'homme Seul" in 1823, and he was considered a wise leader. Billy Attachie believes Mazǫ was a lonesome Charlie, that is, an outsider. John Andre said that Mazǫ was a relative of Duuk'ihsachę. As the cases of Jimathush (Chimarouche) and Duuk'ihsachę indicate, Dane-zaa names often repeat from one generation to another. If L'Homme Seul's son took the name Mazǫ, he could have been the man who shot the Nedǫęslhiine.

John Andre's story identifies the people who waited to ambush the voyageurs as Duuk'ihsachę's relatives.

> One guy was named Mazǫ.
> He was a very proud man. The other Beavers told him,
> "That guy is going to get away. I thought you said you're good."
> Mazǫ said, "I can hit them." He shot a long way,
> and after that man swimming in the water came up, he shot him.
> After the guy came up again, Mazǫ shot at him and killed him.
> People asked, "How could you hit him from so far away?"
> He said, "Like in a beehive, the bee knows his own hole.
> That's how I got him" [meaning that his power came from bees].
>
> There was one Nedǫęslhiine who was following the people back.
> He was alone.
> He had a little dog in his arm, and he walked by crying.
> There was a guy who lived in the post. He told that Nedǫęslhiine,
> "Take off tonight while it's dark." He didn't want to go.
> He was just splitting wood.
> Madaayęą Chish [Madaayęą's father],
> when they killed the HB,
> he was there and didn't want to do anything about it.
> He was Samaloose.
> He camped across the river.
> The guys who killed the HB called across,
> "How come we hear somebody cutting wood?"
> Samaloose said, "There's nobody here.
> I'm the one splitting wood."
> Early in the morning, he told that Nedǫęslhiine to go.
> He gave some supplies to the Nedǫęslhiine. That man told him,
> "There's lots of us over there. We're going to come back."
> That Nedǫęslhiine left early in the morning when it was still foggy.
> After that, they came after them every year,
> but they couldn't find the people who killed the traders.
> (RDA, DZHD09-24)

The events of 1823 brought the trade within Dane-zaa territory to an abrupt halt. All accounts agree that the St. John post at the mouth of the Pine (Beatton) River closed after the killings, and the new Rocky

Mountain Fort was not yet completed. Soon after, the post at Dunvegan also closed. It reopened in 1828, but there was no convenient place for the Dane-zaa of Fort St. John to trade their furs for many years. Memories of the hard times that followed the killing were still alive when Robin interviewed elders in the 1960s. Jack Askoty told Robin a few years ago that Aanaatswęa, born fifty years after the event, still feared retribution when Robin recorded the stories of her husband, Charlie Yahey, in 1966. She must have thought Robin's recordings could be used to punish the people responsible, or their descendants.

With game resources depleted and trade goods difficult to obtain, Dane-zaa communities experienced hard times until the 1870s. In 1966, Augustine Jumbie told Robin a story about how Samaloose, who maintained contact with HBC traders in the forts that remained open, had persuaded the company to open a new post at Gattah Kwậh. According to Jumbie, Samaloose was working for the trader at a post down the river, Dunvegan or Fort Vermilion, when a Dane-zaa delegation arrived at the post (RDA, field notes, 1965-66). Presumably, Jumbie refers not to "old Chimarouche," who died in 1823, but to the son who was probably the man Faries identified as a "fort hunter" in 1823. Jumbie clearly identifies Samaloose as Madaayęa's father – that is, the father of Chief Montney (Madaayęa). This Samaloose is the same person who, according to John Andre, gave refuge to Maranda after the 1823 killings. The incident Jumbie describes probably took place some time after Dunvegan reopened in 1828. A new post at Fort St. John was built in 1857, after the Dane-zaa delegation asked for a new post closer to their own country. John Andre elaborates in this story, translated by Billy Attachie.

> They told the company man,
> "Your post is too far to come from our country,
> all the way down there."
> They wanted him to make a place closer to them.
> Samaloose, Madaayęa-ta [Madaayęa's father]
> was the head man for the trader that time.
> The company man said he would tell Samaloose,
> and they went back.
> The company man told Samaloose what the people had said.
> Samaloose said, "You're the boss.
> You can make the store anyplace you want."
> But the company man said, "No, I don't know anything.

I don't know where people camp, where people come together.
You have to show me where."
So, Samaloose said one boy would show them
where was a good place, and the company man was glad.
So, they said Gattah Kwậh was the best spot.

"That's the main path of the Indians.
That's where they cross the Peace River.
It's not too far from the mountains. That's the best spot."
So, those people sent a boy to show where that place was,
and they chopped down some trees
so the company people coming up the river in boats
won't miss that spot. Then they went back to Samaloose.
The trader made Samaloose boss of all the Indians.
He was supposed to tell them what to do.
The trader would tell him what to tell the Indians,
and then Samaloose would tell them.
They made a house and everything
for the traders at Gattah Kwậh.
They made the trading post there,
and everyone was happy. It wasn't too far to go.

(RDA, JA 1b; Attachie's translation, RDA, DZHD09-1, DZHD09-24)

The HBC established a new post at Gattah Kwậh in 1857, but the company's monopoly began to fade in the 1860s. In 1865, a former miner known as "Twelve Foot" Davis established a trading post opposite the HBC post at Fort Dunvegan. He developed new ways of trading with the Dane-zaa, treated them fairly, and eventually brought in food supplies and a wider range of trade goods. Many Dane-zaa people took the name *Davis* in admiration of the trader, and *Davis* is still a common name at both Blueberry and Doig.

Twelve Foot Davis was born Henry Fuller Davis in Vermont in 1820. After prospecting in California, he came north. Dorothea Calverly, a historian of the Peace River, writes that "he found a twelve-foot unclaimed strip of land between Discovery claims #1 and #2 at Barkerville," which yielded $12,000 worth of gold (MacGregor 1952, 201-11). Although he was illiterate, he had a talent for trading and an ability to relate to Aboriginal people and treat them fairly and with respect. By the 1870s, he was bringing in supplies from Quesnel via McLeod Lake, using a string of packhorses and wranglers. Later, he brought in supplies from Edmonton via Dunvegan.

Aku told a story that reflects the trader's enterprises in both these areas. Margaret Dominic Davis provided this translation.

> Those white men went back up the Peace River
> to McLeod Lake for more groceries.
> Once they saw their boss, Twelve Foot Davis, they told him,
> "We saw some Indians who don't even have any pants."
> "They wear long hair and no clothes,
> and they don't know about matches," they told their boss.
> Davis made a big boat and loaded it down with groceries.
> They had a hard time to get through
> because one place the water was shallow.
> The boat just sat on the bottom of the river,
> and the water couldn't lift it up. They had to build a dam.
> The boat would rise, and then they would break that dam,
> and the boat would go rushing forward on the water
> and then settle on the bottom again.
> They'd have to make another dam.
> They kept having to make a dam. Break a dam,
> make a dam, break a dam for quite a little ways.
> Finally, Davis and his men made it through to Hudson Hope
> with that great big boat. Davis was a storekeeper and a fur buyer.
> They met those Indians again,
> and Davis gave them all their stuff
> from that great big boat, lots of groceries and matches and things.
> And he gave every man one pair of pants.
> He gave them lots of stuff because he was going to buy fur.
> The Tset'ehkwậh [Hudson Hope] people,
> Matsile and her bunch,
> got the Indians from *etsidzane* [likely Rose Prairie]*
> and Gattah Kwậh.
> And they all packed the groceries over the bad place
> in the water.
> It was hard work. Those things in the boat were heavy,
> not like the things Indians pack.
> Davis made a store at Hudson Hope and a store at Fort St. John.
> He picked up the stuff from Grande Prairie,
> and he went back and forth by boat.

---

* Billy Attachie was not sure what this word referred to.

Traders at Fort St. John, 1902. Provincial Archives of Manitoba, N-12892

> He made himself a house, too.
> When the boat came up the river
> from Grande Prairie to Hudson Hope,
> those white guys had to pull the boat all the way. It was hard.
> (RDA, Aku 1966)

Despite competition from independent traders such as Davis, and later from a company called Revillon Frères, the HBC maintained a presence in Dane-zaa territory until after the Second World War. Frank Beaton was the HBC factor from 1899 to 1924. The HBC post provided a convenient location for meetings between the Dane-zaa and government officials, beginning with the treaty commission in 1900. The post continued to be located near the Peace River until it was moved to a site near Charlie Lake in 1924. Beaton's journals indicate that members of the Fort St. John Band visited there frequently to trade and took treaty there every year.

Beaton's journals provide a particularly rich account of Dane-zaa trade relationships. When Robin first read them, shortly after his first fieldwork in 1964, he was amazed to read the names of people who were still alive and whom he had come to know as elders. On 11 March 1911, for instance, Beaton writes, "Acko & a Boy arieved about 12 oclock last nigt they report a lot of sickness in their camp and came in to get some medicine" (Glenbow Archives, M-4560-28).

Acko (Aku), who told Robin many of the stories in this book, was an important elder at Doig in the 1960s. Amazingly, he and Robin were both fathers of new babies in the late 1960s. Shirley Acko, Aku's last child, was born in 1968. Amber, Robin's first daughter, was born in 1969. Amber and Shirley are lifelong friends. Amber is now a folklorist doing research on the Dane-zaa Dreamers tradition, and Shirley is an active member of the Doig River community. Both now have children of their own. Robin also interviewed Johnny Beaton, Frank Beaton's son, in 1966 and heard firsthand about the life of a fur trader. Beaton's journal was particularly useful during our genealogical research for the Doig and Blueberry First Nations treaty land entitlement, during which we confirmed the identity of many people's ancestors.

Because fur prices were generally high in the first decades of the twentieth century, some Dane-zaa families were able to accumulate a large number of horses. Although the Dane-zaa continued to trade with the HBC, several independent traders set up small stores near their winter communities. One of these places was Nig Creek near Montney, where a trader named M. Slyman established a store and trading post in 1929 that serviced a growing number of farmers as well as the Dane-zaa.

Although the fur trade drew the Dane-zaa into a global mercantile system and had a profound impact on their resource base, the Dane-zaa's participation flowed smoothly from their traditional practices of hunting and trapping the animals with whom they shared the Peace River country. The traders and the Dane-zaa were equally dependent on successfully negotiating relationships with each another. Without Dane-zaa hunters and trappers, the traders would have starved and been deprived of profits. Without the traders, the Dane-zaa would have lacked access to the manufactured goods on which they came to depend. It was not until the twentieth century that trade in food items became important. Even then, wild game remained the most important source of food. Imported foods such as flour, rice, and beans were significant because they provided a backup food supply during times when hunting was not successful. In the following story, Doig elder Nachę (Mary Pouce Coupe) describes the transition from an

economy based almost entirely on meat to one in which imported supplies were available. Her grandson Billy Attachie provided this translation.

> When we only ate meat, sometimes we ran out.
> After we finished all the meat, we were starving again.
> We moved all over to kill something.
> When we killed something, we had meat and would keep going,
> moving place to place.
> When we had bannock, after you kill one moose,
> you still have food.
> Now, when you have something to eat like bannock,
> it feels good. But that time we only ate straight meat.
> We went through some very hard times.
> Us, we are still alive. I am still alive.
> Those old people, long time ago,
> they all moved one way.
> When we moved a long way,
> we would all split up into smaller camps,
> maybe four or five groups.
> We moved to Tsiih Kwą̂h [Fort Vermilion].

THE LATER FUR TRADE AND THE HUDSON'S BAY COMPANY KILLINGS

Dane-zaa at Fort St. John, 1906.
Photo by Ancel Maynard Bezanson. Courtesy of Hudson's Bay Company Archives, Archives of Manitoba, N-16881

When we left Tsiih Kwậh, we had to move
all the way back here to the Doig area.
(RDA, NA-1)

The fur trade continued to be an important source of income for most Dane-zaa families until the 1960s. Fur trade companies no longer control the trade, but trapping continues to be important, both culturally and economically. Fur prices are not as high as they have been in the past, and an active animal rights movement has diminished the market for furs. Still, many Dane-zaa families hold on to their traplines and maintain trapping cabins throughout their traditional territories. Dane-zaa hunters and trappers maintain skills that go back to the eighteenth century.

7
Priests and Dreamers

As they traded at the North West Company and Hudson's Bay Company posts, the Dane-zaa learned about the ways of the white men, including the ways in which they worshipped their Christian God. Dreamers such as the Cigne, who traded at the first fort, saw the crosses worn by the Catholic voyageurs. In the Dane-zaa worldview, every animal, material object, and natural feature has power and a story. Dane-zaa hunters wanted to know the stories behind the crosses and all the other new things the traders introduced. They wanted to understand the power behind European firearms and other trade goods. This desire to understand the source of the traders' powers is reflected in the names of Dreamers such as Alédzé (Gunpowder) and Adíshtl'íshe (Paper).

The first Catholic priest to visit the Dane-zaa was Father Henri Faraud, a member of the French Oblate Order of Mary Immaculate (OMI). Faraud first met the Dane-zaa at Fort Dunvegan on 28 October 1859 and later visited Fort St. John. The Dane-zaa of the upper Peace were still trading at Fort Dunvegan, so Faraud met Peace River Dane-zaa from throughout their territory. Before he came to Dunvegan, Faraud had been a missionary in the Athabasca district for ten years and had a good command of Dene Suline (Chipewyan) and Slavey, two Athapaskan languages closely related to Dane-zaa Záágé?. He would have been able to converse relatively easily with the people he met at Dunvegan and Fort St. John. Faraud later went on to become bishop of the Athabasca-Mackenzie District and travelled extensively through the Peace River country.

In his book, *Dix-huit ans chez les sauvages* (Eighteen years among the wild people), Faraud gives a detailed account of his first meeting with the Dane-zaa. He also includes accounts of the conversations he had with the Dane-zaa as part of his attempts to convert them to Christianity. Although he interpreted what they said in relation to his mission, his book provides a fascinating glimpse into Dane-zaa thought after sixty-five years of contact with the fur traders.

> The news of my arrival spread quickly among the wild people. The following day, I heard a distant volley of gunshots coming from both sides of the river. It wasn't long before the explosions were nearby. It was the Beavers arriving in a large group. These poor young people were demonstrating their tactics: as soon as I was willing to present myself, and as soon as they saw me, they shouted cries of joy, which were repeated thousands of times by the surrounding echoes. (Faraud 1870, 102)*

At first, Faraud believed that the Dane-zaa would do as he instructed and quickly convert to Christianity. He did not understand that the Dane-zaa never respond well to commands. To this day, they resist anyone attempting to be their boss. They did, however, listen and learn from what he had to say. "Beginning the following day, I began to train them. The first days, they learned to obey my commands. They listened to my exhortations; many even promised to convert. Throughout the first week, everything started getting better" (Faraud 1870, 102).

Faraud decided that the Dane-zaa were moronic because of their belief in magic and incantation and because of their devotion to gambling in the form of the hand game. He resolved to tackle the game first and hoped to change their core beliefs later. Faraud describes the game as follows:

> This game consisted of hiding a knucklebone in one hand and getting the partner to guess in which hand it was hidden. In our eyes, it seems naive, but to the wild people this game is filled with mystery. So, they reunited in large numbers: behind were the witnesses, and drummers were found at the extremities of the troop. All were rowdy while some chanted and

---

* Kaela Lee and Jillian Ridington provided this and all other translations of Faraud.

others beat their drums and a mystery was completed. It was the guessing game.

The wild people lost powder, balls, lead, clothes and cloth, horses, and, finally, all that they had playing this childish game. This game lasted day and night, during good and bad times. Nothing stopped them, not even the heat or the cold, and all that resulted were sicknesses, arguments, and inhumanities. The Beavers were a barbaric and sad sight. The winners took away the only form of subsistence that the loser had and found pleasure in seeing death, famine, and cold dumped upon the losers. The wrong in what they did was huge and inveterate. Even the women and children believed that no one would survive the day without playing the hand game. (Faraud 1870, 103)

Faraud exhorted the Dane-zaa to give up the game and was pleased that they appeared to be willing to do so, although he must have known that as soon as he left they would continue to do as they had always done.

I attacked it with moderation and gentleness in an attempt to demonstrate the inconveniences and the arguments that followed. After finishing my speech, a Beaver stood up and said, "Father, you are right. Up until now, we played the game to ban anxiety, but now that you have shown us a different way, we will give up."

"When God sees you've stopped," I said, "you shall all be happy." "So," I cried, "do you promise God as well as me, his minister, that you will never again play the hand game?"

"Yes! Yes!" they cried with enthusiasm, "we promise!" (Ibid.)

Encouraged by his apparent success, Faraud moved on to the more delicate subject of baptism.

"My friends," I said, "the moment has come. You will soon leave to go on the hunt. Bring me your children so that I can baptize them."

Nobody responded. I repeated myself, and an elder stood up and said gravely, "The Beavers do not want you to baptize their children."

"Why?" I asked.

> "Because, after being baptized, they are forbidden to practise magic, and if they were to fall sick, they would die."
> It was then that I truly understood the depth of their sorry state, but I could not understand that these men, who had yesterday promised to convert, and these people, who seemed ecstatic about what I had to offer them, were now refusing baptism. (Faraud 1870, 103)

Although the Dane-zaa were willing to say they would give up gambling, they drew the line at giving up "magic and incantation." Baptism, as Faraud presented it to them, meant that they would have to relinquish their medicine powers, something that was and continues to be at the heart of Dane-zaa identity.

> "Unfortunately," I cried, "your almost shameful magic and incantation were no more permitted before baptism than they will be after. If, as you told me yesterday, you really want to convert and become Christians, you need to realize that God's laws prohibit magic. But you must also realize that your incantations will stop neither you nor I from dying. In less than two years, more than half of your brothers have died exerting all they had on your magical science."
> "Father," responded the leading speaker of the Beavers, "incantation is our only medicine. If you want us to stop practising it, you need to bring us several large cases of alternative medicines that will stop us from dying."
> It was hard for me to explain to them that my job as a priest had nothing to do with curing the human body. However, I wasn't against the use of other medicines, and I myself, when I could, gave them remedies to ease their illness without pretending to cure them. The Beavers seemed convinced by what I was saying; however, they still didn't want to bring forth their children for baptism. (Faraud 1870, 104)

Faraud was a missionary who never questioned the superiority of his religion over Dane-zaa spiritual traditions. He met with the Dane-zaa at a time when European diseases and starvation, caused by the fur trade's overexploitation of game, had led to severe suffering. The HBC post at Fort St. John had just been reopened after being closed since 1823. The Dane-zaa relied on traditional healing methods grounded in a larger system of medicine powers and the vision quest. The powers that people obtained on their vision quests defined both individual and social identity in Dane-zaa culture. Faced with Faraud's demand that they give this all up and baptize their children, the Dane-zaa's response was understandable. Unless the priest could provide medicines that would prevent and cure illness, they could not accept his proposition. Faraud, realistically, explained that he was not a doctor and could not provide this kind of assurance. He resolved to try another approach and to find a way to tolerate their deeply held beliefs about medicine power.

> The superstitions of these people saddened me. I finally convinced myself that all my efforts were proving to be useless. The only way to convert them to Christianity was to find a way to allow them to practise this magic and incantation that they called medicine. The medicine of the Beavers is not absolutely evil and is quite different from that of the Crees and Saulteaux, who claim to have dealings with demons. The Beavers invoke neither God nor the devil, but they believe in the power of their songs to cure illness. All the Beavers are doctors but only for their families. (Faraud 1870, 104)

Faraud does not mention Dreamers specifically, but he does describe people he calls "doctors of magic" who used music and the drum to cure illness. Because he did not spend any time with the Dane-zaa in their camps, Faraud had no knowledge of how the Dreamers used their powers to "dream ahead for everybody," as Charlie Yahey described it. Faraud described a typical performance by one of these doctors:

> As soon as someone fell ill, the doctor of magic was called. As he entered the cabin of the one who was ill, the doctor showed him a drum painted in red, blue, white, and black. After that, he would begin a dismal chant accompanied by a loud beating on the brightly coloured head of his drum. Suddenly, he would stop and sit down beside the sick one, simulate a large agitation, and then sniff at every part of the body. Finally, he would say:
> "I see what's wrong. I feel it. It's an evil spirit, and I'm going to destroy it!"
> Then, he would suck the flesh of the sick one from his toes to his face and, when finished, would scream victoriously:

"Here it is ... now I hold it!"

And the imperturbable doctor would show his hand, which contained either a small stone or a small bone that he pretended to have taken from the sick one's body.

If, after the initial scene, the sick one still was not cured, the comedy would start again. The doctor agitated more than ever and screamed like someone who was possessed. He would hit his drum and continue, sometimes for consecutive nights, always removing bones, stones, and pieces of glass from the body of the sick one. When the sickness resisted these knowledgeable operations, the doctor declared that the body of the sick one was filled with too many evil spirits and admitted that he was not strong enough to remove them.

The only thing that kept Mr. Doctor, the professional in magic, from giving up were the payments that he received, which consisted of either dry meat or clothing. The job of doctors is lucrative, even in the land of the Beavers. (Faraud 1870, 104-5)

The idea of sucking evil from a sick person brings to mind Nachę's story about the big fat man (see Chapter 3). Billy Attachie gave us another Dane-zaa perspective on the use of medicine power for healing in an interview in 1999.

Long time ago, they all got power from each animal, those things.
And there were no doctors, no hospital, and if Indians get sick, they're going to die. So, whoever had that kind of power would lay hand on them or give them water or put water on their head, and they would recover.
They would get healed.
(Ridington/Dane-zaa Archive [RDA], DZ99-18)

Faraud attempted to make a bargain with the Dane-zaa: if they gave up gambling and the use of medicines, they could continue to sing and dance. The Dane-zaa refused, and their children remained unbaptized. In fact, baptismal records from Fort St. John did not begin until 1881. From then on, members of the Oblate order visited the Dane-zaa every year and recorded the names of people they baptized, as well as the names and estimated ages of their parents. These records proved to be useful when, together with Mitchell Goodjohn and Pat

Cleary, we prepared a genealogy for the Doig and Blueberry treaty land entitlement claim. We could compare the names that Robin recorded from Dane-zaa elders in the 1960s with the testimony of current Dane-zaa elders and with written records that began in the last quarter of the nineteenth century. Had Faraud succeeded in baptizing the Dane-zaa, the baptism records would have been even more useful, but the erosion of traditional culture might also have been accelerated.

Later historical accounts also indicate that the Dane-zaa continued to play the hand game. In the early twentieth century, trader Philip Godsell reported that men had wagered nearly all their material possessions in the game. Although Godsell was known for exaggerating, this description was probably based on fact. The elders Robin met in the 1960s scarcely mentioned the hand game, although it was still practised, but told him extensive stories about the lives of the Dreamers. The hand game continues to be played on social occasions, but singing and dancing to the Dreamers' songs are now far more important. The hand game is still played at cultural celebrations, but Dane-zaa are more likely to buy a Keno ticket or participate in a bingo game than in the hand game.

In Dane-zaa tradition, the first Dreamer was a man named Mekénúúnatane (see Chapter 8 for stories about his life and death). According to the stories, he lived before the first missionary visited the Dane-zaa in 1859. Another great Dreamer, Mak'íhts'ęwéswąą, preached after that event. Like Faraud, Mak'íhts'ęwéswąą spoke out strongly against using medicine power to harm people. He reaffirmed the importance of maintaining harmonious relationships between humans and the nonhuman animal persons upon whom their lives depended. More importantly, he emphasized that singing and dancing were ways to express that harmony. Dane-zaa Dreamers today repeat the message that singing and dancing is a celebration in the presence of the creator.

Although we can never know for certain what role Dreamers played in ancient times, they likely functioned as hunt chiefs who visualized communal hunts in their dreams and taught people how to deploy themselves in hunts that used drives and surrounds. As the story of Duuk'ihsachę Matáá? indicates (see Chapter 4), they were also prophets. Tsááyaa, the first hunter, served as a model for the first Dreamer. Dreamers knew strangers would be coming to their country, and they prepared their people for these encounters. Mekénúúnatane told the people about the coming of the white men just as Charlie Yahey prophesied that people would come to drill for the "grease of the giant animals." For centuries, prophets have told Dane-zaa people what the future will bring. Although there are no Dreamers at the moment, the Doig River Drummers and Singers, the Yahey singers at Blueberry, and others at Halfway still sing the Dreamers' songs at gatherings at the Doig River and Blueberry Reserves and at other Dane-zaa communities. The songs of the Dane-zaa Dreamers remind the people of the Dreamers' message that singing and dancing are a celebration in the presence of the creator. Singing and dancing are particularly important when people die. They speed the deceased's journey along *yaak'ihts'ę? atanii,* the trail to heaven.

There is a strong connection between dreaming in the vision quest and dreaming of heaven. Aku's story about his father, Azáde (Liver), begins as a vision quest story but then transforms into one that describes the power of dreaming to heaven. Tommy Attachie told us the story as he remembered hearing it from Aku.

> Long time ago, Azáde was looking for a song, for power.
> He travelled all over on the good land.
> He heard, not too far, people laughing and yelling.
> When he got to that place, the noise and laughter got farther away.
> He really wanted to see that place, but it kept going away.
> He just kept following that noise, and he came to one place.
> When he heard that noise again,
> he came to where there was a small spruce, not too tall, lots of spruce.
> It's a place that is really nice with lots of limbs on the spruce.
> He heard those people laughing again.
> When he got to there, he looked around,
> but only saw little spruce branches.
> Then he found a paper right on top of a spruce bough.
> There was no paper that time.
> The paper was just like the paper you write on today.
> He found that paper on one of the good spruce boughs.
> (RDA, DZHD09-24)

The Dane-zaa Záágé? word for paper is *Adíshtl'íshe,* which probably referred originally to birchbark. *Adíshtl'íshe* is also the word for the Bible. A famous dreamer also carried the name Adíshtl'íshe. He, along with others, signed Treaty 8 in 1900. He put his mark on a paper that recognized Dane-zaa hunting, fishing, and trapping rights. Paper, and the idea that it could contain powerful words, became important to Dane-zaa Dreamers after contact with European traders and priests. In the story, Azáde hears words coming from the paper. The first Dreamers observed that the traders wrote on paper. The traders set down how much fur and meat a trapper brought in and the value of the goods he received in exchange. The Dreamers were keenly aware that the traders recorded obligations or debts that would have to be paid off when the next furs were traded. Similarly, they noted that the priests based their teachings on words written in a sacred book. The Dreamers concluded that written words were a source of the Europeans' power.

Aku's story continues:

> He was wondering where that paper came from.
> He rolled it up carefully and put it in his pocket.
> After that, he traveled all over.
> He kept it in his bag with the things from his power.
> He kept it in a clean place. He was wondering what it is.
> He travelled all the time but never told anybody about it.

When people obtained power from a vision quest, they acquired a medicine bundle, which they kept in a special place. Only the power holder could open the bundle, and they did so only on special occasions such as when they needed the power to heal a member of the community or to defend themselves from attack by another person trying to use their own power to cause harm.

Aku's story refers to a medicine bundle that contains symbols of power the boy obtained from paper during his vision quest. If another person opens the bundle, the power will fly back into the bush. The story explains what happens when another person attempts to open someone's medicine bundle:

> Azáde had one younger brother, too.
> When they were moving camp, they had nothing to eat.
> Azáde thought about what happened. He knew what was going on.
> That paper will be taken back. That's why they were starving.
> Every time they moved camp, he hung it up in a good place.
> His younger brother wondered why he hung up that bag all the time,

> so he looked inside and found the paper.
> He wondered where this paper came from.
> It was a really good paper that was rolled up,
> so he picked it up and put it in his pocket.
> He went not too far and killed two big cow moose.
> He thought, "This is a very important thing he got, the paper."
> He thought highly of his brother for looking after really good things.
> When he came back to his older brother's camp,
> he put it back in that same place. He hung it up.
> In the morning, his older brother Azáde said,
> "What have you done? That thing I look after is gone."
> The younger brother went over there and said,
> "Hune [older brother], I'm the one that did it. After you were gone,
> I picked it up and put it in my pocket.
> I went and killed two fat cows. I put it back carefully.
> How is it going to fly out? If it's windy, it's not going to fly out."
> Azáde told his younger brother, "You gave me a pretty hard time.
> I'm supposed to look after it, but the paper already went back to where it came from. It flew back. It's gone."
> (RDA, DZHD09-24)

Aku's story explains a key feature of the vision quest. The experience is a special and privileged relationship between the power seeker and the power giver. Power is a gift that also incurs obligations, much like the gifts animals give to hunters in their dreams. One of the obligations is that upon returning from the vision quest, a child must not tell anyone the details of what happened. To do so would be bragging, which would anger the animal friend. Margie Wolf's story in Chapter 3 relates the consequences of such action.

As people with power mature, they give hints of the nature of their power. A food they cannot eat or an action that they cannot participate in is such an indicator. Through signs such as these, relatives come to know and respect a person's power. By the time people with power have become elders, they can talk about their power more directly. In Aku's story, Azáde gradually reveals that he is becoming a Dreamer.

> Later on, when he was all grown up and got married,
> Azáde started dreaming.

> Pretty soon, he started telling about his dream.
> He told people what is happening.
> Every night, he went to sleep and got up, and the next morning,
> he talked to us in a different language.
> "There's a place in Heaven, and Ahatáa [Our Father, God] is there."
> He told a story about his dream, and pretty soon he was getting more.
> Pretty soon, he was getting stronger.
> Some of those people with really good minds,
> they prayed and sang with him. People with good minds,
> and all the rest of the people, they said,
> "I wish he would tell us more about Ahatáa."
> Pretty soon, it's getting more and more, and he starts singing.
> He knows it more now that there's heaven.
> Even God himself, he's still above heaven.
> (RDA, DZHD09-24)

In another version of this story, translated by Margaret Dominic Davis, Aku describes in his own words how Azáde chose which of the Dreamers he would follow.

> My grandfather sent my father on *Shin kaa*.
> After that, my father started singing *Nááchę* songs [Dreamers' songs].
> After the paper had gone, he started singing the first Dreamer's song,
> but Mekénúúnatane's song wasn't right for him.
> Then he started singing with Mak'íhts'ęwéswąą's song,
> and everything started to straighten out.
> Then he saw a great big evil person *[Dane menechide]* coming to him.
> He kept on singing the song, but that devil just kept on coming.
> The rest of the people couldn't see it.
> Afterward, he told the people there was a great big devil, terrible to look at. He told them,
> "I sang with Mak'íhts'ęwéswąą's song,
> and it turned and left."
> He told the people about the devil.
> He told them not to lie and pack stories around

if they wanted to go straight on the trail to heaven.
He told them the devil was really bad.
After the paper he got when he was training as a little boy was gone,
he went crazy, and he saw the devil.
He sang those Dreamers' songs until it went away.
That paper must have come from Jesus.
(RDA, Aku 1966)

The first part of Aku's story describes a vision quest in which the boy gains power from paper. The second part describes the boy becoming a man and taking on the power of the Dreamers' songs. The story reflects a historical change from dreams as a means to power to dreams as a way of bringing people together. The Dreamer as hunt chief brought people together for communal hunting. The Dreamer as spiritual leader brought people on earth together with their relatives in heaven. Aku then describes what his father learned from dreaming to heaven. People who dream to heaven warn their relatives about the dangers of malicious gossip and discord within a community.

The Dreamers said that packing stories from house to house [gossip] was no good.
Lots of people got killed for that.
That starts the wars.
And swearing and talking like that, that's no good.
You can't get to heaven with that.
If the road to heaven was steep and straight,
no one could make it.
Jesus, when he was killed and made the road to heaven,
he made places to rest so people could make it.
He made that post office
where people stop to see if their name is there.
The one who keeps the gate to heaven [yaak'ihts'ę̄? atanii grati],
he watches over the animals, too, moose, caribou,
everything that lives on the earth.
Sometimes, people on earth don't get many moose.
That's because they don't keep the meat well.
It's just like the Indian Agent who gives out rations.
He knows everything.

>Nobody can hide from him *[ajuu manastwąą wǫ́lę]*.
>On the other side of the gate, there's a really fancy cross,
>and there's a really fancy bird on the cross [see following page].
>
>When a really good person gets to heaven,
>the bird sings, and all the people crowd around to meet him.
>(RDA, Aku 1966)

Tommy's version of Aku's story describes different stages on the trail to heaven. His interpretation of the story clearly reflects the influence of evangelical Christianity in his life.

>Halfway to heaven, on the trail, on the right-hand side,
>is where Jesus slept when he went back.
>He made a place there where people eat and sleep.
>When good people go to heaven, they don't have hard time going.
>They go really fast but want to pass where Jesus rested at night.
>They can't go over there right away. They have to sleep there.
>This is what Jesus made for people. This is the place he told us about.
>After he rested, he took off from there. They come to a place where there is blue sky, and a beautiful bird is sitting there.
>That bird knows when a good person goes through the blue sky to get to the top of the hill.
>The beautiful bird is really happy for people, and it sings, "Heaven is a pretty big place."
>The whole world hears that bird singing.
>When the bird sings, people in heaven wonder who has arrived.
>People wish for their relatives and wonder who has arrived.
>After a person arrives, they see the cross. When a person dies, his relatives make a cross and leave it there.
>That bird is singing, happy for people.
>He is happy when somebody arrives at the place.
>He sees when a person gets to where they wash you and they make you different.
>(RDA, DZHD09-24)

The image of a bird guarding the gate to heaven is part of an ancient shamanic tradition. Dane-zaa Dreamers undoubtedly knew about this

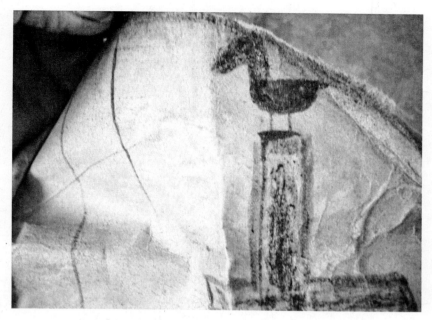

This image of a bird at the gate to heaven belonged originally to Antoine Hunter. Photo by Robin Ridington. Courtesy of Agnes Hunter Solonas

bird long before they encountered Christianity. When they learned about the story of Jesus, they associated it with something that was already part of their spiritual heritage. Aku's father came to think of the bird at the gate to heaven in relation to the Christian symbols.

In July 1968, Robin recorded Charlie Yahey's story about how the first Dreamers learned about heaven from the white men and their priests. The first Dreamers were impressed by paper's power to hold stories. They quickly adapted the idea and put down images on the materials available to them, birchbark and moosehide. The images they drew from their dreams combined elements of Christianity with ancient shamanic ideas. Margaret Dominic Davis provided this translation.

> From the dreamers of long ago we began to know
> that there were some other Indians [people] around.
> Those white men were getting a message from God.
> They had papers coming from God
> that told them about how things were.
> (Ridington 1978, 88)

The Oblate missionaries showed the Dane-zaa pictures of their teachings in the form of the Catholic Ladder, a pictorial catechism used in mission work with people unable to read the Bible. Augustine Jumbie, a Prophet River elder, displayed the Catholic Ladder prominently on his wall. He also had a drawing of heaven done on moosehide by a dreamer named Decuthla. The Dane-zaa do not believe the Catholic Ladder has immediate spiritual power, and Jumbie felt free to put it on public display. In contrast, he brought out the moosehide drawing only on special occasions. Jumbie showed the moosehide and allowed us to photograph it.* The Dreamers who drew images of their dreams about heaven were likely influenced by what they had seen. The Dane-zaa have always felt a strong connection to the spirits of people who have passed on. Stories about the game keepers and the vision quest tell us that the spirits of animals have always been part of their kinship community. In his story, Charlie Yahey describes the heaven that he knew from his own dreams and from the songs and stories of Dreamers who went before him.

> The people who died and went to heaven are looking over the earth.
> God made them again to come down to earth and look at the people.
> God sent them down to earth to be made people again.
> Just before a person gets to heaven, not far from God's place, a land where he stays, from there it is just like a door or gate that someone gets through. On the side of it, where someone goes through, there are beautiful signs.
> All those flowers and grass are painted on it.
> Everyone thinks they are beautiful.
> On the ground in God's land,
> there are beautiful flowers and grass,
> and inside on through it is just like a town, a big camp.
> When you enter the town,
> it starts to get bigger and bigger buildings.
> It is just like that.
> Past the gate, there is a guardhouse dog
> and a person who watches the gate.
> (Ridington 1978, 89-90)

---

* See *Trail to Heaven: Knowledge and Narrative in a Northern Native Community* (Ridington 1987) for photographs of Jumbie's moosehide drawing.

Charlie Yahey's description of heaven closely matches the drawings Dreamers have made over the years. The drawings show houses, crosses, and stylized trails to heaven. As noted, the image of the bird guarding the doorway to the sky world is found in the shamanic traditions of many hunting people. Many of the moosehide drawings show this bird perched on a pole, tower, or cross. Ancient Paleolithic hunters in France painted a strikingly similar image on the walls of a Lascaux cave 16,000 years ago.

This next part of Charlie's story is more shamanic than it is Christian.

> A spirit person sits on sort of a tower. He is like a giant bird,
> maybe like a goose. He has a big mouth and sits on top.
> When a person comes up, he knows.
> When somebody enters there,
> he sort of staggers around and, like in a dream,
> he is shy because it is so strange.
> Those people who have died before and been made again by God,
> they look beautiful, and the new person is shy.
> They all come out of their houses
> and look at the new person coming.
> It is just like here when a strange person comes,
> and all the kids come out and nosey around.
>
> The last one of the Dreamers who died wants to know who it is.
> He is the one who asks, "Does this person come from Him
> or from the other one?" [God or the devil]
> The last Dreamer says what family the new person came from.
> The Dreamer then goes and finds the people in heaven who
> are his relatives.
> When they died and followed the trail to heaven,
> they were made again by God.
> The Dreamer in heaven says to the people arriving,
> "How did you come up to here the hard way?
> I didn't expect you to come by there." That person wouldn't talk.
> They would just talk to each other with their thoughts.
> They would know what that person coming up is thinking.
> The people who are related to the one coming up
> are happy to see him. He is just a shadow,
> but when he gets to heaven,
> he changes back into a person again.
> (Ridington 1978, 89)

The Dreamer's description of people meeting in heaven has obvious Christian influences, but it is also distinctively Dane-zaa. When people from different bands come together for their summer gathering at the place where happiness dwells, Su Na chii k'chige, they greet one another and exchange stories. On earth, they do this by talking, singing, and dancing. In heaven, as Charlie Yahey describes it, they communicate by simply knowing what everyone is thinking. To get to Heaven, the Dreamers say that a person must give up feuds and bad feelings about other people. In this state of mind, there is nothing to hide and sharing thoughts becomes possible. Charlie explains that new arrivals must bathe and be given new bodies before they can join their relatives in heaven.

> There is a big rope. The street is like a big rope.
> The person's shadow goes along this street
> until he comes to the house right at the end of the line.
> It is there that they make people's shadows into bodies again.
> The shadow enters this house, and they say to him,
> "This is the place where they change the shadow into bodies again."
> When the shadow comes up from earth
> and first meets the people in heaven, they feel sorry for him
> and tell him to go to that house to get fixed up
> into a new person.
> If that person who comes up was old,
> they change him into a young person again.
> (Ridington 1978, 89)

This description reflects the Christian idea of baptism and rebirth, but it may also reflect ideas about reincarnation that the Dane-zaa may have held for many years before contact. Charlie's statement earlier in the story that "God sent them down to earth to be made people again" may also refer to such beliefs. People who die and go to heaven may be reborn in the same way that the spirits of animals who give themselves to a hunter come back in a new body.*

Charlie then describes a boss who is like the familiar figure of a game keeper. The person's transformation upon entering heaven is

---

* See Chapter 16 for a discussion of Jean-Guy Goulet's and Antonia Mills's work on reincarnation among First Nations, including the Dane-zaa.

like the transformation that follows encountering a spirit person during a vision quest.

> There is a boss for that place
> where they change shadows into young bodies.
> This manager is the one that takes care of that place.
> They tell the new shadow to take a bath in there.
> When the water comes down on him, he starts to get young again.
> For a good person, they only have to bathe him once,
> but for a bad person, they must do it many times.
> Someone who has been just a little bit bad must do it twice.
> After he has been bathed and has turned
> into a young person again,
> he turns to a mirror and looks at himself to see how good he is.
> There are also pictures hanging up and the new person is told,
> "Choose your own self. Choose how you would like to look.
> Choose the kind of body you would like to have."
> Then he dresses up, and one person is a spokesman
> who leads him around.
> He leads the person around, and the others vote for him.
> He wants to sing a song to find out which one he will dance with.
> (Ridington 1978, 89)

Once the transformation has been completed, the events that take place in heaven parallel those that take place during the summer gatherings. On earth, people sing and dance together to share a common trail and reaffirm the strong bonds of kinship and community. In heaven, they do the same thing.

> They sing a Dreamer's song for you, and the new person dances.
> The one that knew before how to dance, he follows the music,
> someone who danced a lot while he was alive.
> They are all happy. They give them a cheer
> like in the stampede when somebody wins.
> They give him a cheer, and they make him happy.
> If they didn't dance on earth,
> it is hard for them to dance in heaven,
> and they can't follow the music very well
> because their legs feel like they are stiff.
> Somebody has to try for him, someone who died before him.

They dance before him. They dance really well.
So they dance for him, show him how.
They show him how.
Just like something that bounces off something,
just like something bounces off a rock, he dances like that.
He starts to get lighter. He feels like he is getting lighter.
Then he feels like dancing.
That's the way the Dreamer knows
that somebody's gone to heaven.
Then, after they make them back to new again,
they order special food for him, see what he is going to eat.

In heaven, the drinking water is way better
than the drinking water we taste here.
If a person is really sick and doesn't sleep,
when he finally gets to sleep, he sees all the way up to heaven.
His ghost, his spirit, sees all the way up to heaven before him,
even before they give him that water to drink.
After they give him that water to drink,
they take him to everybody to tell about his sins,
what he did on earth when he was little,
and if he tells them all,
not leaving one out, then he will come to heaven.
Then a person will think, I don't know what to do.
I don't know what to do. It's sure hard.
A big person will think that way,
and when a person is ready to go to heaven,
all the people in heaven will just kind of
push him up here and turn him around, and he will go.

If he's really sick and God in heaven wants him to come,
he will dream about that before he dies.
Finally, he will go to sleep.
In his sleep, his spirit will go to heaven.
His spirit will see all the way to heaven.
They give him a drink of water up there,
and when he comes back down to this earth,
he will tell everybody all his sins from when he was living.
When he wakes up back on this earth, he will tell the people,
and after that he will die.
They turn him around and take him back to heaven.

That is the way it is.
The creator made this big world for us, and that's the way it was.
(Ridington 1978, 90-91)

Dane-zaa today combine traditional teachings with Christian beliefs. Funeral services often feature both a preacher from one of the churches in the area and Dane-zaa drummers singing the Dreamers' songs. As Gerry Attachie once told us, "Charlie Yahey and Jesus, they say the same thing."

8
The First and Last Dreamers

Tsááyaa was the first hunter, the first person to gain power from a vision quest, and the first person to follow the swans in his dreams to a land beyond the sky. In the creation story, he continues to fly across the sky, bringing about the turn of the seasons and putting leaves on the trees. Dane-zaa Dreamers take on some of Tsááyaa's attributes. Like swans, they fly through to heaven in their dreams. Elders today say that a Dreamer named Mekénúúnatane predicted the coming of the white people. He took on many of Tsááyaa's ways as he helped his people deal with the disruption caused by the fur trade. His name literally means "His Tracks Earth Trail," but Billy Attachie translates the name more symbolically as "On the Trail – The Doorway – He Opens the Door." The name is appropriate since Mekénúúnatane was the first person to dream about the new ways that the fur trade and Christianity would make necessary. The name suggests that, like Tsááyaa, he followed the sun's path across the sky. Charlie Yahey, who died in 1976, was the last Dreamer, at least until another comes along.

In his stories, Tommy Attachie names the first Dreamers whose songs told people about heaven and urged the Dane-zaa to stop fighting.

> Mekénúúnatane, Mak'íhts'ęwéswąą, Alédzé [Gunpowder].
> They brought peace. They told the people how to live.
> They stopped all the bad people who were fighting.

They stopped the fighting.
After that, the people believed what the Dreamer told them.
They stopped fighting each other.
That's how the Dreamers started.
People said that before them it was really cold.
Tsááyaa made the world really good for us.
He did all kinds of jobs, and he make everything good.
Finally, he got old, but three times,
he made himself young again.
(Ridington/Dane-zaa Archive [RDA], CY Tommy)

Dane-zaa Dreamers are people who have "gone through to heaven and come back to earth in the same body." They follow *yaak'ihts'ę́? atanii,* the trail to heaven, in their dreams by "grabbing hold of" a song sent down by the Dreamers who have gone on before them. Before the Dane-zaa came into contact with Europeans, the Dreamers acted as hunt chiefs who directed communal hunting. Their ability to dream ahead allowed them to visualize the way people should arrange themselves in relation to one another and to the game animals. These dream images symbolized their fundamental message: Dreamers taught the Dane-zaa to live in harmony with one another and with the other creatures of their world. After the Dane-zaa encountered guns and alcohol, the fur trade and Christianity, the Dreamers helped them understand the changes taking place.

Mekénúúnatane was the first Dreamer of this new era. In addition to predicting the coming of the white people, he also dreamed about swans. The chief of the Dane-zaa at Rocky Mountain Fort in 1799 was called the Cigne by the fur trader. The name comes from the French word for swan. It may be that the Cigne was actually Mekénúúnatane, although it is also possible that a later Dreamer took the same name. Tommy Attachie told us a story about how Mekénúúnatane dreamed of daylight coming to him as a spirit person. The spirit asked for his help in making the night shorter. In the video documentary *"Contact the People"* (Ridington et al. 2000) Tommy describes the first Dreamer's connection to Tsááyaa, whose name was Swan and who had power from his namesake.

Even this daylight coming from east.
"This world is too far," Daylight sang to Mekénúúnatane.
When Mekénúúnatane was dreaming, sleeping,

he dreamed about this daylight coming,
that Daylight was singing. He sang a song.
He sang a song, and he told Mekénúúnatane,
"Help me. I want to go fast. I don't go too fast. Help me."
Even that daylight come to him. He dreamed about that song.
He dreamed about all kinds of things.
And he dreamed about Swan, too.
Mekénúúnatane was sleeping.
He dreamed about Swan in a big lake.
There was a big lake with two swans on it.
He dreamed about those swans there, you know in the lake.
Pretty soon, those swans looked at the sky.
This way. Pretty soon, they started to fly.
They started to fly all the way up.
(Ridington 1978, 79)

In the story, even the swans need help flying through to heaven. They pray to the creator with their songs. Mekénúúnatane learns their songs and brings them back to his people.

"When are you going to rest?" he asked the swans.
"You just go around and keep going up.
When you see that blue sky, you want to go through there.
You want to go through to heaven there."
But even those swans can't make it.
They just go around and around.
They can't go through all the way.
And those swans started singing – praying and singing.
They sang a song, and that blue sky just went like this:
it opened up, and they went through.
Only two things can fly through to heaven without dying.
Swans and Dreamers can fly through and return without dying.
That's how the creator is really strong.
That's only one with the power.
Every other thing has to die first.
But Mekénúúnatane dreamed about swans and daylight.
He told people about his dreams.
He sang those songs, and he told everybody about his dreams.
"Two swans went to heaven without dying," he told them.
They were alive, and they went through.

Charlie Yahey and Aanaatswęą (his wife) being greeted as they arrive at Doig Reserve in 1968. Photo by Robin Ridington

> All these things have happened,
> and that's why people believe that
> what the Dreamers say is true.
> There is a heaven. People have to die to get to heaven.
> Lots of people have died and gone to heaven.
> There are a lot of people in heaven.
> These prophets dream about them.
> They see them over there in their dreams.
> The Dreamers never die to get there. That's how they are.
> (Ridington 1978, 79)

The story of how Mekénúúnatane became a Dreamer is set during the early days of the fur trade, when guns made it possible for hunters to kill their game from a distance. We have recorded many versions of this story. Charlie Yahey told Robin the following version on 14 August 1968 at the house of Jack Acko and Eskama on the Doig Reserve. Charlie begins by describing how Mekénúúnatane first left his body and followed the dream trail to heaven.* Margaret Dominic Davis provided this translation.

> The name of Mekénúúnatane was called.
> Something is happening around here.
> They all looked after it.
> One time, Mekénúúnatane went to sleep for a long time.
> The people looked after him always.
> Around noon the next day, in his dream, he went to heaven.
> They knew he was still living,
> but he was someplace, a long ways, in his dreams.
> They just looked after him
> and knew he was in heaven because they could see
> in his throat it was moving. They just kept watching him.
> His throat was still moving, always, so they just watched him,
> and finally, about noon, he came down, and he slept again.
> Then he sat up and started singing.
> He woke up and sat up and started singing.
> He sang that song and told about it.
> He told people about heaven.
> Everything what is wrong and bad.
> That person was called Mekénúúnatane.
> (Ridington 1978, 78-79)

It was particularly poignant to hear the story of the first Dreamer told by Charlie Yahey, who may be the last Dreamer. When the story was translated from Dane-zaa Záágé?, Robin realized that he had been witness to an important moment in Dane-zaa history. It was clear, from the way other people in the room listened, that they had a similar sense of how important it was to hear Charlie Yahey tell the story of Mekénúúnatane. Charlie, as a Dreamer and prophet, trusted that the recordings Robin made would someday carry his voice and stories to future generations.

---

* During his time with Charlie, Robin observed a similar event when Charlie went into a house and began to follow a dream trail as people gathered around and kept a silent vigil. After he came back from his dream journey, Charlie, like other Dreamers before him, sang and delivered messages from the people in heaven.

Charlie continued:

> When a person gets to be like that,
> he hardly eats when there are lots of people around.
> He has a hard time eating meat
> when there are lots of people around.
> Sometimes, he may choke if someone stands up
> when he is eating.
> That is the way it goes. Even now, you have to go look for it.
> (Ridington 1978, 79)

Like Mekénúúnatane, Charlie Yahey lived within an aura of respect. If people stood up while he was eating, his ability to sing the songs from heaven could be choked off. Robin learned this forcefully when he was sharing a meal with the Dreamer and began to get up to pass some food. Sam St. Pierre, who was there, told him abruptly to sit down.

> The people in heaven told Mekénúúnatane
> to eat whatever has been killed with an axe.
> "People will listen to you if they do that for you."
> (Ibid.)

Killing an animal with an axe would sound strange to Dane-zaa today, but before the introduction of firearms, hunting by communal drives and surrounds was common. Once surrounded, an animal could be killed at close range.

> It was sure cold for them, but some of them did not believe him.
> Some of them thought that he was just saying that.
> Some others thought, "He is the one who said this,
> so let's go look for something with just an axe."
> They just took an axe and looked for something.
> They followed a fresh moose track,
> and from the tracks they knew it was a good moose.
> Some of them stood so as to form a surround,
> and one old man with an axe stood in one place by the tree
> and saw the moose running toward him.
> He stood well behind that tree and held the axe.
> Then he threw the axe at the moose.

> He threw that axe, and it stuck in the moose.
> Pretty soon, that moose fell down.
> He fell down, and they all gathered around the moose.
> They butchered it, and all took home lots of meat.
> (Ibid.)

In this part of the story, Charlie is telling people that Mekénúúnatane was originally a hunt chief whose dreams told people how to surround an animal. Mekénúúnatane's dreams told him that if all the hunters in the community surrounded an animal and drove it to a place where it would give itself to them, one man would be able to kill the animal at close quarters with an axe. In practical terms, the Dreamer presented a hunting strategy. Symbolically, he taught the people that if the hunters work together toward a common purpose, the animal person will respect them and sacrifice its life to sustain the lives of the people.

> When they got to camp, he went to one teepee, one camp.
> The people in that camp cooked lots of meat and fed him.
> Then he left that camp and went to another.
> He told the people there that he still wanted to eat
> some more of the meat that had been killed by axe.
> They fed him lots of that new meat every place he went.
> At every camp, they fed him fresh meat, just killed by the axe.
> Finally, after he had seen all the people,
> he went to one old lady's camp.
> He went into there and told them to feed him again,
> but they just fed him the lower part of the moose leg.
> He didn't tell them he didn't want to eat that, but he just ate it.
> When he went out he told them, "Till the end of your lives,
> it is your own fault now that, because you fed me this leg,
> you will always be hungry, always starving."
> The people who fed him well would always have an easy time.
> (Ridington 1978, 79)

Here, the Dreamer reminds people that if they are generous with one another, the animals will respect them and be generous with them. He then tells the people that they should come together to sing and dance. That way, the animals will know that the people are generous and respectful. He rounds up the people in the same way that hunters round up animals.

> Where there are lots of people singing,
> he put lots of rope around to make a pen.
> The people went in there to sing and dance together.
> He told them, "I make you sit in this pen
> because I want all of you to listen to me."
> Mekénúúnatane is the one who made this world good for us.
> After Mekénúúnatane made all this world good,
> there have been lots of Dreamers.
> Long time ago, it was not good.
> Long time ago, before Mekénúúnatane,
> anytime people wanted to kill each other,
> they would just kill each other. It was no good,
> but now, after him, it is good. Mekénúúnatane told them
> that only the spirits of good people are going to heaven.
> (Ridington 1978, 79-80)

Mekénúúnatane knew about the conflicts and medicine fights that had prevailed in earlier times and were intensified by the disruptions that accompanied the fur trade. He must have known Duuk'ihsachę and been familiar with how he used his power to prevent violence. Mekénúúnatane's dream revealed a plan by which people could come together in a hunt that would benefit all. He insisted that they be generous in sharing meat.

During Mekénúúnatane's lifetime, though, the conditions of hunting changed dramatically. With the introduction of firearms, an individual hunter could reach out and kill an animal from a distance. Mekénúúnatane also lived during a time when the demands of fur traders were drastically reducing game supplies. In 1966, Aku told Robin a story about Mekénúúnatane's death. This is Billy Attachie's translation.

> That man, that man who killed Mekénúúnatane,
> he knew something, too. That was his daughter's husband.
> He was a good man.
> In the wintertime, he went up to the Sekani Chief River.
> Mekénúúnatane started to sing in the morning.
> "Just like the boss came to me," he said,
> "God came to me in the morning, and he told me,
> 'You won't suffer any more. Just like God's son,
> he will kill you, too.'"
> (RDA, Aku 1966)

Mekénúúnatane knew that the white men's power came from their stories. The central story of Christianity describes how God's son predicted his own death and taught people about forgiveness.

> Mekénúúnatane and his son-in-law started to hunt.
> Mekénúúnatane went to a different place.
> He saw the fresh tracks of two elk.
> He went one way, and his son-in-law went another.
> "*Sarasin* [my son-in-law], you go around the other way."
> The Sekani chief [Mekénúúnatane] followed the tracks
> and saw them go up the mountain.
> He went up after them.
> He kept tracking the elk.
> He put his axe handle in the tracks
> to see if they were frozen.
> That way he could tell how fresh they were.
> He followed the tracks into a little stand of spruce.
> (RDA, Aku 1966)

The hunt described here differs from the one in which Mekénúúnatane gives directions but does not participate directly. Now, Mekénúúnatane and his son-in-law are hunting as individuals, a technique made possible by guns.

> Mekénúúnatane was wearing a long coat
> made out of a Hudson's Bay blanket.
> His son-in-law had come around below the spruce.
> The son-in-law saw something move there, and he shot.
> He shot Mekénúúnatane in the stomach.
> He should have followed him, but instead he went around.
> At that time, there was not much food.
> Two people couldn't afford to hunt in the same place.
> People had to hunt just like the lynx.
> That way, maybe one would be lucky and everybody would eat.
> (Ibid.)

Here, Aku makes it clear that Mekénúúnatane and his son-in-law were hunting in an environment where resources were scarce because of the demands of the fur trade. The story also makes it clear that the Dreamer wore a manufactured trade blanket rather than traditional clothes made by Dane-zaa women from local resources. HBC blankets were and are made of wool and usually have red and white stripes. The story suggests that the son-in-law was not entirely familiar with the new way of doing things. When he sees a flash of white from the blanket worn by Mekénúúnatane, he mistakes it for the elk he is tracking.

> When the son-in-law shot,
> he heard somebody talking in the little spruce.
> He cried, and he started to run up there.
> The prophet sat down after he was shot.
> He sat right down where he had been standing.
> He told his saazę [son-in-law],
> "I want to see everyone before I go."
> The prophet's son-in-law fired some shots in the air,
> the way people do when they have made a kill
> and want everyone to come.
> Pretty soon, all the hunters came to the place
> and made their camp.
> They sent someone for the women.
> All the women and children came
> and moved their camp there, too.
> Mekénúúnatane did not drink any water.
> All the women and children came to the place,
> and he wanted to tell them. He started to tell his stories.
> "Nobody should make any trouble," he said.
> "You should be friends with that son-in-law.
> I knew that this was going to happen before.
> Just like God's son."
> (RDA, Aku 1966)

Mekénúúnatane reassures the people that just as he had prophesied the coming of the white people, he knows about his own death. In the past, feuds had broken out and continued for generations in retaliation for a single killing. Like the white men's Jesus, he preaches forgiveness and putting an end to the fighting.

> All night, he told stories to the people.
> In the morning, he said, "That's enough.
> When I have given you all the stories, give me some water."
> When they gave him the water, it came out of the hole in his stomach.

Then he went down.
After that the son-in-law wanted to suffer for what he had done.
He cut off his fingers at the joints,
and he burned his hair in the fire. He had said,
"When you are gone I will kill myself,"
but Mekénúúnatane had told him,
"If you do that, you will go to the fire. That is bad."
After that, the son-in-law didn't hunt for a long time.
He just cried for his father-in-law.
Mekénúúnatane was a big prophet.
Before that time, the winters were pretty bad.
Mekénúúnatane said that for a long time
there will be good winters, not much snow.
Since I was a kid, there have been two winters
when there was no snow.
Before those two prophets,
Mekénúúnatane and Mak'íhts'ęwéswąą,
lots of people and game froze to death every year.
After them, some winters have been nice.
Some have been a little cold but not too bad.
Sometimes, there was a little bit of snow on the hills,
but those two winters there was no snow in the flat country.
(RDA, Aku 1966)

In the fur trade, trappers received supplies on credit and paid off their debts later when they brought in furs. The trader kept an account of these debits and credits in a ledger book. In this story, Mekénúúnatane extends the idea of debits and credits into relationships between people. He, like later Dreamers, talks about a person's bad deeds, which are written down on paper. Later Dane-zaa refer to these as cents or sins. Charlie Yahey likewise talked about papers as debts. He lamented that many people no longer listened to what the Dreamers said. He knew he was the last one.

They think the Dreamers are gone.
Many people have gone a long way.
Many people have come back.
There's lots written about them on the papers in heaven.
Lots written about them is there.
Because they trust in the road to heaven,
they don't care about what was written about them,

but there are many papers lying around up there.
(RDA, CY 2)

Doig elder Tommy Attachie told Robin what his grandmother Nachę said to him about the Dreamers. She began by telling him that Tsááyaa had made the world safe for people by driving the giant animals under the ground. Tommy then describes how both Tsááyaa and the first Dreamers "made the world a good place."

> "I believe what the story of Tsááyaa says," Grandma told me.
> "Three times he made himself again.
> He's from the creator.
> When he's getting old, then he becomes young again
> without dying.
> The creator uses him to make everything right.
> All these bad things that kill people,
> some of them, he chased them under the ground.
> And that <u>Ts'iihchuk</u>, Mosquito Man, too,
> I believe the creator uses him that way.
> That's why he did this. He made the world a good place."
> (RDA, CY Tommy 4a)

Tommy described how Tsááyaa provided a model for the first Dreamers, whose task it was to make the world safe from fighting and killing.

> After Tsááyaa, the Dreamers came.
> They dreamed to heaven, and the people all made peace.
> They never fight anymore.
> That's the spirit the creator sent to people.
> That's why people now, some of them are changing
> what they used to do. Those bad things,
> they don't do them anymore.
> They know that only the creator can make things happen.
> Tsááyaa, that time, he made all the world good. No more killing.
> After he did that to all those giant animals,
> after that, all these Dreamers came for the first time.
> (RDA, CY Tommy 4a)

Tommy Attachie is an elder now and a respected song keeper. In 1998, Robin recorded him talking in Dane-<u>z</u>aa <u>Z</u>áágé? about the many different kinds of songs. Madeline Oker Benson translated his words into English.

> There is a song about everything.
> A long time ago, the Dreamers made a song for the west wind.
> If it was very cold, they would sing the west wind's song.
> Sure enough, about two days later, after singing and dancing,
> there would be a chinook wind.
>
> Mekénúúnatane was a great Dreamer.
> He also made a chicken song. One year, it was so cold
> that the chickens [spruce grouse] were freezing
> and falling off the trees.
> Even the chickens would pray to God.
> After that, it did not get as cold any more.
>
> The dreamer named Gayęą made woman songs.
> He also made one chicken song.
> Some people were very bad, but after they heard these songs,
> they would come around and be good.
> If you are good, kindhearted, you will get to heaven.
> (RDA, CY Tommy 4a)

In August 1968, Robin recorded Charlie Yahey as he sang and drummed and spoke to people about his dreams. In one passage, he explains that each of the animals has its own songs to pray for good weather. He warns that if people do not listen to his words and the songs of the animal people, they will bring on harsh winter weather. Tommy and Billy Attachie translated his words.

> All those animals, even they pray to God with their songs,
> but some people don't believe. They are not even scared.
> *[Drumming]*
> Not many people sing and pray in the evening.
> They have all gone the white men's way.
>
> They don't know anything.
> People who don't want to sing or dance
> are not going to live forever.
> Beyond [inside] the sky, that's too far for them.
> This winter, it's going to be pretty hard

Marguerite Yahey (Mrs. Pete) Davis, 2003. Photo by Robin Ridington

> where the Dane-zaa are living.
> That's why I was singing, even during the winter.
> I was singing to make the cold weather stop.
> (RDA, CY 1)

Charlie Yahey's daughter, Marguerite Yahey Davis, gave a similar description of his teaching when we interviewed her in 2003. Her words were translated by her daughter Maryann Adekat and by Lana Wolf.

> Before he went, he said,
> "Only me, a Dreamer comes to me. He walks to me.
> I will not live long. The winter coming, the winter.
> Now, you think it good. It's melting,
> but all of a sudden it will be winter again.
> All growing things the white people grow,
> even all the potatoes they plant, they will not grow well.
> They will not grow. That's why the pigs, chickens,
> even if they have a good house, they will fall all over.

They will fall dead. They will suddenly fall dead all over.
The animals, them, too, they don't pray. Whoever prays,
they are the ones who know, will know, how cold it will be."

My dad, for a long time he's been saying that.
This wind, big wind, will come down.
Let's all pray against it,
so our prayers will come between it.
People should be singing for a long time.
They should be drumming for two days
so our prayers will come between the wind.
There will be a wind, a big wind.
The trees will tear from their roots.
They will fly in the air.
That is why it is hot on this ground the people prayed on.
It's warm where we camp.
A warm wind blows. There is not much winter snow on it.
Now this wintertime, the buds, the buds won't grow.
In my house, I sit and look.
Now, this is the time my dad talked about.
These are the things he said before he died. He said,
"These Dreamers are dreaming. They are leaving this world.
They say, 'Because the people don't listen to us anymore,
we will have to run away from our dreams.'"
They told him about this in his dream.
My dad told me about his dream.
He told me this was happening, and I dreamed about it, too.
(RDA, DZDV02-14)

Charlie Yahey told Robin how Dreamers get their songs. In this story, he begins by saying that Dreamers are like tape recorders – they can bring the old songs to life.

It is just like this tape recorder.
That is the way it is. *Háwǫch'e.*
Over here, they [Dreamers] are singing.
Over here, they are singing, and they bring the song out,
just like in this tape recorder.
That is the way they bring out the song.
That is how they grab it. That is how they grab it there.
They wake up with that song over there.

> They grab one song over there and then another one.
> Over here when the dream is moving.
> They wake up holding that song.
> The people over there [in heaven] are singing,
> and they sing it exactly like that. They do it exactly like that.
> They wake up with it. Over here, when they grab it.
> They know it really well.
> Sometimes, when they are going to lose it,
> it seems like it's covered, and then they don't grab it.
> But when they wake in the morning, they grab it really well.
> It looks like this. It's just there.
> There are many songs like this.
> Dreamers are singing like this.
> And that is how the people listen to it.
> (RDA, CY 11)

Whenever Charlie recorded a song, he wanted to play the recording back and listen to his own voice. He'd laugh and say, "Another man is going to sing," meaning that he wanted Robin to play back the recording. When Tommy Attachie translated some of Charlie Yahey's words, he pointed out that the role of song keeper, which Tommy holds, goes back many generations.

> All these songs, from how many years ago:
> Mekénúúnatane *zhiné?* [songs] and Alédzé,
> Mak'íhts'ęwéswąa, *Nááchę* [Dreamers' songs].
> Look how many years back they go, those old-time Dreamers.
> When you sing it now, just like new.
> Now, we hear their songs on tape.
> But that time, there was nothing like that, no tape recorder.
> But still, in there, generation after generation,
> they sang those songs and made them new.
> Those songs must have saved a lot of people.
> (RDA, CY Tommy)

Many other Dreamers followed Mekénúúnatane. Their names often reflected changes and experiences that came with the fur trade. One of these Dreamers was Alédzé, whose name means "gunpowder." He took the name because of his ability to travel from one place to another in his dreams in the same way that gunpowder makes a bullet fly to its target. There is a place in Doig territory called Alédzé Tsaa (Alédzé

Creek), where the Dreamer often camped and where he died (see Doig River First Nation 2008). Hudson's Bay Company post journals mention a "Powder's Band" in the 1860s (Glenbow Archives, M-4560-26). A later Dreamer was named Adíshtl'íshe (Paper). He took the name because in his dreams he brought messages from heaven back to people on earth. Adíshtl'íshe, a member of the Ts'ibe Dané? Band, married a daughter of Yehlhézęh. Yehlhézęh was Duuk'ihsachę's son and one of the band elders at the turn of the twentieth century. Adíshtl'íshe was also called "the mailman" because in addition to delivering messages from heaven he also carried letters for the Hudson's Bay Company. He first appears in the HBC's records in November 1867, and he, as a designated leader, signed Treaty 8 in 1900 (referred to as "Dislisici").

One of the most important Dreamers, Mak'íhts'ęwéswąą, carried a name that Billy Attachie translates literally to "If He Leaves Things, That's the Way They Would Be" or, more loosely, "His Way Only" or "The Way It Is." Because Mak'íhts'ęwéswąą showed people how to overcome fighting and using their power against one another, the most common translation is "He Shows the Way." Mak'íhts'ęwéswąą was his Dreamer's name. His personal name was Atsukwa. His son, Jack Atsukwa, (Matsíí?dak'ale or White Head) was also a Dreamer (see Chapter 3 for May Apsassin's story about his power). Mak'íhts'ęwéswąą was probably born in the mid-1880s, and he died in 1916. Although he was a member of the Halfway (Hudson Hope) Band, his teachings were important to all Dane-zaa. Some stories say that Mekénúúnatane was Mak'íhts'ęwéswąą's father, but we have been unable to document that genealogically. Certainly, Mak'íhts'ęwéswąą was Mekénúúnatane's spiritual heir.

Johnny Chipesia and Augustine Jumbie both told stories about how Mak'íhts'ęwéswąą came to be a Dreamer. They told Robin that Mak'íhts'ęwéswąą had lived near Moberly Lake as a young man. Another man who lived in the area, named Tseguude, caused widespread fear when he became a cannibal and began to lure people to his camp by bending grass to mark the trail. It used to be that when one camp had enough food to share with others, its members would mark a trail to help people who were starving (see Aku's *wehch'uuge* [cannibal] story in Chapter 3). Johnny Chipesia described (in English) how the cannibal lured people to his camp:

> Tseguude had two wives, an old one and a young one. One day, he told the old wife to kill the young wife

or else he would kill her and eat her.
The old wife killed the young wife with an axe,
and T̲seguude made her cook her in a pot.
After that, T̲seguude, his wife, and two daughters
lived for a whole year on people.
He used to cache the meat just like game.
Once, Mehuu, whose son Old Man Dokey told this story,
came to T̲seguude's camp.
T̲seguude tried to hide the pieces of meat,
but Mehuu saw a head boiling in a pot and asked, "What is that?"
T̲seguude said that it was just a bear head boiling.
Mehuu is the one who later was saved from starvation
by the lynx.
Mehuu saw human bones all around the camp.
T̲seguude went to Moberly Lake and set up his teepee there.
Then he made a trail leading into his camp to lure people in.
It was a trail made of bent-over grass tied with moosehair,
the kind that means, "Come, there's lots of meat."
When hungry people would follow the trail to his camp,
T̲seguude would shoot the men.
Nobody could kill him, no matter how hard they tried.
He took the guns from the people he killed
and kept them loaded in his teepee
so that he could keep up a continuous fire.
When he had killed the men, he sent out his wife
to kill the women and kids with an axe.
In this way, he was able to live for a whole year
eating nothing but people.
(RDA, field notes, 1965-66)

Augustine Jumbie (RDA, Beaver Tales) explained that T̲seguude was already a really bad man before he became a cannibal. He had killed Mak'íhts'ęwéswąą's wife.

Once, before he started eating people,
T̲seguude had killed Mak'íhts'ęwéswąą's wife.
That time, Mak'íhts'ęwéswąą and his wife
were setting snares in the bush,
and T̲seguude and his wife were setting snares in the bush, too.
They didn't know the other was there.
They came close together.

> Tseguude heard something in the bush. He shot at it.
> The bullet went through Mak'íhts'ęwéswąą and killed his wife.
> She was a McLeod Lake woman.
> After that, Mak'íhts'ęwéswąą married
> another McLeod Lake woman.
> Nobody wanted to stay with Tseguude.
> One man wanted to kill him, but Mak'íhts'ęwéswąą said,
> "If you kill him, you will take half his cents [sins],
> and you won't go to heaven." So, they let him go.
> Tseguude travelled by himself after that.

Johnny Chipesia told another chapter of the story:

> Everyone who heard about Tseguude avoided him.
> People just went away from where he was camped,
> but it was a hard time for some people,
> so they were lured in by his trail.
> This was the same winter that Sitle-ta was starving.
> His brother Mak'íhts'ęwéswąą went out to look for him.
> He was afraid that Sitle-ta had been killed by Tseguude.
> Mak'íhts'ęwéswąą found Tseguude and tried to shoot him,
> but he could only shoot him through his behind.
> Mak'íhts'ęwéswąą had a lot of power, and Tseguude was afraid.
> Tseguude offered Mak'íhts'ęwéswąą his two daughters
> if he wouldn't kill him.
> Mak'íhts'ęwéswąą took the daughters as his wives.

At first, Mak'íhts'ęwéswąą tried to kill Tseguude, but the cannibal had too much power. He then took Tseguude's daughters as his wives, but it was not a happy arrangement. The youngest of the wives began having an affair with another man. Johnny Chipesia continued the story:

> That man said to the girl,
> "I'm going to kill Mak'íhts'ęwéswąą,"
> and she said, "OK." He hid a new .38-55 rifle in the bush.
> The wife and Mak'íhts'ęwéswąą went out in the bush,
> hunting rabbits with an old-fashioned muzzle loader.
> The man shot at Mak'íhts'ęwéswąą with his .38-55,
> but he hit the girl instead.
> Maybe God helped Mak'íhts'ęwéswąą.

Then that man ran away.
Mak'íhts'ęwéswąą did not try to follow him.
Instead, he made a song about how that man
was going to the fire.

The Winchester .38-55 breach-loading rifle was first introduced in 1884 and did not come into common use for another decade or so. Johnny's mention of this rifle indicates that the events he described probably took place sometime in the 1890s. The story of Mekénúúnatane can likewise be dated to the period between 1823 and 1860. In the story, the prophet is mistaken for an elk when he wears a Hudson's Bay blanket. The HBC took over from the North West Company in 1823 but immediately closed most of the posts in Dane-zaa territory. It did not re-establish a post at Fort St. John until 1857, although Mekénúúnatane could have obtained a blanket from Dunvegan or Fort Vermilion before that.

Mak'íhts'ęwéswąą had every reason to kill Tseguude and the man who tried to kill him, but instead of taking revenge, he dreamed of heaven. He remembered what Mekénúúnatane had said to his people about forgiving the son-in-law who had shot him. Mak'íhts'ęwéswąą knew that if he killed Tseguude and his wife's lover, he would take on some of those bad men's burdens. It was then that Mak'íhts'ęwéswąą became a Dreamer. Perhaps because his personal story was so compelling, Mak'íhts'ęwéswąą came to be known as the Dreamer "who shows the way." He taught people that it was wrong to seek revenge, no matter how bad an enemy had been. In his dreams, he learned that if you kill a bad person, you take on the consequences of that person's bad deeds.

Tommy Attachie told us a story about Mak'íhts'ęwéswąą while we were writing this book. In his version, Tommy names the man who wants to steal Mak'íhts'ęwéswąą's wife. That man, Wasage (Crying Man), is someone identified in the genealogical record. Tommy emphasizes that Mak'íhts'ęwéswąą preached forgiveness in the same way that Christians do today. Billy Attachie provided this translation.

> We're going to tell about Mak'íhts'ęwéswąą,
> how he became a prophet.
> A long time ago, Mak'íhts'ęwéswąą started.
> He wasn't a prophet then.
> He and his wife were snaring rabbits or something like that.
> They killed some rabbits, and Crying Man, Wasage,

from Moberly, I think, Crying Man, old Wasage,
he wanted to take Mak'íhts'ęwéswąą's wife away from him.
Mak'íhts'ęwéswąą's wife and that Wasage,
they went with each other.
Just the two of them, alone. They made a plan.
Mak'íhts'ęwéswąą's wife told Wasage,
"If you kill Mak'íhts'ęwéswąą, I'll go back home with you."
They made that plan.
Mak'íhts'ęwéswąą and his wife went back
to check their rabbit snares.
They got some rabbits, put them in a sack.
They got a little rabbit there, too, alive. She put it in her pocket.
Mak'íhts'ęwéswąą was standing there.
She started to set that snare
then she sat down. Suddenly, that bullet came.
Wasage shot Mak'íhts'ęwéswąą.
The bullet went right through his chest.
It went right through him and hit his wife
where she was setting snares.
The bullet hit her. It killed her.
It got her right where she was sitting, and that little rabbit, too.

Mak'íhts'ęwéswąą started to run around.
He went all over the place,
looking for Wasage. He was planning to kill him.
He never even slept. Night and day, he was looking for him.

Finally, he fell asleep, and he dreamed about hell.
He saw all those people burning up there
in a fire that never went out.
Mak'íhts'ęwéswąą saw that, and God spoke to him.
"That man made a plan. He was going to kill you,
and she was going to go back where he come from.
He made that plan. That's why bullets just went through you.
And she died there.
If you kill Wasage, you're going to be burn forever."
God showed him the fire there.
Mak'íhts'ęwéswąą saw that, and he quit.
He just stopped.
I think from there on he wanted to live a good life.

Pretty soon, Mak'íhts'ęwéswąą lay down and died.
God had shown him hell and everything that would happen.
He told him everything that would happen if he killed Wasage.
He wasn't a prophet then,
but God showed him what would happen.
He stayed like that for nine days. He died for nine days,
and the people looked after him.
Every couple of days or every second day
they turned him over, like that.
The people gathered around and didn't make any noise.
They tied up all the dogs.
They looked after him in a quiet place.
Every second day, they turned him over,
and they didn't make noise.
They told each other,
"See what happened. He is not breathing."
"But let's wait and see what happens. We'll look after him,"
they told each other. They took nine days, and pretty soon,
during the day, as they sat around him,
his air started coming back.
His wind was coming back from the west to hit his body,
the wind.
Pretty soon, he started thawing out.
As they looked after him, he started thawing out.
Pretty soon, he moved his hand, and they lifted him up.
With their help, he sat up.
He still couldn't talk, though. He looked at all the people.
He thought to himself, which one is a good person?

Then he spoke. He told them, "There's heaven."
He just whispered. They give him something to drink.
Pretty soon, they all began to rub their eyes.
They rubbed all their eyes.
Mak'íhts'ęwéswąą drank a lot of water.
He got up and then sat down.
He told them, "There's heaven." He took nine days.
He just went up there, and God showed him everything.
Then he kneeled down, and God told him, "Go."
But he took nine days. And from there
he learned all these songs we are singing today.

> We believe all these powerful things happened.
> God showed the Native people through Mak'íhts'ęwéswąą.
> That's why we all believe the same way, generations later.
> That's how Mak'íhts'ęwéswąą became a prophet.
> (RDA, DZHD09-1)

Madeline Sagónáá? Davis told us a story about Mak'íhts'ęwéswąą's vision quest power and how it helped him to become a Dreamer. The recording took place in a setting typical of contemporary storytelling. We were riding with a group of elders in the Doig van. Eddie Apsassin was driving. As we passed through traditional territory to identify sites and record stories, Madeline began to speak, and everyone in the van paid close attention. Although the recording conditions were less than ideal, Robin turned on his video camera and began recording. He immediately recognized the story's importance. Madeline's story described how Mak'íhts'ęwéswąą first obtained his power. In the story, Thunderbird, the helper, sends Mak'íhts'ęwéswąą on a dream journey to heaven. The people in heaven tell him that he must not kill the man who killed his wife. If he does, he will take that man's sins upon himself. Instead, people on earth find the man and tell him that he should "work for Mak'íhts'ęwéswąą." Mak'íhts'ęwéswąą's vision quest experience, as revealed by Madeline, replicates a story that Johnny Chipesia told Robin about Thunderbird and his children. Billy Attachie translated Madeline's story.

> Mak'íhts'ęwéswąą, when he started dreaming,
> there was something in his hand.
> My grandma [Nachę]* asked him, "What is that in your hand?"
> "Natane [Thunderbird] put that in my hand," he told her.
> He was with Natane in the mountain.
>
> Mak'íhts'ęwéswąą said, "When the lightning and thunder came,
> I was with Natane's young one. Those young thunders told me,
> 'Our dad comes back with the hail, the big hail,
> and our mother comes back with the rain.'"
> The Natane parents brought something back, maybe a snake.
> They told Mak'íhts'ęwéswąą, "You can't eat this.
> This is what we live on," and they put it in a different place.

---

* Nachę is the grandmother of both Billy and Madeline.

The Natane parents told him,
"You've been with us for a long time.
It's just like you grew up with us, our family.
When the thunder and lightning comes,
these young ones are crazy.
They strike anything. You'd better watch out."

This is what my grandma said about Mak'íhts'ęwéswąą.
Grandma said, "Our grandfather told us about that."
They lived in Yaazon, Clear Hills, Alberta.
This is what Mak'íhts'ęwéswąą said.
Our grandma said, "Asbe* told me this."
Grandma said, "Mak'íhts'ęwéswąą knew about thunder.
He was a very powerful man."

Natane is a really beautiful thing. You don't see him.
You just hear his voice. Natane is a bird made for the sky.
Natane said, "When my kids go through the storm,
anything that's black they will strike.
They are crazy when they are travelling.
Natane told Mak'íhts'ęwéswąą,
"You tell your people."

Even when it's a really strong thunderstorm,
Mak'íhts'ęwéswąą went out wearing his moccasins,
and they don't even get wet. That's what my grandma said.

Mak'íhts'ęwéswąą was mad at somebody
[the man who killed his wife], and he was going to kill him.
Then he went to sleep for ten days.
Natane put him to sleep. He went to sleep too long.
They carried him in the bush.
That time, people took things seriously.
They respected everything.
Over there, they took turns to look after him.
One day, he woke up, and they made soup.
When he woke up, they had soup ready,
and they fed him with a spoon.
He told them, "There's not only land in this world,

---

* *Asbe* means "my mother-in-law, my father's sister." It is also spelled *asbii*.

there's another land over the blue sky, and that's where I went.
I went way over in the sky. That's why I slept a long time."

He brought a song back. He said, "They told me,
'If you kill this guy, you are not going to come back here.'"
"They made me see the fire in hell," he told the people.
"If you kill this guy, you won't make it up here,"
the people in heaven told him.
"When I got to their land in heaven, it was very beautiful."
"I won't kill that guy who killed my wife," he told them.

"I saw my wife over there," he said.
They were looking for the guy who killed his wife.
From heaven, they told him,
"Let this guy work for you until he dies."
After the people on earth found him, they told him,
"The people in heaven said you should work for
Mak'íhts'ęwéswąą."

This is Mak'íhts'ęwéswąą's story.
After that, Mak'íhts'ęwéswąą was singing.
Then lots of people gathered at Mak'íhts'ęwéswąą's camp.
This is why they call Mak'íhts'ęwéswąą "He Sits in Heaven."
In the summertime before he died,
he made a song that was called
"We're All Going to Move to Heaven."
After that, the people all came to him.

"This winter, we are all going to move to heaven."
He told them the story. He sang for the people who follow him.
That fall, lots of people died. After they all died,
he was the last one to die in Suu Na chii k'chige.

There are lots of Dreamers' graves in Dane-zaa nané?.
He made a song that we're all going from the middle of the world,
some place like Dane-zaa nané?.
There was a big storm coming, Natane.

Mak'íhts'ęwéswąą said,
"Natane told me to go to a higher place.
There will be lots of water."

"A big storm is coming," Natane said.
"I'm going to wash this world."
After they moved to the higher place,
all the creeks and the rivers were going up.
People are starving. They couldn't hunt.
They couldn't hunt because there was too much rain.
The people went to Mak'íhts'ęwéswąą and said,
"Asea [my grandfather], we want your help.
There is too much rain."
He went out to the middle of the flat.
He talked really loud to Natane,
and right above him a blue sky opened.
It just cleared up like that.
Natane told him, "I have no choice because of the way I am.
I'm going to wash this world."
Natane told him, "You are going to have lots of meat.
I'm going to bring lots of meat before you."
Then the people who were alive all went out hunting,
and everyone got a moose.
All the animals they killed were really fat.
They really respected Mak'íhts'ęwéswąą.

Wherever Mak'íhts'ęwéswąą travelled,
people from heaven told him
there's going to be meat all the time.
After that, people moved around with him.
It's easy for him to get moose.
"Wherever you move there will be meat ready for you,"
the people in heaven told him.

I don't know what those settlers did with those graveyards.
They messed up all the graveyards.
We don't know where they are.
This is my story. I remember a long time back.
(RDA, DZDV02-27)

Madeline Davis told us another story about a Dreamer who came before Mak'íhts'ęwéswąą. His song was so strong people heard it clearly from camps several days' travel away. Madeline finished the story by talking about Mak'íhts'ęwéswąą and Gayęa, Dreamers who came later.

There was one big Dreamer
before the great Dreamer Mak'íhts'ęwéswąą.
His name was Asusay, and his people lived way north from Doig.
They were camping way up the Doig,
and there were some more people who lived over that way.
This Dreamer was singing. From the heaven they told him,
"Those other people will hear you if you just sing a little bit."
It sounded like the Dreamer was singing really close by.
The people way over in Yaazon, Clear Hills,
could hear him singing.
That Dreamer was singing, and the Yaazon people,
who heard him,
thought they were camping not too far away from him,
so they set out with a dog team to see him.

They all took their food with their dog team,
and still they never got to him.
They made camp and slept one place.
The next morning, got going and slept another place.
Still, they didn't get to him. Every morning when they woke up,
they heard him singing again,
and they thought he was right close by.
That was the Dreamer.
In heaven, they twisted his hair so it just curled up.
That was the Dreamer singing.

He brought tobacco from heaven.
He made some of the people taste it.
The tobacco is really sacred, precious.
That's why he made some of the people taste it.

They travelled how many days before they got to him.
When they finally arrived, they told him,
"In the morning, you sing as if you are close by.
That's why we came
from long ways to get to here."
He told them, "The people from heaven told me that other
people far away are going to hear me singing."
After they got to him, he prayed for them,
singing and drumming.
That prophet with curly hair was a Dreamer for a long time.

After he died, Mak'íhts'ęwéswą̹ą̹ started dreaming.
All those Dreamers, they don't suffer and die.
They don't get sick.
This is what my dad said. After Mak'íhts'ęwéswą̹ą̹,
Gayęą̹ was a Dreamer from the people over there.
He was a Dreamer from Eureka River.
From over there, he sometimes camped with our people.
Gayęą̹ used to come to Dane-zaa nané? to pray for people.
From heaven, they told him,
"You're going to go from right in the middle of the world,
Dane-zaa nané?."
Asbe Malla (Gayęą̹'s wife) used to tell us a story.
Malla told us, "Your grandfather dreamed pretty good."
Gayęą̹ told Malla, "If it's really hard for you,
just hit my drum after I'm gone.
You're going to see it by that time.
Your grandpa told me that."
Malla said, "Yaazon hills, on the other side,
that's where our cabin is."

Gayęą̹ was praying for people and singing
at Dane-zaa nané? in summertime.
When he went back in the fall, he was going back from Montney.
After he crossed Montney Creek, he fell off his horse and died.
After he died, they kept him for a few days,
and then they found out he was really dead.
Somewhere in Montney near the top of the hill, they buried him.
Malla told people that Gayęą̹ told her he was going to leave
from Su Na chii k'chige, right in the middle of Dane-zaa nané?.
After Gayęą̹ died, Asbe Malla went back a long ways
to the other side of Yaazon, where their cabin was.
She went back to their cabin and went back trapping
with Philip Nott and his wife, Nojolie, Malla's sister.
In that winter in Yaazon, there was a lot of snow.
It was too deep.
How are we going to go back? she thought. We got nothing.
She said, "We ate up all our groceries.
After that, for two days, we didn't eat anything."
Malla remembered Gayęą̹'s drum.
She told Philip Nott and Najolie,
"I'm going to hit Gayęą̹'s drum two times."

Malla told them that. They said, "OK."
It was a really cold north wind.
She picked up Gayęą's drum and sang one of his songs.
Malla did that.
In the morning when daylight came, it was not cold.
It was a warm chinook wind.

Asbe Malla told us that Gayęą's drum is powerful.
Gayęą's drum is very powerful. Old man Aki was Gayęą's son.
He lived at Doig and sang when it was very cold.
He's the one who ended up with that drum.
Those Dreamers' drums are already important.
Some of the drums they write on, too. Dreamers write on them.
When people have a problem, they drum with it.
Even the drum they left behind, when people use it,
it comes to help people.
It works all the time.

Long time ago, there were a lot of Dreamers.
When they all prayed, there were lots of people.
This drum comes from heaven.
That's why they look after it really well.
Those drums are left behind for the people
to keep and look after.
When there's a hard time come, they use the drum and sing.
The people from heaven will hear it.
Lots of people die in car accidents.
Lots of people die from drinking.
They die in accidents and drinking.
After they die, it's just like they sit in the dark.
Now, people die, and nobody knows what happened.
When there was a Dreamer,
they would know what happened when a person died.
I was like that this winter.
My spirit came out, and I looked at my body.
Charlotte's mother [Akulli Davis Acko] met me.
When I went out of my body, I saw Charlotte's mother.
She told me,
"Where's Sammy and Annie and Shirley? Tell them to pray."
After she talked to me, I came back in my house,

and I was still lying there sleeping.
I took the blanket over and went back to my body. I woke up.
Funny thing happened to me. I don't forget what happened to me.
This is about Dreamers long time ago.
(RDA, DZDV02-34)

Years before, Charlie Yahey (RDA, Beaver Tales) had told Robin about the teachings of Mak'íhts'ęwéswąą.

Some people don't play the drum.
Mak'íhts'ęwéswąą, that's the singer.
The person who's smart enough to keep his song
won't have any trouble. That's another one of his songs.
Some people are like a crooked stick – all twisted.
Those people don't dance. They don't come to a dance.
They don't sing with the songs.
Some people are like a straight stick.
Those are the good people who dance together,
who give things to others.
When you are friends to everybody, help everybody, that's good.
Drinking, fighting, doing all kinds of smart things, that's no good.
That belongs to the devil. I try to talk to the young boys,
but they tell me I'm not boss for them.
They say I'm trying to boss them. I'm not trying to boss them.
I'm just trying to put them on the right road.

Not long after Mak'íhts'ęwéswąą became a Dreamer, the prophet Gayęą began holding Dreamers' dances for the Fort St. John Dane-zaa. Originally from Eureka River in Alberta, he spent much of his life on the BC side of the border, where he and his wife, Malla (Molly), were much loved and respected by the people. Gayęą painted several drums with images from his dreams of heaven. He became an important teacher in the early years of the twentieth century. Among those who learned from him were Charlie Yahey and Oker, who was the son of Ts'ibe Dané? elder Dechezhę and the grandson of Duuk'ihsachę. Robin photographed Charlie Yahey with a double-sided drum (see page 23) painted by Gayęą. Gayęą dreamed many songs that are still sung today, including the one about Suu Na chii k'chige. He carried on the teachings of the Dreamers who went before him. He dreamed the "Prairie

Amaa Skookum and Marguerite Jumbie at Halfway, 1968.
Photo by Robin Ridington

Chicken Song" while camping at a place where prairie chickens gathered to dance near Sweeney Creek, located to the east of the Doig Reserve.

Like many other Dreamers, Gayęą predicted his own death. He told people that his burial place, like Mekénúúnatane's grave, would always have many game animals. Gayęą died at Suu Na chii k'chige, as he had dreamed he would when he received the song. He was riding just above Montney Creek when he was suddenly taken by a heart attack or stroke and fell to the ground. They buried him near the camp, and for many years his presence there helped people hunt during the summer gatherings. Frank Beaton, the HBC factor, noted his death in a journal entry for 19 June 1922: "Sakona came in and reported the death of Kiah, a Dunvegan Indian who died suddenly at the Reserve today" (Glenbow Archives, M-4560-29).

Gayęą was much beloved by the people. He began life in the fur trade era and died on land surveyed in 1914 and called Indian Reserve 172. Whenever there is a Dreamers' dance, people hear his songs and remember his life. Like the stories of his student Charlie Yahey, Gayęą's words carry on to future generations. After the Fort St. John Band lost the reserve in 1945, much of Suu Na chii k'chige became fields of wheat, barley, and canola. Along Montney Creek, though, the farmers left the bush intact. In 2005, Gerry Attachie took us to the area where Gayęą was buried. To our amazement, the creek valley was teeming with game. We saw moose and many fresh bear tracks. Even after all these years and the changes to the land, the Dreamer's prophecy still held true.

The story of the first and last Dreamers is not complete without mentioning the Dane-zaa women prophets. One of these women, who lived some time ago, is known simply as Ts'iiyuuaęą Nááche (Old Woman Dreamer). The last woman Dreamer was Amaa (or Akize), usually called Mrs. Skookum, who lived on the Halfway River Reserve. Robin recorded Amaa in conversation with Charlie Yahey in June 1966. The two Dreamers were in a teepee at Halfway River with Charlie's wife Aanaatswęą, Augustine Jumbie, and Jumbie's wife, Marguerite (Sawe). Amaa had become a Dreamer several years before after recovering from a serious illness and regaining partial vision following a long period of blindness. She was very old. According to the Halfway River Band list, she was born on 7 April 1873, a year before Aanaatswęą and seven years before Charlie Yahey. She and Charlie Yahey began to talk about what it means to be a Dreamer. Amaa began the conversation, which was translated by Liza Wolf.

> I'm dreaming about people waiting at the gate to heaven.
> The people in heaven are waiting
> for their relatives to come to heaven.
> They are crying for their relatives to come to heaven.
> Everybody in heaven sings that song
> waiting for their relatives.
> That's the gate to heaven song.
> (RDA, OT 19)

Like Charlie Yahey, Amaa Skookum recognized the value of Robin's tape recorder for communicating with people in other communities and in other times, even though she did not particularly like using the medium:

> I don't like to sing for the tape recorder, but I do.
> *[She sings]*
> I don't like to sing for the tape recorder, but I dream that song.
> It's not lying. That's true. That's right.

> I dream of heaven, and somebody told me,
> "You people should play drums and sing
> so you won't have any trouble with meat this summer.
> Sing and drum and you will kill lots of moose this summer."
> The guy I dream about told me to get everyone together
> and sing for the moose, but there's just one person here
> [she means Jumbie].
> (RDA, OT 19)

Amaa then turned from the topic of dreaming ahead to help people in hunting to the more personal and emotional topic of her role as a guide for lost spirits trying to find the trail to heaven. She sang a song the people in heaven gave her.

> I feel like crying when I sing that song –
> Ruby, his song.*
> That's Ruby's song.
> The people in heaven sing that to put him to dance in heaven.
> All his life, he didn't dance when he was on the earth,
> so he had to dance as soon as he got to heaven.
> That's the first time he danced.
> That's the song he danced to.
> Heaven is really nice, really pretty.
> (RDA, OT 19)

When people die, their ghosts must walk in the great shadow of darkness back along the trail they made on earth. Their ghosts must walk at night until they get to the place where it is light enough to rise toward heaven. These ghosts are dangerous. They will try to separate good people's shadows from their bodies and follow them up to heaven. They will startle children and try to follow them up the trail to heaven. When people die with unresolved conflicts or bad deeds holding their shadows down to the tracks of their past lives, their ghosts are particularly dangerous. The living may shorten the dark danger of their shadow trails only by dancing to the songs of the Dreamers. When people dance with their relatives on a common trail that circles a fire whose smoke rises to the highest place, their shadow

---

* Ruby Wokeley, a young man from Halfway River, had frozen to death the previous winter.

trails are shortened. When their feet follow the turns of the Dreamers' songs, their tracks merge with those of their relatives and their minds begin to follow the trail to heaven, yaak'ihts'ę́? atanii.

Amaa began another song. Her unaccompanied voice was husky, growly, and deep. Women do not play the drum. Her song came to an end, and she paused for a moment. Then she sang another song. When it ended, she spoke to the kids who crowded around and listened to the old people. *"Yaak'ihwadané?,"* she declaimed, "heaven people." Then she sang a special song. She explained to the people that it was Ts'ibiisaa's song.

> That's the song from Old Man Chipesia's going to heaven.
> When he got to heaven, this is the song he sang.
> He was really happy.
> He went with his first wife. He was chasing girls.
> I dreamed that when he went to heaven *[she sings]*.
> That's all I know. I'm going to quit.
> (RDA, OT 19)

Amaa rested for a while. Then she began another song. When the last resounding thunder of its final phrase subsided, she mused, as if talking to herself, "I can't think of what to sing." Then a song came to her mind, and she delivered it. When it was finished, she talked about becoming a Dreamer.

> That's my own song.
> About two years ago, I just about died.
> They [one of my husbands in heaven]
> told me to sing that song. I got better.
> That's Nááchęa's [John Notseta's] song.
> I dreamed of him. He is worrying about his kids. He said,
> "I only have one here [Julie]. There's lots of my kids on earth.
> What's the matter?" He wants his kids to go with him.
> (RDA, OT 19)

Later, as Liza Wolf, also Nááchęa's daughter, translated Amaa's words, she commented wryly, "If he loves us, why doesn't he stay with us?" Amaa continued.

> Whichever reserve plays the drum,
> they're going to win all the moose for winter.

> If Prophet River people play all the time,
> they'll get all the moose.
> If Halfway people play, they'll win.
> But nobody plays here.
> I'm not a boy. I can't play.
> I'm the only one who sings.
> People who don't sing can't get any moose.
> I sing well early in the morning.
> I already sang this morning. I can't sing well now.
> I dreamed about that. It's really true. I'm not lying.
> (RDA, OT 19)

Amaa then turned to Charlie Yahey, as if seeing him sitting next to her for the first time. Her term of address, *ashidle* (younger brother), once again reminded us of her seniority. Her next words then indicated that she had finished speaking. Charlie was then at liberty to follow her with his own words:

> Ashidle, I didn't see you sitting there.
> If you heard me, why didn't you sing my songs along with me?
> I'm hungry now. I'm going to quit.
> (RDA, OT 19)

Then Charlie Yahey took up the oratory. He reminded the audience that the two of them were probably the last of the Dreamers. He reminded us that he and Amaa were ending the tradition begun by Mekénúúnatane. He spoke slowly in a strong voice and for a long time:

> I can sing, but I can't sing very well.
> When I sing two or three songs, my wind gets weak.
> My head's not right. I can't sing much.
> I thought that we were going to sing at Halfway.
> That's why I came here, but everywhere it's just the same.
> Only the old people can sing.
> I'm the only one who can sing.
> At Doig, Halfway, Blueberry – everywhere it's the same.
> The young fellows won't help. They think they're white people.
> The young people don't believe me. They go to school,
> and the school teaches those bad children bad business.
> The schoolteachers do that.

> The young people don't believe me.
> When I'm singing, they don't come to help.
> The only time they come to me is after they've been drinking.
> One week, two weeks, and they go a little crazy.
> Then they come to me and say,
> "Help me. Fix me up."
> I'm not going to do much about people like that.
> (RDA, OT 19)

Charlie's words reminded young and old alike that they will find the trail to heaven only when they reach the place where their spirit is light enough to rise on a trail of song:

> There's no ladder into the sky.
> The ghosts have to make it on their own.
> There's a road to the sky, yaak'ihts'ę? atanii.
> You've got to be good to make it.
> It used to be that people who dreamed about heaven
> put water and feathers on the people's heads
> so they could go straight to heaven,
> just the way the priests baptize.
> Now, people don't believe us anymore, so we don't do that.
> No use to talk sense to people like that.
> From now on, if a woman who is going to have a baby
> doesn't think of God every night when she is pregnant,
> she is going to have a hard time when the baby is born.
> The woman, and her husband, too,
> he can help her think about God and pray.
> Then the baby will be born right.
> It used to be that everyone believed
> the ones who dreamed to heaven.
> Now, the young people don't believe.
> No use calling them back because they won't believe.
> All the people who have died already,
> they are the ones who believe.

> Ever since they made new houses,
> people think they are white people.
> This money and drinking – it's a bad business.
> You don't have to hate me for saying that.

> Some Dane-zaa steal lots of money from each other.
> That's why I say that.
> (RDA, OT 19)

Charlie then reminded people that Robin and elders from Prophet River had come to Blueberry the previous winter to support his efforts to make the weather turn for the better. The Dreamer repeated that unless people sing and pray, one winter will follow directly from another.

> They came all the way to Blueberry in the middle of winter,
> when it was very cold, to see me.
> I sang for a long time – two weeks – but it was still cold.
> Then I sang for another week, and the weather got a little bit up.
> I told the people it was going to be cold like that
> if they didn't sing.
> It's their own fault. Nobody sang, and so it was cold.
> I dreamed about heaven, how there were going to be two winters,
> but I sang and sang. That's why it didn't happen.
> But they will make it happen again if you don't believe me.
> Sometime, they will make two winters in a row.
> All the animals will have calves in spring, and they will freeze.
> Nothing will grow, and the white people will starve.
> They won't grow vegetables if this whole world freezes up.
> One person above the heaven looks down on us.
> Everything people do he marks down,
> the good things, the bad things.
> If a person does too many bad things –
> drinking, stealing, lying all the time –
> that person doesn't belong in heaven.
> (RDA, OT 19)

Charlie turned again to Amaa and made a joke about the husbands who send their songs down to her on earth.

> Amaa, when you were young, you had too many husbands.
> That's why you dream about your husbands.
> Your husbands are trying to help you come up.
> You are good to people, kind to people.
> You give things to poor people, but you had too many boyfriends.

That's why you haven't gone to heaven yet.
Some people think nobody knows what they do,
but nothing is hidden.
God knows everything that happens on earth.
There are lots of people who have their name in heaven,
but there are some people who don't have a name there.
It's too bad for them. They should sing like
me and try to go to heaven.
That's the way it goes. That's why I say that.
I'm not lying.
(RDA, OT 19)

Finally, the old man paused in his speaking. He paused, and he began to sing a song. He sang one of the songs that will help a person's shadow make it through to heaven. Then he said,

All over the world, nobody hides from me, the sender of the song.
God stays above heaven. If people in heaven want to see him, they look with binoculars, but you can't see him well.
It's sure bright – shiny, fancy.
The people who go to heaven, he has them stay below him.
He sits in a chair like a big king.
Lots of people who dream to heaven, they don't see God.
They just see the people who are working for God.
Not many see God.
Some people are just like a straight spruce tree,
a spruce tree that grows straight.
Some people go straight to heaven.
The gate is open, and they go right through.
Some people are like a crooked spruce tree that twists around.
When they get to heaven, the gate is closed.
They won't let them through, and then they cry.
Some people don't go the straight way.
They lie, steal, and do all kinds of bad things.
Even though I dream about heaven,
I worry about whether I'll go to heaven.
That's why I dance even though I'm old.
I do that because I want to go to heaven.
Sometimes, when people are singing, I dance.

Just like we feed dogs, just like white people feed chickens,
that's how God feeds us moose.
That's why we have to keep singing and dancing,
so he will give us the moose.
If we don't, it will be hard to get moose.
You will miss them, or they will run away,
or it will be hard to see any.
(RDA, OT 19)

The Dreamer's experience, Charlie Yahey said, is a transformation of a person's normal life on earth. A day on this earth is measured by the sun's passage from horizon to horizon. A day in heaven is measured by the sun's entire seasonal circle of "chicken steps," from its most northerly point of rising and setting at the summer solstice to the most southerly point at the winter solstice.* A complete cycle in heaven is referred to as one day. Each day that the Dreamer is away from his body on earth, his mind experiences a year in the life of the people in heaven. Charlie explained:

In heaven one year is just like one day.
Three years is like three days.
They told me they won't shake hands with me for one day
because I drink too much. Sometimes, I drink when I sing.
That's no good. You people here don't believe me.
You're too crazy. You don't keep what I say.
(RDA, OT 19)

Charlie paused again to sing. This time, he sang a song dreamed by the Dreamer Mak'íhts'ęwéswą̨ą, who followed Mekénúúnatane.

Mak'íhts'ęwéswą̨ą, he's boss for the north part.
He is in charge of sending out songs, dreams, to people.
People in this country don't believe the songs,
so he takes charge of the north country.
He sends songs to the Dreamer at Hay Lake.
People are better there.
(RDA, OT 19)

---

* In Dane-zaa thought, winter and summer are thought of as separate years. Hence, one of our years is equivalent to two Dane-zaa years.

Studies by Jean-Guy Goulet (1998) and Patrick Moore and Angela Wheelock (1990) suggest that the Dreamer from Hay Lake was either Nogha (Wolverine) or his successor, Alexis Seniantha.

In 2001, we visited May Apsassin. As we were about to leave, Jillian asked May whether Dreamers communicated with one another in their dreams. In reply, May told us a wonderful story about a river otter who lures a young Dane-zaa woman away from her father and carries her to his home at Charlie Lake. She becomes his wife and bears a number of children who are half otter and half human. When her brothers try to find out what happened to her, they use their dreaming powers to contact Otter Man. Like Mak'íhts'ęwéswąą and the Dreamer at Hay Lake, the brothers and Otter Man can converse with one another through their dreams. In May's story, which she learned from her father, Charlie Dominic, the brothers reunite with their sister and acknowledge her children as their relatives. The story concludes with Otter Man dreaming and prophesying that strangers will come to Dane-zaa nané? (RDA, DZDV 02-12). Because May told the story in English, our video recording became the basis of *Otter Man's Prophesy,* which was shown at the 2002 Conference on Hunting and Gathering Societies in Edinburgh, Scotland (Oker et al. 2002).

Heaven, according to Charlie Yahey, is like Suu Na chii k'chige. It is a place where people come together and greet the relatives they have not seen for an entire year.

> In heaven, people live in tents and camps just like on this world,
> really beautiful tents. When somebody dies and goes to heaven,
> everyone comes out of their tents to see whose relative it is,
> if it is their relative. The person says where he comes from
> and who his mother and father and any relatives are,
> and the people are really glad to see him.
> It's just like when I come visiting over here
> and everyone comes and asks what's been happening
> and how you got there. It's just the same in heaven.
> They ask, "How did you go here?"
> They say, "It's so hard. How is the world?"
> They ask how their relatives are.
> That's the way it is in heaven.
> "Where's my mother? Where's my father?"
> people in heaven ask. If the newcomer says,
> "He died a long time ago. She died a long time ago,"
> the people cry. They know darn well they went to the other place.

Just like in this world, you ask,
"Where's my brother? Where's my sister?"
and when you say, "They died," you've got to cry.
This is the people crying in heaven.
(RDA, Beaver Tales)

Charlie began another song. When he finished, he reminded people that they must dance if they want to find yaak'ihts'é? atanii. "Dancing on earth is easy," he said. "Getting to heaven is hard." Singing and dancing are ways to clear the path your shadow must take when you die:

It costs you nothing to dance.
It costs you lots to go to heaven,
so you better start singing and dancing.
The world is just sticks and dirt,
but heaven is really fun, really nice,
so you better start singing and dancing.
Sometimes, lots of people don't sing.
Something strange is going on in the reserve, and people don't sing.
There are some people who have bad luck.
A bear eats them up, they drown in the water,
they lose their wife, they go hungry for a little while,
or they don't get many beaver.
Those are the people who don't come to dances.
That teaches them not to think about God.
A person who sings and doesn't drink too much,
doesn't get mad all the time, and prays,
that person has good luck.
They get moose. They don't have a hard time.
Aguulaa. That's enough.
(RDA, Beaver Tales)

9
Kinship and Community

For many centuries before white people came to the Peace River territory, the Dane-zaa moved throughout the land. In fall, winter, and spring they travelled in small bands of closely-related people. Each summer, they came together into a larger group of people related by blood or by marriage. At Suu Na chii k'chige, the summer gathering place, the people sang, danced, arranged marriages, introduced babies, and exchanged stories. Kinship and community defined what people knew about heaven. The Dreamers said that these summer reunions provided an image of what it was like to be reunited with their relatives in heaven. Although the ancestors of today's Dane-zaa signed Treaty 8 in 1900 and were assigned Suu Na chii k'chige as their reserve in 1916, members of the Fort St. John Band continued their seasonal rounds for decades after these events.

Beings with whom the Dane-zaa have relationships include the animals who provide them with life's necessities and sacred stones, winds, rain, tools, and everyday objects, all of which the Dane-zaa view as part of the known world. All of a person's human relatives who have passed away reside above the world in which everyday life takes place, beyond the sky *(Yaak'ih)*. They have followed the trail to heaven, a trail of song *(yaak'ihts'ę? atanii)*. The Dreamers know these trails and are able to maintain contact between these relatives in heaven and the people on earth. On every level and in every direction, Dane-zaa people are surrounded by relatives with whom they have a variety of interactions. Hunters dream to make contact with the spirit of an animal who is willing to give itself to the people. Children make contact with an animal friend. Dreamers make contact with all the relatives in heaven.

The Dane-zaa world is one in which every person is surrounded by a wealth of relations. Animal people give their lives to the hunters who respect them. Winds and rains and rocks and even tools and physical objects are alive with meaning. As Tommy Attachie eloquently said, "Everything is alive." Somewhere between the relations who are animal persons and those who have gone into the place beyond the sky are the human people with whom you experience everyday life. When the Dane-zaa talk about their relatives in Dane-zaa Záágé?, they use terms that do not have exact English equivalents. These terms are much more inclusive than their English translations, because kin terms do more than specify an immediate relative. They identify a person as being in a particular category in relation to the speaker.

Both boys and girls are trained to be responsible members of their community. Tommy Attachie told us a story in English about killing his first moose. In the Dane-zaa world, when young people kill a particular animal species for the first time, they must share its meat with everyone in camp. The ritual is performed even for a small animal such as a rabbit.

> We still got lots, dry meat, everything, but still grandma told me,
> "Go hunt." I remember my dad coming back. He said,
> "Moose run away. I miss him." I was thinking. I told him,
> "Wait till I grow up."
> I started to kill deer when I was nine years old.
> Pretty close. Hit him with .22.
> I don't know how many I shot after.
> And I was proud. And after, I kill a moose. My first moose.
> He buy me a .30-30. I kill moose from there.
> First moose I kill in Pine.
> He teach me how to hunt them up the wind.
> I went top the hill with saddle horse, on the trail.
> Go get my snare.
> Moose track going to the west. I leave my horse. I go way around.
> I started coming back like this. I see him – he lying there.
> I put his head against them trees. I go like this, slowly.
> Finally, I see it real good, you know. I hit him. He told me,
> "When you shoot him with gun, when he lie down,

Alice Askoty, Alice Attachie, Charlie Yahey, Aanaatswęą, Murray Attachie, and Albert Askoty, 1968. Photo by Robin Ridington

just shoot above the snow." He told me.
"You shoot high, you hit him," he told me.
A long time I hang onto that.

Finally, I pull the trigger. I hit him –
he get up, and he run all over – and run to him.
I don't want him to get away, and he already dead.
I run to my horse. I run down to top of the hill,
and I went down to the river. I get excited. He told me,
"What happened? I thought you went to get snare."
"Dad, I kill moose," I told him. He said, "Where?"
"Top the hill," I told him. "I go skin him," he say.
He get a team horse. He ride on that, bareback,
and he went up there.
And he skin him, and he put him in that moosehide.
Sew it together. He put chain in there. He lead the horse.
"It happened," they said.

Our Native way, when your first moose,
any animal you kill, first one,
every one of people going to have one.
Each family, your first one, you give to each,
and that way, in the future, everybody eat what you have.
In our way of living, it's happening.
And I was happy all day up there where I check my snares.
Oh, me, me, I kill a moose today. That was in my mind all day.
All the rest of guys kill something first, you know, they're happy.
(Ridington/Dane-zaa Archive [RDA], DZHD10-1)

In the Dane-zaa world, when young girls were becoming women, they received training in proper behaviour from older women, usually a grandmother. At her first menstruation, a girl was given specific tasks, and the older woman explained how to read a story in the hide. In traditional times, girls were excluded from the camp when they got their first period. More recently, they stayed indoors and did tasks that require great patience, such as picking every needle from a spruce branch or intricate beadwork. While menstruating, the girl could not eat red meat because the Dane-zaa believed that the blood of animals who have sacrificed their lives to hunters should not be mixed with blood that signifies that a woman will not bring forth a new life. When the period ended, the young woman could be asked to make a meal

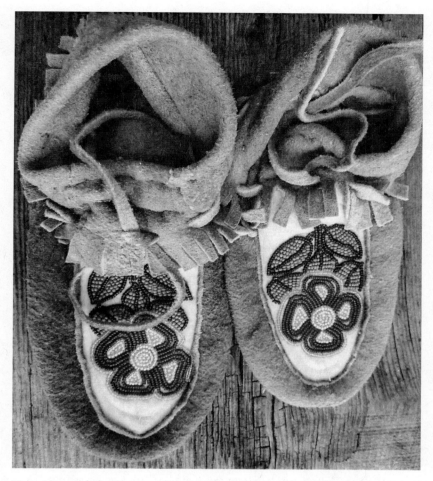

Moccasins made by Margaret Dominic Davis, presented to Jillian Ridington by Doig River First Nation chief and council in 2009. Most Dane-zaa women today are skilled in processing hides and creating garments from them. They make moosehide jackets, vests and moccasins such as the pair shown here for family members, for gifts, or to sell for prices that reflect the skill of the maker and the work involved. Photo by Jillian Ridington

for the family to make sure she is careful in the way she prepares food. The young woman's hair was then washed, and she was declared clean and ready to go back to her community. Although many of these rituals are no longer followed, many Dane-zaa women are skilled in processing hides and creating garments from them. They still decorate moosehide moccasins, vests, and jackets with beadwork. These items are made for family members, sold, or presented as gifts.

The Ts'ibe Dané? and Lhuuge Leą, the people who made up the Fort St. John Band, are descended from a core group of related families who lived in the area when the first Europeans arrived. When we prepared the genealogy for the Doig River and Blueberry River First Nations, we found that most members of those communities could trace their relationship back to these common ancestors. Because of these common bonds, Dane-zaa kin terms classify relationships and regulate marriage. Every person knows or can discover a kin term for every other person.

Traditionally, there was virtually no such thing as a nonrelative in Dane-zaa society. Even people from non-Dane-zaa communities, such as Cree, were assigned appropriate kinship terms. Today, outsiders integrated into the Dane-zaa community by marriage or long-term friendship are included in the wider circle of relatives. When Billy Attachie phones Robin, he always begins the conversation with the Cree word for brother-in-law, *mistau*. Billy and others at Doig call Robin "Labassis," which is their idea of how a Cree person would pronounce his name. The name conveys that Robin is a relative in that he has spent a lot of time at Doig and is close to many of the people. But he's not Dane-zaa. Giving a Cree version of his English name is a way of saying "he's connected to us, but he's someone from a different community." When Billy calls Robin "mistau," he is saying that he's a relative but maybe a distant one. The Dane-zaa Záágé? term for *brother-in-law* is *tlaasé?*.

People who grew up speaking Dane-zaa Záágé? always refer to their relatives with terms that reflect their relationship rather than individual names. Because people have an intimate knowledge of these relationships, it is usually clear from the context of a conversation who is being referred to when the speaker uses terms such as *asbe* (mother-in-law, father's sister), *sǫge* (mother's sister), *astê* (father's brother, uncle), or *si̧ize* (father-in-law, mother's brother). The listener will occasionally have a question about which particular relative is being mentioned. A typical exchange goes like this. After someone talks about his or her sǫge, the listener may ask, "Meaa sǫge?" or "Which aunt?" The answer – "Sǫge lah!" – usually reminds the listener to pay attention. It means "The aunt I am talking about!" That is typically enough explanation. As with Dane-zaa storytelling, the speaker presumes the listener knows the context of what is being described.

The best way to understand Dane-zaa kinship is to imagine that every person with whom you interact is related and can be referred

Aku, Charlie Yahey, and Aanaatswęą, 1968. Photo by Robin Ridington

to with an appropriate term of relationship. The kinship chart in Appendix 2 shows how Dane-zaa kinship terms classify cousins alongside a person's brothers and sisters. Terms in **bold** indicate people the individual should not marry. Terms with <u>underline</u> indicate potential mates. The term for *father's brother* is the same as the term for *mother's sister's husband*. Mother's sister is called by the same term as father's brother's wife. From the perspective of someone growing up within the language and its system of classification, **astê** is always married to **sǫge**. Their children are the same as a person's own brothers and sisters (**hune** [older brother], **ashidle** [younger brother]; **saade** [older sister], **asjé?** [younger sister]). Similarly, father's sister or mother's brother's wife (<u>asbe</u>) is always married to mother's brother (<u>sííze</u>). Their children are called the same as the wives and husbands of the person's own brothers and sisters (<u>tlaasé?</u> [brother-in-law, male speaker sister's husband] and <u>asǫ</u> [which can mean "grandmother" as well as "sister-in-law," depending on the context). A person is not supposed to marry a cousin he or she calls brother or sister, but he or she can marry the other kind of cousin, the children of <u>asbe</u> and <u>sííze</u>. Dane-zaa marriages sometimes even took place across generations. A man could marry his <u>asbe</u> but not his **sǫge**. A woman could marry her <u>sííze</u> but not her **astê**.

There is a logical reason why Dane-zaa call the children of a father's brother and mother's sister by the same term as they would use for their own brother and sister. Anthropologists call these relatives parallel cousins because they are the children of your parent's same-sex sibling (your father's brother's children or your mother's sister's children). In English, the Dane-zaa sometimes refer to these people as cousin-brothers and cousin-sisters. A father's brother is essentially a stepfather: he is like your own father. A mother's sister is like a mother and a potential wife for your father should something happen to your mother or should he, as sometimes happened in earlier times, take an additional wife. The terms for these relatives, *astê* and *sǫge,* convey that sense of closeness. Loosely translated, they mean "my father" and "my mother." The terms for *mother's brother* and *father's sister* are <u>sííze</u> and <u>asbe</u>. <u>Sííze</u> is always married to someone you call <u>asbe</u>. **Astê** is always married to someone you call **sǫge**. Dane-<u>z</u>aa <u>Z</u>áágé? also distinguishes between older and younger siblings. *Older brother* is **hune**. *Younger brother* is **ashidle**. *Older sister* is **saade**. *Younger sister* is **asjé?**.

Cousins who are children of your mother's brother or father's sister are different. Anthropologists call these cross-cousins because they are the children of your parents' opposite-sex siblings. The Dane-<u>z</u>aa <u>Z</u>áágé? words for cross-cousins could be translated as "brother-in-law" and "sister-in-law," but they also have a wider meaning. A woman can marry any man she calls brother-in-law. A man can marry any woman he calls sister-in-law. Brothers and sisters and their spouses often make up the core members of a band.

In a person's own generation, everyone is either called by one of the brother and sister terms or by the terms that refer to a potential partner. As would seem normal to an outsider, you are not allowed to marry a cousin-brother or cousin-sister. The other kind of cousin, though, in addition to being an in-law is thought of as potential husband or wife.* The only people who are possible mates are those who

---

* This doesn't mean that in traditional times people often married their cousins, although that sometimes did happen.

share the same terms with your cross-cousins – that is, children of someone your father calls sister or your mother calls brother. From the point of view of people who are ready to marry someone in their own generation, there are only two possible categories: people they call brother and sister and people that they (or their siblings) can marry.

The genius of the system is the way in which it expands to create a comprehensive circle of relations. From the perspective of a person in the system, you only need to know the kin terms that your parents call the parents of people in your own generation. These terms tell you whether the people are in the sibling or potential spouse or in-law category. Your father's cousin-brothers are people he calls brother, and therefore you think of them as fathers. They are people who can marry your mother or any people she refers to as sisters. Your mother's cousin-sisters are like mothers to you and are people who can marry your father or people he calls brother.* Because you think of your father's cousin-brothers and your mother's cousin-sisters as parents, you call their children brother and sister. These are people you should not marry. The children of your parents' "cousin siblings" of the opposite sex (your father's sister's children and your mother's brother's children) are potential mates or in-laws.

As the system spreads over the generations, every person in your own generation comes to be either a sibling (brother or sister) or an in-law (someone you or your sibling could marry). This is what anthropologists call a classificatory system of kinship. In practice, this system results in a grand division, from an individual's perspective, between relatives who are potential mates and those who are not because you call them brother or sister. The division does not indicate social groups: it simply distinguishes who falls into each category. The system traditionally extended up and down a generation because marriages often took place between people of different ages and generations. A young woman could marry someone her mother called brother (sííze) but not someone her father called brother (**astê**). Similarly, a young man could marry someone his father called sister (asbe) but not someone his mother called sister (**sǫge**). People outside

---

* In the past, men sometimes took two sisters as their wives. The women needed a man to hunt for them and complement their work processing hides and meat. A good hunter could provide for a large camp. Sometimes, a widow married her sister's husband; at other times, a man whose wife had died would marry her sister.

of the Dane-zaa community have sometimes misunderstood the inclusive nature of this classificatory kinship system. They imagined that the Dane-zaa were inbred. The extensive genealogies the elders gave us demonstrate otherwise.*

Genealogies we produced for the former Fort St. John Band, together with the oral histories told by Dane-zaa elders, allow us to reconstruct a portrait of Dane-zaa life during the first half of the twentieth century. Today's elders, born in the 1930s and 1940s, remember travelling with saddle horses, packhorses, and wagons. The elders Robin recorded in the 1960s remembered even farther back, to the time before the Dane-zaa signed the treaty. Aku, born in 1879, and Nachę, born in 1890, told Robin stories about the way things used to be when they were young as well as stories their own elders had given them about Dane-zaa life in the nineteenth century.

Genealogical research and oral history tell us that the common ancestors of the Ts'ibe Dané? and Lhuuge Lęą included Chimarouche and Duuk'ihsache, who were both adults in 1799. They both have descendants in the Blueberry and Doig communities today. Chimarouche, the son of a man referred to in an 1823 Hudson's Bay Company journal as "Old Chimarouche," was also referred to as "Jimathush" in a 1799 North West Company journal. Johnny Chipesia and Aku called young Chimarouche "Samaloose" in the stories they told Robin. Hudson's Bay Company journals from the 1860s refer to him as "Chimarouche," and baptismal records for his children list him as "Echimarouche" (Glenbow Archives, M-4560-26).

Samaloose was the "friendly Indian" who saved the voyageur Maranda and later requested that a new post be established at Gattah Kwậh (see Chapter 6). The elders Robin talked to in the 1960s told him that Samaloose was the father of Chief Montney (Madaayęą) and Apąą. They also told him that the father of Samaloose was named Dane Natsutle (Small Man), which might have been another name for Jimathush. Our genealogical research confirmed that Chimarouche was the father of Apąą. Catholic Church baptismal records from 1894 show that "Old Apąą" was baptized at age forty, which means he was born around 1854. The priest recorded his father's name as *Echimarouche,* which is clearly a French variation of *Chimarouche* (Roman Catholic Archdiocese of Grouard, Fort St. John Baptism Records).

---

* See Chapter 16 for a discussion of Dane-zaa kinship in relation to the anthropological literature.

His other son Montney (also spelled *Mutain, Montagin,* or *Madaayęą*), became chief of the Fort St. John Band. The town of Montney, near Suu Na chii k'chige, is named for him. From the baptismal records of Montney's children, in which the priest estimates the father's age, we can conclude that Montney was born around 1846. One of his daughters married Ch'ǫne? (Old Wolf) and became an ancestor of the Wolf family who are members of the Blueberry River First Nation. Another married Ts'ibiisaa and became the mother of Johnny Chipesia.

Hudson's Bay Company journals from later in the nineteenth century frequently mention Indians arriving from "Chimarouche's Prairie" to trade. On 23 December 1879, the post journal documents a trading visit from the father and son: "Chimarooch, Ahpah, Netea and a few more Indians arrived" (Glenbow Archives, M-4560-26). The name Chimarouche's Prairie was later shortened to Jimrose Prairie by settlers unfamiliar with the Dane-zaa history of the area. It was finally shortened even more to Rose Prairie and is now a small town with a post office where most Doig people get their mail. Few white people today know that what sounds like a good English name actually derives from a Dane-zaa name that goes back to the time of first contact.

Duuk'ihsachę was probably born in the 1770s. His sons, Yehlhézęh and Dechezhę, are the ancestors of many people at Doig and Blueberry, and the links that tie them to many Dane-zaa reflect the importance of kin relationships in Dane-zaa culture. In the North West Mounted Police's 1899 census, Yehlhézęh (spelled *Yeglease*) is described as "Head Chief of the Beaver Indians, known among themselves as The Muskeg Chief" (Library and Archives Canada [LAC], North West Mounted Police, 1899 Census). He is sometimes referred to as *Okimaken,* the Cree word for chief. His brother Dechezhę, whose name is spelled *Detchiyay* in the 1902 Indian register, is listed as *Tagea* (the Great Man) in the 1899 census (ibid.). After his death, his son Sagónáá? is listed as "Techie Succona." Sagónáá?'s grandson, former Chief Kelvin Davis, told us that *Dechezhę* means "an elder who is wise but also young in spirit." The two brothers had many sons and daughters who brought both their wives and their husbands into the band. This practice differed from that of other northern hunting people who preferred to maintain a core group of male relatives and bring in wives from other bands. The Dane-zaa found that if a strong band community developed, it made sense for both men and women to stay and either marry within the band or bring in spouses from other bands. The Yehlhézęh band was particularly successful at this.

Yehlhézęh had five daughters who found husbands from among a larger circle of relatives willing to join the band or camp with them from time to time. Atahin Yehlhézęh's first marriage was to a man named Olah. The couple were the parents of the late Doig elder Charlie Dominic (whose vision quest story appears in Chapter 3) and the ancestors of many people living at Doig and Blueberry today. After Olah died, Atahin married Charlie Yahey, who helped her raise her son. Atahin and Charlie Yahey are the parents of the late John Yahey and the late Marguerite Yahey Davis of the Blueberry First Nation and Jihgenahshihlę (Chikenezia), who married Bob Achla of Halfway River. Yehlhézęh's daughter Watchize married Khatakose Harvey (see photograph on page 257). Darlene Harvey Davis, former chief Kelvin Davis's wife, is Khatakose Harvey's great-granddaughter. Another daughter married Apąą. When she died in 1903, Apąą married Nachę, the daughter of Akena Yehlhézęh and Tl'ok'ih Náázat, whose name means "standing on the prairie." Akena was Apąą's late wife's brother. Nachę's first marriage, to Apąą, demonstrates that the band preferred to retain its core members rather than lose them to other bands.

Nachę would have called Apąą "Síize." Apąą and Nachę lived together until Apąą was killed by a falling tree in 1917. Nachę had a daughter with Apąą and named her Chaole (Helen). Chaole later married Dechezhę's son Sagónáá?. Their daughter is Doig elder Madeline Sagónáá? Davis. After Apąą died, Nachę married Khatakose Harvey, who had been married to Watchize Yehlhézęh. Nachę outlived Harvey, as well as her third husband, Ben, who was Charlie Yahey's brother and Tl'ok'ih Náázat's cousin-brother. Nachę's daughter by that marriage, Alice Ben, became the wife of Murray Attachie. Alice and Murray were the parents of Doig members Billy, Tommy, Gerry, Margaret, Howard, Wally and five others. Nachę is the grandmother often referred to by Billy, Tommy, Gerry and Margaret Attachie – the woman who brought them up and taught them wise stories while Alice was in the tuberculosis hospital. Nachę's last husband was John Pouce Coupe. Through these marriages, Nachę became the grandmother of many important elders of the Doig River First Nation, including Madeline Sagónáá? Davis and the Pouce Coupes. Throughout her marriages, Nachę remained a core member of the Yehlhézęh Band. Another daughter, Muh-chueh'nalin (Pretty One), married Meka Moccasin and became the mother of Alice Moccasin. As a young woman, Alice married the Dreamer Oker, with whom she had Annie Oker, the mother of former chief Garry Oker and the councillor

Nachę (Mary Pouce Coupe), 1966. Photo by Robin Ridington

Madeline Oker Benson. After Oker's death, Alice married Albert Askoty, the song keeper who preceded Tommy Attachie, and had two more sons, Jack and Freddie.

Yehlhézęh's fifth daughter married Apąą's close friend the Dreamer Adíshtl'íshe, who often hunted and trapped with Apąą. Yehlhézęh's sons – Joe Chedeya (Jedney), Akena, and Atsizoke (now referred to as Joe Suzuki) – were also core members of the band. Akena (Birchbark Sap) married Charlie Yahey's cousin-sister Tl'ok'ih Náázat. They were the parents of Nachę and George Miller, who married Yehlhézęh's daughter Muh-cheueh nalin after her first husband, Meka Moccasin, died. Yehlhézęh's brother Dechezhę had two sons, Sagónáá? and Oker. Sagónáá? became chief of the entire Fort St. John Band after Chief Montney (Madaayęą) died of the flu in 1919. His daughter Madeline (see above) is the mother of former chief Kelvin Davis. Sagónáá? and Oker were both grandfathers of many members of the contemporary Doig community.

These marriages indicate how the Yehlhézęh band kept itself together during hard times. Whenever possible, the group as a whole maintained itself as a viable community by finding replacement spouses from among its members. When that was not possible, they recruited spouses from outside the band but within the close circle of people in the appropriate kinship categories. Nachę's first two marriages are a case in point. Her first husband, Apąą, had been her father's sister's husband and, therefore, her sííze, a marriageable relation, rather than her astâ (her father's brother), who would have been like a stepfather. After Apąą's death, she married Harvey, the widower of another Yehlhézęh daughter. The Yehlhézęh band continued to thrive despite the sickness that took many people in 1910-11.

Perhaps it was because of the deaths of key members such as Apąą and the Yehlhézęh daughters who married Apąą and Harvey that Nachę's relatives encouraged her to marry within the band rather than move to another community. The name *Apąą* or *Ahpah* continues and today is written as *Appaw*. The Appaws are members of the Blueberry River First Nation. Helen Appaw married Charlie Yahey's son John and is the mother of many of Charlie's grandchildren, including former Blueberry chief Norman Yahey.

The following story about the time when Nachę discovered a bear's den gives further insight into how the Ts'ibe Dané? lived around the time the treaty was signed. Like every other person of her generation, Nachę refers to people by kinship terms rather than names. She expects that anyone who hears the story will know from the context which individual she means when she uses a kinship term. The story made a particular impression on her grandchildren, and they continue to pass it on to younger generations. Margaret Attachie translated her grandmother's story.

> It used to be we had a hard time. We didn't have horses.
> We had to pack our stuff on our backs.
> We would hunt beaver from boats. It was hard.
> There wasn't much to eat. Sometimes, we would eat a little.
> Sometimes, someone would get a moose.
> We would eat a little, and then it would be gone.
> Then we would move around,
> move from place to place to place until fall time.
> In July and August, we would walk from Moberly Lake
> to Fort St. John to Dawson Creek,
> all over the places where the big towns are now,
> making dry meat.
> That's how far we went for moose. Sometimes, we made a
> round trip from Doig River to Moberly Lake in ten days.
> (Ridington Dane-zaa Archives [RDA], NA-1)

Nachę's story makes it clear just how rapidly Dane-zaa life changed within a single lifetime. She grew up at the end of the fur trade era, when the only white people in Dane-zaa country were traders, government officials, and priests. Even these people seldom ventured to where the Dane-zaa lived and hunted. Like others of her generation, she vividly recalled the trails that lie beneath the streets of towns such as Fort St. John. She and her people spent most of the year walking and moving their camps with dog teams.

> That's what my sǫge [mother's sister or stepmother] told me.
> Some people don't believe that we had to pack all our stuff
> and dry meat on our backs. When *asea* [her grandfather Yehlhézęh] was alive,
> he used to tell me about how they had to make four trips
> back to the places they cached the dry meat.
> In wintertime, too, they had to go back to the cache
> for the rest of the dry meat. Then they got horses,
> and they could make them pack the dry meat back.
> That's how we Dane-zaa used to live in wintertime.
> There wasn't any flour or grub. We ate just straight meat.

> Today, with potatoes and flour and everything,
> you think one moose is lots. You think it will last a month.
> In those days, one moose wouldn't last long, not one month.
> We ate only meat.
> (RDA, NA-1)

Nachę pauses because she thinks her grandchildren Margaret and Gerry Attachie are laughing at her stories about how hard it was in the old days. She jokes with them, "You old buggers, don't laugh at me." She then reminds her grandchildren that the border between British Columbia and Alberta was meaningless to people when she was young. Alberta did not enter Confederation until five years after the Dane-zaa signed Treaty 8, and even after that, the concept of different provincial jurisdictions was not relevant to Dane-zaa life. She reminds her listeners that they ate "just straight meat" and lived without the backup of flour and other staples available in stores in later years.

> We used to go hunting in Alberta.
> We would go hunting for moose.
> There are really good people down there.
> You were never stuck for food. They would always feed you.
> They were really good people. They treated you like a baby ...
> Today, you eat well,
> but it used to be that we went starving all the time,
> all the time, all the time.
> Today, if you don't have meat, you can eat bannock.
> It used to be, when we didn't have any meat,
> we didn't have anything to eat. In the fall time,
> we would bring our dry meat back to Doig River.
> (RDA, NA-1)

After this opening story about how they used to live when she was young, Nachę begins a story about what it was like growing up in the band of her asea (grandfather) Yehlhézęh and his brother Dechezhę. The story describes a time when even the "muskeg chief" and "the great man" had a hard time finding game. The story is not quite a vision quest narrative, but it does suggest that Nachę and her asbe were guided by their spirit helpers to relieve the band's distress.

> One time I was camping with two old men
> [Asea Yehlhézęh and his brother Dechezhę].

> My asbe [father's sister or mother's brother's wife]* was with us.
> Some other people were camping with us.
> We were starving.
> We moved from place to place.
> We moved to another place, and those two men
> didn't even go out hunting for moose.
> So my asbe and I decided to hunt for porcupines.
> (RDA, NA-1)

The story makes it clear that hunting was not the exclusive domain of men. Women and even girls were perfectly capable of going out in the bush on their own to look for food. Women traditionally set snares for rabbits and other small game, and they often set out unarmed and without men to look for slow-moving game such as porcupines. What is notable about this story is how utterly independent and competent these two young women were in the bush. Rather than waiting around feeling sorry for themselves and hungry, they set out on their own to do something about the situation. The self-sufficiency of these and other women, like that of their male counterparts, was fostered by the experience of childhood vision quests.

Nachę was an elder when Robin spoke with her, and she continued to demonstrate great knowledge and authority. It is no wonder that her grandchildren jokingly referred to her as *Samakanis,* the Cree word for a police officer, because of the way she took control of situations.

> We set out, and asbe went along the river.
> I went up along the crest of some mountains.
> It was late wintertime, and there was deep snow.
> I looked down the slope, but I didn't see any porcupines.
> The days were getting long, but already it was getting dark,
> so I started straight down the mountain side.
> There was a river at the bottom, and I thought
> that if I followed it back to camp, I might find something.
> The snow was deep down there, and there was lots of brush.
> I was wearing snowshoes,
> but the snow was too deep for them, too.
> (RDA, NA-1)

---

* Her asbe was probably her father's sister, one of Yehlhézęh's daughters. As noted, she would later marry Apąą and Harvey, both widowers who had been married to two of her asbes.

Nachę was a keen observer of signs in the bush. She knew how to read tracks and how to interpret evidence of places where animals had been feeding. At the time when the story took place, she would already have gone on a vision quest *(Shin kaa)* and would have had an animal friend to guide her. In this case, she is led to a place where a bear has left signs that tell her where he will be sleeping in his den. She observes a breathing hole in the snow.

> I was walking slowly when I saw some sticks
> broken under a medium-size spruce tree.
> It looked like something had broken them.
> I went over there. There were no tracks.
> I was on top of a bear den, but I didn't know it.
> I took off my snowshoes and started to look around.
> There was a small hole where the snow was falling in.
> I took a stick and poked it. It went inside. I looked inside.
> There seemed to be something in there, but I couldn't see.
> It was dark. I poked again with a long stick.
> It felt like there was something in there, but it didn't move.
> It didn't growl. I was wondering what it could be.
> I threw lots of sticks and stones in there, but nothing moved.
> Then I noticed a stick by the entrance that had been chewed,
> so I put it in my pack and started back.
> It was late. I was tired. It was after the middle of the night
> when I got back. Asea was angry.
> "I thought you got a porcupine or something.
> I thought you were carrying some kind of meat in your pack.
> That's why you were late, but you didn't bring anything."
> (RDA, NA-1)

Nachę was not intimidated by her asea's reaction. She knew what she had seen and had brought back a sign as proof. She then guided the people back to the den. Because she had knowledge, they accepted her as a leader in this particular task. While they were busy killing the bear, Nachę took responsibility for building a fire. This part of the story is a perfect example of how Dane-zaa leadership is specific to a particular task rather than a position of absolute authority. This leadership style helps explain why, to this day, the Dane-zaa are uneasy with "bosses."

> I showed asea the chewed stick.
> "I found a bear's den, but I don't know if he is in there now."

Asea called to the other people,
"Hey, my granddaughter found a bear's den."
That same night, we all set out to find it in the moonlight.
I drank tea, and then I went on with them.
We took a dog with us.
After we had gone some way, he could smell the bear,
and he started barking. He wanted to chase after it,
but we held him.
When we came to the hole, we took the bear and killed him.
It was a big black bear, the kind that is almost like a grizzly,
and it was very fat. They started to skin it while I made a fire.
We were so hungry, we ate the bear's liver and guts.
That night, we packed the bear meat back, and we ate it.
The next day, we were feeling better, and we moved camp again.
A chinook wind came, and it turned nice and warm.
Then we got two moose. It was all right then.
(RDA, NA-1)

Nachę's story describes a time when the Yehlhézęh band depended largely on subsistence hunting. Without supplies of store-bought food, they needed to bring in game on a regular basis. The bison, once so plentiful, were gone. A single moose would only last a band of thirty people about a week. As Nachę says, "Sometimes, someone would get a moose. We would eat a little, and then it would be gone." Dry meat, dried berries, and grease allowed the band to continue eating as long as supplies lasted. When the people were forced to reduce their consumption of dry meat, hunters would set out on hunts without adequate nutrition. This is the situation Nachę refers to when she says, "We were starving." Frank Beaton, the Hudson's Bay Company's factor at that time, mentions Dane-zaa coming into the trading post and reporting that people were starving in the camps (Glenbow Archives [GA], M-4560-27). These reports were most frequent during 1910 and 1911 (GA, M-4560-28). Beaton also notes occasions when the people report having plenty of meat. Dane-zaa seem to have particularly struggled in 1910 and 1911. Aku would have been around thirty then, and Nachę would have been twenty. In his entry for 13 November 1910, Beaton describes a number of deaths: "Old Charlie [Usulets or Big Charlie, Nachę's mother's father and Charlie Yahey's stepfather] arieved & Reports the Death of Atcha & Atchayua also Mitchskulla and Ierose and 5 others this makes 19 deaths during the past 5 months amongst the Beaver Indians" (ibid.).

In the first few years that he kept the journal, Beaton made frequent reference to Aku's father, A̱záde (Liver). He mentions Aku for the first time in 1911. His entry for 11 March reads: "Acko and a boy arieved about 12 o'clock last night. They report a lot of sickiness in their camp and came in to get some medicine." On 4 April 1912 of the following year, Beaton wrote: "Acko arieved this evening from the North Pine Lakes [Megawontlonde] and they are all sick as usual." On 14 June 1911, he noted that "Sakona & Oker [sons of Dechezhę] arieved from out North where they have been all winter." On July 8, he wrote: "A few Beaver Indians arieved from up the South Pine and report starvation in their camps" (GA, M-4560-28).

In contrast to Beaton's sparse written records, Dane-zaa oral stories from the early years of the twentieth century are rich and vivid. In 1966, Aku told Robin another story about hunting and trapping in the winter. He remembered living in log teepees made of poles chinked with moss and partially covered with dirt and snow at the base. The fire inside provided both warmth and light. It was only later, when a wider variety of trade items became available, that people began to use log cabins with stoves for heat and lanterns for light. Billy Attachie provided this translation.

> We were going to spend all winter at Cecil Lake,
> me and my father.
> We made a log teepee and got lots of groceries.
> We made lots of dry meat, and we finished our log teepee.
> Then it began to snow a little bit.
> My father and my tlaasé?
> [sister's husband or a male cross-cousin]
> went north to trap some lynx.
> My tlaasé? wasn't too good at hunting.
> He's scared of the bush.
> My ashidle [younger brother] was too young to do anything,
> but he was good for the bush. I was old enough. I knew.
> My father had some dogs.
> A yáá?kwąhne man gave my dad that dog.
> The man's name was Mehatsaen.
> My dad gave them to his son-in-law, my tlaasé?,
> to use for hunting lynx. That same afternoon,
> tlaasé? came right back.
> He thought he had seen a bear in a hole,
> but he was scared, so he didn't go close to it.

He didn't tell us that, but our teepees were close together,
and we heard him telling that to his wife.
My dad said, "My dogs are good. Why didn't you kill that bear?"
My tlaasé? said, "Those bears make too much noise in their hole.
I didn't want to go near them.
The dog didn't want to go near him either."
(RDA, Aku 1966)

The story of Aku's tlaasé? being afraid of what he thought was a bear's den contrasts with Nachę's story of actually finding a den and saving her band from starvation.

Aku continued:

My father said, "That dog isn't scared of anything.
He's killed lots of animals. Why are you scared of it?"
My tlaasé? said, "Mehatsaen ran to that hole then back to me.
He was scared, so we took off."
My dad told him to take us to that bear. So we went out.
Our dogs killed a lynx along the way.
We put it in a tree to pick up when we came back
and then went on. "It's not far from here," my tlaasé? said,
and he pointed to a great big tree stump as big as a log teepee.
He hadn't even gone near it he was so scared.
I went up and looked in it.
There was a hole in it
that was even too small for a dog to get through.
There couldn't be any bears in there.
My tlaasé? hadn't even gone close enough to see.
My dad and ashidle, my younger brother, went ahead.
They knew darn well that wasn't a bear hole,
so they went to hunt some marten. I went a different way.
I was pretty smart for everything,
so I went ahead and hid behind a big tree.
I watched my tlaasé?. He cut a pole and sharpened the end,
and then he went back to that stump
and poked around in the hole.
I just laughed and laughed to myself
to see him trying to make sure there was nothing there.
The next day, my father killed a bear
and four one-year-old cubs somewhere else,
and we showed that to my tlaasé? and told him,

"That's what we call a bear.
Not something that lives in a little tiny hole."
(RDA, Aku 1966)

Aku knew that most of the people hearing the story would know which relatives he was talking about. To be Dane-zaa is to be surrounded by relatives. Dane-zaa kinship has always been all encompassing. Although they do not use the phrase *all my relations,* which is common among many First Nations, the idea of being surrounded by relations is central to Dane-zaa identity. Even animals are relations who have the ability to give life and to bestow power. When a child goes into the bush to seek a song or Shin kaa, he or she enters into the stories of an animal friend. The animal's story becomes the story of the person's life.

10
The 1899 North West Mounted Police Census and Treaty 8

The twentieth century, a century of so-called progress, brought drastic changes to the land and people of the Dane-zaa First Nations. To Dane-zaa living at the time, however, the turn of the century began as any other, at a time when the sun stops its daily movement toward the southern horizon and starts to return to the north. Adíshtl'íshe and Alédzé, like the Dreamers before them, told people that if they did not come together at winter solstice to sing and dance to the Dreamers' songs, the sun would continue to move south until daylight disappeared altogether. Dane-zaa Dreamers and storytellers spent the long winter nights telling stories about the time of creation, the adventures of Tsááyaa, the first hunter, and the exploits of their own ancestors, as they had for thousands of years. But they also sought to prepare their people for the future. They were troubled by the influx of foreigners into their territory.

White men seeking riches had begun to come into Dane-zaa territories by the 1880s. Although the fur trade continued, these individuals who were not connected to the trading companies began to invade Dane-zaa lands and threatened the already diminished game resources. Unlike fur traders, these men had nothing to offer the Dane-zaa. The arrival of these strangers was the first of many changes that would make Dane-zaa traditional land a different place by the end of the twentieth century. Prospectors heading for the Klondike gold fields had no understanding of the delicate balance between the Dane-zaa and their resource base. They sought to exploit the territory without acknowledging that it was Dane-zaa land. As they began to overrun the territory in the 1890s, they sometimes interfered with traditional hunting and trapping.

In 1870, the HBC surrendered its charter to govern the North-Western Territory to the newly formed government of Canada, and in 1871 British Columbia entered Confederation. By the 1880s and 1890s, Canadian policy makers were concerned that conflicts between Aboriginal people and newcomers was getting out of control. In a report for the Department of Indian Affairs and Northern Development on the conditions leading up to Treaty 8, Dennis Madill (1986, 4) writes:

> Reports of hardships in prominent newspapers and continued appeals from the Hudson's Bay Company and missionaries for provisions during the difficult years of 1887 and 1888 finally resulted in government action. During the winter of 1887-88, there were indications that Indians in the Fort St. John area were killing their horses for food. Furthermore, the *Calgary Tribune* reported that rendering assistance to the northern Indians was good policy and would have the timely effect of producing "a good feeling" when a treaty was ultimately made. In 1881, the federal government apportioned $7,000 to the Hudson's Bay Company for relief for destitute Indians in all of the "unorganized territory" and, a year later, Parliament voted an annual grant of $500 to the Roman Catholic bishop of the Mackenzie for the distribution of twine and fish hooks.

Despite reports of hardships among the Indians of Fort St. John, the government of Canada maintained that the Hudson's Bay Company should continue to be responsible for administering social services. This opinion began to change after the government received a report, dated 7 July 1891, that stated that "immense quantities of petroleum" existed in parts of the Athabasca District (Madill 1986, 5). Shortly after receiving the report, the minister of the interior recommended that "negotiations for a treaty be opened up during the ensuing season with the Indians interested in those portions of the Mackenzie River Country, and in the District of Athabaska [sic] including the Peace River Country, as well as in that portion of country which lies south of the District of Athabaska, and north and west of the Northern boundary of Treaty No. 6" (ibid., 6). For reasons probably having to do with politics in Ottawa, the government did not act on the recommendation until 1896, the year that gold was discovered in the

Klondike. When miners began streaming into the Peace River country looking for a route to the gold fields, the government felt compelled to establish its authority over the territory.

A young Swede, whose name was not given, visited Fort St. John in 1898 and later described how the Dane-zaa had reacted to the miners who were abusing their resources. The conflict he describes in the following passage was one of the factors that led the government of Canada to seek a treaty: "In Fort St. John there was an Indian scare. The Beaver and Dog Rib tribes did not want the white man to come and stay in the country which they said was theirs. Some miners stole caches of food, snowshoes, etc. which were hidden in trees. On top of the hill at Fort St. John there were about seventy-five buggies, wagons and Red River carts left by miners. The Indians put the whole works down the hill and I could see afterwards broken wagons and equipment for about six hundred feet down" (Bowes 1963, 203). On 30 June 1898, the *Ottawa Citizen* reported: "There are 500 Indians camped at Fort St. John who refuse to let police and miners go further north until a treaty has been signed with them. They claim that some of their horses have been taken by the miners and are also afraid that the advent of so many men into their country will drive away the fur; hence their desire to stop the travel north" (Fumoleau 1973, 49)

In 1897, the North West Mounted Police (NWMP) were assigned an important role in bringing order to an increasingly chaotic situation. Inspector J.D. Moodie, who was responsible for making a trail from Fort St. John via Fort Grahame to the Klondike, wrote that the Dane-zaa and Sekani Indians were "a miserable lot, half-starved most of the winter, and utterly unreliable" (Madill 1986, 4). He did not note that their impoverished condition had resulted from more than a century of overexploitation caused by the fur trade. Moodie then warned that the arrival of more white people in Dane-zaa territory would cause additional hardship.

> There is no doubt that the influx of whites will materially increase the difficulties of hunting by the Indians, and these people, who, even before the rush, were often starving from their inability to produce game, will in future be in a much worse condition; and unless some assistance is given to them by the Indian Department, they are very likely to take what they consider a just revenge on the white men who have come, contrary to their wishes, and scattered themselves over the country. When told that if they started fighting as they

threatened, it could only end in their extermination, the reply was "we may as well die by the white men's bullets as of starvation." (Ibid., 5)

Canada finally determined that to protect its own interests as well as provide some assurance to Aboriginal people, it would be wise to appoint a treaty commission and negotiate Treaty 8. On 27 June 1898, the Privy Council passed Order-in-Council no. 1703, which authorized the government to proceed with treaty negotiations (Madill 1986, 7). To determine exactly how many Indians were in the territory, the federal government sent the NWMP to conduct a census of all bands in the Peace River region in 1899. The oral history and documents we examined in preparing the genealogy of the former Fort St. John Band (see discussion later in this chapter) indicate that, in some ways, the NWMP census is a more thorough document than the annuity pay lists compiled by Indian Agents following the treaty. However, many people were not included on either list. The census lists 184 "Beaver" Indians at Fort St. John: 46 men, 48 women, 44 girls, and 46 boys. It identifies band leaders and lists all the men by name. It also lists widows and single women. As in the annuity pay lists, married women were counted but not named as individuals. Most of the men listed in the 1899 census are remembered in Dane-zaa oral history.

Below are the men listed in the NWMP census who are prominent in Dane-zaa oral history and genealogy. Our comments are in brackets. (See Appendix 3 for further information about the signatories and Appendix 4 for a facsimile of the NWMP census.)

> Abąą [Nachę's husband and son of Chimarouche]
> Attachie [grandfather of many people at Doig today]
> Azzidie – *Liver* [Azáde, Aku's father]
> Davis [Jebís, father of John Davis (see page 272)]
> Dislisici – *Newspaper* [Adíshtl'íshe, an important Dreamer]
> Jib-ba-jay [Ts'ibiisaa, George Chipesia, father of Johnny and Harry Chipesia, Janice Askoty, and others (see pages 123 and 256)]
> Montagnia – *Chief of the West branch of the Beaver Indians living in Fort St. John* [Chief Montney, son of Chimarouche]
> Muckithay [father of Billy Makadahay and ancestor of many at Doig]
> Thomas Pouscoopee – *a good interpreter; speaks Cree and Beaver, lives at St. John* [Pouce Coupe, ancestor of many at Doig]

Tagea – *The Great Man, a cripple* [Tagea is another name for Dechezhę, son of Duuk'ihsachę and father of Sagónáá? and Oker]

Wolf [Ch'ǫne?, also known as Mister Wolf and ancestor of many in all Dane-zaa communities]

Wuskula [Wuskullie, Bella Yahey's first husband]

Yegclease – *Head Chief of the Beaver Indians known among them as the Muskeg Chief* [Yelhézęh, son of Duuk'ihsachę and ancestor of many at Doig and Blueberry] (LAC, North West Mounted Police, 1899 Census)

At least one man on the list, Jib-ba-Jay (Ts'ibiissa), was alive when Robin began fieldwork in 1964. Many of the people listed simply as "boy" or "girl" in the census can also be identified as people Robin knew. In addition to the Dane-zaa, the census listed five men as Cree and one other as "Half-Breed."

From the Dane-zaa's point of view, the treaty was an agreement about peace, friendship, and the sharing of land. Their main objective in entering treaty was to secure their traditional hunting, fishing, and trapping rights. They had already experienced what amounted to a peace and friendship treaty with the Saulteau who moved into Dane-zaa territory in the late 1800s. According to Stewart Cameron (personal communication, Nenan Youth and Elders Camp, 4 July 2011), a former chief of the Saulteau First Nation, a Saulteau Dreamer named Kayahcogan had been in contact with Dane-zaa Dreamers at the time of the Riel Resistance. Cameron said that through their dream encounters, the Dane-zaa Dreamers agreed to share land with the Saulteau, who would assume the role of peacekeepers. Over a period of several decades, Kayahcogan and the Saulteau Dreamers who came after him led their people from Saskatchewan to Moberly Lake. One of Stewart's ancestors was a Dreamer named Big Drum. Dane-zaa Dreamers still sing his songs today.

The government of Canada's view of the treaty process differed from the Dane-zaa's. To Canada, the treaty was an instrument for extinguishing Aboriginal title and transferring jurisdiction over the land to itself. Although there is "little documentation regarding the ... four meetings in 1900 that occurred from Fort St. John to Fond du Lac and from Fort Resolution to Wabasca," it is clear from Madill's account and from Dane-zaa oral history that the implications of the concept of extinguishment were never adequately explained to the Dane-zaa during treaty negotiations or in meetings regarding adhesions

(Madill 1986, 16). The men who signed the treaty, like all Dane-zaa, spoke Dane-zaa Záágé?. Most Dane-zaa men also spoke Cree, the language of their neighbours to the east and the language most commonly used in dealing with traders. They did not speak English, and the only negotiations that took place were with Kinosayoo's Cree band at Lesser Slave Lake in June 1899. Subsequent signings, such as the one with the Fort St. John Beaver Band a year later, were simply adhesions to the document already in place. Madill (ibid.) reports that "[t]he written terms and conditions of Treaty Eight were finalized during the negotiations at Lesser Slave Lake, and the treaty commissioners decided to make adhesions at all of the other trading posts rather than negotiate several treaties. The commissioners expected that once the Lesser Slave Lake Indians signed treaty there would be less difficulty in obtaining adhesions of the others."

In their report on negotiations with Kinosayoo's band, the commissioners wrote,

> Our chief difficulty was the apprehension that the hunting and fishing privileges were to be curtailed. The provision in the treaty under which ammunition and twine is to be furnished went far in the direction of quieting the fears of the Indians, for they admitted that it would be unreasonable to furnish the means of hunting and fishing if laws were to be enacted which would make hunting and fishing so restricted as to render it impossible to make a livelihood by such pursuits. But over and above the provision, we had to solemnly assure them that only such laws as to hunting and fishing as were in the interest of the Indians and were found necessary in order to protect the fish and fur-bearing animals would be made, and that they would be as free to hunt and fish after the treaty as they would be if they never entered into it ... the Indians were generally averse to being placed on reserves. It would have been impossible to have made a treaty if we had not assured them that there was no intention of confining them to reserves. We had to very clearly explain to them that the provisions for reserves and allotments of land were made for their protection, and to secure to them in perpetuity a fair portion of the land ceded, in the event of settlement advancing. (Madill 1986, 16)

The treaty commissioners were not able to give a clear indication of when they would arrive at Fort St. John. After waiting for them to arrive at the Hudson's Bay Company post in late May and early June 1899, the Dane-zaa family heads returned to their bands, as they had to hunt during the summer to have enough meat for the following winter. The treaty commissioners explained in their report that

> [u]nfortunately, the Indians had dispersed and gone to their hunting grounds before the messenger arrived and weeks before the date originally fixed for the meeting, and when the Commissioners got within some miles of St. John the messenger met them with a letter from the Hudson's Bay Company officer there advising them that the Indians, after consuming all their provisions, set off on the 1st June in four different bands and in as many different directions for the regular hunt ... It may be stated, however, that what happened was not altogether unforeseen. We had grave doubts of being able to get to St. John in time to meet the Indians, but as they were reported to be rather disturbed and ill-disposed on account of the actions of miners passing through the country, it was thought that it would be well to show them that the Commissioners were prepared to go into their country, and that they had put forth every possible effort to keep the engagement made by the Government. (Madill 1986, 16-17)

The relationship between the Fort St. John Band and the government of Canada was finally formalized by the signing of Treaty 8 on 30 May 1900. On behalf of the Dane-zaa, eight men who were leaders of what the government of Canada designated as the "Fort St. John Band" signed a treaty with Her Majesty the Queen. The treaty guaranteed their people hunting, fishing, and trapping rights throughout their traditional lands.

> The Beaver Indians of the Upper Peace River and thereabouts, having met at Fort St. John, on this thirtieth day of May, in this present year 1900, Her Majesty's Commissioner, James Ansdell Macrae, Esquire, and having had explained to them the terms of the treaty unto which the Chief and Headmen of the Indians of Lesser Slave Lake and adjacent country set their hands on the twenty-first day of June, in the year 1899, do join in the cession made by the said treaty, and agree to adhere to the terms thereof, in consideration of the undertakings made therein.

In witness whereof, Her Majesty's said Commissioner, and the following of the said Beaver Indians, have hereunto set their hands, at Fort St. John, on this thirtieth day of May, in the year herein first above written.

Signed by the parties thereto in the presence of the undersigned witnesses, after the same had been read and explained to the Indians by John Shaw, interpreter.

J.A. Macrae, Commissioner

Muckithay
Aginaa
Dislisici
Tachea
Appan
Attachie
Allalie
Yatsoose*

Six of the men – Muckithay, Aginaa, Adíshtl'íshe, Tachea, Apąą, and Attachie – who signed the treaty were well-known family heads remembered by contemporary members of the former Fort St. John Band. The two names *Allalie* and *Yatsoose* have not been linked to oral history or to written documents, perhaps because the men had no living descendants. What is striking about the record is who did not sign the treaty. Neither Chief Montney nor Yelhézęh (Okimakan) signed the treaty, nor did important and influential family heads such as Ch'ǫneʔ (The Wolf), his brother Yakatchie, Thomas Pouce Coupe, Big Charlie, Ts'ibiisaa, and Waskulie.

On one point the government of Canada and the Dane-zaa did have, and continue to have, different understandings. For the Dane-zaa, the treaty was an agreement between two autonomous nations regarding hunting, fishing, and trapping rights. They understood that once the eight leaders signed the adhesion, the Fort St. John Band was collectively guaranteed these rights in perpetuity. As noted above, they had been assured that their hunting and fishing rights would be preserved and that they would not be confined to reserves. Treaty 8 gave

---

* For more information on these men, see Appendix 3, "Research Notes on Beaver Signatories."

the Indians the right to "their usual vocation of hunting, trapping and fishing throughout the tract surrendered as heretofore described, subject to such regulations as may from time to time be made by the Government of the country, acting under the authority of Her Majesty, and saving and *excepting such tracts as may be required or taken up from time to time for settlement, mining, lumbering, trading or other purposes*" (our emphasis). Perhaps the government of Canada had some idea of the development that would follow in the next century. It is certain that the Dane-zaa did not.

Canada believed that eight signatures were sufficient to extinguish title to the Fort St. John Band's entire territory. Commissioner J.A. Macrae pointed out that "even after the adhesions of 1900 were secured, there still remained over 500 Indians who had not been given the option of taking treaty or scrip." He concluded, nevertheless, that "the Indian title ... may be fairly regarded as extinguished" (Madill 1986, 14). It is unlikely that the interpreters were able to explain the concept of land title surrender to the eight men who signed. Historian Richard Daniel and anthropologist June Helm testified on this issue in the Mackenzie Valley Pipeline Inquiry, and their comments are relevant to understanding how the Dane-zaa viewed the treaty. As Madill (ibid., 26) reports,

> Historian Richard Daniel has suggested that available documentation has shown that the treaty commissioners did not explain properly the implications of the phrase "the said Indians do hereby cede, release, surrender and yield up ... all their rights, title and privileges whatsoever, to the lands" ... The explanation is that the commissioners thought that it was a mere formality from the government perspective and that the treaty was "a means of extinguishing the vague aboriginal rights and placating the native people by offering the advantages of a treaty." Also, it is improbable that the commissioners in their hasty journey through the north could have clarified the interpretation of the treaty, particularly the concept of land surrender.

June Helm, in testifying before Justice Morrow, explained the complications:

> How could anybody put in the Athapaskan language through a Métis interpreter to monolingual Athapaskan hearers the

concept of relinquishing ownership of land I don't know, of how people who have never conceived of a bounded property which can be transferred from one group to another. I don't know how they would be able to comprehend the import translated from English into a language which does not have those concepts, and certainly in any sense that Anglo-Saxon jurisprudence would understand. So this is an anthropological opinion and it has continued to puzzle me how any of them could possibly have understood this. I don't think they could have. That is my judgement. (Ibid., 26)

Following the treaty adhesion, individual members of the band thought that registering for an annuity pay list number and obtaining a "ticket" was merely an additional step required to receive the annual treaty payment of five dollars per person and other government assistance. Inspector H.A. Conroy wrote in 1903, "The Indians at this place are very independent and cannot be persuaded to take treaty. Only a few families joined. The Indians there said they did not want to take treaty, as they had no trouble in making their own living. One very intelligent Indian told me that when he was old and could not work he would then ask the government for assistance, but till then him thought it was wrong for him to take assistance when he did not really require it" (Madill 1986, 18).

In 1965, Augustine Jumbie, a Dane-zaa elder who lived from 1895 to 1988, told Robin what he remembered about the adhesion that took place at Fort Nelson in 1910. As he remembered it, the people there, as in Fort St. John, were reluctant to sign the treaty (RDA, field notes, 1965-66). Conroy, in describing the same event, wrote that the Sekani chief (Makenachę [Bigfoot], who raised Jumbie) had told him, "God made the game and fur bearing animals for the Indians, and money for the white people; my forefathers made their living in the country without white men's money and I and my people can do the same" (Madill 1986, 20). Conroy attempted to convince Bigfoot and his people that Indians who were unwilling to sign as individuals were not going to be forced to take treaty but "could go on making their living by hunting and trapping as they always did" (ibid.).

Speaking to Robin in English, this is how Jumbie described the interaction between Conroy and Bigfoot (RDA, field notes, 1965-66). "First treaty man come – people say no – He come again, seven days later. Boss pretty near cry, 'Indian and white man pretty near partner.'

Finally, OK. We can shoot moose anytime."Jumbie's short statement makes the following points: (1) the treaty was made between equal partners or, as we would say today, between autonomous nations – a First Nation and the government of Canada; (2) the government of Canada very much wanted the Indians to take an adhesion to the treaty; (3) and the Indians agreed to the adhesion only upon the understanding that it gave them collective rights to continue their traditional hunting, fishing, and trapping activities. Nowhere in Jumbie's narrative or in those of agents of the Crown is there an indication that these rights would pertain only to individuals who sign on to an annuity pay list. And it is unlikely that the Dane-zaa understood that the provisions of the treaty meant that their rights could be diminished by the granting of land to white settlers and the demands of those who came in search of the mineral wealth of the territory.

In 1914, the government of Canada allocated reserve land to the Fort St. John Band on the basis of the number of people who had been present when the Indian Agent arrived in June to update the band lists and give out treaty money. For each member counted by the agent, the band would be given 128 acres. Suu Na chii k'chige was surveyed as an Indian reserve (IR 172) by Donald F. Robertson in 1914 (LAC, Survey Report of Donald F. Robertson). It was assigned to the Fort St. John Band in 1916. There is no evidence that Surveyor Robertson met with band members to discuss land selection. He took his instructions from the Indian Agent, David Laird.

> ### Survey Report of Donald F. Robertson
> I beg to submit the following report of surveys completed by me during the season of 1914.
>
> In accordance with instructions, I left Ottawa on June 1, 1914, and proceeded to the Peace River Block, arriving at Moberly lake on July 9; and under the conditions of Treaty No. 8 surveyed one block of the reserve for the Hudson Hope band of Beaver Indians at the west end of Moberly lake, laying out an area of 5,025 acres at this point.
>
> At the east end of Moberly lake an area of 7,656 acres was chosen and surveyed for the Saulteaux Indians and a number of the Beaver Indians of St. John band who wished to have their land there.
>
> Both of these reserves are suitable for grazing, and stock has been wintered there very successfully. A portion of each

reserve is well adapted for gardens and mixed farming. Moberly lake has a supply of whitefish and trout sufficient to meet the needs of the Indians. Game is plentiful in this locality. There is an ample supply of timber on each reserve. Hay is plentiful on both reserves.

These Indians live by hunting and fishing. Several at the east end of the lake have small gardens.

On the completion of these reserves, I proceeded to Halfway river, at the west boundary of the Peace River Block, where Assistant Agent Laird had arranged with the Hudson Hope Indians to locate the remainder of their reserve.

Mr. Laird met me at Halfway river and accompanied me to Fort St. John in order that there should be no mistake about the lands at these points, the Indians having scattered before my arrival at either of these points.

At Halfway river a reserve of 9,893 acres was laid out, being the remainder of the land to which the Hudson Hope band was entitled.

This reserve is best suited for grazing. The hunting is good in the mountains near by [sic] and at some seasons trout are plentiful in Halfway river. These Indians live by hunting and fishing.

I proceeded next to Fort St. John and in township 85, range 18, W. 6th, and in township 85, range 19, W. 6th, surveyed a reserve 28 sq. miles for the St. John band of Beaver Indians. This reserve is excellently adapted for grazing and the soil is suitable for mixed farming.

The new reserve at Suu Na chii k'chige was lush land where horses could graze and fatten while the people gathered to sing and dance. It is near the present town of Montney and not far from Charlie Lake, where the Lhuuge Leą and Ts'ibe Dané? fished. It was a traditional summer gathering place for Dane-zaa people. Each summer for generations of lifetimes, Dane-zaa from all over the territory came together there to dance and sing their Dreamers' songs. Young people came together in marriage, infants were introduced, and elders who had gone on the trail to heaven were remembered.

With Suu Na chii k'chige designated their land in perpetuity, the Fort St. John Band continued their traditional way of life. They met at the reserve in the summer months and travelled on their seasonal rounds during the rest of the year. The people continued to gather at Suu Na chii k'chige until 1945, when the Department of Indian Affairs

Dane-zaa at Fort St. John, 22 October 1914. Image I-33180 courtesy of Royal BC Museum, BC Archives

turned it over to veterans of the Second World War who wanted to farm in the area.*

In 2005, we, as researchers for the Doig River First Nation, along with Patrick Cleary and Mitchell Goodjohn, researchers for the Blueberry River First Nation, undertook extensive genealogical research. For every person we proved had been alive at the time of the 1914 survey but not counted, the Blueberry and Doig First Nations would be entitled to 128 acres of land, or its equivalent, and the right to negotiate compensation for loss of use over the intervening years. The research was time-consuming and intensive. Mitchell Goodjohn even studied French calligraphy to decipher the handwriting of the Oblate priests of the nineteenth and early twentieth centuries. Our final report brought together genealogical research completed by Robin and the

---

* Later chapters offer an account of the surrender and the Dane-zaa's attempt to receive justice for the loss of IR 172.

Old Village on the Blueberry Reserve, 1966. Photo by Robin Ridington

elders in the 1960s, oral histories collected over the years, new interviews done specifically for the genealogical project, baptismal and marriage records from the Catholic Church, Hudson's Bay Company journals, and Department of Indian Affairs records. Our work was made more difficult by the use of saints' names rather than common names in church records and by the fact that the Department of Indian Affair's records did not identify women, boys, or girls by name. They were identified only by numbers in columns beside the name of the annuity pay list ticket holder.

One of the pay list holders prior to 1914 was a Cree man from Alberta named Joseph Apsassin (Cree for "small"), who had married Margaret Beaver, the sister of well-known Dane-zaa leader Ch'ǫne?. Joseph and Margaret had two sons, Edward and Dan. Edward married Nora Napoleon, whose mother was Dane-zaa and whose father, Napoleon Thomas, was an employee of the Hudson's Bay Company from eastern Canada. They raised a large family and have many descendants at Doig and Blueberry. Dan Apsassin married a Dane-zaa woman from

Halfway, Juliet Oldman (Wanaii). One of Dan's sons, Bernard, married Charlie Dominic's daughter May Dominic Apsassin, whose wisdom has enriched this book. Another son, Roy, married Erna Harvey, whose father, Harvey, was Dane-zaa and whose mother was Cree. They also have descendants at Blueberry. Today, many people in both Doig and Blueberry bear the surname Apsassin, even though their ancestry is more Dane-zaa than Cree. Many choose to identify themselves as Cree and speak the Cree language as well as Dane-zaa Záágé? and English.

Although the signing of Treaty 8 and the acquisition of the new reserves would have a strong impact on the lives of Dane-zaa in later years, the effects were not apparent to the members of the Fort St. John band immediately following these events. Indeed, the securing of reserves on good land brought some clarity to their relationship with the white immigrants to their land. The Dane-zaa continued to live as their forebears had done and to follow their seasonal trails for the next few decades. But by the end of the Second World War, the influx of white settlers had started to change their lives in dramatic ways.

11
Seasonal Rounds in British Columbia and Alberta

In Chapter 9, Nachę describes how the Yehlhézęh band moved easily between British Columbia and Alberta in the early years of the twentieth century. In 1968, Nachę also gave Robin her first-hand recollections of travelling to Alberta during her youth. She spoke of a time after the buffalo had gone but before "white man groceries" were readily available. Billy Attachie translated this story.

> When we go to trap beaver, we started out from here,
> right up to Hay River.
> There are two rivers over there.
> When we get back to the rivers,
> we get on a raft.
> We get on a raft, and we raft all the way down to here.
> After we get back here with our pack bags,
> we go to Petersen's Crossing.
>
> We are not very wealthy people ...
> If we didn't come from surviving people,
> we wouldn't be alive now, and you guys, too.
> If we came from people who weren't good hunters,
> we wouldn't be alive today.
> People really try hard to live.
> All this time, we were starving.
> We had nothing to eat all the time.

Nachę at Doig, 1966. Photo by Robin Ridington

That's how we lived.
In the springtime, too, when the people had nothing to eat,
we turned to fish.
We lived by fish. We moved to where there are fish.

We camped by the fish.
They packed all the packhorses with dried fish.
And then they moved camp to where there is moose.
Whenever they find moose and kill moose,
that's when the people eat meat.
People moved all the time.
All summer, they don't stay in one place.
And they come back in the fall time.
Sometime in the spring, we miss the winter.
We move to Alberta in spring.
In the springtime, we move to Hay Lakes [Tlugae].
We all stayed down there.
We went that far to get a moose and make dry meat.
Even if you make a lot of dry meat, people still go starving
in the wintertime.
We come from hard-working people, my ancestors,
my generation and my grandchildren.
My aunt told us they don't eat for ten days.
It's not hard.
We told her, "It can't be ten days without food."
My aunt told us, "That's nothing – ten days without food."
Sǫge [my mother's sister – father's brother's wife]
told me they went through really hard times.
When my grandpa [Yehlhézęh] was alive,
we used to move over to that hill, to Clear Hills.
They had heavy packs and packhorses.
They moved ahead to where we were going to camp.
Even they made a lot of meat, the old-timers said,
"You don't make enough meat."
After they came back from Clear Hills, they moved back to here.
When we moved back over here,
we set a big cache from four trees
and put all our stuff on top.
After the snow started, we moved somewhere else.
We moved all winter, all over.

When March time came and the snow got hard,
we moved back to our cache to get our dry meat.
We came back and ate our dry meat.
We only ate straight meat. No bannock. No flour.
When we only ate meat, sometimes we ran out.

After we finished all the meat, we were starving again.
We moved all over to kill something.
When we killed something, we had meat and would keep going,
moving place to place.
When we had bannock, after you kill one moose,
you still have food.

Now, when you have something to eat like bannock,
it feels good, but that time, we only ate straight meat.
We went through some very hard times.
Us, we are still alive. I am still alive.
Those old people, long time ago,
they all moved one way.
When we moved a long way,
we would all split up into smaller camps,
maybe four or five groups.
We moved to Tsiih Kwąh (Fort Vermilion).
When we left Tsiih Kwąh, we have to move
all the way back here to the Doig area.

Right now, it's nothing hard for people.
When we leave that place, High Level area in the fall time,
we moved all the way back up here.
We come from not very wealthy people.
We were always hungry, nothing to eat.
Right now, people don't have a hard time
when they buy something.
When we leave that place, High Level area in the fall time,
we moved all the way back up here.
When you have bannock, you got something to eat.
You feel good, live good.
When you have bannock, when it's gone, you still have
something to eat from white man's groceries.
Before that, when your groceries are gone,
you are starving again.
That is what I know. What do you think about it?
My mom never raised me, and nobody told me stories.
Nobody told me a story. I didn't even know my mom.
I didn't even know my mom.
My grandma used to say that.

(Ridington/Dane-zaa-Archive [RDA], NA-1)

Nachę's contemporary Aku also told Robin a story about the seasonal rounds that the Dane-zaa followed around the time of Treaty 8. In a single year, the band would travel from the mountains west of Fort St. John as far east as Grande Prairie, Alberta. Although the last bison were killed when Aku was young, the movements he describes in the following story show how the Dane-zaa's knowledge of resources in their large territory allowed them to survive throughout the year. Trading was certainly part of the cycle, but food supplies did not seem to have been an important trade item. As Aku says, "Fish and meat were our groceries." Billy Attachie provided this translation.

> Early spring, when the leaves start growing
> and the sap is on the poplar trees,
> when the leaves are full grown and the sap is full,
> people all get together and move to Charlie Lake,
> where the creek joins the lake, where the town is now.
> Just a little ways up the creek, that's where they used to camp.
> People all get together. All the older people,
> they all get together.
> Lots of old ladies. Lots of young boys. Lots of Dane-zaa there.
> Lots of people. Lots of girls. I know about all that.
>
> Lots of Dane-zaa. In Charlie Lake, when the leaves are small,
> people used to camp there for the fish.
> They killed lots of fish there,
> and then they fixed it up. They made fish dry meat.
> They cut them from the neck or from the back.
> They cut them from the side,
> and they don't even have to gut them.
> They just pull it out like that. When they make lots of dry meat,
> they sew it together with sinew. They make it long.
> When women make dry meat, they do the same thing with fish.
> They keep on making it and making it.
> When, after they make lots of fish dry meat,
> after the leaves are big, people all move up to wherever
> they are camping. There were no groceries.
> That time, no flour, the groceries you buy from the store now.
> There was nothing that time.
> With no groceries, what are the people going to eat?
> They just live on the fish dry meat.
> Fish and meat were our groceries.

> Then they moved way back in the bush.
> After they killed lots of moose and made lots of dry meat,
> when the berries were all ripe,
> they went back to Dane-zaa nané?, Su Na chii k'chige.
> (RDA, Aku 1966)

The summer gathering Aku describes was also a time of singing and dancing as larger groups came together during times of plenty. Charlie Lake, which lies between the mountains to the west and the Dane-zaa's hunting territories in what is now Alberta, was an important resource for many thousands of years.

> They picked berries on all those hills [east of the reserve].
> They crossed toward where there are lots of lakes
> (Megawontlonde) toward Cecil Lake.
> All the women picked berries.
> All the days, they just kept doing that, and the men hunted bear.
> There were no white people that time.
> Some of the people hunted bears.
> There were lots of bears on the hills.
> Some of them were fat already. After the berries were over,
> then they made bear grease and dry meat.
> Summertime, when they moved camp,
> they brought all the dry meat and grease
> to where they would spend the winter. It was already winter.
> In the wintertime, they made log teepees for themselves,
> where they were going to stay in the winter.
> They had lots of grease and dry meat.
>
> The berries, too, they dried them and made them like flour.
> Sometimes, they lay the berries on a tarp, and they dry them like that. They boiled the berries and then dried them flat.
> Where it was cracked, they patched it with berry juice.
> They turned it over, and where it was cracked,
> they patched it up with the berry juice.
> (RDA, Aku 1966)

Aku then described how they made birchbark horse panniers and baskets for berries. Moving food supplies from one camp to another sometimes involved several trips.

They used birchbark to make panniers and baskets,
and they filled these up with berries.
They fixed berries two different ways.
One was dry and the other flat, like pemmican.
Those berries and meat, they put it in a cache
where they are going to spend the winter.
They are always doing these things,
and that's why they lived well in the wintertime.
And they made pemmican, too, with the dry meat.
Those women made the pemmican. Good pemmican.
Dry meat pemmican.
They made it with grease and dried berries mixed.
That was good, dry meat pemmican,
grease and berries all together.
That was good. Even a small piece of pemmican,
you carry it when you go hunt.
There were no groceries in the wintertime.
That is how the people used to live.
If a person doesn't do that, then he's hungry.

Then we'd have to move out to the mountains to make dry meat.
That's where we made dry meat.
We'd eat the fish dry meat when we were travelling,
and then we got moose far away,
the other side of Grande Prairie at Tl'ok'ih Saahgii
[literally "prairie river"; Smoky River].
The women picked berries and dried them for winter.
We mixed it with bear grease.
There were lots of bears in the saskatoon berries.
It was around August time. We killed lots of bears
and cached the berries and dry meat,
and we made log teepees for the wintertime.
(RDA, Aku 4)

This seasonal round continued a pattern that elders described in stories about the time of first contact. During the early days of the fur trade, Dane-zaa hunters and their families moved eastward from the Rocky Mountains to beyond Fort Vermilion, Alberta, and back again. The stories about Duuk'ihsache and L'Homme Seul quoted in Chapters 5 and 6 demonstrate the distances the people travelled. Unlike the fur traders, whose journeys were almost always by canoe, the Danezaa used a network of overland trails that connected places hundreds of miles apart. This pattern of travel through their traditional territory, in what later became two different provinces, continued well into the twentieth and twenty-first centuries. People from Doig still go to the traditional camping grounds and remember their annual excursions to Sweeney Creek in Alberta and beyond.

May Apsassin, born in 1940, spoke to us in English about her early memories of this way of life.

> And from there, we stay in Doig and Petersen's Crossing ...
> We say "Saa gatche chu waachene"* when they say that.
> Move to river. We go help them pack up, bring the horses,
> take our teepee down. We put everything good to help our mom.
> When we camp, we pack up our teepee.
> We don't just have little bag, little bag –
> no, them panniers with the moosehide, that kind.
> If we have bunch of dry meat, we just put good, same heavy,
> this heavy, that heavy – same like that.
> If one side heavier, the saddle go like that [sideways],
> and my dad say,
> "It's gotta be the same."
> And all our dishes and everything in another one.
> Food and blankets. And that newer one is for our clothes.
> Put meat in there. Our clothes got its own – out of moosehide,
> just scraped – and they make a big sack for packing.
> And we used to go like that and we're just exciting,
> and we saddle our own. We have little lunch, our own little bags,
> and we put water, tea, there, and we got dry meat and bannock.
> We put it all good in there, and we hang it up on our saddle,
> and when we ready, we just get on and we go.
> (RDA, DZHD09-56)

Billy Attachie is a few months younger than May. The two contemporaries experienced the same events but from the perspectives of different genders. In May 2010, Billy told Robin his memories of that time.

---

* Billy Attachie couldn't determine what this meant.

This is a story about when I started remembering.
I guess you start remember things about six, seven years old.
Some places, I guess I was too young,
where all the people used to camp.
I remember where they camped, and then I don't remember they
moved from there to another camp. I was probably too young.
I was born in '41, I probably start to remember from about 1947.
I was riding behind. Two of us ride saddle horse.
The oldest one rode the horse, and I ride behind.
Every time they move camp, I rode behind people.
There was no transportation.
The only transportation we had was packhorse, saddle horse.
Lots of people, in early fall, they got a little cabin.
The cabin was a log house.
They chink it with mud, and they put the roof, maybe two feet,
foot and a half of dirt. They built a cabin, put on a roof,
and then put moss, grass, and then dirt on top.
If it's about foot and a half, so it won't leak. The water runs out.
So, the cabin is warm when the roof is good. The cabin is warm.
We don't have any floor. Just straight, like little logs.
The bed is made out of wood.
Sometime, they split the wood and make it like lumber.
They make a bed in each corner,
and then they put spruce boughs on the ground.
And they got a stove, and they got a little cook stove
right on the chimney, the stove chimney.
Sometime, they got an oven stove.
They only stayed there till spring. Early spring, they moved out.
They moved out, and they started camping, camping out,
and they camp all summer. This is the main camp in Doig,
just a little way up the hill here from the reserve, east side.
They got a bunch of cabins,
and there's some people have a winter cabin here.
Some of them were in Moose Creek.

First Mygoosh, that's where they camp.
They got a winter cabin there –
Davis, Aku, Old Man Aki. My mom's brother Ben
was married over there. He's over there with them.
And then you go to Milligan Creek, that way.
There's Ts'ibe Dané?. Lots over there, lot of people.

Tommy Attachie at Moose Creek cabin, 1981. Photo by Robin Ridington

They camp at the Big Camp, Mile 52, and Chinchaga.
It wasn't called Chinchaga.
It was called Lake Post. The name was Lake Post,
but I don't know why they changed it to Chinchaga.
Three different places, people used to live.

Ernie Petersen's store was down by the King's Valley.
In wintertime, when we go to the store, we used dog team.
My dad had a good dog. Me, Tommy, Margaret,
we went to Petersen's store with my mom and dad.
They were just like a car, the dog team. From Doig to Petersen's,
take maybe about an hour to get there with a dog team.
They can pull lots, too, dog team.
And then Petersen used to have a bunkhouse
where could people sleep overnight, maybe two nights.
When some people from over by Lake Post, they came down.
And people from Big Camp, they used to meet at the store.
When we get to store, we meet them.
(RDA, Billy Attachie, May 2010)

Between 1999 and 2006, Doig River elders took us to visit campsites they continue to use in Alberta. On 15 July 2002, we accompanied elders to a camping spot near Sweeney Creek, Alberta (McLean Creek) and documented the visit on video (RDA, DZDV02-27). Sweeney Creek is known as Chuu Degaazhih (Blackwater Creek) in Dane-zaa Záágé?. On 14 October 2006, we returned to this site and continued video documentation (RDA, DZDV06 6-7). Robin recorded a statement in English by Tommy Attachie. Tommy described his personal experiences camping in Alberta and related them to stories he remembered from his grandmother Nache. Her husband, Apaa, was a son of Chimarouche. As previously noted, the area now known as Rose Prairie was called Chimarouche's Prairie in Hudson's Bay Company journals. Tommy's narrative tells us that Chimarouche and his band used territory from Fort St. John through Chimarouche's Prairie and well into Alberta.

> I remember when we were kids. Madeline [Sagónáá? Davis]
> is older than us ... about five years older than us.
> We camp up here, way before, with packhorses.
> We go to Blackwater River. We come down this way,
> and there's a pack trail in here, where them trees is.
> That creek behind there, they call it Wolf Creek,
> and this creek is McLean Creek, and about a couple of miles up
> there, Sweeney Creek, and all join together up there.
> We camp in there, years, way before.
> I was maybe about five years old. She's older than us,
> and her, too [Madeline and May].
> And we camp in there with packhorses.
> There's a wagon trail on this,
> one there, you know, right through to Fort St. John,
> through Boundary Lake, Cecil Lake, and right to Fort St. John.
> From Peace River, wagon road, newcomers coming through
> here with the wagon, and Jim Good, who lived in Goodlow, too.
> I remember then [people telling us], you know, that back in the
> thirties, forties, and [I know that] all the way until '58,
> we use wagon here on that Boundary Lake.
> We come this way, and we camp in here for moose every summer.
> That's all we do.
> And these newcomers come in here way before,
> back in the early twenties. They take the farms all over.
> That's where they stay all the time.

After, they sold the farm and go elsewhere, somewhere.
Then other people come in there, take the land, take over.
That's how the white people live.
(RDA, DZDV06 6-7)

Tommy told us that when government agencies pressured the Dane-zaa to remain in one place and send their children to school, the people found this very difficult to do. The hunting-based economy required them to go where the animals were, and the availability of game, fish, and berries was central to the Dane-zaa way of life.

But us Native people live the land all over places
'cause we don't stay in one place.
They think we just stay one place.
Even back in fifties, when we go to school,
every September 9th, it start school them years.
So, before that, we get back to Petersen Crossing
from over here with wagon all the way through,
even though they use saddle horse, you know, wagon for kids,
and we went over there, right straight on, camping.
On the way, too, we kill moose. And after we go to school.
From there, we slow down,
but still we go out trapping and all these.
That's how they make their living.
That's why they know all the trees, all the area,
what kind of trees,
and what kind of area. That's all they know.
They've been in there. They don't have map, you know,
but way they look at the country, even fifteen years ago,
and fifteen years later, they see. Then they know where they are.

And after that, you know, we go into reserve, in 1962.
They start school in there, you know, and farming little bit.
But after that ... they think we stay in one place. We don't.
We still do it. We come up here every year.
And way back, my grandma was young, over here, Clear Prairie
[farther east, near Worsley, Alberta], they got Native people.
All the people come together. Big tea dance in there.
Many people all camp. Different tribes coming there, together
in there.

> My grandma was just young.
> Since then, this trail was in here, pack trail.
> My grandpa's dad, Old Apąą [Chimarouche],
> used to be around here somewhere.
> On this road, he was sleeping in here somewhere.
> There have been three or four generations since then.
> Still, we use this land in here.
> (RDA, DZDV06 6-7)

In the 1930s, an Alberta game warden tried to restrict the Dane-zaa's access to their traditional territory in Alberta. Tommy said that Aku spoke for his people. Aku told the warden that they had the right to hunt under the treaty and questioned the warden's authority. At Aku's request, the game warden in Fort St. John wrote to his counterpart in Alberta and reaffirmed the Dane-zaa's treaty rights. Tommy continued:

> And we were moose hunting over here, you know.
> They say we can't trap in this Alberta border,
> but Leo's grandpa, Sam Acko's dad, Old Man Aku,
> tell Indian Affairs and the game warden. After that –
> I don't know which year they make that BC border –
> after that, he told them, "You going to continue hunting moose over here, not trapping but hunting moose."
> That's what he said, you know. They write it down.
> And game warden in Fort St. John sent the letter to Peace River.
> That letter was up there. Back in 1968,
> me and my dad and family, grandma,
> we were camping up here about half a mile by the road.
> My dad told [the man at the Bear Creek store],
> "I come from Doig. There's a letter up there," he told them.
> "That's right," the man said, "you're from Doig."
> He told him that.
> That's why, you know, Old Man Aku told the game warden.
> We still use it today.
> (RDA, DZDV06 6-7)

In the time of Duuk'ihsache and L'Homme Seul, the Dane-zaa travelled overland by dog team and snowshoe or occasionally by floating a raft downstream. They had a well-established trail system. Later in the nineteenth century, when the Dane-zaa obtained horses, they travelled in summer with saddle horses and packhorses. In the 1950s and 1960s, when oil companies began to cut access roads to service seismic exploration, the Dane-zaa took advantage of the roads and obtained wagons and teams of horses. In an interview in 1999, Tommy said:

> John Davis got team horses,
> and George Sagónáá? got team horses, sleigh …
> In 1956, they make seismic road for the oil, all over …
> After that, we all buy wagons from the farmers,
> tame our own horses, train them.
> So, from there, everybody buy the wagon, you know,
> 1956, '57. Before that – packhorses. That's when I was just a kid.
> I used to ride double with my grandma,
> sometime my auntie Lena.
> With packhorses, that's how people moved.
> Way back up there, just close to Goodlow,
> where old Aki, he died there, in 1962.*
> He used to have a little cabin in there.
> Gary Ben's grandma was buried in there, on that little flat.
> People used to go to Clayhurst, camping there.
> All the women pick berries, you know, grandma and rest of them.
> They sell berries over there, and people buy moccasins,
> tea, and whatever.
>
> Nineteen seventy-seven, they got a band truck. We hunt up there, too, in '77.
> Dick Davis and his wife got a car, pickup, too,
> and the band got that pickup,
> and pretty soon people start to hunt with truck.
> (RDA, DZ99-11)

In 2002, when he recalled memories of camping in Alberta, Tommy stated:

> And we move over here every year, you know.
> That's how we travelling. This is really important for us,

---

* Aki was the last husband of Ano Atsukwa Davis, who married him after Jebís (Old Davis) died. He was the son of the Dreamer Gayęą.

> because our great-grandfather was in here.
> They live, the way they live, we still hang onto it.
>
> That was good, you know. Today, today, I see
> this wagon trail was way before.
> I remember this wagon trail was here back in the '50s still.
> No gravel road. Just a wagon road. Then, right here, where
> Madeline's walking in there, right there, wagon trail there.
> But all the trees are growing up there.
> Not too far up there, that's where we were camping.
> I was riding saddle horse with my dad and all of us kids.
> We were small. And back in 1958, I was fifteen,
> and I look after horses, you know, hunt with people.
> Today, I'm sixty-five. These boys here,
> I remember they were small that time,
> growing up. Today, they still hang onto their tradition.
> And the government thinks we just stay one place
> like the farmers do.
> Sure, we stay in reserve there. Maybe he figure we was there.
> No.
> We still hang onto the bush out there.
> (RDA, DZDV02-27)

People from Doig River continue to hunt in Alberta, but now they do it by snowmobile, all-terrain vehicle, or pickup truck. They remember the places where they used to camp with horses and wagons and often find relics of old camps at those locations. In the 1999 interview, Tommy recalled the following:

> But nothing, we see every different things there,
> these oil wells, everything. Then lots of places over there –
> the Goodlow area, south, Flat Rock area –
> we used to camp in there, too,
> but you know, there's a farmer now, today.
> Very few places we can go, 'cause there's a farmer there.
> That's why we know we were there. We see lots of things.
> On the way back, I was thinking, when we coming,
> it wasn't like that, you know,
> even these boys were looking at the place,
> you know.
> It's really different. We still go out in the bush, you know.

Tommy Davis driving Jack Acko's team and wagon, 1966.
Photo by Robin Ridington

Live off in the bush, get something.
They call this place Sweeney Creek. You can't see anything now.
I remember back, even back in 1958,
you can see long ways, all the prairie.
Just top of them hill, you can see big trees 'round here.
You can see them teepees out there.

They figure we don't use the land no more. No.
We still hang onto it.
That's why, when we translate it where we at,
how we live off the land, we just don't make it out.
We been there, we know it there,

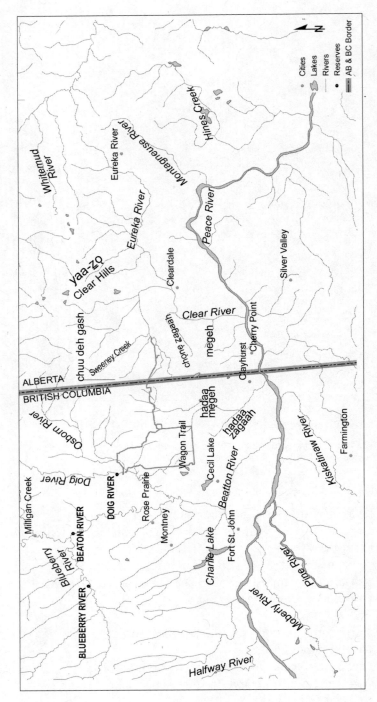

Sweeney Creek area. Courtesy of Doig River First Nation, Leanna Rhodes, and the Treaty 8 Tribal Association

we know where other people at, even though that time, people haven't got no phone or nothing
(RDA, DZ99-19)

Written records from the early twentieth century such as Frank Beaton's Hudson's Bay Company post journal include further evidence of the Dane-zaa's seasonal rounds and their excursions into Alberta. Robin interviewed Frank's son, Johnny Beaton, in 1966. Beaton said that "Attachie used to winter at Clearwater [Clear] River, halfway to Dunvegan" (RDA, field notes, 1965). Clear River is known as Ch'ǫné? Saahgii (Wolf River) in Dane-zaa Záágé?. Beaton also mentioned that "George Chipesia [Ts'ibiisaa] was from Spirit River and has a birth certificate from there." The following excerpts from Frank Beaton's journal (Glenbow Archives, M-4560-27, M-4560-28, and M-4560-29) mention the use of territory in Alberta by members of the Fort St. John band.

> January 23, 1905 Azzeddy [Azáde, Aku's father] and crowd arieved. Joseph and Le Lomus & Achie [either Tachie or Attachie] arrived from Clear water River [Ch'ǫné? Saahgii].

> January 18, 1907 Asquity [Askoty] & 5 Boys arieved from Thomas [Pouce Coupe's] camp. Report the snow very deep at Clear Hills where they are wintering they report moose very plentiful.

> July 28, 1907 the wolf [Wolf] & Joseph's step son arieved from Clear Hill.

> April 4, 1908 Joseph Appassisen and Atcha and a few other Indians patched across the River on their way to SP [Spirit] River to hunt Beaver.

> December 19, 1908 the Wolf & Thomas Boy arieved from Clear water River and report having killed a number of Bear also a few Marten. Burbanks & Chukie ... arieved from Atchas camp bring a few furs report starvation & sickness in their camp.

> January 2, 1909 the Wolf & Azzeddy's son [Aku] arieved from Clear water River.

March 31, 1915 Davis [Jebís] & 2 other Indians arieved from Clear water prairie where they have been trapping during this winter. they have sold all their Furs to Dunvevegan [sic] trader.

June 1, 1917 Thomas Puskupy [Pouce Coupe] has gone to Dunvegan having lost his son at Clear water.

January 7, 1924 the Wolf left for Grande Prairie.

Dane-zaa territories have always included a variety of habitats and ecological communities. Their seasonal rounds covered large areas in what is now the borderland between British Columbia and Alberta. Oral histories by elders such as Tommy Attachie, his grandmother Nache, and Aku tell us that Dane-zaa bands in the nineteenth-century moved regularly from Fort St. John and Rose Prairie (Chimarouche's Prairie) through Sweeney Creek (Chuu Degaazhih) and Clear Hills and farther east toward Dunvegan. The Hudson's Bay Company's post journals and our interview with Johnny Beaton confirm that both of Tommy's grandfathers, Apaa and Attachie, regularly wintered in what is now Alberta, and the journals mention other members of the Fort St. John Band following a similar seasonal round. As Tommy said, "Native people live the land all over places, 'cause we don't stay in one place. They think we just stay one place ... They figure we don't use the land no more. No. We still hang onto it ... That's how they make their living. That's why they know all the trees, all the area, what kind of trees, and what kind of area, that's all they know. They been in there" (RDA, DZDV02-27, Tommy Attachie).

12
The 1918 Flu Epidemic

By the time the Department of Indian Affairs assigned Indian Reservation (IR) 172 to the Fort St. John Band, the First World War had already begun, and when it ended, returning soldiers brought home the "Spanish flu." The flu epidemic of 1918-19 killed more people throughout the world than did the war itself. The flu found its way to Dane-zaa territory, and when it was over, many key leaders of the Fort St. John Band had died: Chief Attachie, Chief Montney (Madaayęą), Big Charlie, Yehlhézęh, and Adíshtl'íshe.

The Spanish flu epidemic claimed 70 to 100 million lives worldwide, and young adults with strong immune systems were its primary victims. Among the Dane-zaa, it killed the hunters and mothers who were most essential for the people's survival as well as the leaders mentioned above. These deaths had long-term consequences for the Dane-zaa, and it took several generations for the population to recover. Johnny Chipesia, who is the grandfather and great-grandfather of many members of the Doig and Blueberry communities, was six years old when the flu struck. In 1966, he told Robin his memories about that time. Johnny was a master storyteller, whether he spoke in Dane-zaa Záágé? or, as in this case, English. His story is long, but we include it in its entirety because it gives a vivid picture of Dane-zaa life in the years immediately following the reserve land survey, particularly how life was changed by the flu.

Johnny's story begins with a description of his family's seasonal rounds from Spirit River, Alberta, to Fort St. John and the life they led in the years immediately preceding the flu.

Johnny Chipesia with Robin's truck, 1966. Photo by Robin Ridington

Nineteen fifteen, we left Spirit River [Alberta].
I was about three or four.
I remember walking on the trail.
My uncle Charlie stayed at Spirit River,
and my dad spent the winter with him.
My uncle shot a beaver on the ice in April, the first beaver out.

My mother said, "Where you get that beaver?
We can take it to St. John and buy food for the kid."
My dad said, "OK, we leave for Fort St. John."
Just early we left, and we got to Peace River late in the evening.
My brothers, Louis and Aballi [ages one and two], camped with us.
My dad said, "We can't sleep late.
We have to cross on the ice early in the morning."
We made camp and ate beaver and moose meat.
(RDA, 1966-67)

Johnny's mother was Atohe (Ann) Montney, the daughter of Chief Montney (Madaayęa) and granddaughter of Samaloose (Chimarouche). She is listed as "Bella Madaie" on her children's baptismal records. Johnny's story describes the seasonal rounds in which people travelled regularly between their hunting territories in Alberta and Gattah Kwậh, Fort St. John. Johnny's father was Ts'ibiisaa (George Chipesia), originally from the Spirit River area. The marriage between Atohe and Ts'ibiisaa illustrates how Dane-zaa communities maintained ties between different communities through marriage. Like most men of his generation, Ts'ibiisaa spoke Cree as well as Dane-zaa Záágé?.

Johnny continues the story by describing the spring beaver hunt and the family's return to Fish Creek via Cecil Lake and the Pine (Beatton) River.

In the morning, my dad made a fire across the river,
and then we went across. My dad said,
"There are some beaver here, so we'll camp here.
I try to get a beaver for the kids to eat."
In the evening, he came back with one beaver
and gave it to my mother to skin.
We ate everything, feet, meat.
Then my dad got one more beaver with one shot.
Now, we had three beaver, because my uncle had given us one.
My dad had three dogs.
He had horses, too, but he kept them at Montney in the winter.
The next day, we camped at Cecil Lake,
and my mother set snares for rabbits.
She got one and boiled the meat with beaver fat in a kettle.
She woke me up, and my dad said, "We got to go to Pine River,
T'ohtsuugaa? [Beatton River], today.
We have to cross that river today.

Ts'ibiisaa (George Chipesia or
Japasa), 1929.
Photo by J.C. Boileau Grant

We passed lots of Indian horses on the way.
Thomas Pouce Coupe's horses. That was my dad's uncle.
But my dad said we can't take them
since we don't have any saddles.
We started to go to Pine. My mother made a fire.
We were all wet with wet snow,
and there was lots of water running on the ice.

My dad took a stick to try to cross, and one place
there was a hole on the ice, and he went through to his neck.
Then he tried another place,
and the water only came to his waist.
My mother then crossed, packing the kids.
My dad had to make lots of trips to take our stuff.
I packed kettles. Dogs packed bedrolls and stuff – teepee, axes.

"Tomorrow, we get to St. John," my dad said.
We passed Fish Creek.
Little spruce and muskeg where Indians used to camp all the time.
Four miles from river. Nobody else there. Everybody in bush yet.

Khatakose Harvey, 1929.
Photo by J.C. Boileau Grant

"You tired?"
"Yes." Little boy played out.
We made fire and ate beaver meat. No flour.
Just straight beaver meat. We went again.
We got to St. John and got to Harvey's place,
where St. John is now.

We put the teepee there.
Little spruce and muskeg where Indians used to camp all the time.
Four miles from river. Nobody else there.
Everybody else in the bush. My dad said,
"I go to St. John to get stuff." He came back late with a big pack.
"What you got there?" He had cans, cigarettes, tobacco, flour, tea,
lots of stuff. My dad talked Cree to Old Beaton.
Beaton told my dad, "Tomorrow, you come here,
downriver to spend two days."
Down there was camped Tsila,
who couldn't walk and lived off rations.
One, my dad's mother's sister *(sǫge)*.
Mekodas [Red Pants, Cree] stayed there, too.

Next day, we move over to her place.
She give me blueberries that she'd kept since summer.
She [Johnny calls her *aso̧* (grandmother)] told my dad,
"That big hill, I killed silver fox, fisher, marten. I got money.
You my relation. I buy you big tent."
She buy me mitts at Hudson's Bay, toque too,
just like big woman tits. Should be she buy in winter.
Springtime, I can't wear mitts.

Mekodas told my dad,
"Up Cache Creek, Old Thomas and Old Wolf.
About two weeks ago, they were at Hudson's Bay
and went back to Cache Creek between Halfway River."
Old Madaayȩa̧, my mother's dad, had lots of horses around top of hill. My dad found some of his horses, too.
We had saddles and pack saddles cached at Fish Creek.
All the Indians cached their things there.
Then we rode with six horses up to Charlie Lake.
Three pack- and three saddle horse.
I rode one saddle horse with the two boys behind me.
Fish Creek and Charlie Lake.

(RDA, field notes, 1966-67)

Johnny's frequent references to Fish Creek reveal that this area was an important reference point in the seasonal rounds. It was also the home territory of important elders such as Big Charlie and Johnny's grandfather Madaayȩa̧. The Lhuuge Lȩa̧ and Ts'ibe Dané? continued a pattern that, with some variations, went back over ten thousand years. In earlier times, the Dane-zaa had used fire to keep the area grassland and to support the bison population (see Chapter 4). In Johnny's time, the grasslands provided habitat for large herds of horses. Ts'ibiisaa hunted and trapped into Alberta during the winter and kept his horses in his father-in-law's territory for use after the beaver hunt.

My dad saw bear track in snow. Just out, bear, and my dad go out.
Long time he was out. My mother made camp.
Finally, he came back with meat and bear hide –
fifty dollars for hide.

First time I see bear, hide. My dad said to my mother,
"Long time he go, but I got him."
We had brown flour, rolled oats, brown sugar.
My mother cleaned hide. Next day, my dad said,
"No feed for horses. We move camp, and I look for bear again."
My mother make grease in kettle and fill bear guts with grease.
She stretch hide. We start to eat bear meat, lots of fat.
Bear soup with rolled oats, pretty good.
My dad looked for bear but didn't catch nothing.
Next morning, my dad get horse, and we start to go.
We camp halfway to Cache Creek, Red Creek. My dad say,
"I go ride around up creek, look for bear."
He take three dogs. Long time he gone,
and finally, at dark, he come back. "What you got?" "I got bear.
Sure fat. Too heavy for one horse. I get it in morning."

"No place to put the grease," my mother said. We got lots.
Next morning, my mother clean hide and put it on stretcher.
We stay there three days. My dad said,
"I look for my uncle at Cache Creek, maybe ten mile."
Late, he come back. Big stout guy, big chest, with him.
We scared for that big guy.
He tease me, and I hide behind my mother. That's Big Charlie.
He didn't kill bear, and he want bear meat and fat.
We got too much.
Next day, my dad give him half. He tell us,
"Way up Cache Creek, old Thomas stay over there."
Next morning, we move and camp by big creek one night.
Next day, we move again. Tomorrow,
we get there to Thomas camp.
My dad say, my mother say, "You play there with other kids."
Seven teepees: Attachie, Thomas, Wolf, Chekyass,
Dick (whose wife come from Spirit River), Ustan [Justin] Attachie,
John Davis wife first man [Burbank].
They told my dad, "Lots of water. Lucky you don't kill these kids."
"We stay Cecil Lake and kill rabbits," my mother say.
Davis _sı́ze_ [my father-in-law] had daughter, Ahahaen.
I play with her.
"Lucky you don't kill kid. Long trip," Thomas said.

We start to move around and get to 111.*
Dane dawehtsats, people dance. Alédzé make big party there.
Everybody hunt bear. Thomas was head guide to move.
Just like chief. He tell people which way to go.
Some boys get the horses. When we got whole bunch together,
people started to go hungry. Some roots we ate down by river.
Wild corn, some people know [probably cattail, *T. latifolia*].
We cook it in kettle, and kids eat good. But no meat.
We start hungry. That time, too many Indian and not much moose.
Thomas say, "It's hard to get bear."
He come in morning, and all men sat down outside.
He say about three people take packhorse
and go to St. John to get flour. We can't get meat.
Finally, three days, they come back with flour, beans, and
rolled oats, and they pass around.
They got it on credit.
Every family got his order on credit.
Beaton know just what the Indians wanted.
He marked down bills, "1111" and "x."
Indians all knew how to read these marks.
That time, not much money, just debts. He give you slip, no cash.
Ustan, Attachie went. After, somebody got a bear,
maybe Chekyass, and everybody got meat and bear fat.
(RDA, field notes, 1966-67)

Johnny's comment that Thomas was "just like chief" because "he tell people which way to go" illustrates that Dane-zaa leadership is based on knowledge and experience rather than on the authority of a title. People are willing to follow a leader who knows the way, just as they follow Dreamers who know *yaak'ihts'ę? atanii,* the trail to heaven. The dancing ground at Mile 111 is still considered a special and sacred place by the Blueberry people.

We start to move, Montney, St. John.
About June, everybody come back.
Moberly Lake, Rose Prairie, Montney people.
Thomas say, "Another ten days. Everybody go."
We got summer cache at Blueberry.

---

* Near what is now mile 111 on the Alaska Highway.

> Had cache and my dad met him there.
> He had moose, lots of fresh meat. I see him.
> "Asea [grandfather], you take lots of dry meat."
> Everybody go to St. John, sometimes five kids on one horse.
> Attachie had two wives and about eleven kids.
> His sister's kids, too.
> His sister's kids. One was Mrs. Field, Attachie's uncle's kid.
> Ustan was her dad, but he died.
> Ustan and Peter Attachie were twins.
> Each had two girls.
> (RDA, field notes, 1966-67)

In the next passage, Johnny describes the ancient practice of creating fish weirs in Fish Creek, the stream that runs out of Charlie Lake. According to the archaeologists excavating the Charlie Lake site, the area has been stable for thousands of years. The pattern of taking suckers from the stream probably goes back to when the first people lived in the area. Sadly, the elders told us that when white people built a dam at the end of Charlie Lake, the dam blocked their spawning run. The white people also stocked the lake with jackfish, which quickly devoured the suckers. Within one generation, a resource the Dane-zaa and their ancestors had managed for ten thousand years was eliminated. A pub called Jackfish Dundee's now occupies land at the end of the lake.

> We camp at creek, and everybody go after fish.
> Put lots of stick in water, and some guy chase them,
> and they get caught in there. Lots of fish, suckers in every camp.
> Kids just ate the tongues and eyes and cheek meat.
> Too many bones for them. Old people could watch it and ate meat.
> After, we go to St. John and met lots of Indians.
> Fairview. Hudson's Hope. Rose Prairie. Just big stampede.
> Long jump. High jump. Play. Gamble. Dance.
> Pretty soon, no meat. Get lots of fish. Some more dance.
> Lots of brown flour. Hudson's Bay smart.
> Everything second-hand.
> He eat white flour, but poor trappers get second-grade flour.
> Good trappers get white.
> If mice got in warehouse and spoiled flour,
> that's poor trapper's food.

Summertime, people just had fun. Just like a stampede.
They stayed at St. John for a month.
After, maybe three, ten families went into bush.
Hythe. Beatton River. Pink Mountain. Fontas.
In the fall time, they all came back.
My father and twenty other families, about August –
St. John, Jack Pine, Peace River, Smoky, Spirit River –
and back hunting moose.

My mother started to get sick.
No doctor that time.
They tried the medicine man, but he couldn't help.
Old Crees Apsassin and Calahazen tried but can't stop it.
Finally, she couldn't ride, and they made a stretcher.
For six days, four guys carried her in this blanket stretcher.
Every three or four miles, they changed people
and made ten miles a day. They went to St. John,
Happy's place [Suu Na chii k'chige],
and all Indians came back there in fall.

My mother lost her mind and just talk.
Two white people, old Muhwuk lived there
and tried to do something.
He made hot towel and looked after her for three nights.
My mother passed out [died].
That time, when people died, they put them on stick in tree.

I was just kid then, and I don't know. I think she sleep.
I start to sing, one Cree song.
Old Madaayęą [Johnny's mother's father]
saw me singing, and he got mad. He swear.
"You sing, your mother die." He swear at me. Now she died.
Then I stood under where she hung and cried. I held a blanket.
Madaayęą cried then, too. But he told me she was gone.
I said, "No, she's over there yet."

November she died.
Hudson's Bay man brought whipsaw lumber,
and people made a nice box for her. I watched.
I don't know why they put my mother in the ground.
That night, little snow. Fox, he come to graveyard.

Dad told Peter Attachie to set trap there.
He wants to die, too.
Next morning, we got silver fox worth $1,200.
Maybe that fox friend.

Then I got a new mother – Old Man Madaayęą, his wife.
But then my dad took me and Aballi
back to Spirit River, and we had a hard time.
Other kids beat us up. My mother, before she died,
told him not to get a wife for ten years, and he did that, too.
My mother smart. Maybe another woman beat us up.
Five years we live around Fairview, Peace River,
Hay River, Spirit River.
Mother died same summer as Mak'íhts'ęwéswąą, 1916.
(RDA, field notes, 1966-67)

In his journals, Frank Beaton notes the death without further comment on 29 October 1916: "Japasia's wife died early this morning" (Glenbow Archives, M-4560-29. In Johnny's story, however, it is clear that Beaton did what he could to give Johnny's mother a burial in the white people's way. Johnny's father died in 1964, and Robin witnessed the event. Before he died, silver foxes came to visit him and say goodbye. At that time, Johnny told Robin the story of Ts'ibiisaa's vision quest, during which the foxes came to him for the first time (see Ridington 1987, 51-61 for the full story). After Johnny's mother died, one of Madaayęą's wives took over caring for her grandsons, including Johnny. At the time, Madaayęą had two wives, an older and a younger one. The older one, Katige, would have been in her late fifties or early sixties at the time. The younger one, Achue, was only twenty-two and had a two-year-old girl named Maria to look after. We cannot be certain which of these women became Johnny's "new mother," but it was likely the older one.

My dad came back to St. John then, 1917.
I wasn't even seven.*
We stayed around St. John all summer.
Old Muta-iin (Madaayęą,) stayed around Nig Creek
winter after my mother died.

---

* Our genealogy shows that Johnny was born in 1912. He would have been five years old in 1917.

> In winter, twenty families stayed together.
> Not many moose but lots of beaver.
> Finally, Madaayęą said, "Same bunch together; maybe we starve."
> St. John, Fish Creek, we had lots of caches.
> Some killed rabbits. Old Madaayęą's wife sure smart
> and got one rabbit every night.
> Some kids just ate the bones.

Madaayęą was a wise leader who understood that a large group of people living together was more likely to starve than several smaller groups spread out over a wider area.

> Pretty soon, all the kids were crying.
> Too much snow to find the wild corn. My dad said,
> "I see two caribou tracks." Old Madaayęą said,
> "Well, we go after the squirrels."
> He shot a squirrel, and we ate it.
> Then Madaayęą got two caribou.
> Old Attachie ran away to St. John with one wife and three kids.
> He left all the rest with Madaayęą to take care of.
> Madaayęą came back to St. John. He said,
> "Not like a man to leave a wife and kids there."
> When he got to St. John, Beaton's bookkeeper Sabacis
> came over with team, with food.
> Attachie broke road, and ten families stayed together.
> Madaayęą got caribou, and we ate everything, even blood.

> One night, we heard dog bell, and big dog team came with grub.
> Attachie had asked for it. Cook big bacon and bannock.
> That bacon was as big as a door.
> He brought lots of food, and all the kids were happy.
> Everybody had lots of fur, and the Hudson's Bay man took it back.
> People used to live in teepees of split trees, wind hole.
> Man would leave family in teepee
> and hunt and trap by himself five nights.
> After they cleaned up one place, headman would say,
> "OK, we move."
> They would go twenty miles, stay maybe one, two weeks.
> They'd make a road out to where they trapped.
> After Hudson's Bay man went back,

> Chinook came, and we got three moose.
> Madaayęą knew they were there.
>
> Madaayęą got a moose. Maybe ten families stayed there.
> Some women got no man.
> "Well, we got to go to St. John before June and get a bear."
> My dad pretty near starving then.
> He broke trail, sweated, didn't eat all the time.
> We just ate rabbit guts. We went over there.
> Douya [Wonla], Charlie Dominic's dad,
> he broke trail down north of Rose Prairie.
> There were ten families camped there. We started off.
> Madaayęą said, "We go there. Maybe we ..."
> Yehlhézęh, an old man from Rose Prairie, told Douya
> to tell Madaayęą to come there and shoot beaver.
> We didn't have rubbers or socks, just moccasins,
> and they just got wet.
> Pine River high. Old Mazuukii made a raft.
> Too old to hunt. He just cut raft and made trail.
> He helped with camp and with women.
> Mezuke helped us all across. Somebody got a small moose,
> and we had some white people food. So we ate.

Johnny's story at this point parallels Nachę's story in Chapter 9. In both stories, the Dane-zaa's fortunes vary from season to season and from year to year. Early spring could be particularly difficult. Food from the traders made it possible for people to survive when game was scarce.

Johnny continued his story by describing how the Lhuuge Lęą and Ts'ibe Dané? helped each other.

> We started to get to Yehlhézęh place. Big beaver dam place.
> Lots of people there. Yehlhézęh told Madaayęą,
> "We leave kids here, and we all go hunt beaver.
> Young people go far – Fontas, Hay River. Everybody go."
> That time, I cried from hunger.
> Madaayęą, Yehlhézęh tried but couldn't get moose.
> Maybe just one beaver. Lots of people to feed,
> maybe a hundred people, so beaver didn't go far.
> Jim, Yehlhézęh's boy, sent to St. John.

Took horse to St. John to get grub. Madaayęą told him,
"If you see Harvey, tell him to bring our horses."
Long time he's gone. Then big noise on the trail,
and he brought down lots of horses.
Everybody made their own saddles then
from spruce roots and babiche.
People made own ropes, too, from babiche.

Harvey came. I knew him before.
He brought fancy, long stick candy.
First time I saw he gave me lots of clothes.
He brought horses close to Pine, to Petersen place, Bone Creek.
Yehlhézęh and Madaayęą stayed in camp,
but all young men went out to get beaver.
Maybe fifty women. Harvey had brought lots of food.

Madaayęą told Harvey and George and Jim,
"Take eight horse, more food to Fontas, Hay Lake."
And he went over there.
Halfway, he met Yehlhézęh boys and Abąą.
They all made moosehides just like woman.
My dad brought seventeen beaver, and other got maybe five or six.
Came Rose Prairie, Petersen place.
Everybody started to come back.

Old Madaayęą, around end of June, went to St. John.
Yehlhézęh and Madaayęą made raft across Pine River,
and all day they took people across.
Have to pull raft up each time. People camped on the other side.
Ustan and Peter Attachie came from St. John and saw my dad.

Then everyone went to St. John.
Lots of old Cree sold medicine to Indians.
My dad buy from old Wabi [Whitehorse].
My dad had lots of cross at Hudson's Bay.
"I give you good moose medicine. You see moose tracks,
open medicine, put food and medicine in tracks. You get him.
You get branch moose eats, you put it in track."
"Sounds good. How much?"
"Two horse, $300. Good medicine. You can sell 'em anytime."
All time, Cree beat Beaver.

My dad had fancy cross belt and put medicine in it.
OK, my dad he got medicine now. Madaayęą say,
"I heard you got good medicine. Old Thomas, too."
Next year, he went across Smoky.
Old Madaayęą. Attachie. Big Charlie.
Asea Billike. Mudis [Modeste]. Madzuusgwalaa.
All summer, we go around Dawson, Pouce Coupe,
and come back to St. John, October.
Left horses, then took dog teams.

That time, new store set up. Different people, not Hudson's Bay.
Good man there. Wood box of candy.
First of July, money man came and give everybody five dollars,
kids too.
This time, we went to Hudson's Bay to buy candy.
Fall, we come back to town,
and everybody go to Cache Creek to trap.
Up to Cameron Creek, this side of Halfway, twenty families.
We started hungry. Three, four days, no moose. We got hungry.
Ate porcupine, everything we could find.
My dad had little camp for himself and two dogs.
Old Madaayęą came over one night.
"Saazę [son-in-law], I heard you got good medicine.
We starving now.
I want to use. I buy him three cross, two horse besides tobacco."
"OK," Dad said. Old Mudis [Modeste] with him, too,
and sang medicine song. My dad couldn't sing that time
[because of a personal medicine taboo].
We go to place for moose. I go, too, with snowshoes.
"Don't look. Medicine might hurt your eyes."
Moose last food. He break stick, and Mudis sang song.
Put medicine on stick in tracks.
Finally, an hour, we had gun ready, but no moose.
Sundown, and we cold. No moose. My dad, cold.
Maybe we not put right that medicine.
Tomorrow, we try just fresh tracks. I don't go next day.
Too cold. Same thing next day. Just like that man tell him.
He wait four hours, but no moose.
Then he throw that medicine away.
Beaver Indian just buy for nothing.
Sometimes buy Hudson's Bay candy with feathers on it.

Johnny offers a wry commentary on the difference between Dane-zaa medicine and that of the Dahshíne (Cree). When a Dane-zaa person receives power from an animal friend, it is personal and private. The animal friend would be offended if a person tried to brag about or sell his or her power. Cree medicine, at least as the Dane-zaa saw it, was quite different. Crees were willing to sell medicines they claimed would be useful in love or hunting. As Johnny reports, these promises seldom materialized.

> That spring, we went up the Pine, Nig Creek, 147
> [Mile 147, Alaska Highway]
> to Pink Mountain by spring time.
> We went down Cache Creek and Cameron Creek,
> and by June we got to St. John again. That was a hard time.
> Holy geez, sometimes we got nothing to eat.
> Cameron Creek, bear start come out, and someone kill one,
> but too many people for one bear.
> Got wild corn chopped from ice. Eat lots.
> Dick Atsukwa got two moose across Cameron Creek
> and made raft.
> Women packed meat across. Young people got horses at St. John
> and brought them to Cameron Creek.
> Then we went to creek by Charlie Lake,
> and suckers started to run there. Whole bunch camped there.
> Old guy, Huhe, said, "You come right time. I made fish trap."
> Everybody camped and got big sacks of fish.
> Kids ate tongues and eyes. Made soup.
> Lots of fat in fish guts.
> That's good, I figure, that time. I don't know nothing.
> My sǫge, Madaayęą and Katige, Charlie Mudis, Ano Davis, all
> went to Fish Creek, St. John, Rose Prairie, Dunvegan.
>
> Everybody boss himself. Madaayęą not boss.
> My old lady [Julie] got two sisters and one brother.
> There around ten families: Madaayęą, George, Dick
> [Atsukwa, Johnny's wife's father].
>
> Made lots of fish dry meat. That's summer lunch.
> Not many moose that time. People had to stay together.
> Not many good hunters.

Ano Davis (Dedama) on horseback, 1950s.
From Charlie Dominic's photo album

If good hunter tracks a moose, he's got to get it.
Harvey came then and told Madaayęą that Big Charlie
and lots of old people were at Fish Creek.
We took horse and dry meat and went down there.
That's first time I saw Old Apsassin.
I played with Dan Apsassin, a boy my own age.
Old Apsassin gave me bacon and bannock.
His old lady [Margaret Beaver] cooked dry saskatoon berries.
I saw his mouth was just black. That old lady, too.
Every day, Dan and Ed [Apsassin] and I went swimming at Fish
Creek. I didn't know how. Before, I put a big stick to help me.
Two weeks, I swim good.

All kinds of Indians there. Saulteaux from Moberly Lake, Cree.
One night, Saulteaux dance. One night, Cree.
One night, our people.
Old Beaton and all his family, just same Indian. They dance, too.
Some night, you have to pay to dance.
Some night, old Cree song, you got to trade something.
I want to dance. Maybe Sam. I give him hat.
Then Sam give me moccasin. Poor people can't dance,
just trade, but sometimes Cree beat Indian too much.
Policeman stop it. Ferried across river. Big dance two weeks.
Old Madaayęą, Attachie, Big Charlie, all head guys, said,
"You stop it. You beat us too much."

That summer, 1918,
people went across Peace River to the Pine River.
So many horses went across,
they stretched all the way across the river.
Each camp had four or five dogs. Hudson's Bay boat ferried.
Gee, talk about dogs. When people move, the dogs fight.
So many people and dogs and horses,
the first people were an hour ahead of the end.
Not many saddles that time, or halters.
Lots of people ride with just blanket.

People say lots of moose over Smoky River. Everybody go there.
My dad said, "Too many people for boat. I make a raft."
Way up the river, he made a raft
and put on axe, gun, kettle, saddle.
I had one Asea Billike made me. My dad paddled on back,
had two paddles.
I stayed on front, Aballi [Johnny's brother] behind.
He told me to hold on to rope, not move.
My dad, "Where we go?" Well, we went too far up.
Pretty soon, we get to place.
I saw big pile of people stuff on shore, and we landed there.
Before flu, hundreds of people. Not much to eat, though.

My sister started to marry that time. Old Man Davis got her.
Two years. Two women then. One was Appama.
Just all on one hill. All day, canoe cross. No place to camp.
I saw one horse drown. John Davis got one horse.

> His head down, up, then down. He went under.
> Then I saw him float, belly up. John just cried for his horse.
> One Halfway guy said, "Don't cry for horse.
> That blue horse, you break him." Not relation, too.
> He got too many horse, that man.
>
> We move then, different people.
> One old Cree named "Laughing Lots."
> Pouce Coupe, there was one store and police house.
> Policeman had stick across road. Few little cabins around.
> Policeman say, "Not supposed to be you St. John people
> come to Alberta. Where you going?"
> Madaayęą say, "I go to my daughter's sister's boy.
> I'm Indian. I can go anywhere to live, make dry meat."
> Policeman just look down. Finally, say, "OK."

Aku recalled a similar confrontation with Alberta game wardens who attempted to prevent the Dane-zaa from hunting in their traditional territories on the Alberta-side of the border (see Chapter 11). Both Madaayęą and Aku successfully cited the treaty to remind officials of their hunting, trapping, and fishing rights throughout their traditional territories.

Johnny continued his story:

> Down to river from Pouce Coupe, Madaayęą and us camped.
> Horse Lake. Hythe. Little Smoky River. Lots of moose then.
> That's the last time. For nothing they make all that dry meat.
> Aku's mother started to die. She walked with two sticks.
> She raised my dad, that old lady.
> That poor old lady pounded dry meat,
> and Sam threw a bunch of mud to tease her.
> Old Aku just about choked him for that.
> That old lady, Ahguuhgaa, walked with her crutches.
> "Don't hit him," she said.
> She fell over, little windfall, and fell over.
> She didn't get up then. We tried to get her up, but she died.
> Her tea was still in the cup in her camp.
>
> This was the last trip to the river.
> They came back with lots of dry meat,
> so much that they would have to take horses to next camp

Jebís (Old Davis) and son John, 1929. Photo by J.C. Boileau Grant

   and then go back for another trip.
Down by Jackpine, white man with one eye [Hue] got canoe.
Three days it took to go across at that place.
People stay Cecil Lake
and then to muskeg, where St. John is now.

Johnny's story continues and relates the terrible flu of 1918. Davis (Jebís) knew the flu was coming and brought down a song to warn people.

   That prophet, Gayęą, came over there.
Old Davis, too. Old Madaayęą. All big old-timers.
In the morning, that prophet, medicine man, made a new song.
The people danced three days. That song, talking song,
"People Move to Heaven." After that, start cold.
Everybody went to stores at St. John and took stuff,
blankets and all. Old Madaayęą went three camps away;
Big Charlie, Charlie Lake.
My dad, Asea Billike, Davis, Djari took me to
Spirit River. Lucky, he take me, too.

We stay winter at Clear Prairie, this side Hines Creek.
Nobody know flu.

One morning, Old Davis, funny song he sing.
Charlie Wolf left his old lady. Charlie Wolf, Dan Wolf,
Taneshun, Aske Kuleą, and Wolf's sons stayed with my dad.
Davis sing in morning. What kind of song.
He say, "Nobody live. Pretty soon, you hear bad story."
He say, "Everyday, shoot down the road to chase away flu."
Old Aku know old people story. He told my dad,
"We gots lots ammo. We go try."
Five nights they did that.
Old Davis stood outside teepee and talked.
"You lucky. You shoot him."

Pretty soon, Jim Jedeya [sic], Yehlhézęh boy,
and Jack Appaw come.
Lamas, white people from Spirit River, came with team.
Had store. Aku went to store with team. I got one weasel.
"What you want?" "Brown sugar."
Three night he came back with one big sack brown sugar.
Fur good price then. "You get me sugar.
Hwana [elder brother], you carry my sugar."

Sundown, we heard people cry, coming from St. John.
Something happen. Jim and others coming. "What happen?"
"You see. Nobody left." I cry and dance when I hear that.
Then, Fairview people came, too.
Nobody left there, too. Alex Moose people.
My dad went to St. John and made grave for Madaayęą.
Six days we travel. I go too. I walk little snowshoes.
My dad, Charlie Wolf, me, Aske Kuleą went.
Some relations left, and we made grave.
Attachie, Big Charlie, Madaayęą – gone. We got to St. John.
Madaayęą's wife, Katige, we met her.
Harvey's sister, Jack Appaw's wife, his other wife.
Asea stay there too long. We went up to Montney.
Put good clothes on him. He was still in tree.
About ten people dead there. My dad made big spruce box.
Madaayęą had big bag full of silver.
My dad put it in the box with him. Prospectors give him silver.

> He don't use money at St. John.
> He just save it.
>
> Atluke and Wolf there, too, and helped.
> From Charlie Lake, just Charlie Yahey and wife,
> Yehlhézęh daughter. Peter Attachie [his wife died],
> Aanaatswęą [Bella Yahey], and Julie Chipesia.
> When we got to Charlie Lake, graveyard just half-finished.
> Some people, ears, nose gone. Mice put house in lungs.
> You take blankets off old people, mice all run.
> After we finish, we go back again. We no get flu.
> Must be we shoot that make it OK.
> We go Spirit River.
> Old Djari and seven people playing cards. All dead.
> Money all around. My dad take that Djari money.
> Djari old lady die making wood.
> My dad work lots making graves.

Old Man Aku (Ray Acko) was a generation older than Johnny Chipesia. He was in his eighties in 1966, when he told Robin his memories about the flu (RDA, Beaver Tales), and would have been in his late thirties in 1918. Liza Wolf translated this story.

> We used to live at Fort St. John.
> One summer, we all moved to the mountains.
> Charlie Kulęą [Big Charlie, for whom Charlie Lake is named],
> all of us used to live there.
> It used to be that the Ts'ibe Dané?, Muskeg people, lived there.
> A whole bunch of us moved to the Hanás Saahgé? River
> (Doig River).
> One day, we all got colds.
> We all started coughing, every one of us.
> My *hune* [older brother] Kulęą Nachę,
> Old Man Wolf's oldest brother,
> was the only one who wasn't sick.
> We moved away from there,
> but one family was too sick to move.
> So we moved, and every night, every night,
> we were getting worse and worse.
> My dad and our family moved along the Hanás Saahgé? River
> by ourselves, even though we were sick.

Atluke, 1929.
Photo by J.C. Boileau Grant

The sickness was really bad.
When we eat meat, it tasted no good.
It tasted just like a tree. We couldn't eat much.
That sickness was really strong. Yehlhézęh's wife died,
and two of Damas's [Thomas Pouce Coupe's] sons died.
Three were dead.
It was a strong sickness, but that is all that died.

Aku's small band was lucky. Among other groups, the death toll was much worse. Scientists have recently learned that the flu virus causes an overreaction of the body's immune system. That is why it ravaged the bodies of young adults with strong immune systems. There were fewer deaths among children and older adults. This explains why many of those who died were hunters and women of child-bearing age, the people most needed to keep a population strong and healthy. It took many, many years for the population to recover.

Many leaders were also among the dead. In his journal, Frank Beaton reports that on 23 January 1919, "The Deaf Boy and 3 others arieved from the North and report the death of Adisles [the Dreamer Adíshtl'íshe] and Matchakie [Felix Makadahay] and all the women in Camp" (Glenbow Archives, M-4560-29).

Billy Attachie's grandfather, Chief Attachie, 1915.
Used with permission of Billy Attachie

Chief Attachie and most members of his family also perished. He was buried on a bluff overlooking the confluence of the Peace and Halfway rivers. Cora Ventress, Marguerite Davies, and Edith Kyllo's *Peacemakers of the North Peace* (1973, 17) includes a report that a girl named Narlie, about six years old, was found in Attachie's camp during the winter of 1918-19. Although Narlie had lost her foot from frostbite, she survived. All others in the camp were found dead. She was raised by white people and later lived in Edmonton.

13
Losing Suu Na chii k'chige, the Great Fire, and Petersen's Crossing

While the Dane-zaa dealt with the influenza epidemic, a threat even more devastating to their traditional way of life was coming to their territory. Political and boundary changes that would affect them long into the future were taking place in a changing and developing Canada. Northern Alberta was included in the North-Western Territory until 1870, when it and Rupert's Land became Canada's North-West Territories. The district of Alberta was created as part of the North-West Territories in 1882. British Columbia had joined Confederation in 1871, and in 1884 it granted the federal government a twenty-mile-wide belt on either side of the Canadian Pacific Railway in return for aid during the CPR's construction. To compensate for the non-arable land included in these railway lands, the dominion government would also gain 3.5 million acres in the fertile Peace River area. Disputes between the federal government and the provincial and territorial governments delayed the transfer. But after Alberta became a province in 1905, the land was surveyed, and the federal government took possession of the Peace River Block in 1907. The boundaries of the block extended thirty-five miles north and south of the Peace River and seventy-four miles west of the Alberta–British Columbia border – all of which was within the Dane-zaa's traditional territory. In 1912, the government announced that the land would be thrown open for homesteading (York 1981, 7).

Settlers soon followed. The Cadenhead family, "the first settlers to arrive with the intention of settling" in the Peace River area, arrived in 1912 (Ventress, Davies, and Kyllo 1973, 16). The number of newcomers increased slowly in the years following the First World War. Under the terms of Treaty 8, the Dane-zaa retained the "right to pursue their usual vocations of hunting, trapping and fishing throughout the tract surrendered ... saving and excepting such tracts as may be required or taken up from time to time for settlement, mining, lumbering, trading or other purposes." Conflicts were bound to arise, but in the early years of the agreement accommodation was the norm. The Peace River area had space in abundance, and contact between the Dane-zaa and the newcomers was limited for years. The settlers either respected the Dane-zaa or ignored them. Monica Storrs, "God's Galloping Girl," a woman who did missionary work for the Church of England in the area from 1929 to 1939, hardly mentions the "Beaver Indians" in her otherwise comprehensive diaries (see Storrs 1999 and Morton 1979). The Dane-zaa adapted to the settlers' presence, as they had always accommodated to change.

A few settlers became friends with the Dane-zaa. In 1982, Billy Attachie introduced Robin Ridington to some of these old-timers, including Slim Byrnes, who came to the Peace River country in 1928. During an interview, Byrnes introduced himself with decorum and talked about how his early fear of the Dane-zaa turned to respect and friendship.

> I'm going to talk a little bit about the early days here, when I first came into this country – that was back in 1928. It seems I never really get tired of talkin' about the early days – the trappers, the Native people, cowboys, and all the people that come up along the old trails and all this. When I first come in, I was a teenager, and I was quite bashful. And when I used to meet some of these Indians ridin' along on these fancy horses in them days – they were tall people, and they were very shy, too – and they might just nod to me and just talk a little bit of sign language to start with, because I was almost shakin' in my boots. I didn't know just how to take these people, and us people comin' in here, and the homesteadin', and, uh, kinda infringin' a little bit on the huntin' grounds. They probably felt the same way toward us.
>
> So, it was quite a little while before I found out that they could talk pretty good in a mixture of Beaver and English or whatever you want, maybe a little French throwed in for good measure. And I could communicate with these people pretty

Slim Byrnes, 1982. Photo by Robin Ridington

good. And 1928 is when I come in, the summer of 1928, and I filed on a homestead here at Cecil Lake, in the fall of 1928. And, uh, I worked for a fur trader that winter up at Montney, where he run a sort of a tradin' post and some stuff up there, and I was a kind of a chore boy and a good man Friday around there because, at that time, they didn't seem to be very anxious to take me right into the middle of the fur trade at my age, in 1928. So, it wasn't until the followin' year that I really got involved with 'em in a big way.

I think my first venture meetin' with the Indian people ... Lee Stringer and I, a friend of mine from Saskatoon, Saskatchewan, who was up here, and we used to ride together quite a bit, we were comin' across from Rose Prairie, which was then named Whiskey Creek, and comin' through what we called the Big Flats here on the Beatton, on what we used to call the Old Cree Trail [actually a Dane-zaa trail] – we still do, whether that's the right name for it or not I'm not sure – when we got to the top of the hill on this side. We looked back down into the valley, and that whole valley down in there below Clark's was filled full of teepees, and there must've been at least a hundred head of horses. And it was in midsummer, and it had been a

Winnis Baker, 1982. Photo by Robin Ridington

very, very productive summer, and the horses were fat, and they were shiny. They built their campfires down there and started playing their drums, in 1929, which is fifty years ago. It done somethin' to me that I shall never forget, with kind of mixed feelings, and we stayed up there and stayed and stayed on top of the hill and grazed our horses and looked down into the valley and watched their campfires and seen them dancing around the fires. And that was my first really big experience with the Indians. They called it a tea dance. And, now, why they all joined there or not I don't know. It wasn't too far over to what was then the big Indian reserve at Fort St. John, what later was all broke up and sold to the soldiers' settlement and that kind of people. (Ridington/Dane-zaa Archives [RDA], G-28)

The first half of the twentieth century brought the Dane-zaa new neighbours who practised farming and ranching. Some of them were contractors, engineers, and troops with the US Army who came through in 1942 to build the Alaska Highway and decided to stay. Winnis Baker came to the north Peace River country with her husband, Garfield Baker, at that time. Billy Attachie introduced us to her in 1982, and she told us about those days.

> I remember when we first came here to work on the Alaska Highway. A lot of the boys had these most beautiful buckskins, embroidered, you know, on the coats. These boys, of course, when they went back east with these beautiful coats, you know, you never see anything like that down there. Tell you, they just walked down the street, everybody's eyes would open up, you know. "Where did you get a thing like that?" 'Cause they really made a beautiful job of those things.
>
> You see, nearly everyone that worked here on the highway, the civilians, were from back east, because at that time there weren't any construction outfits in the West that were large enough. Like you had to have fifteen to twenty cats [Caterpillar tractors], or they wouldn't even hire you, you know. Two cats was no good. It was too much looking after to have a camp for two cats, so they got bigger contractors from down east.
>
> My husband was what was known as a cat skinner, and they had to have the operators for these big machines to build the road. They were big machines then, but they were pretty small machines by our eyes now. But they were pretty big machines coming into a country where people had only been used to horses and that. It was quite a thing for the people to see those, the construction, and how fast they moved. You know, when you think of that distance to be done in eight months, it's – I bet they couldn't do it today. (RDA, G-31 and G-32)

Baker was right: the Dane-zaa were astounded by the big machines. In the 1960s, Johnny Chipesia told Robin that when the first "cat" came through the woods near where the people were camping, one older woman who was picking berries hurried back to their camp shouting, "Úsá? k'éguch! Úsá? k'éguch!" or "Kettles walking! Kettles walking!" She had seen and heard the bulldozers crashing through the bush and used the only terms she knew to describe a noisy machine that emitted exhaust that looked like steam. Other roads and seismic lines were built. They gave white men's vehicles easier access but often obliterated ancient Dane-zaa trails. Gerry Attachie told us about how the Dane-zaa reacted to the cats and other machines.

> First time they said they seen cats, eh, boy they were surprised.
> I guess they went to follow the cats going in the bush.
> Then they, them old, some old people, they remember.
> Somebody told them they gonna make a bridge at Peace River, at Peace River now. They just laughed. They wouldn't do that, they said, "It's too wide, and then they gotta have long posts, you know, long big trees." But this guy told them, that Hudson's Bay manager, Beaton, I guess he told them, "Oh, they gonna build a bridge here. Fort St. John will be big town." And they don't think, they just laugh. They should see that now!
>
> (RDA, Broomfield et al. 1984)

Tommy Attachie recalls being told that the Alaska Highway was originally going to begin at Peace River, Alberta, but "the farmers don't want that big highway through there" (personal communication with authors, 10 July 1984). Without the consent or knowledge of the Dane-zaa, plans were changed, and the highway began at Dawson Creek, BC. The building of the Alaska Highway and the end of the Second World War accelerated the pace of change in the Peace River country. As part of their attempt to help war veterans get re-established on their return to Canada, the federal government offered "vets" farmland in remote areas. One of the areas they thought suitable for farming was Indian Reserve (IR) 172.

Despite the importance of Suu Na chii k'chige to all the Dane-zaa, the Departments of Indian Affairs and Veterans Affairs believed that veterans returning from the war would need the land more – that they, unlike the Dane-zaa, would cultivate it. A detailed discussion of the events leading to the "surrender" and the loss of IR 172 in 1945 appears in Chapter 14. In the decades immediately following the loss, few Dane-zaa understood what had happened. The Dane-zaa were promised money for the reserve, but the $70,000 the band received was credited to the Fort St. John Band's account with the Department of Indian Affairs, and individual band members saw little benefit. In the 1970s, Charlie Dominic and other elders still wondered what had happened to the old reserve. As Charlie told us in 1979:

> Two times we get, uh, ten dollars apiece. Little kids, too.
> Just now, I see reserve, lots of oil. All over.
> Montney, this way town, all over.

> That time he [the Indian Agent]
> never told people about the oil, huh?
> That time, first time he say, he say,
> some place on reserve, oil. He say maybe get the oil.
> (RDA, RR-2)

After the surrender, the old reserve was developed as farmland, and the Dane-zaa were not allowed to go back to it. The Ts'ibe Dané? and Lhuuge Lęą lost their primary gathering place. They continued their seasonal rounds and met together to camp with small groups of relatives, but they could no longer meet in the large groups that had once camped together at Suu Na chii k'chige. Poor and bewildered at the loss of their reserve and their mobility, they also often went hungry. Gerry Attachie's grandmother Nachę told him, "People never get together again. Even relatives. They don't see each other again, and then some of them died" (Gerry Attachie, personal communication with authors, 1 July 1984).

Charlie Dominic's daughter May Apsassin, now an elder of the Blueberry River First Nation, remembers feeling the loss of the reserve as a child:

> I remember we were camped at that Montney Reserve they take away from us.
> I cry. I say, last time we go back in there, they chase us away. Galibois [the Indian Agent at the time] come with that army jeep, and policeman was with him. He say,
> "You guys go back here. This guy going to take you."
> From there, my dad he say that to us,
> "No more we going to go back in there. They take it. That's theirs."
> From there, we never go back, but we always say,
> "Our reserve, we want to go see." But they said, "No. You go jail." They just take it like that.
> (RDA, DZHD09-56)

Without their reserve, the Dane-zaa continued to camp throughout their traditional territory, even though more and more settlers were coming into the area and farmers were growing crops close to the Dane-zaa's campsites.

After they were exiled from the "Place Where Happiness Dwells," the people had to find other places to come together. Winnis Baker recalls the gatherings that took place on the land where she and her husband settled, on the road from Cecil Lake to Fish Creek.

> We left it for them because we didn't mind them coming. They never harmed anything or anybody, and we didn't need that land. It was on the riverbank, and they would put stakes in the ground, and they'd tether their horses, and the stake was made so it would turn around. It was real neat. And, so, they left their poles there year after year ... and they always came and hunted for the moose, and they hunted with .22 rifles, and they got their moose just the same as the guys with the big guns. It was quite funny, you know. And the women, they'd be busy cuttin' meat and drying it. (RDA, G-31 and G-32)

When we asked Baker if she had seen or heard the gatherings, she replied, "No, we were too far. It was twelve miles away, but the kids used to speak of it, about them doing it. You know, they had no drink with them when they were here. Everybody was just their own natural selves. I know they did, did do dances, because there would be places, you know, where the grass would be worn out" (ibid.).

In early September 1950, some of the members of the Fort St. John Band were camped at Milligan Creek when a brush fire got away on a farmer. The fire spread so quickly that the Dane-zaa families out hunting and camping didn't have a chance to get to a safe place. Seven of the Ts'ibe Dané? perished in the fire. Alice Moccasin (later Askoty) was already married to her first husband, Oker, so she was not with the family. Alice's mother, Chwénalę (the Precious One), died in the fire along with her husband, George Miller, and their four children. Chwénalę was the grandmother of Johnny and Freddy Askoty and Annie Oker and the great-grandmother of many members of today's Dane-zaa First Nations. The people who survived lost their cabins and all their horses, the main means of transportation at that time. Each family had twenty or more horses, which meant that when they travelled they could take only what they could carry with them. After the fire, they joined the other members of the band at Petersen's Crossing.

The late Sally Makadahay's grandfather Joe Atsisoke (Suzuki) Yehlhézęh died in the fire, and all the victims were members of her extended family. Sally, a teenager at the time of the fire, told Jillian Ridington about the fire as they drove near the site in 1979. It was a quarter century or more after the fire, but Sally still remembered all the details and was close to tears as she related the loss of so many

Sally Makadahay, 1979. Photo by Jillian Ridington

relatives, all at the same time. Elder Tommy Attachie likewise recalled that his family was camping near Sweeney Creek when the fire broke out. From the campsite, he could see the sky glowing red. In September 2008, May Apsassin, who would have been ten years old at the time of the fire, told Jillian about her memories of the event.

> That's where my grandpa used to camp always, Joe Kulęą.*
> By a big lake, toward Fontas, he got a cabin.
> We even had a cabin because we live with them one year.
> We all had a cabin: Pouce Coupe, Dan Wolf, George Miller and his family, his wife and his daughter,
> his youngest son, and George and Grandpa.
> Grandpa, they didn't find his body over there.
> Two women and that boy and his dad, they find their body there one place,
> and this side close to Pine, they find another two boys.

---

* Joe Atsisoke was May's grandfather's cousin-brother and, in the Dane-zaa language, a classificatory grandparent.

One was George Miller's son.
The two boys die not too far from town.
Big fire, you could see it all the way from Petersen's.
It was really hot summer, in August, summer, September, end
of August, in there somewhere maybe.
Nobody know how that fire went the way like that.
Even that white man living in there, Moig Flat, his name was Dan,
and they know him. He lived there, and he see this fire.
He see the fire up there, come down, across.
He got all these horses, dogs. He's a trapper.
He let everything go. He grab a blanket.
He went jump in the water. He touched that water.
He said that water was kind of boiling, in the river.
He said that he came back, and there's a place where that river,
it's kind of broken. You can crawl over there like that.
He say he go under there, and one side he got face burned,
all his hair, but he survived.
My dad see him in Petersen's store, and my dad said,
"Why didn't you go in the water?" and he said,
"Don't say that – that water hot. I can't get in there."
We didn't know about it. We went to Sweeney Creek.
Charlie Yahey, Alec and Theresa [Chekiiyaas],
they all move with us
to Sweeney Creek. We went to Moose Creek.
We used to call it Moose Creek. It's Goodlow now.
After that, we moved to Sweeney Creek. We live over there.
That's where we saw that big smoke start,
just big smoke. Just white. Must be big. My grandpa died in
the fire, my Grandpa Joe.
Inside teepee, it was dark, but sun was up here.
My mom and my dad tied horses –
put pack saddles and everything on the horses –
and my mom pack up all the dry meat, everything.
My aunt, Mrs. Pouce Coupe, she still alive. Her, too –
she got all her horses, tied them. Everything packed up.
She got lot of people work for her, a lot of young guys.
And she say, my auntie, that Mrs. Pouce Coupe, Nachę,
she say, "It's going to be dark, that fire, that's why we can't see."

"Maybe that Joe Kulęą die." That's what she said.
Grandpa Charlie Yahey was there, so all of us, we say,

"Grandpa's here. We're not scared." But Grandpa say,
"No, but that fire come. We gotta do something."
And from there, Grandpa say, "I'm going to go down to the creek.
Gonna wash. Get ready everything. All your rain gear."
So, Grandpa went down to the creek and wash his head.
Pretty soon, we just heard thunder, thunder just hitting around,
and we see smoke on this side,
and that thunder just coming this way.
And all the horses were tied up. Then, right away, it just stopped,
and Grandpa was just singing away. He say,
"Joe Kulęą, something happened to him.
That's why that fire turned white. Maybe he show us that he died."

After that, we stay there, and all those old people,
Aki, Nachę, they all stay in one place, came down to one place.
They all say, "We gotta go home.
We all gotta go find out what happened.
That Joe Kulęą died."
My dad can't believe it for long time.
He say, "Síize [mother's brother] is a strong man.
He know everything. He can't die.
He know when something coming.
I don't think he died." But they still think he not alive.
So, from up there, we all came back. We camped once,
then we came back to Doig, and from there Grandpa Charlie
[Yahey] and everybody moved back to Pine [Petersen's Crossing].
My dad still didn't know. He went to see Petersen.
He asked if the young boys had come back to get groceries.
Petersen said, "No, them people are gone. There's a big fire.
I bet those people died."

Same time, my mom say, "I think you kids gonna go to school.
They building that big school. They just about finished, looks like.
Nachę got one house. Oker got one house. Just like that."
We got excited. But one thing I still think about
how my grandpa Joe died in the fire.
(RDA, DZDV08-12)

Joe Atsizoke's body was never found, and the people experienced profound grief and sadness. Oker dreamed about where Joe's body was and told Billy Makadahay and others who set out to look for him.

However, because Joe had been a spiritual person, they were told to leave his body exactly where Oker saw it in his dream. At Petersen's Crossing, the heads of families built cabins for their own households and for all the people who had lost their homes. It was many years before the land recovered from the fire, but when the grass and trees grew back, some people moved back to the area. For Alice Askoty, the loss had been so great that she often cried when they camped in the area for the summer.

The new settlement at Petersen's Crossing incorporated the first school that Dane-zaa children could attend. Verbal assurances concerning education rights were mentioned in the "Report of Commissioners for Treaty No. 8" (see Madill 1986, 24). However, the government made no attempt to educate Dane-zaa children in the white people's education system. Schools were built in the Dane-zaa's traditional territory before 1950, but only white children attended them. An account in *The Peacemakers of the North Peace* states that Rose Prairie School, which opened in 1929, was "the first school in the district" (Ventress, Davies, and Kyllo 1973, 284). In the same book, Amy Smith describes her experience teaching at the North Pine School in 1930. Either no one considered the possibility of Dane-zaa children attending these schools or the migratory lives of the Dane-zaa made attendance impractical. Overall, considering the negative experiences that many First Nations children had in residential schools, it is probably a good thing that young people were able to stay with their families and learn traditional skills.

May Apsassin described seeing the new school when her family came to live at Petersen's Crossing in 1950:

> When we come to Pine [Beatton River],
> we go to check around. We see that big school.
> Everybody was just working on it. My Dad and Billy,
> they help each other. They build one log house,
> so Asa Billy [Makadahay],
> they live with us all winter. We stay in one cabin, all of us.
> (RDA, DZDV08-12)

Although land had been set aside for the Doig River and Blueberry River reserves in 1950, the school was built at Petersen's Crossing because, according to the regional schools supervisor, "it was centrally located from these reserves, and was chosen on which to erect a school and homes for parents whose children are attending it" (Doig River First Nation 2003). The area south of Rose Prairie where a bridge crosses the Beatton River was named Petersen's Crossing after a settler named Ernie Petersen, who came to the region as a trapper. Dane-zaa oral history tells us that Petersen lived in a cave that he dug out himself and lined with straw. Later on, he built a shed and various buildings and got to know the Dane-zaa who came to Petersen's Crossing on their seasonal rounds. He learned Dane-zaa Záágé?, and built a store on the south side of the Beatton River. The Indian Agent made him responsible for handing out rations to the Dane-zaa. The people were given rations of flour, tea, beans, and other staples from Petersen's store. Sally Makadahay, who lived at Petersen's Crossing most of her life, remembered that the flour sometimes tasted like kerosene. Tommy Attachie has clear memories of both the school and the store.

> We go to school there in 1950. There's a store down across,
> where the King's Valley [a Christian camp] is now.
> Nancy and Joe Apsassin used to live there.
> They lived by that store.
> I remember I go with my grandma sometimes.
> On this side of the hill there's a trail.
> She go to the store there,
> went across. I remember a lot of pack horses all over.
> Ernie Petersen built his store there.
> Got a lot of groceries in there.
> And people all living there, they'd buy their stuff.
> They got a place, a bunk house there too.
> Indians from Milligan Creek came there too.
> They'd buy the groceries,
> and by the river they would make a fire.
> Sometimes they'd spend the night,
> sometimes they'd come to Doig.
> And after so many years, you know, that store,
> other guys took over.
> That was before 1959 – '49, I think.
> All of us kids, we know him;
> we used to work for him.
> (RDA, DZ99-39)

The school was built on land near the north bank of the river. Joe Galibois, the Indian Agent, told Fort St. John Band members who were parents of school-aged children that they must stay at Petersen's because if their children did not attend school, they would be taken away from them. He also told parents they would lose their family allowance payments if they failed to send their children to school. These monthly payments were made to all Canadian mothers with children under the age of sixteen, but children aged seven to sixteen were required to attend school. The thought of losing their children was intolerable, and although the family allowance was only five dollars per child per month, the money was important to the parents, especially those with many children. The families lived on the north bank of the Beatton, across the river and a mile from Petersen's store. They cashed their family allowance cheques at the store, where they also traded furs for food.

Gerry Attachie, who grew up at Petersen's Crossing, talked about life in the area when he spoke to students at Upper Pine School on 17 January 1992.

> I was raised at Petersen's Crossing.
> They built a school there in 1950.
> We went to school there until 1961. After '61, we moved to Doig.
> But between '50 and '60 we were at Petersen's Crossing –
> all the people from Doig.
> I remember when we're at Petersen's Crossing,
> we used a team of horses, and in summertime a wagon
> and in wintertime, sleigh.
> And then we used horses all year round.
> And I remember when we're at Petersen's Crossing,
> I wanted to go to Doig.
> When I was a kid, I wanted to get out of there.
>
> We had log cabins. There's maybe about twenty cabins there.
> And there are two log houses there still standing.
> One burned down, and the other one they taught in.
> There were no bridge there, nothing.
> Only way to get across is by raft.
> Each family had their own raft.
> Only the teacher had a boat there.
> It had a kicker [outboard engine].

Gerry Attachie at the Beatton River near Petersen's Crossing, 2009.
Photo by Jillian Ridington

> We had to go to school until the end of June.
> Right after school was out,
> we usually moved to Doig.
> Then from Doig we moved to north of Goodlow.
> We camped there two to three weeks, north of Goodlow.
> And later on, we moved to Alberta, Sweeney Creek.
>
> We didn't just camp one day to get over there.
> We camped in between.
> Going toward Sweeney Creek, Alberta,
> I remember that the ladies usually
> made moccasins, gloves, mukluks.
> When we get to Sweeney Creek there,
> the people hitchhiked to Worsley, Alberta,

where they sold moccasins.
And then they could bring food back,
and then we liked that.
While we're going to school,
our parents usually trapped.
They trapped all winter. We go to Doig, and then, sometime,
they went out for two or three weeks.
There was no welfare at that time. Sometimes, when we get,
we come back early from the moose hunt in Rose Prairie,
some of our parents
– the people usually go to work for the farmers, thrashing,
stooking.
It's how we get by. I've seen hard times.
Just part of it, it's really – it's tough.
(RDA, field notes, 17 January 1992)

May Apsassin is eight years older than Gerry and went to the school at Petersen's Crossing as soon as it opened in 1950. In September 2008, May told Jillian about her experiences.

M.A.
From 1950, we go to school.
They built us cabins, and we all get ready to go to school.
We don't know. We don't eat like white people.
My mom, she put bannock [in our lunch boxes].
My dad went to store.
He put bologna and stuff like that.
He say, "White man eat like that."
We go to school, mostly Kindergarten,
big Kindergarten, me!
J.R.
How old were you then – about ten, eleven?
M.A.
Something like that. Even Lena Pouce Coupe, she's big, older than us. She go to school, too.
J.R.
I guess you didn't know English.
M.A.
We needed a lot of help. You know I used to remember –
Granny Nora Apsassin, she used to go to school,
before she married,

at Moberly Lake.
She write really good.
She write "ABCD." She teach us.
Help my mom too. Came over and teach us.
She help me lots, because she talks Beaver.
So, she say, "This gonna be like that."
Her kids just really good, but us, we need help. So she help us.
And I thank God, you know. Even when we were young,
she teaches us lot of white ways. I remember that.

We all lived in Pine. Grandpa Charlie Yahey went back.
They move back to Blueberry,
but us, we all live in Pine and go to school.
We learn little bit. We talk to teacher father [priest] about …
Grade 1, Grade 2, 3, 4, Grade 5. I went.
Nineteen fifty-six, I was in Grade 5.
I was sixteen, and the Indian Agent said,
"May, you're a big girl. You're sixteen now.
You can't go to school.
There's nothing we can do. Get married."
But I'm thinking,
all the time people go to school at higher grade.
They want to keep us like that – not knowing much.

I remember Margaret Olla, all of them. They were living in Pine.
Every time they come to Pine, Johnny Chipesia, Sam Pierre –
we didn't see his wife or his kids. But him, he always there.
And Grandma [Bella Yahey] just sit in that big teepee
Grandma got. Margaret Olla live with them.
Help for her. And Jack Wolf and his oldest son, that Ralph.
Margaret Wolf, when Grandma make dry meat,
she put up rack for her. She wash her clothes.
Her clothes hanging on that line, and Grandma say,
"Margaret, I want water. Margaret, I want wood."
So, my dad tell me,
"You kids, go gather little bit wood
and pile it up in Grandma's yard.
That one girl work too hard. You help, too."
So, me and Tommy used to go find wood,
little bit of wood, and pile it.
She speak, everybody quiet. And everybody respect her. She say,

"This gotta be done. That gotta be done,"
and everybody do what she want.
And Grandpa Charlie, too.
J.R.
Who was your teacher?
M.A.
Father Green and Father Warren.
J.R.
Were they Catholic, Catholic priests?
M.A.
Yeah. Christmas, they have candy. We never see that before.
Excited! Just having candies, and little oranges.
I wondered where those come from.
J.R.
Did they let you speak your language, or did you have to do everything in English?
M.A.
I think we talk our own language, but I think after that,
Father said, "You can't talk. Talk our own English."
But that Father was mean.
When he whipped our hand, it really hurt, just raw.
Little strap he got. He always carry it.
If he see that we don't do writing,
he just whip our hand. But it hurt. So we all scared of him.
(RDA, DZDV 08-11)

The school at Petersen's Crossing was destroyed by fire sometime in the 1960s. Gerry Attachie took us to the site of the school in 2009. Gerry talked about his experiences at the school (RDA, DZHD09-60). He gave the names of the people and families who had lived there: Pouce Coupe, Jack Acko, Billy Makadahay, Charlie Dominic, all the Attachies, and Nache, Gerry's grandmother. He showed us where the school had been. It's easy to find because the chimney and the foundation still exist. The school was close to the river, and Gerry remembered looking out the window and longing to be outside. To stop the students from gazing at the view, the teacher put up a sheet.

At the time, only a footbridge crossed the river, and people crossed over with rafts when the water was high. In the summer, they crossed the river by horse or on foot; in the winter, they walked across the ice or travelled by sleigh or horse and wagon. On Sundays, they attended church services in the school, and Gerry remembers Christmas concerts for which people came down from their houses carrying lanterns.

People still relied on trapping and hunting. Nache provided well for Gerry and many of his siblings. According to Gerry, "She grew up in bush. She trapped. She used to get forty to fifty squirrels and got forty cents each for them at Petersen's. That was good money in those days. She bought pork chops and fed us good" (Gerry Attachie, personal communication with authors, 6 August 2009). Gerry remembers a time when a muskrat came across the river. Someone shot it and got paid at the store for the fur.

Fred Jumbie, Harry Chipesia, and "a whole bunch of people" stayed with Gerry's dad while Gerry's mother, suffering from tuberculosis, was in the Charles Camsell Hospital at Edmonton, Alberta. They came from the other reserves to sell furs at Petersen's store. It was a one-day trip to Blueberry by horse or horse and wagon. Gerry remembers that the water in the Blueberry River was clear then. "It was clear at Doig, too, and at Three Mile Creek. All are muddy now, and people can't drink the water." They used to hear threshing machines on the nearby farms at harvesting time. Gerry and his brothers worked on them when he was a teenager: "long, long days, hard work" (Gerry Attachie, personal communication).

It was hard to live in Petersen's Crossing at the time because firewood was hard to come by. In the late 1950s, some people left Petersen's Crossing. They didn't want to spend another year there. It was too hard to get wood and moose, and it was too cold. Charlie Dominic and Murray Attachie decided to move their families back to the area around Doig River, where they had cabins and where things weren't so hard. Some families followed them back to Doig, while others went to the area along the Blueberry River. When they were told they would lose the family allowance, they said, "Keep it, we can't do this anymore." The Attachies moved to cabins at Cameron Creek, just upriver from Doig. The place later became part of the reserve. Around that time, transporting goods was getting a little easier because seismic roads made travel by wagon possible. Tommy Attachie told us about that change:

> In 1956, they make seismic roads for the oil, all over. That time, 1956, John Davis got a team of horses, and George Sagónáá? got a team of horses and a sleigh ... After that, we all buy wagons from the farmers. Tamed our own horses, train them. So, from

Rene Dominic and Gerry Attachie, Doig River Reserve, 1966.
Photo by Robin Ridington

> there, everybody buy wagons, you know – 1956, '57.* (RDA, DZ99-11)

Madeline Sagónáá? Davis, who was born in 1936, recalled the 1950s in an interview with Amber Ridington in July 2007.

> Once Joe Galibois start Indian Affairs, he cut off everything. He cut off our family allowance, too. Our kids ... we got nothing, no ... nothing to eat. No, no wood. No moose. No nothing. Nothing. Some people got no food. Nothing. We move to over here, reserve. We live in that old cabin over there. Some people move, too. Maggie [Dominic Davis] and them move with us, too. Abou *taa* [Abou's father, Aku] move too. Grandpa Jones

---

* Tommy also talks about this era in the Virtual Museum of Canada website *Dane Wajich: Dane-ẕaa Stories and Songs – Dreamers and the Land* (Doig River First Nation 2008).

[John Davis] – all those people moving in the reserve [the area that is now the Doig River Reserve].
May 1958. Joe Galibois cut us off of the family allowance. "Why you guys move? You won't have family allowance." He cut us off. We don't care. We make hide. The men go hunting and trapping, stuff like that. Joe Galibois – they have a meeting with him. He said, "After you finish that Doig, set up the school. That time, I'll take your family allowance back." He never give it back. Nothing. (RDA, ARDZMD#5-2007-07-29 GP004-2)

The Davis family, Jack Acko, and the Attachies trapped and grew hay around Doig, but the school remained at Petersen's Crossing. Margaret Dominic Davis, Charlie Dominic's daughter and the band manager at Doig for many years in the 1970s and '80s, talked about the building of the first Indian Affairs houses:

We were living in those log cabins in 1961.
Department of Indian Affairs, they came around with helicopter
when we were living in those log cabins on top of the hill.
They came around by helicopter, and then they flew down,
and they asked a few people where they think
they would like the school to be built.
So, they were told they should build the houses in here.
So, they done soil sample and stuff like that,
and then we didn't hear
anything any more until in the fall.
And they start putting the road from
Cecil Lake, and then they move all the supplies down here.
They just started building right then.
They built six houses plus the
teacherage and the school.
From October till next June.
(RDA, HB-85)

In the winter of 1962, a teacher finally came to Doig. George Sagónáá? went to Petersen's store and came back with the message "Teacher's coming." The teacher's name was Simon Flynn. He taught at Doig and took pictures of the people, including one of Alice Askoty packing ice from the river. He reported that the kids were hungry and wrote, "This is how people live." His report was published in the

Roundup at Doig, 1979. Photo by Jillian Ridington

paper, and he got fired. After that, it was hard to get teachers for the Doig school. Teachers could not get away on the weekends because the location was isolated. There was no bridge over the Doig River until the late 1970s, although Marshall Holdstock, a linguist who has long worked with the Dane-zaa, did build a bucket-and-pulley system in the 1960s so that people could get back and forth to Doig when the river was high. The Dane-zaa raised cattle at Doig, and the Catholic Church built a church, which was taken down in the 1980s. Saviour Stoney, Dick Davis, and Tommy Dominic managed the farming and cattle operations.

The only Dane-zaa left at Petersen's Crossing were the families of Jimmy Pouce Coupe, Albert Askoty, Billy Makadahay, and Dan Wolf. Billy's wife, Sally Makadahay, recalled that she and Billy gave Indian Agent Galibois one dollar for their trapline in 1963. At that time, white settlers were taking over the traditional hunting areas of the Dane-zaa people, who were forced to lease traplines to continue trapping in their territory as they had always done, even though the practice was contrary to the terms of Treaty 8.

Today, a few members of the Doig River First Nation still live in the Petersen's Crossing area, which is located on the road between the Doig River Reserve and Fort St. John, only fifteen minutes away from the reserve by car. People travel back and forth regularly. Petersen's Crossing is forty minutes from town, and the trip from town to the reserve takes less than an hour. Younger children are bussed to Upper Pine School in Rose Prairie while the older ones go to high school in Fort St. John.

The Dane-zaa continue to experience change. By the 1980s, their traditional lands had been radically transformed as oil and gas, the grease of the giant animals, were extracted from beneath the earth with increasing intensity. Sam Acko recalls a times before large-scale industrial development, a time when they camped at Sweeney Creek in Alberta.

> I remember fall time, September, first week,
> when all the leaves start blowing off. People start moving back.
> Packhorses full of dry meat. Wagon full of dry meat,
> moose grease, bear grease.
> People have way more than what they need for the winter.
> Even berries.
> And then we move back to cabin, live in the cabin,
> and keep all those dry meat, bear grease, berries,
> and everything like that.
> In wintertime, even they collect those wine bottles,
> those big jug of wine bottle.
> My mom used to collect those,
> and she fill it up with blueberries,
> and it keep good in there.
> Just like fruit jar.
> In wintertime, you just open it and pour it in a bowl
> and eat it with bannock.
> That's our dessert.
> And many times,
> I think we eat better that time than today.

Later, Sam told us:

> I don't like these rigs.
> Oil wells. I don't like them.
> Too many roads.
> Animals have been disturbed,
> and even our traditional camps, like that.
> We are disturbed.

Tommy Attachie added:

> Just like we hold them back, last few years.
> But still, every place you go,
> there's going to be oil wells happen there.
> Anyplace.
> No matter muskeg is how many thousand acres.

Sam concluded:

> What my dream is, I hope that the oil wells will get dry,
> so they're not going to come back and disturb some more.
> I hope they will disappear someday.
> No more oil. No more gas.
> (RDA, DZ00-18)

By the end of the century, the Dane-zaa language was written by tribal linguists but not spoken by most Dane-zaa children. These losses, however, were accompanied by the Dane-zaa's increased ability to cope with the white man's world. Although Gerry Attachie disliked school, the skills he learned in that small building at Petersen's Crossing enabled him to investigate what had happened to the old reserve and bring about some restitution. As Thomas Berger states in the chapter of his memoir devoted to "The Montney Treasure," Gerry was the prime mover of the legal challenge, from its launch in 1957 to its resolution two decades later in 1977.

> Jerry [Gerry] Attachie, chief of the Doig River band, had for twenty years been the champion of the Montney case. He had taken the file to a lawyer in the first instance. He had, after the trial judgement went against the Indians, urged an appeal. He had, together with Joe Apsassin, the chief of the Blueberry River band, and [lawyer] Harry Slade, come to see me to ask me to take the appeal to the Federal Court of Appeal. He had come to Ottawa for the hearing before the Supreme Court. No one had been associated for as long as he had been with the Montney claim. I think his band members must at times have wondered about his obsession with the pursuit of the Montney cause. But every cause needs someone who will not give up. Jerry was there at the finish. He was there when the settlement of $147 million was reached.

Jerry had always realized something was wrong. How had the band lost Montney? Why had others become wealthy from the riches beneath Montney while the Indians remained impoverished? To be sure, when you have observed the loss of your patrimony, when you are yourself a casualty of what seems a kind of arbitrary injustice, it often serves to sharpen the mind.

[Gerry] was not well educated in a formal sense; he did not know the law. But he kept asking a question that had never been answered until we had reached the Supreme Court of Canada; How could a people's patrimony have been lost? He believed there must be a remedy. It turned out that he was right. (Berger 2002, 271)

14

The Place Where Happiness Dwells, Indian Reserve 172

In 1978, more than three decades after they lost Suu Na chii K'chige, the members of the former Fort St. John Band sued the Crown (the government of Canada) for "allowing it to make an improvident surrender of their reserve."* They charged the Department of Indian Affairs (DIA), which is supposed to look after the best interests of all First Nations people in Canada, with a breach of fiduciary duty. They argued that the DIA had not protected the Dane-zaa's interest in the land, as it was obliged to do. In July 2005, former chief Gerry Attachie discussed the history of the case with Amber Ridington and Kate Hennessy:

> In 1900, the Treaty was signed down at the old Fort. One of my grandfathers signed the Treaty, put his "X" on it ... They signed the Treaty [because] the early settlers, the gold miners, wanted to go up north to Alaska, Yukon, to look for gold.
>
> But they can't get by here, our people won't let them go through. They don't want anybody around here to go through. So they stopped them and then it took them, I don't know how long. Finally, they negotiated and then they signed the Peace Treaty – And about, around 1916, they gave us Montney

---

* *Apsassin v. The Queen*, [1988] 3 FC 20, [1993] 2 CLNR 20; *Blueberry River Indian Band v. Canada (Department of Indian Affairs and Northern Development)*, [1995] 4 SCR 344, [1996] 2 CLNR 25.

Reserve. It is about seven miles north of Fort St. John – 18,000 acres. So we call that "Where Happiness Dwells," our gathering place. So we were there from 1916 up to 1945. (Attachie 2002)

Thomas Berger, who presented the appeals in the *Apsassin* case, devotes Chapter 10, "The Montney Treasure," of his 2002 memoir, *One Man's Justice: A Life in the Law,* to the case. He points out that settlers wanted the land contained in IR 172 as soon as they first began arriving in the area. But the land could not be opened up for agriculture unless the federal government obtained a surrender of the reserve from the band. Government policy was to retain reserves in Indian ownership, although reserve land was sometimes leased out to local farmers. Mineral rights could also be leased. Indeed, the mineral rights to IR 172 were surrendered to the Crown for lease in 1940. As late as 1944, Howard McGill, director of Indian affairs, recommended to the deputy minister that the best agricultural land in IR 172 be leased rather than sold. But McGill retired at the end of 1944. In June 1944, the DIA sent its employee John Grew to make treaty payments and to discuss the surrender with the Fort St. John Band. Grew met with the band and discussed the possibility of selling the reserve (Berger 2002, 243-48).

On 22 September 1945, Grew summoned the male members of the Fort St. John Band to a meeting at Petersen's Crossing. The DIA brought some of the men to the meeting by truck. Others arrived on horseback. Following the meeting, the place where happiness dwells was surrendered and transferred "for lease or sale" to the DIA. The department sold it to the Department of Veterans Affairs, which then auctioned the land off to veterans. Although Chief Sagónáá? and a few other adult males had put their marks on the surrender documents, it is not clear they understood the impact of what they were signing. Information compiled by former chief Gerry Attachie and the testimony of elders at the trial in 1987 reveal that the majority of members of the Fort St. John Band did not understand what had happened. Nor did they knowingly agree to the surrender.

Gerry Attachie, who was born in 1948, is too young to remember when the Fort St. John Band had IR 172, but he spent a great deal of time in the 1970s and 1980s talking to the elders about what happened at that time. None of the elders who had been alive at the time of the surrender could read or write English. They did not necessarily understand the difference between the surrender of mineral rights

Chief Norman Davis with his great-grandfather Chief Sagónááʔ's coat.
Photo by Robin Ridington

and the sale of IR 172. They knew they had received money for the mineral rights for a couple of years but did not receive any money after that. They knew that they had lost the reserve. Gerry has only a few years of formal education, but like his Dane-zaa ancestors, he is extremely good at following trails. He followed the paper trail that showed that the rights of his people had not been well served by the machinations of the government departments who decided the fate of IR 172.

In his interview with Kate and Amber, Gerry recalled how his elders talked about the loss:

> But while we grew up down at Petersen's Crossing, people were talking about what happened to Montney reserve ... According to some people, when it was sold in 1945, some of the people came back to the reserve. But it was fenced off in some places, and they said, "You can't come back here. It was sold." And that's when they knew, some of the people knew, it was sold, in 1945.

> About that time, in the early 1940s, the government and the people in Fort St. John, they wanted that Montney land, for farmers. They thought it's good for farming, and that our people, First Nations, don't use it. That's what they said.
>
> But some people that work for the Department of Indian Affairs, they said, "The Indians will be farming one of these days, and in the future they will farm." But about 1943, '44, they put a lot of pressure on Chief Sagónáá?, our Chief. They wanted that land, and then finally in 1945 they set a date. On September 22, 1945, the surrender took place down at Petersen's Crossing, which is ten miles west of here.
>
> They brought some of the people back from the bush, but some were way back, they couldn't find them. And they brought some people back there at Petersen's Crossing, but not very many. Some were gone. They brought some people in from Prophet River. And I don't remember what happened. Some of them, according to some of our people, they didn't vote.
>
> Anyway, the land was sold. 18,000 acres for returned soldiers. And today, forty-two farmers own the mineral rights in British Columbia. It's the farmers at Montney. I.R. 172. (Attachie 2002)

In his memoir, Berger (2002, 247) points out that the land could have been leased rather than sold, for the surrender was "in trust to sell or lease ... to such person or persons, and upon such terms as the government of the Dominion of Canada may deem most conductive to our welfare and that of our people." But the government never seemed to have considered leasing the land.

Gerry Attachie also talked about the loss of Suu Na chii k'chige and the subsequent court case at a symposium organized by Lorraine Weir and Robin Ridington at UBC in 1988:

> What happened was back in 1945 we lost good land there, just about eight miles north of Fort St. John. We had 18 sections of land there. And we live there all our lives, and up until 1945. We lost it and ... the Government promised our People at that time they could get a lot of money, so they gave up the good land ... they were promised that they would get lot of money every year and then for a couple of years they received, I believe, ten dollars apiece – each person ...
>
> Later on the money stopped coming in, so they kind of wondered why they don't get any more. Ever since I remember,

back about in the late 1950s, people would get together lot of times ... and then they said, "I wonder what happened ... We don't get any more money," and just amongst themselves they discuss this problem, and then, off and on we would mention that they been promised that they could get a lot of money every year – for a long time. I don't know how long.

Then, there's lots of oil over there, and gas. I remembered what people were complaining about before. And, one day, I sat down with some Elders, and then they told me exactly what happened. (Ridington 1990, 278-79)

Gerry referred to the fact that, in addition to its value as agricultural land, IR 172 was located in an area rich in mineral wealth. Although the Dane-zaa had no use for the minerals in traditional times, their stories did refer to the deposits as "grease" from the giant animals that Tsááyaa (the Transformer) had placed under the earth.

There is evidence that the federal government knew about the riches in the area even before Treaty 8 was signed. Dennis Madill (1986, 5) notes that the government received a report, dated 7 July 1891, which stated that "immense quantities of petroleum" existed in parts of the Athabasca District. The federal government was also made aware of the probable presence of oil and gas in the Peace River area (though not specifically in the Montney area) in 1918, when, in a report for the Department of the Interior, F.L. Kitto (1918, 6-7) stated: "Springs of natural gas and tar rising to the surface at several points in the valley of Peace River suggest that reservoirs of both these substances exist at depth in the rocks below. Drilling has been undertaken at two or three points to tap these reservoirs, and in a well near Peace River a heavy flow of gas was struck, at a little over 1,000 feet in depth. Some heavy oil was also obtained, which, by pumping, would amount to a few barrels daily." The existence of gas and oil under IR 172, if not the amount present, was certainly suspected by 1940, when the band asked the DIA to take the mineral rights "in trust" and to lease them for the benefit of the band. As Gerry (Attachie 2002) put it: "The oil company asked for permission to drill around, in I.R. 172. So our people gave them permission to go ahead. And they did. They did some drilling."

The ownership of the mineral rights would become an important issue during the trial and a focal point during the appeal to the Supreme Court of Canada. But, when Gerry first began looking into the events leading to the loss of IR 172, those events were yet a long way in the future.

Although Gerry's childhood at Petersen's Crossing was difficult, his schooling did bring literacy and gave Gerry the tools he needed to find out what had happened. When he was elected to the Fort St. John Band Council, he had an opportunity to do so.

> About, around 1970, '74, I became Councillor. In 1976 I was elected for Chief, for Blueberry and Doig together [the bands separated in 1977]. That's when ... I read some books, a book called "Peacemaker" *[Peacemakers of the North Peace]*. And I was looking at that, and then I read a story about Pine View. Pine View reserve, it says, I.R. 172. They even had a map, parcel, each quarter, and it said that the former reserve, Montney, was sold in 1945 and then the mineral rights to that I.R. 172 were forgotten, they said. So I thought, the people were talking about that. They only had ten dollars for two years, twenty dollars, each person. They call it *nan soniiye,* money. Land money, *nan soniiye*. What happened to *nan soniiye,* they said. So that's when I started to look into that more, and then tried to communicate with Indian Affairs. (Attachie 2002)

Gerry had read a chapter in *Peacemakers of the North Peace* titled "History of Fort St. John Indian Reserve 172 and Pineview" by Nora Sall. In it, Sall (1973, 27) states, "In 1950-51 it was discovered that the Mineral Rights which adhere to an Indian Reserve, were forgotten, at the time of the sale of farms to the veterans and the V.L.A. obtained these for the 42 veterans, and it is written in Red Ink on the Farm Title. Understand too, that they were the only 42 farmers of British Columbia who own Mineral Rights." Sall provides evidence to substantiate the claim that the DIA had assigned the mineral rights to the Department of Veterans Affairs in 1948 without consulting with the Dane-zaa. Leslie Pinder and Louise Mandell, lawyers working for the Union of British Columbia Indian Chiefs, pointed out the lack of diligence in this transfer when they visited Doig Reserve on 10 May 1981 and spoke to the people about the case as it had evolved up to that time. They noted that the surrender of the land did not make any reference to the mineral rights. To them, this indicated that "the mineral rights did not merge back with the land and get transferred." Because the mineral rights had already been surrendered for lease, the subsequent surrender of the whole reserve could not have included the minerals. Certainly, they were not specifically mentioned in the 1945 surrender. Pinder and Mandell argued that they would have been referred to had they been included (Ridington/Dane-zaa Archive [RDA], G-2b). Nor were the mineral rights included in the appraisal of the value of the land. Therefore, the mineral rights were not part of the 1945 surrender and should have been retained by the Crown for the Fort St. John Band, even after the 1945 surrender of the surface rights. The band was never paid for the mineral rights, yet it lost them. The $70,000 purchase price for the reserve was for the surface rights only (ibid.).

According to correspondence cited in court by Mandell and Pinder, "sometime down the road," the Department of Veterans Affairs asked the DIA whether the mineral rights had been included (RDA, G-2b). The DIA, which did a perfunctory search of its own records, did not look at the documents from 1940, which showed that the mineral rights had been transferred in trust to the DIA for lease on behalf of the band. The DIA told the Department of Veterans Affairs that the rights had been part of the 1945 surrender. The transfer of the mineral rights was not in line with the government's usual practices and policy. The oil companies who wanted to lease the mineral rights were uncomfortable with the assurances that mineral rights went with the land they had received, and they asked their lawyers to examine the matter. As Mandell put it, "they never closed their books on it" (RDA, G-2b). Berger (2002, 252) notes that the DIA seemed to have given the rights away, "apparently in a state of absent-mindedness."

At the meeting at Doig in 1981, Mandell and Pinder also pointed out that the price that the DIA had asked for IR 172, "a minimum of $100,000," had been lowered to $70,000 because the Department of Veterans Affairs said that "it didn't have much money." The Fort St. John Band was not consulted about this change (RDA, G-2b).

Documents generated by the DIA state that the reserve had only been used by large groups as a gathering place for a few weeks each year. According to the Dane-zaa, however, smaller bands also used the land on a regular basis as part of their seasonal rounds. Furthermore, as a summer gathering place for all Dane-zaa people, the land was an essential part of the Dane-zaa's social and ceremonial life. Hunter-gatherer cultures depend on seasonal gathering places, which are part of an annual system that exists as a whole. If you pluck out one segment of the annual system, you threaten the whole system. If you pluck out the summer gathering place, the one spot where all the various bands meet to exchange crucial information and goods, you are mounting a direct assault on the system as a whole.

As Gerry talked to the elders who remembered the loss of IR 172, he found out more about their recollections of that time. According to Gerry,

> My grandmother was still alive, and every time I took her to town she said, "We lost a good land." And then, she told me a story about how people got together there every year. They celebrated and then people all have a good time together there. And after 1945, when the land had been sold, then people never got together again. Even relatives didn't see each other again and then some of them died ... I just talked to some farmers around there, just recently. They said, one time there were about four or five hundred tipis, and then they could hear drums about 20 miles away. People were having a pow-wow in there. Our people. (Ridington 1990, 279)

Drawing on government records and elders' recollections, Gerry pieced together the complete story. The Fort St. John Band was fortunate that C.S. Johnston-Watson (whom the Dane-zaa called Johnny Watson), the Indian Agent for Fort St. John at the time that Gerry was making inquiries, was a good man. Johnson-Watson was helpful in getting the claim to court. Gerry continued:

> After I found out what happened to I. R. -172, I set a meeting with the Indian Affairs Superintendent that worked in Fort St. John. His name was Johnny Watson ... we set a date and then we sat down and we talked about I. R. -172 and then he said, "There's something wrong in here," he said. "Something happened in here." And, he brings out all the documents. About three feet high – papers. And, oh boy [he laughs] that was how it all started, and we got a lawyer and then we hired a local lawyer there. His name was Gary Collison and he started doing some research and he went to Vancouver, I believe. (Ridington 1990, 279).

The Union of British Columbia Indian Chiefs (UBCIC) learned about the case, and Leslie Pinder and Louise Mandell began to work on the file. As Leslie Pinder said in a recent conversation with us, "I began to go through all the files and the case law and went back to the office and said to Louise, 'This is going to be a really complicated case'" (personal discussion with authors, June 2010). Mandell and Pinder, who left UBCIC in 1982 to start their own practice, worked on the case for the next ten years. In 1984, the *Guerin* case established that the relationship between the Crown and First Nations involved fiduciary obligations and was not just a "political trust."* This advancement in the law eventually became the legal foundation for the *Apsassin* case.

Even with the support of the UBCIC, the bands had to find money for travel, expenses, and the like. "We finally got the money from a small Band [the Horse Lake Band] just across the border. And sometimes people could say, you know, 'Indians should help one another.' But sometimes, when it comes down to something like this, it's different. We struggled. We travelled lots. Finally we got some money to start. In 1987 we went to court" (Attachie 2002).

Because the Doig and Blueberry Bands had shared IR 172, Joe Apsassin, chief of the Blueberry First Nation and grandson of a man present at the surrender, joined in the case. The case was heard in the Federal Court, Trial Division, in 1988 and in the Federal Court of Appeal in 1993. The case was called *JOSEPH APSASSIN, Chief of the Blueberry River Indian Band, and JERRY ATTACHIE, Chief of the Doig River Indian Band v. HER MAJESTY THE QUEEN IN RIGHT OF CANADA as represented by the Department of Indian Affairs and Northern Development and the Director of the Veterans' Land Act.* The case is cited in legal journals and in court decisions as *Apsassin v. The Queen* or *Blueberry River Indian Band and Doig River Indian Band v. Canada,* leaving off the name of the man who was the prime mover of the action (see footnotes for citations).

Robin had a sabbatical from teaching anthropology at the University of British Columbia for the 1986-87 academic year and spent a great deal of time at the trial. He kept scrupulous field notes during the trial and organized a conference at the International Institute for Structural and Semiotic Studies, which was held at UBC in 1988. Gerry Attachie and Hugh Brody, witnesses at the trial, and Leslie Pinder and Art Pape, legal counsels, spoke at the conference. Both the conference

---

* *Guerin v. The Queen* [1984], 2 SCR 335.

and an article authored by Robin and published in *Canadian Literature* (Ridington 1990) were called "Cultures in Conflict: The Problem of Discourse." The article began with a discussion of "the problem of discourse" between the Dane-zaa and the law, two cultures with no common or shared understandings. The article was based on Robin's field notes from the trial, his experience while attending the trial, and testimony given at the conference.

Here is an excerpt from Robin's field notes for the first day of the trial, 12 January 1987:

> Leslie Pinder began by reading an elegant and compassionate prepared brief, the essence of which was that the action "concerns at its deepest level, the whole class of people to which the plaintiffs belong," and that it seeks to establish "the proper legal relationship between Her Majesty and the Indian people." The court, she said, "will be called to understand them as themselves." It will have to consider "the problem of discourse ... Between any two cultures there is a gap. Both must know their similarities and differences in order to communicate. The problem of discourse is of critical legal significance when the result of the discourse is legally binding."
>
> The Judge became very disturbed by Leslie's assertion that the central issues in the case were that the Indians did not give informed consent and that the defendant failed to provide the required information. His problem centred on the question of the consensual nature of their decision. At one point, Justice Addy remarked:

> > I have difficulty understanding how any society can operate *qua* society, for instance, go to war, without some sort of authority. Once consensus is obtained, what is the mechanism for putting the decision into action? ... Do you have to get every member of the band to indicate consent? There is the problem of discipline, too. If somebody is murdered, who would carry out the discipline? ... The main concern is who was authorized? What would have been proper?

Robin noted that the judge could not grasp the concept that the Dane-zaa have their own distinctive culture and decision-making process and that it is indeed possible for a group of people to operate without formal hierarchical authority structures.

Art Pape, who was also acting for the plaintiffs, outlined the events of 1944-48. "You are going to be asked," he told Justice Addy, "was this behaviour the kind of behaviour that the courts expect and demand of a fiduciary? The Department *knew* about these kinds of conflicts between settlers. They knew what they had to do and had developed policies. You will hear the development of that policy." He reminded the judge that the sections of the Indian Act dealing with surrender derived from a fiduciary responsibility that goes back to the Royal Proclamation of 1763. At that time, King George III reserved the western lands for "several nations or tribes of Indians" under his "protection" as their exclusive hunting grounds. As sovereign of this territory, however, the king claimed ultimate dominion over the entire region. The proclamation gave the Crown the right and responsibility to deal with all Indian lands. Only five years before *Apsassin* came before the court, the proclamation was referred to in section 25 of the Constitution Act, 1982, which notes that there is nothing in Canada's Charter of Rights and Freedoms to diminish the Aboriginal rights and freedoms recognized by the Royal Proclamation.

Robin's field notes from the court case reveal the contrast between the perception of justice held by the judge and that of the Dane-zaa and the lawyers representing them. Art Pape continued:

> We do not say that compliance with procedures necessarily proves fulfilment of the fiduciary relationship, but we *do* say that non-compliance is a breach of it – unequivocally opposed to alienation of land that would be of possible value to them. Under-utilization was *not taken* as a reason for surrendering lands. Generally, no surrender was contemplated.
>
> We are talking about human beings who are competent in their world and are being asked to deal with a matter out of their world. The fiduciary already has an agenda and wants to get an agreement and that situation has great potential for mischief. He has to act with knowledge and understanding of the ward. The fiduciary relationship requires treating the Indian wards honestly and intelligently.

In response, the judge asked why he needed to hear more evidence beyond an affidavit of the surrender sworn before a justice of the peace. The judge and Pape then discussed the legal positions:

Judge: I'm saying what the legal position is, not its policy. You may know that government policy is often an illegal one. That's part of your case. You've got to convince me that facts after signing have got anything to do with the issue. If I sign an agreement today, unless I waive my rights or you waive yours, no facts have bearing on the legal issue. If it was obligated to transfer the mineral rights, the veterans could have sued. If they were not, then that's a different kettle of fish. Unless the facts are a change in the original contract.

A.P.: Never looking at what the rights of the Indians are? For 10-15 years, they are in the hands of the Director.

Judge: Yes, I hear you. There are agreements for sale. That is policy. That is elementary law. Agreements for sale are elementary law. If I agree to sell you, 5 years hence, for one dollar, I am obliged to do so.

But until then, I'm the owner. But subject to the agreement for sale. If the Crown was obliged under its original agreement to transfer mineral rights to the Veterans, how can its behaviour subsequent to that have anything to do with the situation insofar as granting of the mineral rights, not with respect to the rights of the Indians?

A.P.: They never did undertake to grant it.

Judge: Your case is that there was no obligation?

A.P.: Our case is based on the 1940 surrender.

This discussion was followed by a lengthy presentation of historical correspondence between officials of the two departments regarding mineral rights. One of these letters was from D.J. Allen of the DIA, who wrote Joe Galibois, the Indian Agent, to ask for his opinion. Galibois – "the small Indian boss," as the Dane-zaa called him – responded that he thought the rights had been transferred to the Director, Veterans' Land Act. Justice Addy listened carefully to this part of the story but then interrupted: "When you allege a breach of trust, there is no onus on a person because there is an allegation to prove there is not. The defendant breached its obligations because it did not take legal advice."

A.P.: You will be asked to decide whether they should have taken advice.

Judge: I gather from your pleadings that you claim that even though the land was granted to the VLA that there was a

fiduciary relationship of the Director *qua* Director toward the Indians. Among the alternatives, you're going to have to convince me of that. I think his powers are very limited. Whether he's capable of acting as a fiduciary for anyone else is the sixty-four dollar question.
A.P.: Yes, that is one of the big questions. It's a big issue in fact and a big issue in law. Our pleadings are that ownership of rights was never in control of the Director, but *if he got them, he got them burdened with obligations.* (RDA, field notes)

Justice Addy seemed at one point to be far more concerned about the rights of the veterans who had acquired the land after the surrender than he was about the rights of the land's original inhabitants.

Judge: I'm a little concerned about this case now. Supposing that at the end, I conclude that the original surrender is void. It follows as night does day that the grant of Veteran lands is void. If you can't – Although you're not claiming against the Veterans' title, what will be the effect on the Veterans if they try to dispose of their land? Should they not have a word to say in this thing now? Here's someone with a real interest in this in the sense of realty, and you're attempting to knock down the entire structure on which their entitlement rests. This is a real kettle of fish ... Where does that put the Veterans? ... I realize my findings will not *directly* affect their rights. If it's publicized in every paper in B.C. "Federal Court rules title to lands to be void," what does that do to their rights? If I say they haven't got the title, it's going to create a lot of harm. I think they would be heard. If I say the original surrender was void and therefore the title is still in the DIA, there's a problem; surely the interests of the veterans come in here ... The commercial value of the lands will plummet.

On Wednesday, 21 January 1987, Gerry Attachie took the stand. Leslie Pinder began by asking Gerry about his time on the band council. The following excerpts are from the transcript of Gerry's testimony.*

---

* *Apsassin v. Her Majesty the Queen,* 1987, Federal Court of Canada, Trial Division, Docket T-4178-78.

G.A.: In 1976 they elect me for Chief. In '79 I resign. In '74 ... I was out in the bush and I came back and they elect me for Chief, not for councillor ... I thought about it for a little while and then I figured it was OK, I guess ...

L.P.: Tell the Judge who your father was.

G.A.: Murray Attachie ... He is the son of Chief Attachie, one of the chiefs that used to lead the people there in the Fort St. John Area.

L.P.: Do you know when Chief Attachie, Murray's father, died?

G.A.: I believe around 1918 ... The big flu that came through about that time killed a lot of the Native People there. He was one of them ...

L.P.: And your father, Murray Attachie, when did he die?

G.A.: 1969 ... he was 53.

L.P.: And your mother, what was her name?

G.A.: Alice Ben ...

L.P.: Ben was her maiden name?

G.A.: Yes ...

L.P.: And I understand there were 12 children in your family? You had 11 brothers and sisters?

G.A.: Right.

L.P.: And 10 of those children are still alive?

G.A.: Um-hmm ...

L.P.: Do you know ... who it was that raised your father?

G.A.: I think John Davis raised him mostly ...

L.P.: And who was it that raised you, brought you up as a child? ...

G.A.: Yeah, I believe about around 1950 – '49 or '50 – my mother, she had TB, and she had to go to hospital, Charles Council [Charles Camsell] Hospital in Edmonton, a TB hospital for natives. They sent her out there ... My grandmother took me. She looked after me until she returned from the hospital. It was about two years later. She went back again ... She spent about 5 years total in TB hospital. I believe she went back there about '53 or '54.

L.P.: You were raised during this time by your grandmother. What was her name?

G.A.: Mary Pouce-Coupe [Nachę] ...

L.P.: And Mary Pouce-Coupe was your mother's mother, Alice's mother ...

When you were raised by Mary, where was that? Where were you living as a boy?

G.A.: Petersen Crossing. It's the other side of Rose Prairie ... A guy name Petersen, he owned the store there, Ernie Petersen, so they name the place for him.

The Court: You were between two and four?

G.A.: Right. After my mother come out of hospital I still stay with my grandmother ... until maybe eight or ten.

L.P.: Do you remember the place you lived at Petersen Crossing? ...

G.A.: We live in a cabin that my dad built there about '50, I believe ... My dad had his own cabin and my grandmother had one. Like daytime I go back to our house and hang around there when my dad is home, but mostly he's out the bush. At night-time I go back to my grandmother ... Me and my sister ... Margaret ...

L.P.: Were there other people who had a cabin, who had cabins at Petersen Crossing?

G.A.: Yes, there's about, oh, 15 of them ... Some from Blueberry, you know. Yeah, about 15 families. We went to school in an old log building. We had a wood heater there. Sometimes in morning ... we have to sit around the stove until it get warm ... Really cold. It's in the valley. Sometimes it to 60 below there ...

L.P.: What made it so cold there?

G.A.: The place where I was raised, the log cabin, didn't build too good. The ceiling was really high, and you had one planks there for the roof, and then tarpaper on top of it. I remember I could see the draft from the ceiling. When we warmed up the house, water dripping from the ceiling ... I remember one time my dad got a stove from a farmer, a gas barrel stove, 45 gallon drum. That was a big stove, and when we used it, we used to put a whole bunch of wood in there, and then we used to stand around the stove, I remember, just before we would head for school.

L.P.: The cabins you told us about, the 15 families that were there, were the cabins the same, or were they different from one another?

G.A.: They were different. They didn't build those cabins right. We had another village there at Doig about that time. These cabins had sod roof. Like, they put dirt on top of it and chink really good. They were pretty warm. But at Petersen's Crossing, didn't build too good.

L.P.: What did you people do for wood? How did you get wood for the stoves?

G.A.: Yeah, I remember we cut wood by axe and Swede saw, and team horses too. We have to go eight miles to get wood, sometimes nine miles.

L.P.: Why was that?

G.A.: Well, it's hard to get wood around there. Mostly small trees. When we have to get good wood we have to go eight or nine miles east of there.

Robin recorded the following about the testimony in his notes:

> Gerry said in court that he thought they would go to a lawyer and the DIA would give them the money right away, maybe a few weeks. This trial is very much Gerry's accomplishment. He really is acting as a chief. He has the agreement of the various segments of the community and he is constantly aware of the need to check back with people about what is happening.
>
> Later, Gerry then said that when he was giving his first testimony about what it was like growing up at Petersen's Crossing, he was feeling sad as he told about how they lived at Petersen's Crossing. He really meant what he said. It wasn't a sob story. He really had a very hard time there feeling powerless and cold and hungry and victimized by circumstance. I think it was only his grandmother who really pulled him through. I can see a lot of her in Gerry. Maybe she was some kind of chief during those years. Gerry said she was a trapper all her life.

Dane-zaa elders who were alive at the time of the surrender testified about that day. Albert Askoty, who was born in 1920, was among the younger men present in 1945. He testified on 3 February 1987. Lana Wolf, a member of the Blueberry River Band, interpreted.*

> *A.P. [Art Pape]:* Good morning, Albert Askoty. I will ask you about things that happened a long time ago, and you can tell the judge about those things. When were you born?

---

* Ibid., vol. 13, pp. 1548-51.

Albert Askoty and his wife, Alice Moccasin, 1960s.
Photo by Robin Ridington

A.A.: 1920.
A.P.: Who raised you when you were a young boy?
A.A.: I can hardly remember. My father was blind and I stayed with people.
A.P.: And when you were a little bit older, who took you trapping and took care of you?
A.A.: My Dad's younger brother, Charlie Yahey.
A.P.: Please tell us about the Indian land at Montney where the people went in the summers.
A.A.: In the summertime they moved there.
A.P.: Did the old people have a name for that place in the Beaver language?
A.A.: "Where Happiness Dwells."
Mr. Haig [J.R. Haig, attorney for DIA]: I'm sorry, I didn't get the answer to that.
The Court: It was known as "Where Happiness Dwells," in the Beaver language.
A.P.: What did the people do at that place in the summer?

A.A.: They hunt bear, deer and pick berries.
A.P.: Were there some cabins at that place?
A.A.: Two places this side Montney.
The Court: Cabins in two places, or two cabins?
Lana Wolf [Interpreter]: Two cabins, on the east side, I seen the cabin, he said.
A.P.: Whose cabin was that?
A.A.: This side Montney, Joe Apsassin's wife, had a cabin there.
A.P.: Who built the other cabin?
A.A.: By the creek, Mudeese [probably Charley Modeste].
A.P.: Were there graves at that place?
A.A.: On the other side. Oker has a cabin there, there were lots of graves.
A.P.: In the summertime, which Indian people used to come to that place?
A.A.: Everyone.
A.P.: What else did they do at that place besides hunting and getting berries?
A.A.: Ceremony. I guess they dance and sing.
A.P.: What did people do at the ceremony?
A.A.: They have a prophet.

Later in his testimony, Albert Askoty talked about the meeting regarding the surrender.

A.P.: Did Billy Mosquito [the translator for the surrender] say things to you and the other people who were outside the cabin [where the signing took place]?
A.A.: He was talking, but me, I didn't understand ...
A.P.: The two white men [Galibois and Grew], did they talk to the people outside that day?
A.A.: No, they only talked to those inside.
A.P.: At that place, on that day, did you talk to anybody about the land?
A.A.: Nowhere ...
A.P.: At that place near Petersen's house, that day, did people talk about getting other land at other places?
A.A.: No.
A.P.: Albert Askoty, when you were there near Petersen's house on that day did anybody ask you if you wanted to sell the land?

> *A.A.:* That land, people were saying they were going to sell it. It's a good land.
>
> ...
>
> *A.P.:* Albert Askoty, on that day near Petersen's house did anybody ask you if you want the land to be sold?
> *A.A.:* Right then nobody said anything.*

Albert was then cross-examined by J.R. Haig, who was acting for the DIA.

> *Mr. Haig:* Mr. Askoty, will you agree that the following people hunted with Charlie Yahey and yourself. Jack Appaw, John Yahey, Jack Wolf, Pete Davis, Frank Attachie, George Chipesia, John Attachie, George Cheekyass?
> *A.A.:* George Cheekyass was staying with his older brother – Jack Appaw was there. John Yahey wasn't there. I saw Pete Davis. Frank and John Attachie.
> *Haig:* I want to put to you again, before you ate the meal, while you were sitting with Charlie Yahey and others, do you not remember the white man speaking to the people?
> *A.A.:* No, I don't remember.
> *Haig:* Do you remember being asked where you wanted a new home that day?
> *A.A.:* There, they didn't – nobody said anything ...
> *Haig:* Did you ever see the Indian boss and the tall man [Grew] outside?
> *A.A.:* They were there, but they weren't saying anything.
> *Haig:* Did they speak to the people through interpreters?
> *A.A.:* No, they didn't say anything.
> *Haig:* I have no further questions, my Lord.†

According to the genealogy of the former Fort St. John Band that we prepared in 2005, John Davis, an elder of the Doig River Band who testified at the trial, was born in 1904. He spent his life in the bush, trapping and hunting. He had never been to Vancouver before the trial. Robin Ridington made notes during Davis's testimony: "Once again, there was a problem of discourse. The old people had one way of speaking about things, the court another. Art's job was to put the two

---

* Ibid., vol. 13, pp. 1565-69.
† Ibid.

together. John Davis is a determined and proud man. He is like every other Beaver Indian in having his own highly individualistic style of doing things. His response to something he doesn't like is simply to walk away or to say nothing" (RDA, field notes, 28 January 1987).

The lawyers for the Dane-zaa had a reasonable understanding of both Dane-zaa and judicial cultures, but Justice Addy was literal-minded. He did not seem to understand or appreciate Dane-zaa ways of thinking and speaking. After a morning of preparation and practice with the style of translation, John Davis and translator Lana Wolf went on the stand in the afternoon of 28 January. Robin noted in his field notes:

> When John Davis took the stand there was almost a sense of wonder among the people watching. Only Mr. Justice Addy seemed unmoved. Indeed, during the break Art came up to me and whispered that he was amazed and saddened that this man is so limited that he failed to take advantage of such an opportunity for learning and communication as John Davis provided.
>
> Despite the integrity of this man's speaking and of his assurances that he spoke from what he knew from experience, the Judge was impatient and cranky. He complained whenever it seemed that John Davis was telling what he had heard other people say rather than what he has heard himself. For John Davis, something he heard another person say is primary evidence, not hearsay. For George Addy, it is inadmissible because it is not "of probative value" toward what he thinks is the simple and straightforward matter of fact that he still believes is at the heart of this case. In this, he is both right and wrong. There is a straightforward matter of fact, and that is that the Government forced the Indians into something that was both against their wishes and contrary to their best interest. But Mr. Justice Addy is looking for a finer and more limited domain. He wants to know simply whether there was a meeting and a vote as was attested to by the justice of the peace, a junior judge whose testimony he is by disposition more inclined to trust than that of illiterate Indians, no matter how noble and needy they may appear to have been.

Art Pape asked John Davis simple and direct questions, using a style of address that approximated a simple declarative form of

Dane-zaa Záágé?. Each question began with the old man's name, said loud and strong.

> A.P.: John Davis, I want you to tell the Judge stories about when you were a little boy and no white men were in your country. Tell the Judge where you and your family lived when you were a little boy, before the white men came.*

When Pape mentioned a time when there were "no white men in your country," he did not mean first contact but rather a time before settlement became widespread. This was the world John Davis grew up in. The white people he knew then were storekeepers and fur traders. John Davis responded:

> J.D.: Long time ago, when there was no white people, there were two stores. One of the storekeeper's name was Davis. What I can remember I will say. What I do not remember, I will not say. I cannot read and write. I only can remember. Before the whitemen came, we were bush people. When they came, where we live, they said, "this is my land," and we have no more. We can't read or write. We only can remember it. Since not too long ago that my people started to go to school.
> A.P.: When white people came, what did they do on the land?
> J.D.: First time two men came and they started building cabins.
> Judge: We should know how old you are.
> A.P.: The Judge wants to know how old you are. Can you tell him?
> J.D.: I don't know my age.
> Judge: For the record, let's say he looks old to me. He's not a teen-ager.
> A.P.: When those white people came, what was the place where your family lived in the summer?
> J.D.: Place we call, "Indian Lands."
> A.P.: Did some other families live there at that place with your family?
> J.D.: ... Jack Acko and Acko Senior.
> A.P.: Okay. That Indian land, did the white men give that Indian land to your people?

---

* Ibid., vol. 10, pp. 1431.

J.D.: They didn't. But it's a good land, we live there, until the white people came and we have to move back.
A.P.: In those times long ago, where did you go in the winter with your family?
J.D.: Petersen's Crossing.
A.P.: Did you go other places too, like Moose Creek?
J.D.: I stayed at Moose Creek and when I run out of things, I go to Petersen's Crossing. When we were little I stayed at Moose Creek.
A.P.: Tell the Judge about when Dr. Brown [former Indian Agent] gave you treaty money at Fish Creek.
J.D.: He gave us treaty money. That's all I remember. No land money.
A.P.: How much treaty money did he give you every year?
J.D.: Five dollars.
A.P.: Tell the Judge about Old Succona, the Chief.
J.D.: He was our Chief but he doesn't know paper. All the people don't know paper.
A.P.: Did he have special clothes?
J.D.: He has trousers like policeman, clothes like policeman.
A.P.: When did Succona wear his special clothes?
J.D.: When he goes, he says he's gonna talk.
A.P.: Who did Succona talk to?
J.D.: Small Indian Boss [Galibois], when he calls him.
The Court: Succona talked to Small Indian Boss, is that it?
A.P.: Yes.
A.P.: When the Small Indian Boss called him, what did the Small Indian Boss tell Succona?
J.D.: He talks about the land.
A.P.: What did the Small Indian Boss say about the land?
Judge: ... the small Indian Boss is speaking English, so he couldn't know what the Small Indian Boss was saying ... unless it was hearsay ...
A.P.: I'm trying to elicit this witness's stories so he will tell us what he knows.
Judge: He is subject to the basic rules of evidence, i.e. what you say, heard, or experienced yourself.
A.P.: I wish to prove the nature of the relationship between the Indian Agent and the Chief.
Judge: I have no objection to repeating anything that was said in front of a translator, but I can't see the probative reason or

purpose of what he heard that Succona said. If it's a question of background, I've got plenty of background. I want to get back to the facts, provable facts ... I don't want him to say what he thinks Succona said. I'm not paying any attention to it.*

Justice Addy's refusal to listen to John Davis's words stood in remarkable contrast to John Davis's testimony that "What I do not remember, I will not say ... I cannot read and write. I only can remember." John Davis was an honest man who would not say anything he was unsure about. Justice Addy's narrow conception of truth, which conformed to a code of evidence completely foreign to Davis, left no room to respect Davis's knowledge and wisdom. Art Pape, forced to ask questions in a way that the judge would find more acceptable, continued:

> *A.P.:* Well, one of the facts that has to be proven, my Lord, is the perception that ... these Indian people had 40 years ago and 50 years ago, about the power that the Indian Agent had over their lives.
> *Judge:* Ask him that ... but don't start asking what the conversation was, or what the Indian Boss said.
> *A.P.:* John Davis. When Dr. Brown talked to Succona, was there an interpreter to tell Succona what Dr. Brown was saying?
> *J.D.:* A guy named Johnny Beaton [son of Frank Beaton, the HBC factor].
> *A.P.:* When Johnny Beaton talked for Dr. Brown, could the Indians understand what Dr. Brown was saying?
> *J.D.:* Johnny Beaton could speak a little bit of Beaver.
> *The Court:* A little bit of Beaver.
> *A.P.:* Did you sometimes hear Johnny Beaton speak for Dr. Brown?
> *J.D.:* No, I can't understand English.
> *A.P.:* Did you understand Johnny Beaton, when he spoke Beaver?
> *J.D.:* Yes.
> *A.P.:* Can you tell some things that Johnny Beaton said in your language for Dr. Brown?
> *J.D.:* About the land. People don't want to sell, but it was still sold.

---

* Ibid., vol. 10, pp. 1435–41.

Elder John Davis, 1995. Photo by Amber Ridington

A.P.: Did Johnny Beaton tell Succona in your language about the land when he talked for Dr. Brown?
J.D.: The Indian Boss wants to sell the land.
A.P.: What did Johnny Beaton say in your language would happen after the Indian boss sold the land?
...
J.D.: Johnny Beaton was speaking for people. He was helping the Indian people for long time. The Small Indian Boss wasn't helping.
A.P.: Do you know the name of the Small Indian Boss?
J.D.: Galibois ...
Judge: Is Galibois the Small Indian Boss, or is it Dr. Brown?
A.P.: Galibois ...
J.D.: He was the Indian Boss but he never help Indians.
A.P.: John Davis, what did Johnny Beaton say to Succona about selling the land?
Court: The answer doesn't mean anything unless it's situated in the proper context.
A.P.: The story you have just told about Johnny Beaton, did you hear Johnny Beaton say that to Succona?

J.D.: I was there, I hear.
The Court: All right.
A.P.: Did Johnny Beaton say those things in your language when he talked to Succona?
J.D.: He speak a bit Beaver ... He told him not to sell it, that the Indians are poor, they should be left there.
Judge: What did Succona say?
J.D.: He doesn't think so. Johnny Beaton told him, but the Chief doesn't think so.
A.P.: What did the Chief want to do?
J.D.: He just want to go out hunting and he sold the land.
A.P.: Why did the Chief [want to] sell the land?
J.D.: "Gonna be lots of money," the Indian boss told him. They just took it. They never saw nothing from it. To this day there was no money.
A.P.: Which Indian boss told Succona there would be lots of money?
J.D.: The one who sold the land, the small Indian Boss, Galibois.
A.P.: Did Succona talk that day to the people about selling the land? Did he tell them anything about selling the land that day?
J.D.: He told people he was going to sell it, but a lot of people were against selling it ...
A.P.: Who was against selling the land?
J.D.: A lot of people. Aku, Jack, myself, my dad, Jedney, the other people said no. We never received anything from it. There's lot of white people on it today.
A.P.: On that day, did you tell Succona no?
J.D.: We all told him no.
A.P.: Did you talk to Chief Succona on that day?
J.D.: When he was going to the meeting I told him, "No, don't sell the land."
A.P.: What place were you at when you told him that?
J.D.: The Indian land where we were living before we sold it.
A.P.: When you told Chief Succona, "No," what did he say to you?
J.D.: "There's gonna be lots of money for it." Now there's no money for it.
A.P.: On the day when you were outside at Petersen's shack, did other Indian people talk to Chief Succona about selling the land?
J.D.: Not many people spoke to him.

A.P.: Did Chief Succona ask every Indian person that day what they want to do?
J.D.: There were a few sitting around with him.
A.P.: Did Chief Succona ask each one to say what he thought about selling the land?
J.D.: There were a few talking to him and some were against selling it. They want to talk.
A.P.: When Johnny Beaton [translating for Galibois] told that to Succona, was a tall man you called Ottawa [John Grew] there too?
J.D.: He was with the Chief where we live.
A.P.: What place was that?
J.D.: Doig River.
A.P.: Did you see Ottawa at Doig River?
J.D.: He was with Indian Chief. From the outside I saw him.
A.P.: Were they in a tent?
J.D.: Little cabin.
Judge: Are you going to explore what the Small Boss told about the money? Was there an interpreter?
A.P.: When the Small Indian Boss told Chief Succona about the money, was there someone who put the words into Beaver?
J.D.: Mosquito ... Billy Mosquito.
A.P.: Where did Billy Mosquito come from?
J.D.: He was from down [Alberta], yes? He doesn't translate for people. *[John Davis then lists the men who were there.]*
A.P.: The people you saw there, did you sit with them outside?
J.D.: Some were inside, some outside.
A.P.: Which ones were inside?
J.D.: Succona, George Miller ...
A.P.: Did Joe Apsassin go inside?
J.D.: He was outside.
A.P.: Did Daniel Apsassin go inside?
J.D.: I didn't watch that. I only can tell you what I saw.
A.P.: What was the building they went inside?
J.D.: Log cabin ...
A.P.: Whose cabin was that, do you know?
J.D.: Petersen, Ernie Petersen ...
A.P.: The people outside with you, what did they do outside?
J.D.: They weren't doing anything. They were just sitting outside.
A.P.: Who told them to come there that day?

J.D.: Indian Boss.
A.P.: Did the Indian Boss tell you to come there?
J.D.: No.
A.P.: Who told you to come there?
J.D.: Nobody tell me. There were a lot of people there.
A.P.: Where were you before you went to that place?
J.D.: At my place, by the river.
A.P.: What is the name of your place by the river?
J.D.: Petersen's Crossing.
A.P.: Did anybody talk to the people outside about selling the land?
J.D.: Nobody ...
A.P.: Did Succona talk that day to people about selling the land? Did he tell them anything about selling the land that day?
J.D.: He told people that he was going to sell it but lot of people were against it.
A.P.: What did Succona say – why he was going to sell it?
J.D.: There's going to be a lot of money for that land. To this day, never saw no money.
A.P.: Who was against selling the land?
Judge: Wait a second. I want to get the answer. There were a few and some were against selling the land. They didn't speak to him?
A.P.: Who did not speak to Succona?
J.D.: When he told them that he was going to sell the land, they turn away and didn't speak to him.
A.P.: Who were they?
J.D.: I know some of their names.
A.P.: Would you tell the Judge their names?
J.D.: Joe Jedney, Jedney, Aku, Jedney's older brother, myself. Those I know.
A.P.: Can you say what Murray Attachie said about selling the land?
J.D.: He said no.
A.P.: Can you say what Dan Wolf said about selling the land?
J.D.: He too said no. There's a lot of them who said no.
A.P.: Do you know about what Charlie Yahey said about selling the land?
J.D.: He too said no.
A.P.: When you were outside, did Billy Mosquito say some things to you and the other Indians there?

J.D.: He said, "They're selling the land." He told the Chief, "You're going to have lots of money." There's no money.
A.P.: Did you hear Billy Mosquito tell that to the Chief?
J.D.: Yes. Sometimes he spoke Beaver.
Judge: Did anybody say yes outside of Succona?
J.D.: Very few. Some went to town. They said they gonna get to town, get money, and they ask us to come, but we went the other way ...
A.P.: Which Indians wanted to sell the land?
J.D.: The Chief, the Small Indian Boss. Those days, people don't know paper. White people, they know paper. They go by it.
Judge: Who among the Indian band outside of Succona were in favour of selling the land, if any?
J.D.: Jedney's older brother[;] George Miller.
Judge: Ask him, "Did Joe Quilan [Kulẹa] want to sell the land?
J.D.: They do as Chief tells them to. They don't listen to other people.
Judge: Are you saying that Joe Quilan agreed to sell the land because the Chief told him to?
J.D.: Yes, the Chief was to make the last decision.
Judge: Among those who were in favour, were there only two? Jedney's older brother, Joe Quilan, and George Miller? ...
A.P.: Were there some other Indians who also wanted to sell the land?
J.D.: That's all I know.
A.P.: Did Joe Galibois say the names of all the Indians who were there?
J.D.: He called them to come. Just a few came. There were people against selling the land.*

The court adjourned for the day. Robin wrote the following about the day's proceedings:

> After John Davis testified he spoke with Gerry. Later, Gerry said that John Davis had told him that ever since he was a young man, all he had to do was get up in the morning, saddle up his horse, go out hunting for moose. He would just do what he wanted to and nobody would ask him anything about what he was doing.

---

* Ibid., vol. 10, pp. 1141-56.

The ritual taking place in this courtroom and the ritual that was imposed on the Ft. St. John Indian people in 1945 are parallel and intimately connected to one another. In 1945, Joe Galibois imposed his own agenda on a community that could only vote no by walking away. In 1987, Art Pape and the painstaking research that supports him in court today, provide a context in which the Beaver People can finally be heard, at least to a certain extent. As a piece of ritual theatre, the justice of their cause is self evident. Even in the rule of law, it is building into a powerful demonstration. The only problem is that in the mind of Mr. Justice Addy, the Indian people and their way of being are still wholly foreign. At best, he may be open to an argument that the trust relationship is like that of a child to its protector. So far, he has shown little or no signs of understanding the power and autonomy and knowledge of the people whose testimony he has been hearing. He still sees them as backward and victimized people.

When the day was over, everybody but the counsel for the defence was glowing. Many of us went up and shook the old man's hand and patted him on the back. He seemed pleased. David [Davis, John's son] was proud and beaming. Haig and company were obviously uncomfortable, as indeed they should be in their situation.

John Davis spoke in the highly contexted form of discourse that assumes a knowledge of the fundamental facts of the situation. I think at the end, the Judge at least satisfied himself that he knew what John Davis was saying, even though it is unclear whether he believed it to be an accurate account of events brought back in memory from forty years past. (RDA, field notes, 28 January 1987)

The next morning, John Davis continued on the stand, and Lana Wolf translated. The Crown attorney, J.R. Haig, thought he had spotted something in John Davis's testimony that indicated that the Dane-zaa had been called upon to vote. When asked whether Galibois said the names of all the Indians who were there, John Davis answered, "He called them to come." Haig declaimed, "We say that is a very important acknowledgment that the names of all the Indians were called out at this meeting. We will argue that that can only mean that the names were called out to vote." Haig started his cross-examination with that point: "John Davis. Good morning. Please tell us some more about what you said yesterday when you told us, 'Joe Galibois told us to come.' Please tell us more about that story" (RDA, field notes, 29 January 1987)."*

Art Pape pointed out that Haig had taken one sentence out of a longer answer. Haig then quotes the full statement from which his excerpt came: "*A.P.:* Did Joe Galibois say the names of all the people who were there then? *J.D.:* He called the names. Just a few came." Pape interjected, "I'm glad that Mr. Haig wants to accept the first sentence and not the second or third." Mr. Haig then pursued another line of questioning. At the end of the arguments, Pape summarized the Dane-zaa's case: "This is a case where Indian People did not say, 'give me something,' but had something taken away. The answer is in the asking. Until 1960, Indians did not even have the vote."†

Gerry Attachie, Eddie Apsassin, and Joe Apsassin were in court throughout the final week. Gerry told Robin that it was particularly hard to be in the city, but he managed to stick it out. Robin noted: "Sometimes I forget how much he and the others are so much persons of their country. Sometime during his final argument Art pointed out that it is important to remember that replacement land is not within the Indian sense of meaningful options. For them, 'place is everything.' It is place and not location that is important. Montney is the place 'where happiness dwells.' The fundamental idea of Indian land is different from that of white land. For Indians, land is inalienable while in white law the test of ownership is its alienability" (RDA, field notes, 29 January 1987).

When Gerry spoke with Amber Ridington and Kate Hennessy in 2005, he talked about the outcome of the case.

> We lost. They said we were six months late over limitation. Thirty year Limitation Act which came into BC in 1974, and we run into that, and we run into a rough, pretty redneck Judge, George Addy, his name.
>
> We appealed it, before three Judges, in 1992. One was a black Judge named Isaac [Chief Justice Julius Isaac]. These two other whites, those white Judge went against us, but the coloured guy, Isaac, he said the Indians have a good case here. And so we appealed it to Supreme Court in Canada in 1995, and won it there. We just settle it out of court. (Attachie 2002)

---

* Ibid.
† Ibid.

In 1989, when Gerry spoke at the "Cultures in Conflict" conference at UBC, the appeal had not yet been heard. He had more immediate thoughts on the case:

> Yeah, I just want to say another thing. We – we had people that were at the 1945 Surrender. We had people that were still around. They were still alive, and hopefully they could settle this while they were still alive. [Over the] last few years, when we started working on this case, a lot of people were wanting to get involved, the people that were there at that time. And just recently there's some farmers, local people in Fort St. John that, when they heard about this case, heard that we lost the first round – they were upset. They said that hopefully you people will get something out of this. You know, they felt really bad, and we had some people that were involved at that time. Some people from outside, like teachers and some priests, Catholic priests. They had good testimony, and we taped some of them ... what I believe is we should have these people before the court case, and then would have been different too. (Ridington 1990a, 280)

As Gerry notes above, the bands appealed the decision. They asked Thomas Berger to argue the case. Gary Nelson worked with him, and Leslie Pinder and Art Pape continued their work on the case. Berger alleged that Justice Addy had failed to fairly assess the evidence and to apply the law and that Addy "had not applied a fiduciary standard but had instead applied a test of informed consent" (Berger 2002, 225). Berger explained further: "This distinction was not esoteric, but basic. The law of fiduciary duty is that a fiduciary must look after a beneficiary's property with the same prudence he would use if it were his own property. A prudent owner would not have given away the mineral rights. A prudent owner would have done exactly what DVLA [Director, Veterans' Land Act] did on behalf of the veterans; *lease* the minerals rights to oil companies" (ibid., 255-56).

Berger argued that a fiduciary has responsibility for all the consequences, foreseen or unforeseen. A fiduciary has an obligation of honour. Berger also pointed out that in another important fiduciary duty case (the *Canson Enterprises* case), which the Supreme Court of Canada had decided some four years before the *Apsassin* case, Justice McLachlin had written, "A breach of fiduciary duty is wrong in itself, regardless of whether a loss can be foreseen" (Berger 2002, 256). But the Federal Court of Appeal sided with Justice Addy. In Berger's opinion, the reasoning of the majority "did not take into account the special elements of loyalty and trust that give rise to the fiduciary duty. Moreover, it did not take into account that no advice had been provided to the Indians regarding their best interests, and no attempt made by the Crown to protect their best interests." Berger noted that "Judge Louis Marceau, writing for the majority, went on to shrink the Crown's obligation to the vanishing point ... the Crown as fiduciary is not to be held to the same standard as an individual, because the Crown always has to deal with the perfectly legitimate needs of other constituencies" (ibid., 258).

Yet, as Berger pointed out, the Crown does not owe a fiduciary obligation to these other claimants, not even to veterans. In his dissenting judgment, Chief Justice Isaac determined that the Crown had breached its fiduciary duty in transferring the mineral rights. Isaac also stated that the lawsuit had commenced within the thirty-year ultimate limitation under BC's 1975 Limitation Act. "The first alienation of legal title to the lands did not take place until 1952. Isaac would have allowed the band's appeal and sent the case back to the Trial Division for assessment of damages" (Berger 2002, 259).

Because of Chief Justice Isaac's strong dissent, the bands were given leave to appeal to the Supreme Court of Canada. On behalf of the Dane-zaa, Berger argued that the surrender had not been valid and that the land should never have been lost to them. Once a government takes on a responsibility, he contended, it must meet its responsibility in a proper manner. In this case, the 1945 surrender had been manifestly improvident and, he argued, the Crown had been well aware of that because DIA officials had consistently refused, until 1945, to ask the band to surrender. The surrender had been contrary to departmental policy, which was "solidly against alienation by sale of lands for which there is any likelihood of Indian need in future years." This is what the minister of Indian affairs had advised Parliament in 1945, the very year in which the surrender took place (Berger 2002, 263).

Despite this argument, Berger concentrated on the mineral rights issue, which formed the basis of Chief Justice Isaac's dissenting opinion. As Berger (2002, 264) states in his assessment of the case:

> We adopted the reasoning of Chief Justice Isaac, who had said in this dissenting judgement:
> If the Crown intended that the 1945 surrender was both to divest the Indians of their entire interest in the reserve and to

relieve itself of the willingly assumed obligation to administer the mineral rights to the reserve in the Indian's best interests, *it would have been under a positive duty to inform the Indians that this was the case.* [Emphasis added]

In the appeal, Berger (ibid., 264-65) also quoted a letter that A.F. McWilliams, a lawyer in the Department of Veterans Affairs, had written to his director in 1961:

> It has been known here The Director, the Veteran's Land Act is the owner of the mineral rights underlying the Fort St. John Indian Reserve. *It has always been a mystery to the writer how he acquired these mineral rights, and our file on the Fort St. John Indian Reserve does not disclose how this came about.* We would be interested to know, therefore, under what arrangement did The Director, The Veteran's Land Act acquire the mineral rights under the Fort St. John Indian Reserve. [Emphasis added]

Berger also pointed out the reply to McWilliams's query, which was written by H.R. Holmes, the superintendent of the Securities and Property Division of Veterans Affairs.

1. I think the simple answer to your query of June 14th is that the reason we acquired the mineral rights when we acquired the surface rights is because the Letters Patent which issued did not reserve the mines and minerals.
2. The chief and principal men of the St. John Beaver Band of Indians executed a Surrender dated the 22nd of September, 1945, and the Governor in Council by Order in Council PC 6506 dated the 16th day of October, 1945, accepted the Surrender and authorized the Minister of Mines and Resources [under which ministry the DIA fell at the time] to sell or lease the said lands subject to the conditions of the Surrender and the provisions of the Indian Act. *During purchase negotiations with Indian Affairs, there was no reference, to the best of my knowledge and belief, to the question of mineral rights. As I have already said, the mines and minerals, either deliberately or inadvertently, were not reserved with the result that we acquired them. I think possibly the failure to reserve the sub-surface rights was inadvertent.* (Berger 2002, 263, emphasis added)

Berger argued that the Crown had failed to take any steps to protect the band's interest when it transferred and leased the rights to minerals underlying the former IR 172. In 1949, the DIA took the view that the minerals had been transferred to the Director, Veterans' Land Act (DVLA) in 1948. The DVLA then leased the mineral rights to oil companies for the benefit of the veterans. The DVLA later transferred the lands to the veterans in fee simple. Berger said that the Crown had failed to take any steps to protect the band's interest in the mineral rights or to obtain any benefit for the band. As he put it, "How could it be said that this failure fulfilled the Crown's duty under the 1945 surrender to dispose of Montney upon such terms as would be, according the language of the surrender signed by the Indians, 'most conducive to our welfare and that of our people'?" (Berger 2002, 265-66)

But even if the Supreme Court accepted Berger's argument, there was still the problem of the thirty-year limitation under BC's Limitation Act. Fortunately, Justice McLachlin pointed out a little-known section (section 64) of the 1927 Indian Act, which authorized the DIA to revoke any sale made in error. Berger seized on it to argue that the DIA was under a continuing obligation, even after the sale to the DVLA, to cancel the sale and return the mineral rights to the band. In essence, the band could claim that the Crown had a fiduciary duty to revoke the mineral sale to the DVLA and reacquire the mineral rights. This fiduciary duty continued to lie with the Crown until the date on which the mineral rights had been sold to the veterans and, therefore, could no longer be reacquired under section 64. This meant that the limitations clock did not begin to run until 1948, when DVLA had passed the rights on to the veterans (and, therefore, the DIA could no longer cancel the sale or reacquire the mineral rights). If this was the case, the lawsuit had been filed just before the thirty-year limitation ran out.

The decision came down on 14 December 1994. The Supreme Court found that the 1945 surrender of the surface rights had not been a breach of the Crown's fiduciary duty. The Crown had intended that alternative reserves would be acquired for hunting and trapping. It was, the court held, a defensible decision. The judgment of Justice McLachlin (who wrote for the minority, but laid the groundwork for the majority decision, as well) reads as follows:

> In 1940, the Band surrendered the mineral rights on its Fort St. John reserve to the Crown, in trust to lease for its benefit ...

At the end of World War II, the federal government instituted a program under which agricultural land was made available to veterans for settlement ...

[T]he Band agreed to surrender its reserve to the Crown ... so that it could ultimately be distributed under The Veterans' Land Act ... After negotiations between the Department of Indian Affairs ("DIA"), and the Director, The Veterans' Land Act ("DVLA"), a price of $70,000 was agreed upon and paid to the DIA by the DVLA ...

Between 1948 and 1956, the land which had formerly been the Band's Fort St. John reserve was sold to veterans by way of agreements for sale. In 1948 gas was discovered about 40 miles southeast of the reserve. In 1949 oil companies expressed interest in exploring the land for oil and gas ... In 1976, oil and gas were discovered. The revenue from this discovery (an amount not determined in the current proceedings, but estimated by the trial judge to be roughly $300 million) went to the veterans or their assigns ...

The measure of control which the [1927 Indian] Act permitted the Band to exercise over the surrender of the reserve negates the contention that absent exploitation, the Act imposed a fiduciary obligation on the Crown with respect to the surrender of the reserve ...

The true object of the [relevant sections] of the *Indian Act* was to ensure that the surrender was validly assented to by the Band. The evidence ... amply established valid assent ...

The appellants have not established that the Crown wrongly failed to prevent the surrender of the Fort St. John reserve in 1945 ...

In the face of this evidence, it cannot be said that Addy J. erred in concluding that the sale of the land to the DVLA was not in breach of the Crown's fiduciary duty. A number of options – lease, partial sale and outright sale – were considered ... In retrospect, with the decline of trapping and the discovery of oil and gas, the decision [to sell rather than to lease] may be argued to have been unfortunate. But at the time, it may be defended as a reasonable solution to the problems the Band faced.*

---

* *Apsassin v. The Queen*, [1995] 4 SCR 344 at paras 26-28, 36, 44, 51.

No Dane-zaa made any statement about wanting to be closer to their traplines. The elders had stated as clearly as possible that the Place Where Happiness Dwells was intimately related to their well-being. They had spoken about the good hunting and berry picking at the old reserve. It would seem evident, given that the new reserves were not acquired for many years after the loss of IR 172, that the loss of the reserve did contribute to their poverty in the period immediately following the loss.

As Robin points out in "Cultures in Conflict: The Problem of Discourse" (Ridington 1990a), and as Jean-Guy Goulet reiterates in "Legal Victories for the Dene Tha?" (Goulet 2010), First Nations concepts of justice differ from the dominant (white) conception of justice. To a member of the former Fort St. John Band, the problem was that their reserve had been sold without the consent of the majority of the adult men who were on the band list in 1945 (female band members had no vote at that time). The Supreme Court took no account of the fact that these men could not read or write – there was no school until five years after the surrender. At all levels at which the case was heard, judges made decisions based on statutes that would have been unfamiliar to the band members of 1945 – and, indeed, were still unfamiliar to the elders who testified in 1987. The Supreme Court of Canada took into consideration the Indian Act and the BC Limitation Act. The judges' interpretation of the band members' wishes must have been taken from Indian Agents' reports filed in Ottawa rather than from the words of the men who were present at the surrender. Although the Indian Agent "Johnny Watson" supported the band's case, it appears that his testimony was not given as much weight as words written by Crown servants four decades before the case was heard.

The former Fort St. John Band did, however, win on the mineral rights issue. Justice Gonthier, who wrote the majority decision of the Supreme Court of Canada, noted that IR 172 had been surrendered in trust in 1945 to "sell or lease." Therefore, in Gonthier's view, the surrender contained "no clear authorization from the Band which justified the DIA in departing from its long-standing policy of reserving mineral rights for the benefit of the aboriginals when surface rights were sold." Justice Gonthier concluded that "[i]t was a violation of the fiduciary duty to sell the mineral rights to the DVLA in 1948."*

---

* Ibid., McLachlin J., companion decision, para 19.

Madame Justice McLachlin wrote a lengthy companion decision in which she set out the background facts on which the majority judgment had been based. In it, she notes the "wonderment" of various officials when they discovered that the IR 172 mineral rights had not been retained by the DIA but had instead been transferred to the DVLA. Years later, wonderment persisted as to why the mineral rights had been passed to the DVLA. The wonderment was understandable given the well-known policy of the DIA to reserve out mineral rights and the fact that the only interest of the DVLA was to obtain land for agricultural purposes, not to enrich veterans through procuring mineral rights for them. The best explanation of how the mineral rights came to be transferred to the DVLA appears to lie in simple inadvertence."*

Did the inadvertence amount to a breach of fiduciary duty? Although Justice Addy had said that nobody at the DIA had had any reason to believe the mineral rights were other than worthless, Justice McLachlin disagreed: "The finding of the trial judge that the Crown could not have known in 1948 [when the mineral rights were transferred to the DVLA] that the mineral rights might possess value flies in the face of the evidence on record. Accordingly, this is one of those rare cases where departure from a trial judge's finding may be warranted ... After taking the surrender [of the mineral rights for lease] in 1940, [the Crown] issued a permit for prospecting for oil and gas on the property. The 1940 permit alone was worth $1,800, a not insignificant sum."†

McLachlin found that Addy had "confused potential with actual value" (Berger 268-69). She continued:

> If indeed the mineral rights had minimal sale value in 1948, it does not follow that a prudent person would give them away ... since it would cost nothing to keep them, they should be kept against the chance, however remote, that they might acquire some value in the future. The wisdom of the latter course is demonstrated by the Crown's policy with respect to its own mineral rights; it reserved them to itself, regardless of actual value. It lies ill in the mouth of the Crown to argue that it should have done less with the property entrusted to it as fiduciary to lease for the welfare of the Band.

---

* Ibid., para 94. See also Berger (2002, 267).
† Ibid., paras 98-99.

The trial judge's emphasis on the apparent low value of the mineral rights suggests an underlying concern with the injustice of conferring an unexpected windfall on the Indians at the Crown's expense.*

In the majority's decision, Justice Gonthier concluded:

> As a fiduciary, the DIA was required to act with reasonable diligence. In my view, a reasonable person in the DIA's position would have realized by August 9, 1949 that an error had occurred, and would have exercised the s. 64 power to correct the error, reacquire the mineral rights, and effect a leasing arrangement for the benefit of the Band. That this was not done was a clear breach of the DIA's fiduciary duty to deal with I.R. 172 according to the best interests of the Band.
> Thus, I conclude that the appellants may recover any losses stemming from transfers by the DVLA after August 9, 1949 as such losses fall within the 30-year limitation period imposed by the British Columbia *Limitation Act,* and are not barred by any other provision of that Act as explained in the reasons of McLachlin J.†

Gonthier agreed with McLachlin's disposition of the case in which she stated that she "would allow the appeal and set aside the judgments below" and "[t]he Bands are entitled to damages against the Crown for breach of fiduciary duty with respect to such mineral rights as were conveyed by agreement for sale after August 9, 1949."‡

At that point, no one knew how much oil and gas lay beneath the land sections ceded to veterans after 9 August 1949. When Berger and the other lawyers consulted oil and gas experts (Berger 2002, 270), they learned that the sections did have oil and that two were big producers. "All that remained was to determine the actual value of the oil produced from the 6.75 sections" (ibid.). That took another two years.

The former Fort St. John Band did finally receive compensation, but not until ten years after the initial trial, and not for the loss of the land itself. In 1997, the Doig River and Blueberry River First Nations

---

* Ibid., paras 102-3.
† Ibid., majority decision, paras 22-23.
‡ Ibid., McLachlin J., para 123.

(the former Fort. St. John Band) negotiated a settlement. They were pleased to accept this compensation, but they did not feel that they had received true justice. To the Dane-zaa, the decision seemed to disregard the testimony of the elders at the initial trial. In Dane-zaa culture, as in any culture with a long oral history, elders are deeply respected and honoured as the keepers of the wise stories. The Dane-zaa viewed the courts' seeming refusal to accept their words as valid truth as unjust and disrespectful. Nor had the courts acknowledged the Dane-zaa's deep roots in the area. Despite the pain they felt for their elders, they resolved to look to the future and to use the money to make life better for future generations.

Gerry summarized the outcome of the case with these words:

> And with that money we built this hall here, this complex, the rodeo ground, and some of the buildings. And the sad part is, when we start this court case, some of the Elders said they were happy, they said. Finally they want justice done, because they've been suffering in the past too long. They passed on.
>
> But now we're just looking forward to the future, to setting up something for our next generation. One thing lacking right now is our language – it's slowly dying off. But we are fighting that. We're trying to bring it back. That's why we brought you people in. The museum here too. I hope we don't lose our language, and I just want to end there. (Attachie 2002)

15

Today and Tomorrow

Although the judgment in the *Apsassin* case might not have been all that the members of the former Fort St. John Band had hoped for, the financial settlement enabled the Doig River and Blueberry River First Nations to improve their quality of life. With some additional support from local businesses and oil companies, Doig River First Nation opened its new band hall and cultural centre on 18 July 2003. It is now the centre of cultural life in the community.

The chief and councillors have their offices in the complex, as do the band manager and support staff. In addition, the building houses a nursing centre; a museum that displays historical photographs and artifacts, as well as recordings and photographs from the Ridington/Dane-zaa Archive; offices for members working on a variety of projects; a kitchen where band members help themselves to coffee, tea, and other refreshments and where cooking is done for community gatherings; and a gym with changing rooms and saunas. All kinds of community events, from basketball games to wakes and funerals, take place in the complex. Blueberry River First Nation now has a similar building, which opened in the summer of 2010.

According to its website, the city of Fort St. John and surrounding area now has 60,000 inhabitants. There are currently about 250 members of the Doig River First Nation and 400 members of the Blueberry River First Nation. With the addition of Dane-zaa at Halfway River (227 members) and Prophet River (223 members) and those who live off reserve or at other reserves not as close to Fort St. John, there may be about 1,500 Dane-zaa alive today.

Doig River First Nation Band Hall and Cultural Complex, 2010.
Photo by Jillian Ridington

Sam Acko teaching boys to drum in Doig River First Nation Band Hall and Cultural Complex, May 2010. Photo by Jillian Ridington

One hundred years ago, Aboriginal people formed almost 100 percent of the area's population. Now they represent only about 2.5 percent. Fort St. John calls itself the "Energetic City," and its website states: "Early pioneers built Fort St. John into the largest city in British Columbia's northeast region." It fails to mention the contribution of the Dane-zaa. There is some evidence that white "locals" are now paying more attention to the area's original people. In May 2010, we were invited to speak to Sci-Tech North, a group of professionals from the Fort St. John area, at the North Peace Cultural Centre. They were a receptive and appreciative audience and asked many thoughtful questions about Dane-zaa culture. Elder May Apsassin, her daughter Sandra, the Doig Drummers, Chief Norman Davis, former chief Garry Oker, and many other Dane-zaa were present.

Dane-zaa youth and elders are participating in Nenan Dane-zaa Deh Zona, an organization that comprises First Nations people, social workers, and other professionals from northeastern BC who are negotiating to take over Aboriginal family and children's services from the BC Ministry of Children and Family Development. Youth and elders from all the Dane-zaa bands joined Saulteau and Metis at Youth and Elders Camps that Nenan organized in the summers of 2009, 2010, 2011, and 2012. Elder May Apsassin has been an important contributor to the camps, as have Tommy Attachie, the Doig River drummers, and the Blueberry River singers and drummers. The Honourable Mary Polack, who was then BC's minister of children's and family development, took part in the 2010 gathering and promised to support the initiative. Her successor, the Honourable Mary McNeil, attended the 2011 camp at the Pink Mountain Ranch, which is now owned by the Blueberry River First Nation. The 2009 and 2010 gatherings took place at Bear Flat Campground (near where Alexander

Gathering for a meal at Nenan Youth and Elders Camp, 2009.
Photo by Robin Ridington

Mackenzie made his famous journal entry quoted in Chapter 5). All four gatherings have been successful. The 2012 camp attracted over five hundred participants. Robin videotaped all four camps, and his videos are being used to publicize and further the work. A professional film titled *Home Is the Place Where Happiness Dwells* (Nenan Dane-zaa Deh Zona 2011) documents the 2011 camp and the organization's objectives.

Another important summer gathering is the Doig River rodeo, which takes place on Doig's well-maintained rodeo grounds, just below the band hall and cultural centre. It is well attended by First Nations people and white residents who come from throughout the area to compete or just to enjoy the gathering.

Outside of Fort St. John, the Peace River area is still a land of farms and mixed poplar, pine, and spruce forest, but its economy is now based more on oil and gas production than on farming. The Dane-zaa now run companies such as Renegade Construction, owned by Trevor Makadahay, that provide services to oil companies. Trevor is a great-grandson of Dechezhę, grandson of the late song keeper Billy Makadahay and Sally Takola Makadahay, and son of Doig River First Nation linguist Billy Attachie and Rita Makadahay. Trevor's fleet of trucks supplies oil rigs throughout the area. Trevor's cousin Wes Rothlesberger owns another company, Beaver Dam Ventures.

The Dane-zaa must respond to and engage with changing circumstances in ways unique to First Peoples. They are willing to take advantage of employment and investment opportunities in the oil and gas industry but do not necessarily share the mindset of developers. They are aware that grease from the giant animals is a finite resource, and they see their role as making the extraction industry more environmentally sound and accountable to local communities. They see their first responsibility as being to the land and its people. Many Dane-zaa are working as monitors to ensure that damage from development is prevented or minimized. Sandra Apsassin, a member of the Blueberry River First Nation, developed an excellent presentation on the history and beliefs of Treaty 8 First Nations, the implications of Treaty 8, the relationship between the people and the land, and other topics. She presented it to the employees of several oil and gas companies, often accompanied by her mother May. The presentation has been well received.

A generation ago, the oil and gas industry did not respect Dane-zaa rights. Companies constructed wells, seismic roads, and compressor stations without consultation. In the process, they often obliterated

Old Blueberry Reserve from Charlie Yahey's camp, 1966. Photo by Robin Ridington

Garry Oker teaching at training session for environmental assessment team. Boardroom, Doig River Band Hall and Cultural Complex, 2009.
Photo by Jillian Ridington

traditional village sites, graves, and trapping cabins. In July 1979, a sour gas well forced residents of the Blueberry Reserve to evacuate. "Poison gas came down like a fog" and made all the residents fearful of further damage from the well (audio documentary, Broomfield and Ridington 1981, Ridington/Dane-zaa Archive [RDA]). After a court case and long negotiations, the reserve was moved to another location farther away from the well. Jillian Ridington and Howard Broomfield documented these events in "Suffering Me Slowly," a program broadcast on CBC Radio's *The Hornby Collection* in 1981. The Dane-zaa have become more effective in their dealings with the oil companies, and the oil companies have become more respectful of the Dane-zaa, although many issues are still being contested.

Doig River First Nation has become an active participant in an agroforestry program called the Doig River First Nation Demonstration Project. This positive environmental initiative is testing the concept of creating hybrid poplar and aspen forests in conjunction with native grasses to produce a sustainable source of forest products within Doig territory. Coordinated by band member Carl Pouce Coupe, the Doig First Nation views the project as furthering its overall mission "to enhance the quality of the life of the members of the Doig River First Nation, today and in the future, through culture, education, social and economic development."

Dane-zaa people are concerned about the impact that the construction of the Site C dam, the third dam on the Peace River, will have on their traditional territory and the game they have hunted for millennia. The proposed dam would flood hundreds of acres of traditional Dane-zaa territory near Attachie and Bear Flats, the area where Alexander Mackenzie landed. The water would flood islands where moose give birth to their calves. In addition, if the project goes ahead, a new highway will replace Highway 29, and its path will be close to the old pack trail that Dane-zaa used for centuries and near the graves of Chief Attachie and other ancestors.

On 6 May 2010, we travelled with councillors and elders, including three of Chief Attachie's grandsons, and local farmer Bill Tompkins to Chief Attachie's grave. Tompkins's father had, in 1919, homesteaded the land where the grave is located. Bill Tompkins now farms it, but the land was sold to BC Electric (now BC Hydro) when the W.A.C. Bennett Dam was built. Bill feels that he has no choice but to leave, but he is unhappy at the prospect. Other farmers resisted BC Electric's offers back then, but their descendants now fear being expropriated. The Site C dam's possible effects on wildlife, traditional grave sites,

Tommy and Billy Attachie at their grandfather's grave, 6 May 2010.
Photo by Jillian Ridington

and First Nations rights under Treaty 8 is being assessed by the Treaty 8 Tribal Association, an organization of First Nations in the Peace River Basin. Well-known environmentalist David Suzuki also visited the site on 14 July 2012 when he participated in the "Paddle for the Peace" event. He also visited Chief Attachie's gravesite near the confluence of the Halfway and Peace rivers and met with Tommy Attachie there.

On 16 and 17 September 2010, the Doig River First Nation joined the Treaty 8 Tribal Association in sponsoring a First Nations Leadership Summit to plan a response to the proposed Site C dam. Participants included the Halfway River, McLeod Lake, Prophet River, and West Moberly First Nations; the Dene Tha'; and other First Nations along the Peace-Mackenzie drainage system. During the summit, the Doig River, Halfway River, Prophet River, and West Moberly First Nations issued a declaration, which pointed out that the signatories to Treaty 8 agreed that "First Nations have the right to continue with our way of life for as long as the sun shines, the grass grows and the rivers flow," and they have the right to do so without interference. The declaration stated that the dam would:

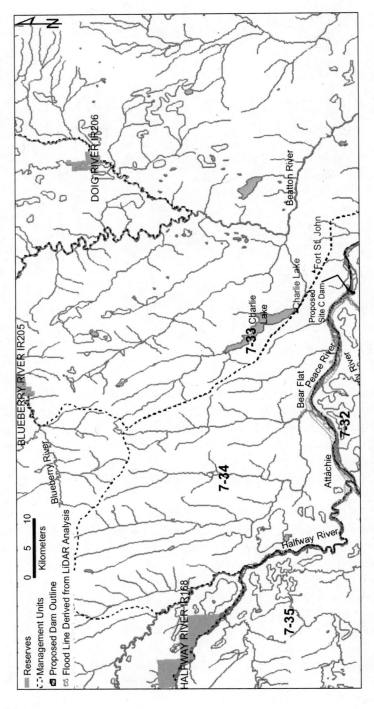

Wildlife units within proposed Site C reservoir. Courtesy of BC Hydro

- Disrespect and destroy the graves of our ancestors.
- Eliminate critical warm lowlands where both predators and prey survive harsh northern winters.
- Demolish habitat and disrupt migration routes for bull trout and other fish species at the top of the Peace River aquatic food chain.
- Annihilate the islands in the Peace where cow moose deliver their calves. Submerge key ungulate calving grounds for moose, mule deer and elk.
- Eliminate regionally rare and important ecosystems, including old growth deciduous and mixed wood forest of the Peace, Halfway, and Moberly rivers, riparian forests important to fur-bearers, habitat for red and blue listed neo-tropical migrant birds, and traditional and medicinal rare plant communities.
- Destroy more than 7,000 acres of class one and class two farmland and along with it the opportunity for food security in northeast BC.
- Together with the reservoirs created by the two existing dams, create a cumulative barrier to fish and wildlife movement, especially grizzly bear, at the narrowest waist of the continentally important Yellowstone to Yukon wildlife corridor.
- Exacerbate the negative environmental impacts caused by the first two upstream Peace River dams to the Peace-Athabasca delta and other wetlands down the Peace, Athabasca and Mackenzie River watersheds through Alberta and the Northwest Territory all the way to the Arctic Ocean.
- Add 147,000 tons of carbon dioxide to the atmosphere.
- Eliminate the very land upon which our people hold annual cultural camps to maintain the heritage of our relationships between our Elders, our youth and the land that is our duty to pass on to future generations in a healthy, vibrant state.
(Treaty 8 Tribal Association 2010)

Following the leadership summit, Chief Norman Davis, Councillor Gerry Attachie, several elders and members of the Doig River First Nation, staff and officials of the Treaty 8 Tribal Association, farmers and settlers from the Peace River Valley, and members of First Nations from throughout BC travelled to Victoria to participate in Paddle to the Premier. The journey culminated in a demonstration at the provincial legislature. Liz Logan, the Treaty 8 tribal chief, and Gerry

Attachie were among those who spoke eloquently about the importance of the valley and its fertile land. Gerry stated:

> We want to thank the Good Lord that we came here over one thousand miles to tell you that we want to stop the dam, another dam. This will be the third one if it comes true. It's going to cause a lot of grief. Our elders really oppose it. We all do, too, because we're from northeastern BC. I'm Dane-zaa, one of the Dane-zaa from over there. We were the first Fort St. John Beaver Band, they call us. We signed the treaty. My grandfather was one of the leaders that put his "x" on the treaty. (Ridington/Dane-zaa Archive, video documentary, Ridington 2010b)

Unlike fifty years ago, when the Bennett Dam flooded the area just west of Dane-zaa territory, indigenous people are aware of the proposal for the Site C dam and the problems and devastation it may bring. In this struggle, long-time white residents are joining First Nations in an effort to save the land they all love. As a speaker remarked during the rally, "It's cowboys and Indians together on this one!" Since the rally, Liz Logan has travelled to New York to appeal to the UN to intervene, and a report has been issued that shows that the dam would cost far more than the original estimates and would cause a 50-percent increase in the bills of BC Hydro customers. The environmental review process is now underway. The Doig River First Nation and other Treaty 8 First Nations are monitoring the situation and will respond as they see fit.

The advent of television and the Internet has decreased the use of the Dane-zaa language. Children of the Blueberry River First Nation attend elementary school on their reserve. Lana Wolf teaches them their traditional language, but they do the majority of their work in English. Children from Doig River First Nation attend the Upper Pine School with other elementary students from the area. Every year, all students from North Peace elementary schools come out to the Doig Reserve for Doig Days. At these events, members of the Doig River First Nation demonstrate traditional skills such as hide preparation, bannock making, and snowshoe crafting, and they perform traditional stories and songs.

Few young Dane-zaa speak Dane-zaa Záágé?, although most understand some phrases. Dane-zaa linguist Billy Attachie has worked with Marshall and Jean Holdstock of Trinity Western University and the

Jack Askoty demonstrating snowshoe making to area schoolchildren at Doig Days, May 2011. Photo by Jillian Ridington

Summer Institute of Linguistics for almost fifty years. They have made a significant contribution toward preserving Dane-zaa Záágé?. Throughout the years, they have developed an illustrated Dane-zaa Záágé?-English dictionary and translated many Bible stories into Dane-zaa Záágé?. Together with Madeline Oker Benson, Billy is writing down traditional stories and translating stories recorded in Dane-zaa Záágé? in the Ridington/Dane-zaa Archive. Several young Dane-zaa have attended the Gulf Islands Film and Television School and have used the skills they gained there to create films and websites. Their work was fundamental to producing *Dane Wajich: Dane-zaa Stories and Songs – Dreamers and the Land,* the website created by Amber Ridington and Kate Hennessy for the Canadian Museum of Civilization's Virtual Museum of Canada.

Dane-zaa artists are also making themselves known in the larger world. Brian Jungen, a great-grandson of the dreamer Oker, graduated from the Emily Carr College of Art and Design. His work has been shown in many galleries around the world, including the Vancouver

Art Gallery and the Tate Modern Gallery. Jungen became the first living Native American artist to have his own show at the Smithsonian National Museum of the American Indian. Titled *Strange Comfort,* the exhibition was on view from 16 October 2009 to 8 August 2010. The write-up for the show referred to Jungen as "the foremost Native artist of his generation, [who] transforms the familiar and banal into exquisite objects that reference themes of globalization, pop culture, museums, and the commoditization of Indian imagery" (Smithsonian Magazine 2009). In 2010, Jungen received the $25,000 Gershon Iskowitz Prize from the Art Gallery of Ontario for his outstanding contribution to visual arts in Canada. An exhibition of Jungen's work was on view at the gallery from May to August 2011. Jungen, like Tsááyaa, is a transformer and shape shifter. He takes ordinary objects such as Nike runners, cuts them apart, and reassembles them into forms meaningful in First Nations culture. Some of his constructions are relatively small, but others are large enough to occupy an entire room.

Despite his international fame, Jungen maintains close contact with his Dane-zaa relatives. In 2009, Robin was driving through Doig territory with elders when they came upon a bush camp where people were butchering a freshly killed moose. The event was important because the moose was the first kill for Carl Pouce Coupe's daughter Jasmine. There, helping with the butchering, was Brian, looking like a typical young Dane-zaa man rather than an internationally famous artist.

Brian's cousin, former chief Garry Oker, has also studied art and clothing design and has produced several films based on Dane-zaa stories and history. He describes his role as a cultural curator and designer. Oker collaborated with Robin and Jillian Ridington and filmmaker Stacy Shaak on a 2000 film, *Contact the People,* which received critical acclaim at the Sundance Festival (RDA, video documentaries, Ridington et al. 2000). He is currently involved in both cultural and entrepreneurial projects. Garry is a singer of traditional Dane-zaa songs, but he has also produced a CD called *Spirit Dreamers,* which blends Dane-zaa music with instrumental improvisation by Vancouver percussionist Sal Ferreras and others. Garry describes what he sees as the connection between traditional songs and the new media: "If you're walking on the trail to heaven, your shadow may scare you, and you become a wandering spirit. I was told always to look for my songs, and today I've found my songs, the traditional songs and the new ones that I made in a modern way, inspired by those traditional songs. It's my own. I've created my own songs, and

Brian Jungen, *The Men of My Family,* 2010, rawhide, metal, paint, and freezer, 272.0 × 122.5 × 70.5 cm. Collection of the Vancouver Art Gallery, Vancouver Art Gallery Acquisition Fund. Photo by Rachel Topham, Vancouver Art Gallery. Courtesy Brian Jungen and Vancouver Art Gallery

that's what Grandma and Grandpa told me. Keep looking for it. Don't let it go" (in discussion with Robin Ridington, 2 May 2010).

Garry is designing a video animation based on the story of Tsááyaa that he calls "A Hero's Journey." In 2011, Garry designed, organized,

Artwork by Garry Oker, on display in the boardroom of the Doig Band Hall and Cultural Complex. Photo by Robin Ridington

and taught digital media workshops for Dane-zaa youth. He calls the project "Dane-wajich TV": "Like many Aboriginal communities Doig River is experiencing rapid advancements in their technical infrastructure which now both allows for, and requires, the transliteration of cultural activities and traditional cultural archives into digital media formats" (email communication with authors, 1 November 2011). Young people today are learning video techniques and the art of interviewing and are encouraged to use traditional myths as the basis of explorations in new technologies. In 2011, Doig River received broadband Internet service throughout the community. This enables Garry and future students to share videos with other First Nations communities participating in a nation-wide media initiative called "First Mile."

The elders of today were raised by elders who lived most of their lives during the fur trade era. They grew up speaking Dane-zaa Záágé? as their first language. They learned the wise stories and wise practices that sustained Dane-zaa on their lands for many generations. Young Dane-zaa now attend high school with non-Aboriginal youth in Fort St. John, and some study at Northern Lights College. This education is providing them with the skills necessary for success in today's world, but it is not teaching them about their own culture. As part of their effort to make their history known to future generations of Dane-zaa, as well as to their non-Dane-zaa neighbours, the Doig River First Nation initiated the project that resulted in this book.

In an effort to protect their traditional lands, the Doig River First Nation, working with Silva Ecosystem Consultants, has drawn up plans for a tribal park to protect the culturally and ecologically important area known as K'ih tsaa?dze. They describe the project in a press release issued 2 October 2011:

> Doig River First Nation announced today that it has declared 90,000 hectares of land within its traditional territory in northeastern British Columbia and northwestern Alberta as a Tribal Park. The area, known to Doig River as K'ih tsaa?dze, is one of the few remaining areas where Doig River members can continue to exercise their Treaty and Aboriginal rights. The declaration of the Tribal Park was made necessary by the impacts of ongoing resource development on the First Nation's traditional territory. The Tribal Park will be identified with signage and Doig River plans to monitor how the Park is used by its members and others.
>
> "Our First Nation has invested significant time and resources in order to protect K'ih tsaa?dze from the impacts caused by oil and gas development and forestry activities," said Chief Norman Davis. "We will continue to protect this area for future generations by implementing our long-term vision for K'ih

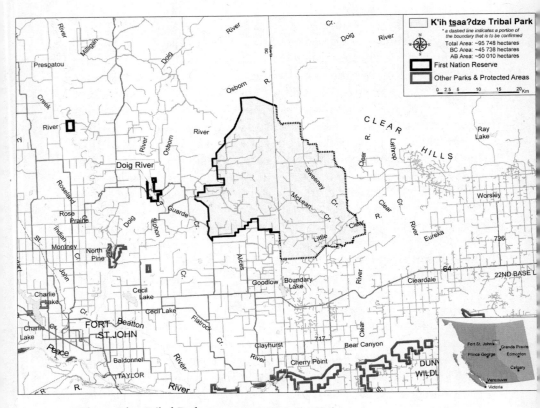

K'ih tsaaʔdze Tribal Park. Courtesy Doig River First Nation

tsaaʔdze." Chief Davis advises that Doig River has developed an Ecosystem-Based Management Plan in collaboration with Silva Ecosystems, which will guide the First Nation's management and protection of the area.

Councillor Gerry Attachie explained that, "in the Dane-za language, K'ih tsaaʔdze means 'old spruce.' This area has been sacred for generations. It contains the place that never burned – there are very old trees there that have survived forest fires and there are many healing plants."

"K'ih tsaaʔdze also contains balsam fir," added Councillor Marlene [Madeline] Oker Benson, "which is a very rare tree species in this part of the country." In 2006, a specimen taken from K'ih tsaaʔdze was confirmed to be balsam fir *(Abies balsamea)* by Richard Hebda of the Royal British Columbia Museum.

The announcement came at a time when the province of BC is acknowledging the need to protect more lands in its northeastern sector. On a visit to Fort St. John in 2011, Terry Lake, BC's environment minister, recognized that the region was underrepresented in terms of parks and protected areas and pledged to make the northeast a priority. Similar parks were established by First Nations in BC and are now official provincial parks. The federal government and the government of Alberta have not yet agreed to enter into discussions about the creation of the park. The Dane-zaa know that their culture, their language, and their land are all part of a larger whole. They are aware that the land must be protected and available for their use if their culture and language is to remain alive.

The reach of Dane-zaa oral history is extraordinary. The stories we have documented go back well before the first white people came to Dane-zaa country. They describe times of conflict and times of reconciliation and accommodation to drastic changes in the region's resource base. Stories from early times describe the threat of violent conflict between individuals and groups. After Aht'uutlętahsalats, the "Dog Piss on Arrow War," the people, who had failed in their attempts to make peace, dispersed into different territories. In the late pre-contact period, the Dane-zaa were challenged by Cree moving into their territories. They also experienced conflicts when people from different bands who were related by marriage found themselves involved in raids and skirmishes, like the one described in the story of Matsíí?dáásasádlę. These conflicts intensified during the early fur trade period. Powerful men such as Duuk'ihsachę and Chimarouche used the power from their vision quests to avoid conflict rather than provoke it.

Soon after them, the Dreamers Mekénúúnatane and Mak'íhts'ęwéswąą began teaching about peace and forgiveness. Today's challenge is to translate stories and practices from life in the bush to life in a complex, industrialized society. As Garry Oker pointed out when discussing his digital media workshops, "We're still dreaming; there are still dreamers among us. Dreaming is about envisioning the future and moving in positive ways toward that vision" (email communication with authors, 1 November 2011). More than one hundred years have passed since Chief Attachie, the Dreamer Adíshtl'íshe, Duuk'ihsachę's son Dechezhę, Duuk'ihsachę's grandson Aginaa, Chimarouche's son Abąą, and Muckithay, the father of the great singer Billy Makadahay, signed Treaty 8. Those men, in turn, grew up in a fur trade economy that was already more than a hundred years old in 1900.

We trust that one hundred or two hundred years from now the Dane-zaa who still live in Dane-zaa nané? will continue to learn from the wise stories and wise practices of their elders. We have done our best to make the stories of the oral tradition available in writing as well as audio and video documents for future generations. Future generations will not be able to learn how to hunt moose by reading this book, but we hope that they will continue to feel a connection to the generations that came before. It has been our privilege to learn from Dane-zaa elders and to be instrumental in making their knowledge available for others to share.

16
Dane-zaa Stories and the Anthropological Literature

The chief and council of the Doig River First Nation specifically asked us to write about their history in language accessible to community members, the general public, as well as to an academic audience. For this reason, we avoid excessive footnotes and references to the vast anthropological literature about northern people and cultures in the main chapters of this book. For those who would like to know more about the Dane-zaa and their neighbours, this short essay cites and offers comments on the ethnographic and theoretical literature relevant to the stories we have documented here.

We begin by listing academic sources on the Dane-zaa and their immediate neighbours. Pliny Earl Goddard was the first anthropologist to write about the Dane-zaa. His publications "The Beaver Indians" (1916) and "Beaver Texts, Beaver Dialect" (1917) were based on fieldwork with the Dane-zaa in Hay River, Paddle River, and Dunvegan, Alberta, in the summer of 1913. He briefly visited Fort St. John but reported that upon his arrival "the Indians had left or were on the point of leaving for the fall hunting" (1916, 203). Nevertheless, the stories he collected provide a point of reference and comparison with oral histories provided by the elders of the Fort St. John area. Although Goddard spent only a short time with the Dane-zaa, he was a student of Athapaskan languages and therefore able to translate a number of Dane-zaa Záágé? texts. Some of the stories he recorded are similar to those the elders have shared with us. Others reflect a somewhat different culture and experience.

Robin first met the Dane-zaa in 1959 and began fieldwork in 1964. He was accompanied by Antonia Mills in 1965, and she went on to write about concepts of reincarnation among First Nations people, including the Dane-zaa (Mills 1982, 1988). Hugh Brody's book *Maps and Dreams* (1981) describes his work with the Halfway River Dane-zaa and has led to wider public knowledge of the Dane-zaa in general. He captured the spirit of a hunting way of life in his portraits of the people he knew, even though he gave them pseudonyms. His book on the legacy of hunting and gathering peoples, *The Other Side of Eden* (2000), places the Dane-zaa in the wider context of traditions that go back to a time before the advent of farming and urban life.

The Virtual Museum of Canada's website *Dane Wajich: Dane-zaa Stories and Songs – Dreamers and the Land* (Doig River First Nation 2008), created by Amber Ridington and Kate Hennessy, makes representations of Doig experiences available online. Amber is currently working on a PhD dissertation about the Dane-zaa Dreamers' songs and stories. Kate Hennessy's dissertation, "Repatriation, Digital Technology, and Culture in a Northern Community" (2010), surveys our work with the Dane-zaa in relation to current interest in cultural repatriation.

There has been considerable work done on the Dane-zaa language, Dane-zaa Záágé?, starting with the pioneering, in-depth studies of Marshall and Jean Holdstock, of the Wycliffe Bible Society, who lived in Doig River in the early 1960s (unpublished material in possession of the Doig River First Nation). They now live in Fort St. John and are still collaborating with Doig language expert Billy Attachie. More recently, Patrick Moore and Julia Miller have done linguistic work at Doig River and other Dane-zaa communities. For this book, we relied on Billy and Pat to help us represent Dane-zaa words and names in an orthography consistent with the one developed by the Holdstocks and used in the *Dane Wajich* website.

The Sekani, the Dane-zaa's neighbours to the west and south, were documented by Diamond Jenness in 1924 (Jenness 1931) and later by Guy Lanoue (1983, 1992; Lanoue and Desgent 2005) and linguist Sharon Hargus (1988, 1993, 2005). According to Hargus (personal communication with authors, 1 April 1992) and our own research, the Sekani also call themselves *Dane-zaa*, although in recent years they also use the Carrier cognate term *Danne'-zaa* for "big man" or "chief." The name *Sekani* simply means "people of the rocks" or "Rocky Mountain people." As Chapter 5 reveals, stories from the early fur trade period document both intermarriage and conflict between the Peace

River Beaver and Sekani, in the late eighteenth and early nineteenth centuries. For instance, Duuk'ihsachę and his father were both from the mountains. Aku's story begins "Duuk'ihsachę was from somewhere up in the mountains, near where the Halfway River people live, but he went to Milligan Creek and married into the Ts'ibe Dané? band." Marriages between McLeod Lake Sekani and Halfway River Dane-zaa occurred in the twentieth century. We have also done work for the McLeod Lake Indian Band of Sekani, work relevant to their adhesion to Treaty 8 in 2000. More recently we interviewed Sekani elders about the impact of the Bennett Dam, which flooded many of their traditional hunting and trapping areas in the 1960s.

The Dane-zaa's neighbours to the northeast are the closely related Dene-Tha', whose language and culture have been documented by Patrick Moore and Angela Wheelock (1990) and Jean-Guy Goulet (1998). Their neighbours to the north are the Slavey and Kaska, documented by John Honigmann and John Mason (1946), Michael Asch (1980, 1988), and others. Farther to the north, Dominique Legros has worked with the Northern Tutchone and written an ethnohistory that documents their culture from 1840 to 1920 (Legros, in press). Julie Cruikshank (1990, 1998) has worked with the Southern Tutchone and written extensively about their oral history.

There are many theoretical issues relevant to our work with the Dane-zaa. These issues span the disciplines of cultural anthropology, folklore studies, First Nations studies, history, law, and even literary criticism. Anthropologists have been particularly interested in the dynamics of band organization among northern hunting people. Frank Speck, for instance, did pioneering work on James Bay Cree social organization in the early years of the twentieth century. Eleanor Leacock and Harvey Feit added to this discussion, as did Colin Scott (1996), who has written about the ecology, social organization, and systems of knowledge among the James Bay Cree.

In the 1960s, June Helm (1961, 2000) proposed a classification system for bands such as the Tłįcho (Dogrib) and other northern Athapaskans. She suggested that rather than having one single form of hunting band, northern Athapaskans adapted to the landscape by developing a flexible relationship between their social organization and ecology. Helm pointed to the task-specific nature of band organization and leadership. Our work with the Dane-zaa supports her conclusions. Regional bands such as the Ts'ibe Dané? and Lhuuge Lęą join with others seasonally in places such as Su Na chii k'chige but split into smaller multifamily groups during the winter. Other groups formed for particular tasks, such as the spring beaver hunt.

One of the most theoretical applications of information about Dane-zaa kinship and band organization is John Ives's *A Theory of Northern Prehistory* (1990). Ives compares the Dane-zaa's kinship and marriage patterns (based on Ridington 1969) with those of the neighbouring Slavey as described by Michael Asch (1980, 1988) to explain how fundamentally similar sets of kin terms can be used to generate different systems of band organization. Among the Slavey, he writes, "Parallel kin are placed within the local group while cross kin and potential affines are segregated in others." Among the Dane-zaa, "internal marriage links [are] endorsed by local groups, but the generational span within which suitable potential marriage links may be found is widened as well" (Ives 1990, 100). While the Slavey prefer to exchange spouses between bands, the Dane-zaa prefer to keep marriages within a successful band whenever possible. As we discuss in Chapter 9, the Yehlhézęh band of the Muskeg people (Ts'ibe Dané?) is an example of this preference at work. Nachę's marriages clearly illustrate the cross-generational connections used to keep a band intact within the Dane-zaa system. The loss of people because of introduced diseases probably intensified this pattern as a means of preserving a viable group.

Our work with the Dane-zaa clearly demonstrates that both men and women took part in childhood vision quests (see Chapter 3 and Ridington 1988). The vision quest among women has been less clearly documented among other Athapaskan groups. We are unable to say whether the Dane-zaa are different or whether women's vision quests have simply not been as well documented elsewhere. As we noted previously, Dane-zaa people spoke more freely about their vision quests when they were elders and when they were speaking to contemporaries. It may be the case that many anthropologists do most of their fieldwork while in their twenties and are less likely to get confidences. As a married team, now in our seventies, we are fortunate to have been told vision quest stories by both men and women, some of whom we have known most of our adult lives.

Information about the Dane-zaa is relevant to an anthropological discussion of knowledge and power among band-level hunting societies. For a comprehensive survey of how anthropologists have written about knowledge, power, and the individual in subarctic hunting societies, see Robin's article in *American Anthropologist* (1988). Jean-Guy Goulet's narrative ethnography *Ways of Knowing: Experience,*

Knowledge, and Power among the Dane Tha also contributes to this discussion (1998). Goulet points out that "learning through personal experience is the cornerstone of the Dene way of life" (ibid., xxx) and states that what cannot be learned from personal experience can be learned through stories, what Billy Attachie calls "wise stories." Every other researcher writing about ways of knowing among northern First Nations has reported a similar emphasis on personal experience and oral tradition. Ronald and Suzanne Scollon (1979, 177-209) contrast what they call the "Chipewyan" bush consciousness to the modern consciousness of their own academic way of thinking about information: "Knowledge that has been mediated is regarded with doubt. True knowledge is considered to be that which one derives from experience" (ibid., 185). Doig elder John Davis made this point clearly in the *Apsassin* case when he said, "What I can remember I will say. What I do not remember, I will not say." The Dane-zaa share with other Athapaskans the practice of avoiding conflict by removing themselves from potential disputes. In the meeting regarding the surrender of Indian Reserve 172, John Davis and others walked away without voting rather than showing disrespect for Chief Sagónáá?.

Although Goulet's work highlights many similarities between the Dene Tha' and the Dane-zaa, their recent history has been quite different. The Dene Tha' were gathered into the larger community of Assumption in 1951, and Dene Tha' children attended residential school between 1951 and 1969 (Goulet 1998, xxi). There are differences in their systems of belief as well. The Dene Tha' had more consistent and sustained contact with Roman Catholic priests than did the Dane-zaa. Yet the Dene Tha' continued to respect their Dreamers. Goulet writes that one of them, Alexis Seniantha, "lives as a dreamer for whom Christ is real in a sense that missionaries never anticipated" (ibid., 200). Patrick Moore and Angela Wheelock have collaborated on a book of Dene Tha' translations, *Wolverine Myths and Visions: Dene Traditions from Northern Alberta,* which presents stories about an important Dreamer named Nógha or Wolverine (Nówe in Dane-zaa Záágé?).

Goulet also reports that a belief in reincarnation is widespread and an important part of the Dene Tha' worldview. He quotes Antonia Mills (1988, 25) as saying that among the Dane-zaa, "all people are said to be the reincarnation of souls who have been on earth before." Mills's work suggests that families sometimes identify children with the spirits of people who have passed on. In our interviews, Charlie Yahey focused his attention on the idea of heaven as a place where one's relatives go, a place like Su Na chii k'chige, where happiness dwells. He also said that "the people who died and went to heaven are looking over the earth. God made them again to come down to earth and look at the people. God sent them down to earth to be made people again" (see Chapter 7). He did not tell us exactly how this process takes place. Nor did he mention it in any of the other texts we recorded. Some people we spoke to rejected the idea of reincarnation, while others identified particular children as embodying the spirits of relatives who have passed on. We conclude that the emphasis on reincarnation that Goulet noted among the Dene Tha may not apply to the Dane-zaa.

Another difference between the Dene Tha' and the Dane-zaa appears to be the influence of evangelical Christianity. Goulet makes no mention of it, while many of the Dane-zaa we interviewed, including song keeper Tommy Attachie, made a point of citing the ways in which Christian (i.e. evangelical) teachings correspond to those of the Dreamers. Like the early Dreamers who incorporated teachings from the Oblate missionaries into their iconography, contemporary Dane-zaa leaders emphasize places where evangelical Christianity accords with the Dreamers' tradition.

Goulet has also written about recent legal decisions that recognize the federal government's failure "in its fiduciary duty to consult with the Dene Tah of northwestern Alberta concerning the Mackenzie Valley Pipeline" (Goulet 2010, 15). He points out that the question of underlying relations between First Nations and the Crown is an unavoidable one and asks "is justice and constructive co-existence between the settler state and Aboriginal Peoples possible in Canada today?" (ibid.). He concludes that "the relationship to Aboriginal peoples was defined unilaterally by the Crown who did not question the subjection of others to its policies" (ibid., 25). Both the Dene Tha' and the Dane-zaa are signatories to Treaty 8 and face similar issues in their relations with the Crown.

Another theme that anthropologists discuss is the relation between cultural ecology and narrative, an important theme in Robin's dissertation (1968a). Later, in *When You Sing It Now, Just Like New*, we proposed that Dane-zaa "narrative technology requires negotiating relations with sentient animal persons [and] communicating these relations with fellow humans" (Ridington and Ridington 2006, 93). We concluded that "Aboriginal people of the North American Subarctic have evolved adaptive strategies that place great emphasis on the authority of individual intelligence within the social responsibility required of a system in which animals and humans alike are interdependent members of a single community" (ibid., 203). The exercise of individual intelligence guided by wise stories is at the heart of Dane-zaa hunting technology. Similarly, when a child goes on his or her vision quest, or *Shin kaa,* stories about the game keepers and their powers guide the experience.

Dreamers also gain their power to see ahead through the stories that others have told them. When Mak'íhts'ęwéswąą first dreamed, he encountered the power of Thunderbird. The story of his visionary experience is exactly the same as a story about thunderbirds that has been told for generations by Dane-zaa and other First Nations storytellers. Johnny Chipesia told Robin a version of the Thunderbird story in 1966 (Ridington/Dane-zaa Archives [RDA], field notes, 1965-66). Mak'íhts'ęwéswąą literally dreamed his way into the story. Thunderbird is an important figure among many First Nations, but the Dane-zaa have integrated this powerful being into the traditions of their Dreamers.

Julie Cruikshank also makes important contributions to the literature on northern Athapaskan storytelling and knowledge. In *Life Lived Like a Story* (1990), Cruikshank presents the life stories of three female Yukon elders. These storytellers, she writes, "understood that human beings and animals were born into a world suffused with and animated by power; at the beginning of time, animals and humans shared certain attributes such as language ... Traditional narratives are powerful because they are constructions rooted in general social concerns, even though they are refracted through individual tellers by the time we hear them. Like all good stories, they contain multiple messages: they explore social contradictions women have faced, but they also dramatize a cultural ideal women recognize" (Cruikshank 1990, 340-41).

Cruikshank's *The Social Life of Stories* (1998, 4) presents the argument that First Nations "narrative storytelling can construct meaningful bridges in disruptive situations." Her discussion of prophecy narratives is particularly relevant to understanding the Dane-zaa Dreamers' tradition. Like the Upper Yukon River people Cruikshank describes, the Dane-zaa Dreamers predicted the disruptive influences of white contact and the fur trade. In both cases, First Nations people responded to early Christian influences "by incorporating Christian concepts and making them part of their own indigenous narratives as a way of strengthening their own influence" (ibid., 121).

Another theoretical issue discussed in the anthropological literature has to do with understanding interpersonal and intergroup conflict.

Robin has written about the Dane-zaa medicine fight as an instrument of political process (Ridington 1968b). He argues that among the Dane-zaa and perhaps other northern hunter-gatherers, medicine fights can result when an unsustainably large number of people hunt within a particular area. This situation often results in smaller groups moving to different territories, thus relieving the pressure on resources. As Guy Lanoue (1992) documented for the Sekani, being forced to live in an unsustainably large reserve community causes interpersonal conflicts that cannot be resolved by moving to different areas. The considerable literature on the cannibal known as Windigo among northern Algonkians ties into this issue. In "Wechuge and Windigo" (1976), Robin argues that the character of the Dane-zaa wehch'uuge, although similar to Windigo in many ways, reflects the people's need to respect the medicine powers of individuals. Rather than being a form of culture-bound mental illness, it is a culturally significant way of demonstrating personal power.

Understanding Dane-zaa oral tradition also relates to issues in literary criticism. In *Orality and Literacy* (1982), Walter Ong argues that writing brings about a transformation of consciousness and that the "oral literature" of people such as the Dane-zaa is qualitatively different from written literature. His ideas are interesting in light of the Dane-zaa's belief that writing is a creative power. Writing became part of the Creator's way of making the world after the Dane-zaa had contact with traders and priests. The Dreamers quickly adopted metaphors from the fur trade practice of keeping written accounts of furs traded and goods received. They likened the bad deeds a person commits to his "bills" in the fur trade ledger books. On a more abstract level, they noted the importance priests placed on scripture and the Catholic Ladder pictorial catechism (Thiel 2009). Indeed, one of the Dreamers who brought messages back from heaven to earth was named Adíshtl'íshe (Paper) (see Chapter 7). Despite their recognition of the power of writing, Dane-zaa storytellers continue to perform entirely within an oral tradition. This book puts some of their stories on paper as one way of passing them on to later generations, but we have also given the community extensive audio and video recordings of their storytellers working within the oral tradition. This archive will be available for future generations.

Anthropologist Dennis Tedlock suggests that even within oral tradition there is a difference between the recitation of texts from memory and oral performance. Plato and Aristotle made a similar distinction between diegesis and mimesis, narrative and imitation. Unlike some Native American cultures (such as the Omaha, with whom Robin worked [Ridington and Hastings 1997]) in which specialized priests carry out the recitation of formal prayers, songs, and ritual formulas, Dane-zaa oral tradition is entirely diegetic or narrative. Tommy Attachie made this point to us clearly when he said, "When you sing it now, just like new." We understand this to mean that, even when telling a traditional story or singing a Dreamer's song, the storyteller or singer is also the author of an original performance. He or she fits the song or story to a particular audience and situation rather than simply repeating something learned by rote. Okanagan storyteller Jeannette Armstrong states that in her tradition, storytellers are both creative narrators and conduits for the expression of ancient voices. She writes, "Through my language I understand I am being spoken to, I'm not the one speaking. The words are coming from many tongues and mouths of Okanagan people and the land around them. I am a listener to the language's stories, and when my words form I am merely retelling the same stories in different patterns" (Armstrong 1998, 181).

First Nations writer Thomas King writes in *The Truth about Stories* (2003), "I think of oral stories as public stories and written stories as private stories." His argument, like that of Walter Ong (1982), is that "the act of reading is a private act ... whereas oral stories generally have an audience in which there is a group dynamic" (King 2003, 154). The stories we recorded from Dane-zaa storytellers are clearly public in that the storytellers chose to perform them for us and others, and in some cases, they specifically intended that the stories become part of this book. They also understood that the group dynamic included readers or listeners they may never know personally. We believe that their stories continue to be public and performative, even when they are part of a published work that may very well be read by our own descendants and those of the storytellers. Audio and video documents make it possible for people who are not physically present at an oral performance to have some feeling of its nature.

We trust that future generations of Dane-zaa will understand how to bring the stories of their ancestors back into the oral tradition. We hope that as you read these stories, you will think about bringing them back to life within an oral tradition in your own tellings. By telling, or even simply paraphrasing, a story you have read, you make the stories "just like new" and add your own creative authorship to the truth that is contained in Dane-zaa stories.

Sam Acko performing a story for schoolchildren at Doig Days, May 2011. Photo by Jillian Ridington

Native American writers themselves have used stories from oral tradition in novels, plays, and critical essays. Beginning with the pioneering novels of Mourning Dove and D'Arcy McNickle, First Nations authors and biographers have told true stories about how the lives of individuals continue to exist in conversation with spiritual traditions. Those authors who are well known today include N. Scott Momaday, Leslie Marmon Silko, James Welch, Louise Erdrich, Gerald Vizenor, Louis Owens, Thomas King, Tomson Highway, Eden Robinson, Jeannette Armstrong, Jo-ann Archibald, and Greg Sarris.

Okanagan storyteller Harry Robinson (Wickwire 2004) is a special case in that he is both an author and a performative translator of stories from his tradition, even though he does not physically compose in writing. Thomas King cites Robinson's work as a prime example of what he calls an interfusional First Nations literature that combines features of oral and written tradition (King 2003). We prefer to think of Robinson as an author rather than as a writer in the literal meaning of the term. The interfusionality of his work comes about as a result of his collaboration with Wendy Wickwire, a good listener, learner, and editor. As Stó:lō scholar Jo-ann Archibald (1992, 161-62) has observed, listener-learners "make meaning from the storyteller's words and ... put meaning into everyday practice."

We hope that our work with the Dane-zaa has transformed us into listener-learners. Our late colleague Howard Broomfield always told us to "clean your ears." He reminded us that Dane-zaa tradition involves both speaking (oral performance) and listening (aural listening). Some scholars have suggested replacing *oral tradition* with *aural tradition* to emphasize the listening component of the relationship between speaker and listener, but we feel that *oral* best represents the performative skills of Dane-zaa storytellers. Besides, it seems counterintuitive to create a distinction using words that sound the same but have a different meaning in written form.

Perhaps the most amazing thing about the Dane-zaa stories is the depth of cultural memory they represent. Amber Ridington describes Dane-zaa oral history as the product of oral curation (see Ridington and Ridington 2011). Remarkably, by remaining oral and being passed on from generation to generation, events that happened more than two centuries ago are still being made new to contemporary listeners. Stories of the time before contact, the early fur trade, and the experiences of Dane-zaa Dreamers will remain alive as long as they are passed on in Dane-zaa Záágé?. A new generation of Dane-zaa young people is growing up without speaking or understanding the language of their elders and ancestors. We have done our best to collaborate with fluently bilingual translators such as Billy Attachie, Madeline Oker Benson, Lana Wolf, Maryann Adekat, and others to provide written versions of these stories.

Robin is also creating video documentaries in which written translations of the stories appear along with the audio and video. Dane-zaa who do not know the language will be able to get a sense of the content and performative style of their oral tradition. We, along with a number of other scholars, discuss new media in relation to oral tradition in our contributions to *Born in the Blood: On Native American Translation* (Ridington and Ridington 2011; Ridington et al. 2011). We describe several of Robin's videos, including "The World Will Listen to My Voice," a subtitled video based on an audio recording of

Charlie Yahey's creation story, and a subtitled translation of Aku's Duuk'ihsachę story, which is presented in written form in Chapter 4. These videos and others are listed in the Works Cited under "Ridington/Dane-zaa Archive."

Appendices

APPENDIX 1
Transcription of a Portion of the Charlie Yahey Creation Story
(RDA, CY 11)

EDDIE APSASSIN AND PATRICK MOORE

Háá guulaa héwǫ́hch'e laa. *That's how it was.*	00:27
Háá edaawajííh ésę̌ ǫ̌, *Even though he [Robin Ridington] knows everything,*	00:30
háá ǫ́ke edaawajííh kuujii. *he wants to know it twice.*	00:33
Chiideh jii nan <u>ts</u>ííyuuwíí? ǫláá?, *When God first made this land,*	00:38
gúúh ahtesíi sǫ̌ ajuu lhǫ wǫ́lę. *there was not much on the earth.*	00:41
Wǫ́lę jii chuu zǫh wǫ́lę ghęlé? ghǫ̂. *There was only water.*	00:47
Ayii nan ǫláá? dah wats'ęh, *He made that land, and from there,*	00:53
háá lhę̌t'ǫ́h jii nan nazheh, nazheh. *all this land started to grow and grow.*	00:57
Lhę̌t'ǫ́h jii nan necháá? aajáá?. *All of it, until all this land became big.*	01:00

Gáá guulaa dane éhjii laahsii?.	01:03
That's what people say.	
Ayii chuu zǫh wǫ́lę.	01:06
There was only water.	
Zhe k'iihaa nan wúúlé??	01:09
What will be on the earth? [he thought].	
Adę sǫ̂ wǫlíi mak'iih wǫ́lę.	01:13
There must be something on it.	
Aláá? gúlé?, wáje gúlé?.	01:16
He must have had a boat.	
Adane adę awúúdle;	01:20
He would make things by himself.	
háá ii sǫ̂ ké?ę̣hch'ii wóh?ǫh.	01:25
What he thought about appeared for him.	
Ęhketane?ii nachíi ǫláá?.	01:27
He made a big raft in the form of a cross.	
Ayii dahdę́hlhaat ǫ̂.	01:30
He floated that raft.	
Dahdę́hlhaat úúh, gúúh sǫ̂,	01:32
He floated the raft, at that time.	
gúúh háyę́láá?.	01:39
He must have done that.	
Dah wats'ęh wǫ́lę,	01:40
Something was	
yę́kááję, jii nan.	01:41
looking for this land.	
"Chéhnah?aadze!"	01:42
"Go into the water!" he told them,	
ǫ̂ ajuu wǫlii.	01:45
but there was nothing.	
Haje hǫ́hch'ii wǫlii tǫ́h,	01:47
Just like that, then,	
hǫ́hch'ii tǫ́náágoch,	01:49
they crawled out of the water like that.	
hǫ́hch'ii.	01:51
It was like that.	
"Hajii, Chehk'áa?, chéhyę́h?áh!" najwé.	01:52
"Wait, Muskrat. You go in the water!" he said, and Muskrat was gone.	

Háá jii nan natsadlii ayii ʔeh hóghęchiich, 01:57
  Muskrat pushed up a little bit of land,

ę yaak'ih néneʔǫʔ. 02:03
  and he put it on the cross raft.

Háá úújǫ sǫ̂ yaak'eh hááyénlíí tl'ǫh, 02:05
  He placed it there carefully and said,

"Nawǫ́yehe!" 02:09
  "You will grow!" [He said, speaking to the land]

Háá yéhjii adíshtl'ísh ǫlááʔ. 02:10
  What he said was written [as commandments].

Háá lhę́lǫh ę wats'ęh eh ii wats'ęh nazheh, nazheh, nazheh. 02:13
  From then on, the land was growing, growing, and growing.

Háá lhę́lǫh lhę́lǫh, gáa lhę́lǫh, 02:19
  Then finally, finally, then finally,

gúúh sǫ̂, daahcheh sǫ̂, naayehi. 02:25
  it must have been then, it must have been, that it was growing.

Ii laa dane éhjii. 02:34
  That's what people say.

Juu tlęzaa tlę adédlááʔ. 02:41
  The dogs made themselves into giant dogs [also word for horses].

Tlęzaa tlę adédlááʔ. 02:46
  The dogs made themselves into giant dogs.

Háá hǫ́hch'e. 02:49
  That's how it was.

Háá, "Jii nan daahtese gáa ii mamaa dętleha!" yéhjii. 02:50
  *"This earth is so big, run around it!" he told them
  [to determine how large it was].*

Háwǫ́jetl, wodase nedéʔę. 02:56
  After that it [the dog] disappeared.

Ajuu wǫdzedze wodaziid úúh, 03:02
  It was gone a long time,

gúúh sǫ̂ ach'uu nan aadǫlaaʔ gúlé. 03:06
  and it must have travelled to a different land.

Danegónéʔ elhę́ʔ nááchęlh. 03:12
  And when it returned, it brought back a person's arm.

"Aja hǫ́hch'ii ghaa laa anaslhaʔ," laahjiih. 03:16
  "That is not what I made you for," he told it.

Hǫ́hch'e laa dętset. 03:19
  Then he sent it away.

"Jii tsą dane nahaake?.   03:22
    "This dog will sit behind us people.

Nahaake? atsets dezǫh!   03:24
    You will only eat behind us now!

Ii dezǫh sǫ̂ naawǫlędze awǫjésę̂."   03:27
    Now you will stay where you belong."

Lhę́t'ǫ́h ajuulii.   03:32
    There was nothing.

Lhę́t'ǫ́h ajuulii.   03:34
    There was nothing at all.

Dane yekeh edaawojííh.   03:55
    People know about it.

"Jii nan waduusadzi sę́."   03:37
    "They will run on this land," he said.

ę gáa hǫ́hch'e k'aajuu ch'uuné?,   03:40
    And then the wolf

ayii k'aajuu tlęzaa naadédlaa?,   03:43
    changed back into a dog,

ayii wats'ęh gáákaa hǫ́hch'e got'ǫ́h nedé?ę hǫ́hch'e.   03:48
    *and from there it disappeared for a long time like that
    [travelling around the world].*

Gáá lhę́lǫh,   03:54
    Then finally,

gáá lhę́lǫh najwé.   03:56
    finally, it was gone.

Gáá lhę́lǫh najwé.   04:04
    Finally, it was gone.

"Aa?, salě?, maasje úúh najwé dáájáá ǫhch'e?"   04:07
    "Ah, what happened to the dog I love?"

Háá edaayejííh ǫ? aalaade.   04:12
    He knew how things would be.

"Haché?, dats'ané? ghąh dahwuudę!",   04:15
    "Wait, he shall live by his legs!" he thought. [So it could catch game.]

kuujii adíshtl'ísh.   04:21
    As he thought these things, they were written [as commandments].

Yawuú? saatsóné? ǫlaa?.   04:23
    He made its teeth out of metal.

Háákaa juuhdzenéh: 04:27
    They are still like that today.

woḷii wuhchut dah,	04:29
when it grabs something,	
háje bes.	04:30
its teeth are just like a knife.	
Gaahiilaa, gúúh sǫ̂,	04:32
And then, back then,	
jii nan necháá? ǫlii ?éh.	04:35
he must have made this earth big.	
Háá tehtlah hǫ̂.	04:37
Even though the dog ran away, it could not hide.	
Háá aalaade hááyę́laa?,	04:41
The dog wilfully disobeyed his orders,	
ii juu dane éhjii.	04:44
that's what people said.	
Háá lhę́lǫh woḷii yek'eh eh?as;	04:46
Then something was coming on the land,	
woḷii yek'eh eh?áázi.	04:49
coming en masse onto it.	
Hájá woḷii nadéélh ke?iih,	04:51
It was just like birds landing in flocks.	
háá lhę́lǫh dááwahtese.	04:54
There were so many.	
Godah dane aadáájędeh,	04:58
He went where people stayed in different places,	
Aje dane aa?ii kaa.	05:00
but not just to visit people.	
Gúúh sǫ̂ dane mak'eh awúújíi.	05:03
At that time, there were starting to be people.	
Háá sǫ̂ dane lhígé? dane,	05:07
There must have been one person;	
dane lhígé? dane wóḷii, háá hǫ́hch'e wadzis?ę́ne woghaayeh?ii.	05:11
there was one person whom he chose to use. [Tsááyaa]	
Háá edęwaadzęh k'ę́adashde wats'ęh,	05:18
He walked around,	
guu woḷii mats'eliih dane z̲ehhel.	05:21
and wherever he found bad people, wherever he found bad animals, he would kill them.	
Háá dane yech'áá?, yech'áá?	05:24
Those bad ones ran away from him, away from him;	

taawahdehsiit. 05:28
they ran away from him.

Ǫ ii dane k'eh k'ęadashde. 05:30
He walked around following those people.

Háá ędah, guuzéhhel, 05:35
When he sees them, he kills them.

Guuzéhhel. 05:38
He kills them.

Ii gaa ayii, wǫlii nachíí ayii juu. 05:40
He killed the giant animals.

Háá ii juu yazéhhę; 05:44
Those, too, he killed;

ii juu yazéhhę. 05:47
he killed them as well.

Háá nááyedenet'aats hǫ́hch'ii, 05:48
He cut them up like that,

hǫ́hch'ii. 05:53
like that.

Hájé háátsadlii nááyedenet'aats, yaayííhshuudah, 05:55
He cut them into small pieces and threw them.

"Ayii kewúúye wǫ́lę," yéhjii dah. 06:00
"That's how you will be named," he said to them.

Háá ye ębaa ghatl'el, 06:03
When he threw one piece, there was a weasel running along.

ii laa yaayííhshúúdah 06:07
When he threw another,

ii wats'ęh uuschę̂ ghatl'el. 06:08
there was a marten running.

Ii wats'ęh aahtesii. 06:11
Every type of animal came from there.

Gúúh nǫ́we ayii laa cházís mejiihé? alę, 06:15
At that time, Wolverine was the boss of all the fur-bearing animals,

dane yéhjii. 06:20
people said.

Aht'e guu tsázís ghadaa. 06:21
He kept all of the furs.

APPENDIX 2
Dane-zaa Kinship Terms

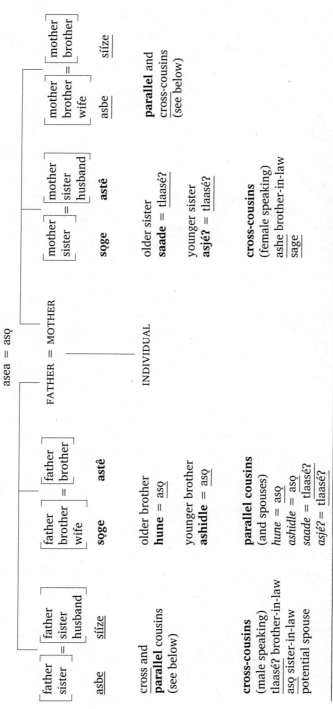

Notes: Terms in **bold** are parallel relations. Marriage between people in parallel relationships is not allowed. Terms with underline represent cross-relations who may marry. Every person knows every other Dane-zaa person and associates them with these categories. Parallel cousins are the children of a parent's same-sex sibling and are referred to as "brother" and "sister." Cross-cousins are the children of a parent's opposite-sex sibling and are referred to as "brother-in-law," "sister-in-law," or "possible spouse."

APPENDIX 3
Research Notes on Beaver Signatories

Muckithay

"Tsekute's sons were Kayan and Makedge, Billy Makadahay's fa. Another son was Wasconli who married Bella Atachie." Ridington 1965 fieldnotes p. 30 quoting Johnny Chipesia as the source.

Muckithay first appears on FSJ Beaver Band annuity paylist in 1900 as #10. I. D. 333; Felix McKidie is recorded as baptised in 1891 at about the age of 50 years, making his birthdate approximately 1841. He would have been 60 years old at time of treaty. Muckithay can be identified as Ridington's "Makedge," the father of Billy Makadahay. Billy Attachie told R & J Ridington in 2000 that Billy was adopted by Oker (brother of Hazizhe, his mother) when his father died. The APL for 1930 shows Billy transferring from Oker's ticket to his own. A 1905 baptismal registration gives "Aloyisius" as a boy born to Mekedie?e and Hazhizhe (I. D. 326). I. D. 396 identifies this boy as Billy and concludes that Felix died about 1907 or 1908.

Aginaa

Aginaa first appears on the FSJ Beaver band annuity paylist in 1900 as #9 (first spelled Agiuaa and then Aginaa). He appears to have died in 1911 (remarks on #9 are "Man dead. Woman dead"). The name is variously spelled Aginta and Agenta. Aginaa appears on Ridington's genealogical chart as Akena, son of Yeklezi (APL #15, Yeglease). A baptismal record from 1893 records "Louis Okimakan" as being born in 1863. Okimakan is the Cree word for headman and appears as a synonym for Yelies & Sliedze (I. D. 1000), i.e. Aginaa's father. A baptismal record from 1891 gives the mother of Lucie Akinn as "Jus du Boleau" (birch sap) and her father as Akinn (I. D. 1002). Ridington reports that the Beaver word for poplar sap is Kina and Garry Oker (2001) confirms that Akena's name means poplar sap. The baptismal record apparently gives a French translation of Akena as the mother's name and the Beaver word (Akinn) as the father's name.

Ridington's chart gives Akena's wife as Klukenazit. She appears on baptismal records as Tloke Nazhoet and other varients. The Registered Indian Record (inactive list, FSJ Band) refers to her daughter (who can be identified as Eskama on Ridington's chart) as "Prairie Standard's daughter." Billy Attachie told R & J Ridington that Klukenazie means "Standing on the Prairie," i.e. what an Indian agent heard as "Prairie Standard."

Dislisici

Dislisici first appears in the FSJ Beaver Band annuity paylist as #6, Dislisica (I. D. 78). He is listed as being elected Headman in 1912 and as dying in 1919. Beaton reports the death of "Adisles" in January, 1919. He is also known as Littlehead on Ridington's chart and is listed as the father of Katakhose Harvey, thus having many descendents.

The name derives from the Beaver word for paper or birchbark, Adisklise. There is extensive oral tradition about Adisklise as a prophet or dreamer who is the author of many songs in the dreamer's dance repertoire. The name is a metaphor for his role as a dreamer who carries messages (paper) from heaven to earth. "Disclise" is mentioned in the HBC post journal for May, 1884. It is likely that Dislisici inherited a name that has been used in previous generations. "The old Bark" is mentioned in the 1823 HBC journal of Hugh Faries (Burley et al. 1996, 169).

Tachea

Tachea first appears on the FSJ Beaver Band annuity paylist as #2, Tagea or Tachea, later written as Tachie or Sachie. He is listed on the APL as dying in 1911. His name is also written as Detchiyay (baptismal records of Succona and Oker) and Dechiin (Ridington genealogies 1968). The connection between the different spellings is proven by a listing of "Boy Succona" on #2's ticket in 1903. Succona's baptismal record lists his father as Detchiyay. Beaton's reference to "Achie" in April, 1904 is probably Tachea. The FSJ post journal of February 18, 1867, refers to Aceea & on November 2, 1867 as Ah-ceea. Ridington's chart shows Dechiin as brother to Yeklezi.

Appan

Appan first appears on the FSJ Beaver Band annuity paylist as #3 in 1900. He is listed as dying in 1918. The story of his death by a falling tree is well known by contemporary people at Doig River. His death is also recorded in the Beaton journal. His wife at the time was Nachin (Mary Pouce Coupe) and she told the story to her grandchildren. The contemporary family name Appaw comes from Appan.

The name Appan goes back to a previous generation. The HBC post journal refers to Ahpah's band on September 30, 1868. On December 23, 1869, the journal says, "Chimerooch Ahpah Netea and a few more Indians arrived." Baptismal records list Baptiste Apaen as being baptized in 1875 at the age of 25. That would place his birth at 1850, which would make him too young to be a band leader in 1868. Baptiste Apaen's father is listed as Esemarouche which corresponds to Chimarouche in the HBC record. HBC post journals refer to "Old Chimerooch" on March 24, 1870. The HBC post journal of 1823 refers to the death of "an old Indian (Chimarouche)" (Burley et al 1996:164). A generation earlier, the North West Company post record refers to Jemathush on January 9, 1800 (Burley et al 145). It is probable that the Jemathush of 1799 is the same person as Chimarouche who died in 1823. Johnny Chipesia told Robin Ridington that Chief Montney's father was named Samaloos and was witness to the HBC "massacre" in 1823. Since we know one Chimarouche died in 1823 and another was the father of Baptiste Apaen in 1875, the second one could have been the Samaloos of Johnny Chipesia's narrative.

According to Peace River historian Martin Kilo, the name Rose Prairie derives from Jimrose Prairie which in turn derives from Chimerooch's Prairie (HBC journal October 7, 1869; Chimaroo's Prairie Dec. 31, 1894).

Attachie

Attachie first appears on the FSJ Beaver Band annuity paylist as #4 in 1900. His death in 1918 is recorded in the Beaton journal as well as in the APL. Ridington records one of his wives as Isuan. Baptismal records identify a number of children whose father is "Atcadi" and whose mother is variously spelled "Iaou'e" and "Ezjan." Two of these children are twins, Peter and Justin. Johnny Chipesia told Ridington that two of Attachie's children were twin boys, Peter and Ustan. The phonetic spelling for "Ustan" corresponds to the way a French priest would pronounce "Justin." Hence, the oral record is substantiated by the baptismal record and confirms that "Atcadi" is actually Attachie. Attachie has many descendents among contemporary Dane-zaa.

Allalie

The only FSJ Beaver Band annuity paylist record for Allalie is an indirect one. The 1900 list for #5 is "Telialis Widow" with a remark, "pd son Allalie." The ticket notes for #5," Thatis widow (per Allalie)." In 1909 she is referred to as "Thatis (Widow Allalie)." Baptismal records refer to a man whose name is variously spelled Tilaye, Dekaye, and Delaia (I. D. 320) and whose wife is "Onkedze" or "Okedze," a name that means "number two" in Beaver. A marriage record lists "Alexis Delaia" marrying "Okedze" in 1891 at the age of thirty. He appears to have died by the time of Treaty, which was signed by his son, Allalie. For reasons unknown, Allalie never received his own paylist number. He apparently died without issue.

Yatsoose

Yatsoose first appears on the FSJ Beaver Band annuity paylist as #8 in 1900. He is only on the list for 1900 and 1901. It is not clear where he belongs genealogically. No name that connects to this one can be found in either the oral or the written record.

Conclusion

Six of the men who signed treaty in 1900 were well-known family heads who are remembered by contemporary members of the former Fort St. John band. These include Muckithay, Aginaa, Dislisci, Tachea, Appan and Attachie. Allalie must have been quite young at the time and we have not identified Yatsoose in relation to names in oral history or to written documents.

A number of important men did not sign the adhesion, although this may be simply because they were in their territories at the time. These include chiefs Montney and Yeklezi (Okimakan), The Wolf, his brother Yakatchie, Big Charlie, Ootah and Yuschua Wuskulli.

APPENDIX 4
Facsimile of the NWMP Census

Beaver Indians at St. John & Nelson - Peace River - The Nelson Indians trade at Fort St. John -

Names	Men	Women	Boys	Girls	Total	
Appan	1	1	1	1	4	
Attochock (Big Eagle)	1	3	6	–	10	Has 3 Wives
Attackie	1	2	2	4	9	" 2 "
Ayyudie (Liar)	1	1	1	–	3	
Aginian	1	–	–	–	1	
Aginaa (Chief's son)	1	1	–	2	4	
Allellia	1	–	–	–	1	
Bob Big Head	1	1	2	1	5	+ This man - the chief of the Nelson Beaver Indians at St. John
Boss (Big Feet) x	1	–	2	2	5	
Charley	1	2	3	4	10	Has 2 Wives
Cudgee (Young Moon)	1	1	1	–	3	
Cat Eater	1	2	1	1	5	
Clouty	1	–	–	–	1	
Davis	1	1	1	1	4	
Dislisici (Newspaper)	1	1	–	2	4	
Ha Lillie	1	–	–	–	1	
Iskotay	1	1	–	–	2	
Jib-ba-jay	1	–	–	–	1	
La Bonne (one eye)	1	–	–	1	2	
Lilla	1	1	–	1	3	# This man - the chief of the head branch of the Beaver Indians living at St. John
Little Head	1	1	1	1	4	
Montegnie # (Chief)	1	1	–	1	3	
Muckiscola	1	2	2	1	6	Has 2 Wives
Modesto	1	–	–	–	1	
Mantsuakie	1	1	3	3	8	
Muckithay	1	–	–	–	1	
Bill Muckithay	1	–	–	–	1	
Pat Muckithay	1	1	–	1	3	
Total	46	48	44	46	184	

RG 18, Vol. 1435, File RCMP 1899 No. 76, Pt 2-81

Works Cited

Archival Sources

Glenbow Archives, Calgary, AB
Peace River Country Research Project, Series 1
   M-4560-26, Hudson's Bay Company, Fort St. John Journal, 1866-1870
   M-4560-27, Hudson's Bay Company, Fort St. John Journal, 1899-1907
   M-4560-28, Hudson's Bay Company, Fort St. John Journal, 1908-1915
   M-4560-29, Hudson's Bay Company, Fort St. John Journal, 1916-1924

Library and Archives Canada, Ottawa, ON
North West Mounted Police, 1899 Census. RG 18, vol. 1435, f. "RCMP 1899 No 76."
Survey Report of Donald F. Robertson, Department of Indian Affairs Annual Reports, 1914. RG 10, Black Series, vol. 4065, f. 410 786-3.
Treaty Annuity Paylists, Department of Indian Affairs. RG 10, Series B-8-d.

Ridington/Dane-zaa Archive (RDA)

Manuscripts and Papers
Beaver Tales, a collection of Dane-zaa stories.
Chipesia, Johnny. "The Boy Named Swan."
   "Tsááyaa's Encounter with Big Man and Big Woman."
   "Tsááyaa Made Himself Just Like God."
   "Everyone who heard about Tseguude avoided him."
Jumbie, Augustine. "Aht'uutlętahsalats". Translated by Liza Wolf.
   "Tseguude." Translated by Liza Wolf.
Nachę. "One time, there was a boy who married young."
Robin Ridington Papers
   Field notes, 1965-66
   Field notes from *Apsassin* case, 1987
Yahey, Charlie. "Some people don't play the drum."

Oral Stories in Audio and Video

Aku 1966. Aku, audio recordings by Robin Ridington, 1966.
"Early spring, when the leaves start growing," translated by Billy Attachie.
"I don't know this story well," translated by Billy Attachie.
"My grandfather sent my father on Shin káánatah," translated by Margaret Dominic Davis.
"That man, that man who killed Mekénúúnatane," translated by Billy Attachie.
"There used to be a white man," translated by Margaret Dominic Davis.
"They went there and got lots of ammunition and guns," translated by Margaret Dominic Davis.
"This guy's story is not very long ago," translated by Billy Attachie.
"Those white men went back up the Peace River," translated by Billie Attachie.
"We used to live at Fort St. John," translated by Liza Wolf.
"We were going to spend all winter at Cecil Lake," translated by Billy Attachie.
ARDZMD#1-2007-05-21 GP2003, Margaret Attachie, video interview by Amber Ridington, transcript, 2007.
ARDZMD#5-2007-07-29 GP004-2, Madeline Sagónáá? Davis, video interview by Amber Ridington, July 2007.
Attachie, Billy, "This is a story about when I started remembering," video recording by Robin Ridington, May 2010.
CMC 8-1, Charlie Yahey, Creation Story, Version 1, audio recording by Robin Ridington, August 1965, translated by Billy Attachie.
CY 1, Charlie Yahey, song and drumming session, August 1968, audio recording by Robin Ridington, translated by Tommy and Billy Attachie.
CY 2, Charlie Yahey, audio recording by Robin Ridington, 1968 (discussion of translation: DZ01-6, 24 April 2001).
CY 8, Charlie Yahey, Creation Story, Version 2, audio recording by Robin Ridington, July 1968, translated by Eddie Apsassin.
CY 11, Charlie Yahey, Creation Story and "It is just like this tape recorder," audio recording by Robin Ridington, 26 July 1968, translated by Billy Attachie.
CY Tommy, Tommy Attachie, translation of Charlie Yahey's stories, audio recording by Robin Ridington, 7-9 July 1998.
CY Tommy 4a, Tommy Attachie on Dane-zaa songs, audio recording by Robin Ridington, 1998, translated by Madeline Oker Benson.
DZ00-16, Sam Acko, "I remember fall time, September, first week," audio recording by Robin and Jillian Ridington, 21 July 2000.
DZ00-18, Sam Acko, "This boy, Eskama's great-great-grandpa," audio recording by Robin and Jillian Ridington, 24 July 2000.
DZ99-11, Tommy Attachie interview, audio recording by Robin Ridington, 27 July 1999.
DZ99-18, Billy Attachie interview, audio recording by Robin Ridington, 28 July 1999.
DZ99-39, Tommy Attachie interview, audio recording by Robin Ridington, 14 October 1999.
DZDV02-14, Marguerite Yahey Davis, Story of Abąą's Death, video recording by Robin and Jillian Ridington, 10 July 2002, translated by Maryann Adekat and Lana Wolf.
DZDV02-27, Madeline Sagónáá? Davis, "Mak'íhts'ęwéswąą, when he started dreaming," video recording by Robin and Jillian Ridington, 15 July 2002, translated by Billy Attachie.

–. Tommy Attachie, visit to Sweeney Creek, Alberta, 15 July 2002, video recording by Robin and Jillian Ridington.

DZDV02-34, Madeline Sagónáá? Davis, recorded by Robin and Jillian Ridington, 17 July 2002, translated by Billy Attachie, September 2010.

DZDV06 6-7, visit to Sweeney Creek, Alberta, 14 October 2006, interview with Tommy Attachie, video recording by Robin Ridington.

DZDV08-11, May Dominic Apsassin, interviewed by Jillian Ridington, 10 September 2008, video recording by Robin Ridington.

DZDV08-12, May Dominic Apsassin, interviewed by Jillian Ridington, 10 September 2008, video recording by Robin Ridington.

DZDV09-31, Margie Wolf, Story of the Two Brothers, recorded by Robin and Jillian Ridington, 17 July 2002, translated by Billie Attachie, 21 May 2009, video recording by Robin Ridington.

DZHD09-1, Tommy Attachie, interviewed by Robin and Jillian Ridington, 18 May 2009, translated by Billy Attachie and Madeline Oker Benson, video recording by Robin Ridington.

DZHD09-20, Remi Farvacque, interviewed by Robin Ridington, 28 May 2009, video recording by Robin Ridington.

DZHD09-23, Tommy Attachie, interviewed by Robin and Jillian Ridington, 30 May 2009, translated by Billy Attachie and Madeline Oker Benson, video recording by Robin Ridington.

DZHD09-24, Tommy Attachie interviewed by Robin and Jillian Ridington, 30 May 2009, translated by Billy Attachie and Madeline Oker Benson, video recording by Robin Ridington.

DZHD09-56, May Apsassin interview by Robin and Jillian Ridington, 4 August 2009, video recording by Robin Ridington.

DZHD09-60, Gerry Attachie talks about Petersen's Crossing, August 2009, video recording by Robin Ridington.

DZHD10-1, Tommy Attachie, interview by Robin and Jillian Ridington, 2 April 2010.

DZHD10-15, Sam Acko and Tommy Attachie, Story of Aht'uutlẹtahsalats, 8 May 2010, translated by Billy Attachie, video recording by Robin Ridington.

G-2b, Leslie Pinder and Louise Mandell, presentation to Doig River First Nation, 5 October 1981, audio recording by Robin Ridington.

G-28, Slim Byrnes, in discussion with Robin and Jillian Ridington, 8 August 1982, audio recording by Robin Ridington.

G-31 and GD-32, Winnis Baker, in discussion with Robin and Jillian Ridington, 13 August 1982, audio recording by Robin Ridington.

HB-12a&b, Albert Askoty, "The Cree and Dane-zaa met on the Peace River," recorded by Howard Broomfield and Robin Ridington, 6 August 1981, translated by Billy Attachie, audio recording by Howard Broomfield.

HB-46, 24 June 1981, audio recording by Howard Broomfield.

HB-85, Margaret Dominic Davis, interviewed by Howard Broomfield and Robin Ridington, 4 April 1982, audio recording by Howard Broomfield.

JA-1b, John Andre, audio recording by Gerry Attachie, no date.

NA-1, Nachẹ, interviewed by Robin Ridington, April 1966 and July 1968, translated by Billy Attachie. Old tape remaster, audio recording by Robin Ridington.

OT 19 (digital remaster AM1), Amaa Skookum in conversation with Charlie Yahey, recorded by Robin Ridington, June 1966, translated by Liza Wolf, audio recording by Robin Ridington.

RR-2, Charlie Dominic, in discussion with Robin and Jillian Ridington, 15 June 1979, audio recording by Robin Ridington.

Audio Documentaries

Broomfield, Howard, and Jillian Ridington. 1981. "Suffering Me Slowly." *The Hornby Collection,* CBC Radio (repeated on several dates). 60 min.

Broomfield, Howard, Jillian Ridington, and Robin Ridington. 1980. "Trails of the Dunne-za: A Suite of Four Radio Pieces." *Our Native Land,* CBC Radio. Four 5 min pieces.

Broomfield, Howard, and Robin Ridington. 1979. "Soundwalk to Heaven." CFRO Vancouver. 50 min.

–. 1981. "Nextdoor Neighbors." CFRO Vancouver. 30 min.

–. 1982. "Old Time Religion." Presented as a slide-tape docudrama at the 1982 Canadian Ethnology Society meeting. 60 min.

–. 1983. "In Doig People's Ears." Composed for "The Sociology of Music: An Exploration of Issues," Trent University, August. 42 min.

Oker, Garry, Robin Ridington, and Stacy Shaak. 2000. "Dane-zaa Dreamers' Songs, 1966-2000." Vol. 1, Suu Na chii K'chi ge (The Place Where Happiness Dwells)."

Ridington, Robin. 1988. "Miracle." Presented to American Anthropological Association session on "Narrative Ethnography," November. 27 min.

Ridington, Robin, and Jillian Ridington. 1990. "Why Baby Why?" To accompany a paper in a special issue of *Canadian Journal of Native Studies* 8, 2: 251-74. 21 min.

Video Documentaries

Broomfield, Howard, Jillian Ridington, Myrna Cobb, and Robin Ridington. 1984. "In Doig People's Ears: Portrait of a Changing Native Community." 30 min.

Oker, Garry, Jillian Ridington, Stacy Shaak, and Robin Ridington. 2002. "The Otter Man's Prophecy." 2002. Shown at the "Conference on Hunting and Gathering Societies 9," Edinburgh, Scotland, 11 September. 24 min.

Oker, Garry, Stacy Shaak, Robin Ridington, Jillian Ridington, and Dane-zaa Elders. 2002. "They Dream about Everything." 50 min.

Ridington, Robin. 2004a. "Finding Gayęą's Grave." 16 min. Documentary about the search for the grave of a Dreamer who died in 1923.

–. 2004b. "Kuu Ghadii Aliin Ku." 4 min. Realization of Charlie Yahey text by Robin Ridington from recording ca. 1966. Translation by Garry Oker, Billy Attachie, and Eddie Apsassin.

–. 2006. "The World Will Listen to My Voice." 24 min. Subtitled translation of Charlie Yahey's creation story set against video background of environmental scenes.

–. 2009a. "Doig Days, 2009." 16 min. Document of annual event.

–. 2009b. "Nenan Youth and Elders Camp, 2009." 36 min. Document of event for Nenan Dane-zaa Deh Zona.

–. 2010a. "Nenan Youth and Elders Camp, 2010." 32 min. Document of event for Nenan Dane-zaa Deh Zona.

–. 2010b. "Paddle for the Peace, 2010." 8 min. Document about rally at the British Columbia legislature.

–. 2010c. "A Tree For My People." 5 min. Realization of Charlie Yahey text translated by Billy Attachie for Nenan Dane-zaa Deh Zona.

Ridington, Robin, Jillian Ridington, Garry Oker, and Stacy Shaak. 2000. "Contact the People." 24 min. Shown at Third International Conference of the Northern

Studies Association, Sapporo, Japan, 12 October 2000. A revised 24-minute version with English subtitles was presented at the Canadian Indigenous Native Studies Association meeting in Saskatoon, Saskatchewan, 3 June 2001.

Roman Catholic Archdiocese of Grouard
Fort St. John Baptismal Records, FSJ-HP, Baptimes, 1881-93, and FSJ-HH, Baptimes, 1894-1920

Other Sources

Archibald, Jo-ann, and Ellen White. 1992. "Kwulasulwut S yuth [Ellen White's teachings]: Collaboration between Ellen White and Jo-ann Archibald." *Canadian Journal of Native Education* 19, 2: 150-64.
Armstrong, Jeannette. 1998. "Land Speaking." In *Speaking for the Generations: Native Writers on Writing*, edited by Simon J. Ortiz, 175-94. Tucson: University of Arizona Press.
Asch, Michael. 1980. "Steps toward the Analysis of Athapaskan Social Organization." *Arctic Anthropology* 17, 2: 46-51.
–. 1988. *Kinship and the Drum Dance in a Northern Dene Community*. Edmonton: Boreal Institute for Northern Studies.
Attachie, Gerry. 1988. Speech given at "Cultures in Conflict," UBC Symposium, Vancouver, BC, August.
–. 2002. Interview with Amber Ridington and Kate Hennessy, Virtual Museum of Canada. *Dane Wajich: Dane-ẕaa Stories and Songs – Doig River First Nation*. http://www.museevirtuel-virtualmuseum.ca/.
BC Oil and Gas Commission. 2002. Commissioner's Update, vol. 1, no. 2, May-June.
Berger, Thomas. 2002. *One Man's Justice: A Life in the Law*. Vancouver: Douglas and McIntyre.
Bowes, Gordon. 1963. *Peace River Chronicles*. Vancouver: Prescott Publishing.
Brody, Hugh. 1981. *Maps and Dreams*. Vancouver: Douglas and McIntyre.
–. 2000. *The Other Side of Eden*. Vancouver: Douglas and McIntyre.
Bryce, George. 1910. *The Remarkable History of the Hudson's Bay Company*. Toronto: William Briggs.
Burley, David V., J. Scott Hamilton, and Knut R. Fladmark. 1996. *Prophecy of the Swan: The Upper Peace River Fur Trade of 1794-1823*. Vancouver: UBC Press.
Cruikshank, Julie. 1990. *Life Lived Like a Story*. Lincoln: University of Nebraska Press.
–. 1998. *The Social Life of Stories*. Lincoln: University of Nebraska Press.
Doig River First Nation. 2003. "Specific Claim of the Doig River First Nation Concerning the Failure to Secure Reserve Lands at Petersen's Crossing." Treaty 8 Tribal Association Reference no. 0548-601.
–. 2008. *Dane Wajich: Dane-ẕaa Stories and Songs – Dreamers and the Land*. Virtual Museum of Canada website curated by Kate Hennessy and Amber Ridington. http://www.virtualmuseum.ca/Exhibitions/Danewajich.
Faraud, Henri. 1870. *Dix-huit ans chez les sauvages: Voyages et missions dans l'extrême nord de l'Amérique britannique de Mgr. Henry Faraud*. Edited by Fernand Michel. Paris: Nouvelle Maison Perisse frères.

Fumoleau, Rene. 1973. *As Long as This Land Shall Last: A History of Treaty 8 and Treaty 11, 1870-1939.* Toronto: McClelland and Stewart.
Goddard, Pliny Earle. 1916. "The Beaver Indians." *Anthropological Papers of the American Museum of Natural History* 10, 4: 203-93.
–. 1919. "Beaver Texts, Beaver Dialect." *Anthropological Papers of the American Museum of Natural History* 10, 5-6: 297-545.
Goulet, Jean-Guy. 1998. *Ways of Knowing: Experience, Knowledge, and Power among the Dene Tha.* Lincoln: University of Nebraska Press.
–. 2010. "Legal Victories for the Dene Tha? Their Significance for Aboriginal Rights in Canada." *Anthropologica* 52: 15-31.
Hargus, Sharon. 1988. *Lexical Phonology of Sekani.* New York: Garland Press.
–. 1993. *Studies in Lexical Phonology.* San Diego: Academic Press.
–. 2005. *Athabaskan Prosody.* Philadelphia: J. Benjamin's Publishers.
Harmon, Daniel Williams. 2006. *Harmon's Journal, 1800-1819.* Surrey, BC: Touchwood Editions.
Helm, June. 1961. *The Lynx Point People: The Dynamics of a Northern Athapaskan Band.* Ottawa: National Museums of Canada Bulletin 176.
–. 2000. *The People of Denendeh: Ethnohistory of the Indians of Canada's Northwest Territories.* Iowa City/Montreal and Kingston: University of Iowa Press/McGill-Queen's University Press.
Hennessy, Kate. 2010. "Repatriation, Digital Technology, and Culture in a Northern Community." PhD diss., University of British Columbia.
Honigmann, John J., and John Alden Mason. 1946. *Ethnography and Acculturation of the Fort Nelson Slave.* Yale University Publications in Anthropology 33-34. New Haven, CT: Yale University Press.
Innis, Harold. 1930. *The Fur Trade in Canada.* New Haven: Yale University Press.
Ives, John. 1990. *A Theory of Northern Athapaskan Prehistory.* Boulder, CO: Westview Press.
Jenness, Diamond. 1931. "The Sekani Indians of British Columbia." *Proceedings and Transactions of the Royal Society of Canada,* third series, 25: 21-34.
King, Thomas. 2003. *The Truth about Stories.* 2003 Massey Lectures. Toronto: House of Anansi Press.
Kitto, F.H. 1918. *The Peace River District Canada: Its Resources and Opportunities.* Ottawa: Department of the Interior.
Lanoue, Guy. 1983. "Continuity and Change: The Development of Political Self-Definition among the Sekani of Northern British Columbia." PhD diss., University of Toronto.
–. 1992. *Brothers: The Politics of Violence among the Sekani of Northern British Columbia.* New York: Berg.
Lanoue, Guy, and Jean-Marc Desgent. 2005. *Errances: Comment se pensent le Nous et le Moi dans l'espace mythique des nomades septentrionaux sekani.* Quebec: Musée Canadien des Civilizations.
Legros, Dominique. In press. "Northern Tuchone Athapaskan Indians Ethnohistory, 1840-1920." http://www.ebookpp.com/at/athapaskan-doc.html.
MacGregor, James G. 1952. *The Land of Twelve Foot Davis: A History of the Peace River Country.* Edmonton: Applied Art Products.
Mackenzie, Alexander, and W. Kaye Lamb, ed. 1970. *The Journals and Letters of Sir Alexander Mackenzie.* Toronto: MacMillan of Canada.

Madill, Dennis. 1986. *Treaty Eight Research Report.* Treaties and Historical Research Centre, Indian and Northern Affairs Canada, Ottawa.

McCormack, Patricia. 2007. "Deconstructing Canadian Subarctic Grasslands." Paper presented at the European Environmental History Conference, Amsterdam, 5-9 June 2007.

Mills, Antonia. 1982. "The Beaver Indian Prophet Dance and Related Movements among North American Indians." PhD diss., Harvard University.

—. 1988. "A Preliminary Investigation of Cases of Reincarnation among the Beaver and Gitksan Indians." *Anthropologica* 30, 1: 23-59.

Moore, Patrick, and Angela Wheelock. 1990. *Wolverine Myths and Visions: Dene Traditions from Northern Alberta.* Lincoln: University of Nebraska Press.

Morton, W.L., ed. 1979. *God's Galloping Girl: The Peace River Diaries of Monica Storrs, 1929-1931.* Vancouver: UBC Press.

Nenan Dane-zaa Deh Zona. 2011. *Home Is Suuné'chi'ii Ké'chi'iige: The Place Where Happiness Dwells.* Vancouver: To Be Heard Productions.

Ong, Walter. 1982. *Orality and Literacy: The Technologizing of the Word.* London: Routledge.

Ridington, Robin. 1968a. "The Environmental Context of Beaver Indian Behavior." PhD diss., Harvard University.

—. 1968b. "The Medicine Fight: An Instrument of Political Process among the Beaver Indians." *American Anthropologist* 70, 6:1152-60.

—. 1969. "Kin Categories versus Kin Groups: A Two-Section System without Sections." *Ethnology* 8, 4: 460-67.

—. 1976. "Wechuge and Windigo: A Comparison of Cannibal Belief among Boreal Forest Athapaskans and Algonkians." *Anthropologica* 18, 2: 107-29.

—. 1978. *Swan People: A Study of the Dunne-za Prophet Dance.* Mercury Series Canadian Ethnology Service Paper No. 38. Ottawa: National Museum of Man.

—. 1987. *Trail to Heaven: Knowledge and Narrative in a Northern Native Community.* Iowa City/Vancouver: University of Iowa Press/Douglas and McIntyre.

—. 1988. "Knowledge, Power, and the Individual in Subarctic Hunting Societies." *American Anthropologist* 90, 1: 98-110.

—. 1990. "Cultures in Conflict: The Problem of Discourse." *Canadian Literature* 123-25: 273-90.

Ridington, Robin, and Dennis Hastings. 1997. *Blessing for a Long Time: The Sacred Pole of the Omaha Tribe.* Lincoln: University of Nebraska Press.

Ridington, Robin, and Amber Ridington. 2011. "Performative Translation and Oral Curation: Ti-Jean/Chezan in Beaverland." In *Born in the Blood: On Native American Translation,* edited by Brian Swann, 138-67. Lincoln: University of Nebraska Press.

Ridington, Robin, and Jillian Ridington. 2006. *When You Sing It Now, Just Like New: First Nations Poetics, Voices and Representations.* Lincoln: University of Nebraska Press.

Ridington, Robin, Jillian Ridington, Patrick Moore, Kate Hennessy, and Amber Ridington. 2011. "Ethnopoetic Translation in Relation to Audio, Video and New Media Representations." In *Born in the Blood: On Native American Translation,* edited by Brian Swann, 211-41. Lincoln: University of Nebraska Press.

Sall, Nora. 1973. "History of Fort St. John Indian Reserve 172 and Pineview." In *The Peacemakers of the North Peace,* edited by Cora Ventress, Marguerite Davies, and Edith Kyllo, 1-102. Fort St. John: Self-published.

Scollon, Ronald, and Suzanne B.K. Scollon. 1979. *Linguistic Convergence: An Ethnography of Speaking at Fort Chipewyan, Alberta.* London: Academic Press.

Scott, Colin. 1996. "Science for the West, Myth for the Rest? The Case of James Bay Cree Knowledge Construction." In *Naked Science: Anthropological Inquiry into Boundaries, Power, and Knowledge,* edited by Laura Nader, 69-86. New York: Routledge.

Simpson, George. 1970 [1872]. *Peace River: A Canoe Voyage from Hudson's Bay to Pacific by the late Sir George Simpson ...* Edited by Malcolm McLeod. Toronto: Coles Publishing Company.

Smithsonian Magazine. 2009. "Brian Jungen Show Opens at American Indian Museum." *Smithsonian Magazine,* 15 October.

Storrs, Monica. 1999. *Companions of the Peace: Diaries and Letters of Monica Storrs, 1931-1939.* Toronto: University of Toronto Press.

Thiel, Mark G. 2009. "Catholic Ladders and Native American Evangelization." *US Catholic Historian* 27, 1: 49-70.

Treaty 8 Tribal Association. 2010. Declaration of the Doig River First Nation, Halfway River First Nation, Prophet River First Nation, West Moberly First Nation Concerning the Proposed Site C Dam on the Peace River, British Columbia.

Ventress, Cora, Marguerite Davies, and Edith Kyllo, eds. 1973. *The Peacemakers of the North Peace.* Fort St. John: Self-published.

Wickwire, Wendy. 2004. *Write It on Your Heart: The Epic World of an Okanagan Storyteller.* Vancouver: Talonbooks.

York, Lillian, ed. 1981. *Lure of the South Peace: Tales of the Early Pioneers to 1945.* Fort St. John/Dawson Creek: South Peace Historical Society, 1981.

Acknowledgments

The Doig River First Nation wishes to acknowledge and thank the following for their valuable financial contribution to the development of this book: Doig River Trust, Taqa North, Talisman Energy, Suncor Energy, Devon Canada, Shell Canada, Encana, CNRL, Eric Mohun of Trans Canada, the Treaty 8 Tribal Association, Mclean Budden, and Phillips, Hager & North. We thank them for their generous support.

The authors wish to thank Leeanna Rhodes of the Treaty 8 Tribal Association who skilfully prepared the maps. We are immensely grateful to Darcy Cullen of UBC Press as well as to the peer reviewers who provided helpful advice in preparing the manuscript.

Leslie Hall Pinder gave advice and assistance on Chapter 14, and Elinor Langer, Jody Wyatt, and the late (and much missed) Gail Buente made helpful comments on the manuscript. Howard Broomfield will always be a part what we do, and we are forever grateful for all he taught us. Lindy-Lou Flynn worked tirelessly as a research assistant at UBC preparing typescripts of the collection we call "Beaver Tales." We are also grateful to another former UBC research assistant, Myrna Cobb, for organizing the catalogue of slides and negatives and placing them carefully in binders for safekeeping. Our talented granddaughters, Undine Thompson and Kaela Lee, assisted with charts and French to English translations. We are indebted to them all, and thank them for their contributions.

We could not have completed this project without the cultural and financial support of the Doig River First Nation. Chief Norman Davis and former chiefs Garry Oker and Kelvin Davis have been helpful throughout and have all given great support. At Blueberry River, former chief Norman Yahey, Maryann Adekat, Sandra Apsassin, and Lana Wolf have been generous with their assistance. We are deeply indebted to them and to all the Dane-zaa for sharing their lives with us over the years and for trusting us to tell their stories well.

Above all, we give thanks to our own "tribe" – our children, Karolle Wall, Diana Lynn Thompson, Michael John Thompson, Eric (Aballi) Ridington, Amber Ridington, and Juniper Ridington; our thirteen grandchildren; and our great-grandchild. Our children and our older grandchildren understand our preoccupation with this project and our commitment to the Dane-zaa. We trust that the next generations will share this understanding.

Index

Note: "(f)" after a page number indicates a figure; "(m)" after a page number indicates a table.

Aanaatswęa (Bella Attachie Yahey), 12, 120, 129, 159(f), 187,199(f), 274, 293
Aboriginal title, 223
Achla, Amos, 12
Achla, Bob, 11, 208
Acko, Akulli Davis, 184
Acko, Annie, 184
Acko, Charlotte, 184
Acko, Jack, 70, 91, 159, 249, 294, 297, 322
Acko, Ray (Acko Sr.). *See* Aku
Acko, Sam, 8, 70, 184, 299
Acko, Shirley, 133, 184
Addy, Justice, 311-14, 321-29, 332, 336, 338
Adekat, Maryann, xi, 50, 169, 369, 383, 390
Adı́shtl'íshe (Atisklise) (Dreamer), 143, 172, 210, 219, 226, 253, 276; as word for "paper or birchbark," 143-45
Aginaa, 357
agroforestry, 346
Ahatááʔ (Our Father), 13, 146
Aht'uutlętahsalats (Dog Piss on Arrow War): story, 72-75, 86-88, 357, 382, 384

Akena, 208, 210
Aki, 184, 247, 287
Akoga, 271
Aku (Acko), 9, 91, 111, 128, 133, 203, 206, 216, 238, 242, 246, 251, 252, 271, 296, 328; stories told by, 63-65, 81-86, 104-5, 106-7, 131-32, 143-48, 163-66, 216-18, 238-40, 274-75
Alaska Highway, 6, 281-82
Alberta, 234, 277
Alberta-BC border, 212, 246, 252, 277
Aledze (Gunpowder) 156, 171, 219, 260
Algonkian language family, 5
Allalie, 226
Alula, Charlie, 11
Andre, John, 384; his story of HBC killings, 126-29
anthropological literature, 1, 359-70
annuity pay lists, 222
Apąą, 1, 49, 92, 109, 206, 208, 210, 222, 226, 244, 252, 357
Appaw, Helen (Chaole), 208, 210
Appaw, Jack, 273, 320
Apsassin, Bernard, 232
Apsassin, Dan (Daniel), 232, 269, 327

Apsassin, Eddie, xi, 19-20, 46, 178, 331, 371, 383
Apsassin, Edward, 232, 269
Apsassin, Erna Harvey, 232
Apsassin, Joe, Jr., 300, 310, 331
Apsassin, Joseph (Joe Sr.), 232, 251, 262, 269, 289, 300, 319, 327
Apsassin, May Dominic, 8, 54-59, 56(f), 195, 232, 244, 283, 288, 343; stories by, 60-62, 241, 283, 285-87, 292-94
Apsassin, Nancy, 289
Apsassin, Nora, 232, 292
Apsassin, Roy, 232
Apsassin, Sandra, 343, 344
Apsassin v. The Queen, 300, 302-40, 341
Archer CRM, 68, 69
Arctic-Pacific Divide, 5
Asch, Michael, 361, 362
Askoty (Asquity). *See* Askoty, Billike
Askoty, Albert, 9, 75, 91, 199, 199(f), 210, 298, 317-20, 318(f), 384, 199
Askoty, Alice Moccasin, 9, 199, 199(f), 210, 284, 288, 297, 318(f)
Askoty, Billike, 251, 267, 270, 272, 318
Askoty, Freddy, 210, 284
Askoty, Jack (Johnny), 8, 19, 129, 210, 284, 351(f)
Askoty, Janice, 222
Atsisoke (Joe Kulea, Joe Suzuki), 210, 285, 287, 288, 329
Atsukwa. *See* Mak'íhts'ęwéswąą
Atsukwa, Ano Davis, 247
Atsukwa, Dick, 268
Atsukwa, Jack. *See* Matsííʔdak'ale
Athabasca District, 220, 306
Athapaskan language, xi, 1, 5, 72, 75, 136, 227, 359, 361-62, 369
atlatls, 68
Atluke, 274, 275(f)
Attachie, Alice Ben, 199(f), 208, 295, 315
Attachie, Bella. *See* Aanaatswęa (Bella Attachie Yahey)
Attachie, BC, 102, 346
Attachie, Billy, xi, xii(f) 1, 2, 8, 46, 46-49, 91, 126-27, 141, 202, 208, 241-43, 278, 281, 344, 347(f), 350, 360, 363, 378; as translator, 2, 12, 57, 63, 72, 75, 81, 91, 114, 124, 129, 134, 156, 163, 168, 172, 175, 178, 216, 234, 238
Attachie, Chief, 3, 102, 107, 222, 226, 252, 259, 261, 264, 267, 270, 276(f), 315, 357, 380; death, 273, 276; gravesite, 347, 347(f)
Attachie, Frank, 109, 320
Attachie, Gerry (Chief), 1, 8, 77, 126, 155, 187, 208, 212, 290-92, 291(f), 296 (f), 356; and Alaska Highway, 281; early life, 290, 294-95, 314-17; family, 208, 212; in *Montney* case, 283, 300-10, 314, 317, 329, 331-32, 340; Site C protest, 349-50, 356
Attachie, Howard, 208
Attachie, John, 320
Attachie, Margaret, 8, 159, 208, 211, 212, 243, 316
Attachie, Murray, 102, 199(f), 208, 295, 315, 328
Attachie, Narlie, 276
Attachie, Peter, 261, 263, 266, 274
Attachie, Tommy, 3, 8, 22, 56, 93(f), 100, 109, 208, 124-26, 210, 243(f), 285, 289, 293, 295, 296n, 300, 343, 347, 364, 367, 347(f); and Doig River Drummers, 343; early life, 198, 244, 246-52, 282, 285-88, 289; Duuk'ihsachę stories, 91, 113-15, 128, 295; song keeper, 62, 72, 367; stories of Dreamers, 156-59, 175-78
Attachie, Ustan (Justin), 259, 260, 266
Attachie, Wally, 208
Asusay, 182
Azáde (Liver), 143-46, 216, 222, 251

Baker, Garfield, 281
Baker, Winnis, 280(f), 281, 284
baptisms, 5, 138-42, 152, 206-7, 232, 255, 378-80; baptismal records, 206, 232
BC Hydro, 348(m)
Bear Flats, BC, 343, 346
Beaton, Frank, 132-33, 186, 215-16, 251, 257, 260, 263-64, 270, 276, 282
Beaton, Johnny, 133, 252, 324-25, 327

Beatton River (Pine River), 3, 113, 129, 255-56, 262, 266, 288-89, 291
beaver, 72, 97, 104, 106, 211, 234, 251, 264, 266; hats, 99
Beaver, Margaret, 232, 269
Beaver Indians. *See* Dane-zaa
Beaver language. *See* Dane-zaa Záágé?
Beaver River. *See* Moberly River
Beaver Tales, 2, 29, 38, 42, 51-53, 86, 173, 185, 196, 274
Ben, Alice. *See* Attachie, Alice Ben
Ben, Gary, 247
Bennett Dam, 346, 350, 361
Benson, Madeline Oker. *See* Oker Benson, Madeline
Berger, Thomas, 300-1, 303, 305, 308, 332-35, 338-39
Bible, 10-11, 13, 22, 46, 143, 150, 351, 360
Bigfoot. *See* Makenachę (Bigfoot)
Billike, Asea. *See* Askoty, Billike
bison, 3, 64, 67-70, 72, 110, 104, 110-11, 119, 215, 238, 258; extinction of 3, 68, 70, 111, 119
Blueberry River, 3, 260, 295
Blueberry River First Nation (Blueberry River Band), xi, 3, 6, 8, 11, 143, 192, 202, 207, 231, 283, 288, 300, 310, 316, 317, 339, 350, 390; Blueberry River Singers and Drummers, 343; new band hall and cultural centre, 241; reserve move, 346
Brody, Hugh, 310, 360
Broomfield, Howard, 6, 7(f), 8, 75, 346, 369
buffalo (bison) sickness (story), 70-72
buffalo scrapings boy (story), 63-66
Burford, Aidan, 69
Burley, David, 68, 106-7, 109-11, 113, 118-22, 379
Byrnes, Slim, 278-80, 279(f)

Canadian Museum of Civilization, xi, 351
cattle, 298, 298(f)
Calverly, Dorothea, 130
Cameron, Stuart, 223
Catholic church, 220, 232; Catholic ladder, 150, 366; at Doig, 7, 298; Oblate Order, 49, 136, 141, 150, 231, 364; priests, 5, 13, 38, 136-42, 191, 211, 321, 292, 294, 332, 363, 366-67
CBC, 7-8, 346
Cecil Lake, BC, 216, 239, 255, 259, 279, 284, 297
census (North West Mounted Police), 222-23, 381
Charlie Lake, 3, 11, 112, 132, 195, 230, 238-39, 258, 261, 268, 272, 274; archaeological site, 67-70
Charlie, Big, 11, 12, 215, 226, 253, 258, 259, 272, 273, 274, 278
Chedeya (Jedney), Joe, 210
Chekyass, 259, 260
Cheekyass, Alec, 286,
Cheekyass, George, 320
Cheekyass, Theresa, 286
chief and council, 1, 8, 201, 341, 359
Chikenesia. *See* Jihgenahshihlę (Chikenesia Yahey)
Chimarouche (Jimathush, Samaloose), 91, 106, 109, 122, 125, 127, 129, 206-7, 222, 244, 246, 252, 255, 281, 357, 379
Chimarouche's Prairie. *See* Rose Prairie, BC (Chimarouche's Prairie)
Chinchaga, 243
Chipesia, Aballi, 270,
Chipesia, Atohe (Ann) Montney, 255
Chipesia, George (Japasa, Ts'ibiisaa), 189, 207, 222, 251, 255-56, 263, 320, 256(f), 320
Chipesia, Harry, 222, 295, 295
Chipesia, Johnny, 9, 29, 31, 38, 42, 178, 206, 207, 254(f), 365, 378, 379; stories by, 122-24, 172-73, 174-75, 253-74, 281, 293
Chipesia, Julie, 274
Ch'one? (Old Wolf), 207, 223, 226, 232, 251, 252, 259, 274
Christianity, evangelical, 13, 148, 364
Christmas, 294, 295
Chwénalę (Precious One). *See* Muh-chueh'nalin
Cigne (the Swan chief), 107, 136, 157
Clear Hills, AB, 179, 182, 236, 251-52
Clear Prairie, AB, 245, 252, 272
Clearwater River, 251
Cleary, Patrick, 8, 141-42, 231
clovis point, 68, 69

INDEX

Confederation, 212, 219
Contact the People (documentary), 157, 353
Conroy, H.A., 228
creation story, 10-24
Cree (Dahshíne), 5, 75-78, 80, 86-87, 90, 99-100, 114, 127, 133, 140, 172, 181, 183, 202, 207, 213, 222-24, 232-33, 255, 257, 262, 266, 268, 270-71, 279, 310, 357, 361, 378
Cree-Beaver war, 99; story, 75-77
Crown. *See* Government of Canada
Cruikshank, Julie, 361, 365

Dahshíne. *See* Cree (Dahshíne)
Dane Wajich (website), xi, 6, 8, 351
Dane-zaa: knowledge, 2, 13; storytelling, 2; thought, 36
Dane-zaa nane? (the people's land), 3, 4(m), 8, 26, 68, 183, 195, 219-20, 358
Dane-zaa Záágé? (Beaver language), xii, 1, 2, 6, 8, 10, 12, 13, 70, 136, 198, 202, 224, 251, 289, 296, 300, 318, 340, 350, 351, 360
Danezaa Záágé?-English dictionary. *See* Doig River First Nation, dictionary
Davies, Marguerite, 276, 278, 288
Davis, Ano Atsukwa, 247n, 268-69, 269(f)
Davis, Darlene Harvey, 208
Davis, David, 330
Davis, Dick, 159, 247, 298
Davis (Jebís), 222, 242, 247, 252, 270, 272-73, 272(f)
Davis, John, 9, 222, 247, 259, 270-71, 272(f), 295, 297, 315, 320-29, 325(f), 343, 363
Davis, Kelvin (Chief), 207-8, 210
Davis, Madeline Sagónáá?, 8, 51, 178, 181, 208, 210, 244, 247, 296-97
Davis, Margaret Dominic, xi, 8, 146, 201, 296, 297; translations by, 46-47, 104-5, 131-32, 146-48, 149, 160
Davis, Marguerite Yahey, 9, 50, 169, 169(f), 208
Davis, Mary Dominic (Daeda) Davis, 9
Davis, Norman (Chief), 8, 43, 304(f), 349, 355-56

Davis, Pete, 320
Davis, Tommy, 29(f), 249
Davis, Twelve Foot, 130-32
Dawson Creek, BC, 211, 282
Dechezhę (Detchiyay, Tagea, Tachea), 80, 95, 185, 207-8, 210, 212, 216, 223, 226, 344, 357
Decuthla, 150
Department of Indian Affairs and Northern Development (DIA), 220, 253, 282, 297, 302, 303, 303-8, 333, 335, 338
Department of the Interior, 306
Department of Veterans Affairs, 303. *See also* Veterans' Land Act
des Groseilliers, 97-98
discourse, highly contexted, 3, 311, 320, 330, 337
"doctors of magic," 140-41
Dog Piss on Arrow War. *See* Aht'uutlętahsalats (Dog Piss on Arrow War)
Doig River (Raft River [Hanás Saahgé?]), 3, 211-12, 274, 275, 295
Doig River First Nation, xi, 3,172, 289, 298, 339, 355; Agroforesty program, 346; band hall and cultural centre, 341, 342(f), 345(f); chief and council, 1, 8, 201(f), 307, 359; dictionary, xii, 351; Doig Days, 350; history of, 2, 346-47, 360; Doig River Drummers, 343; farming at, 298; rodeo, 344
Dokie, Old Man, 173
Dominic, Charlie, 9, 46, 54, 60(f), 195, 208, 265, 282-83, 294, 295; vision quest of, 60-62
Dominic, Renee, 296(f)
Dominic, Tommy, 298
Dreamers, 2, 5, 9, 12, 26, 125, 140, 144, 146, 155, 219; Dreamers'songs, 150-53, 170-71
Dunvegan, AB (Fort Dunvegan), 109, 113, 114, 118, 122, 129-31, 136, 175, 186, 252, 268, 359
Duuk'ihsachę, 43-44, 80, 113-14, 126-28, 163, 172, 185, 206, 207, 223, 240, 246, 357, 361, 370; stories about, 81-86, 91-96, 114-18
Duuk'ihsachę Mataa?, 80, 142; story about, 80-86

395

education. *See* school
Emily Carr College of Art and Design, 351
Eskama (Mary Ann Acko), 70, 71(f), 159, 378
Eureka River, AB, 183, 185

family allowance payments, 290, 295, 297
Faraud, Henri, 49, 52, 136-42
Faries, Hugh, 109, 119-21, 127, 129
farmers, 5, 4, 69, 133, 187, 247-48, 282-83, 292, 295, 303, 305, 307, 309, 332, 346, 349
Farvacque, Remi, 69, 70
Federal Court of Appeal, 300, 333
Feit, Harvey, 361
fiduciary duty, 332, 333, 335, 337, 338, 339
Finley, Fiona, 122
Fish Creek, 255-56, 258, 260, 284, 323
Fladmark, Knut, 68, 106-7, 109-11, 113, 118-22, 379
Flynn, Simon, 297
Fort Chipewyan, 100
Fort St. John (city), 5, 7, 11-12, 69, 104, 211, 238, 246, 282, 298-99, 303, 305, 315, 332, 337, 341-44, 355, 357, 360
Fort St. John (fur trade fort), 80, 113, 118-22, 129, 130, 132, 135-36, 139, 141, 175, 211, 220-21, 224, 253, 255, 359
Fort St. John Beaver Band, xi, 3, 8, 11, 19, 100, 107, 132, 185, 187-88, 197, 202, 206-7, 210, 220, 222-31, 233, 238, 244, 251-53, 255, 260, 280, 284, 290, 302-3, 307-9, 320, 334-37, 339-40, 350, 380
Fort St. John massacre, 119-29
Fort Vermilion, AB (Tsiih Kwąh), 5, 99, 113, 115, 117, 134, 175, 237, 240
fur trade, 69, 75, 86, 91, 95, 97-135, 139, 156, 157, 159, 163, 166, 171, 211, 219, 221, 240, 279, 355, 357, 360, 365, 369
fur trade journals, 90-91, 109, 119, 120-22, 126, 132-33, 172, 186, 206, 207, 215-16, 232, 244, 251-52, 263, 276, 379-80
fur traders, 3, 5-6, 96, 105-6, 133, 137, 163, 219, 241, 279, 322

Galibois, Joe ("small Indian boss"), 283, 290, 296, 297, 298, 319, 320, 323-27, 329, 330
gambling, 137, 139, 141, 142. *See also* hand game
game keepers, 47, 48, 53, 54, 63, 150, 152, 365
game wardens, 246, 271
Gattah Kwąh (Fort St. John area), 104, 118, 127, 130-31, 206
Gayęa, 22, 168, 181, 183-87, 272
genealogy, 8, 133, 142, 202, 206, 222, 231-33, 320
giant animals, 16, 43-44, 47, 66, 67; grease from, 143, 299, 306, 344, stories about, 27-29, 38-43, 53-54, 57-58, 62-64, 80-86, 91-95, 167, 376
Glacial Lake Peace, 68
Goddard, Pliny Earl, 359
Godsell, Philip, 142
Goodjohn, Mitchell, 8, 141, 231
Goodlow, BC, 247, 248, 286, 291
Gonthier, Justice, 337, 339
Goulet, Jean-Guy, 152, 195, 337, 361-64
Government of Canada, iv, 220-21, 223, 225-27, 229, 302, 305, 333, 335, 338-39
Grande Prairie, AB, 100, 132, 238, 240, 252
Gurein v. The Queen, 310
Grew, John, 303, 319, 320, 327

habitat, 3, 68, 70, 110, 252, 258, 349
Haig, J.R., 320, 330-31
Halfway River, 103(f), 258, 267, 276, 347, 349
Halfway River Band, 11-12, 114, 172, 186-88, 190, 208, 230, 232, 242, 271, 341, 360-61; Halfway River Singers, 143
Hamilton, Scott, 68, 106-7, 109-11, 113, 118-22, 379
hand game, 137-39, 142

Hargus, Sharon, 360
Harvey, Erna. *See* Apsassin, Erna Harvey
Harvey, Khatakose, 208, 210, 213, 233, 257, 257(f), 266, 269, 273, 361, 378
Hay Lake, AB, 194-95, 236, 266
Hay River, AB, 234, 263, 265
heaven: animals flying to, 26-27, 30; description of, 148, 191-98; dreaming to, 16-17, 143, 146-55, 163, 175, 177-78, 180, 187-89, 379; trail to, 26, 60, 148-51, 157, 260, 352
Helm, June, 227-28, 361
Hennessy, Kate, xi, 6, 8, 302, 304, 331, 351, 360
Heron, Francis, 121-22, 126
High Level, AB, 114-16, 125, 237
Holdstock, Jean, xi-xii, 2, 350, 360
Holdstock, Marshall, xi-xii, 2, 298, 350, 360
Holmes, H.R., 334
Honigmann, John, 361
horses, 248, 258, 266, 271, 278-80, 284, 286, 290, 295
Hudson's Bay Company, 86, 88-90, 98, 113-36, 164, 172, 175, 206-7, 215, 220, 225, 232, 244, 251-52, 258, 261-62, 264, 266-67, 270, 282
Hudson's Bay Company post journals. *See* fur trade journals
Hudson's Hope, BC, 113, 124, 131, 261
Hudson's Hope Band, 229
Hughes, Guy, 121-22
hunt chiefs, 9, 142, 147, 157, 162
Hunter, Antoine, 149
Hunter, Thomas, 12
hunters, 5, 22, 45, 67, 69, 99, 101, 104, 110, 112, 120-22, 133, 135-36, 145, 151, 159, 162, 165, 197-98, 200, 215, 234, 240, 253, 268, 275, 295, 308; relationship to animals, 45-46; techniques, 68; women 212-13
hunting and fishing rights, 224

Indian Act, 335, 337
Indian agents, 147, 222, 229, 283, 289, 290, 293, 298, 309, 313, 323-24, 337. *See also* Galibois, Joe ("small Indian boss")
Innis, Harold, 99, 104
Isaacs, Chief Justice, 333
Ives, John, 362

Japasa (Jib-ba-jay, Ts'ibiisaa). *See* George Chipesia (Japasa, Ts'ibiisaa)
Jedney, 328
Jedney, Joe, 328
Jenness, Diamond, 360
Jesus, 38, 147-49, 155, 165
Jihgenahshihlę (Chikenesia Yahey), 11-12, 208
Johnston-Watson, C.S. (Johnny Watson), 309, 337
Jumbie, Augustine, 9, 12, 86-87, 90-91, 129, 150, 172-73, 187-88, 228-29, 295
Jumbie, Fred, 295
Jumbie, Marguerite, 186(f), 187
Jungen, Brian, 351-52, 353(f)

K'ih tsaa?dze Tribal Park, 355-57, 356(m)
King, Thomas, 367-68
kinship, 197-218; chart, 377; terms, 198, 202-6, 362
Kitto, F.L. 306
Klondike, 219-21
Kulea, Joe. *See* Atsisoke (Joe Kulea, Joe Suzuki)
Kyllo, Edith, 276, 278, 288

Laird, David, 229-30
Lake, Terry, 357
Lake Athabasca, 5, 75, 100
Lesser Slave Lake, 99, 224-25
Limitation Act (BC), 333, 335, 337
L'Homme Seul (Man Alone, Mazo), 107, 109, 113-14, 118, 127-28, 240, 246
land claims, 6
Lanoue, Guy, 360, 366
Leacock, Eleanor, 361
Lhuuge Lęą (suckerfish people), 3, 5, 8, 202, 206, 230, 258, 265, 283, 361
Logan, Liz (Chief), 349-50

Mackenzie, Alexander, 3, 5, 72, 75, 77, 99-103, 110, 119, 343, 346
Mackenzie Valley Pipeline Inquiry, 227, 364
Madaayęą-ta, 129
Madaayęą (Chief Montney), 109, 125-26, 128-29, 206-7, 210, 253, 255, 258, 262-73
Madill, Dennis, 220-21, 223-24, 228, 306
Makadahay, Billy, 222, 288, 294, 298, 344, 357, 378
Makadahay, Felix (Muckithay), 222, 276, 288, 357
Makadahay, Rita, 344
Makadahay, Sally Takola, 9, 11, 159, 284-85, 285(f), 289, 298, 344
Makadahay, Trevor, 344
Makenachę (Bigfoot), 91, 228
Mak'íhts'ęwéswąą (Atsukwa), 59, 142, 146, 156, 166, 171-83, 185, 194-95, 263, 357, 365
Malla (Molly), 183-85
Mandell, Louise, 307-8, 309, 310
Maranda, 122, 125-26, 129, 206
Marceau, Judge Louis, 333
Mason, John, 361
Matsíí?dak'ale (White Head, Jack Atsukwa), 59, 172
Mazo. *See* L'Homme Seul
McCormack, Patricia, 70
McGill, Howard, 303
McLachlin, Chief Justice Beverly, 332, 335, 337n, 338
McLeod Lake, BC, 113, 131, 125-26
McLeod Lake Sekani, 174, 347, 361, 347
McRae, Commissioner J.A., 227
McWilliams, A.F., 334,
medicine bundle, 144
medicine power, 12, 49, 51, 64, 86, 100, 115, 139, 140-42, 144, 366. *See also* Shin kaa
Mehuu, 173
Mekénú únatane, 142, 146, 156-57, 159-66, 168, 171-72, 175-76, 186, 357
menstruation, first, 200
Miller, George, 284, 285-86, 327, 329
Miller, Julia, xi-xii, 360

Milligan Creek, 284, 289; fire, 284-88
Mills, Antonia, 6, 152, 360, 363
mineral rights, 303, 304, 307-8, 334, 335, 387-88
miners, 221, 225, 302
Ministry of Family and Children's Services, 343
Moberly Lake, 172-73, 211, 223, 229, 260, 270, 293
Moberly River, 103, 121, 349
Moccasin, Alice. *See* Askoty, Alice
Moccasin, Meka, 208, 210
moccasins, 61, 179, 201(f), 247, 265, 291-92
Modeste, Charlie, 268
Modeste (Mudis), 267, 319
Montney, BC, 133, 183, 186-87, 207, 230, 255, 260, 273, 279, 283, 306
Montney case. *See Apsassin v. The Queen*
Montney, Chief (mutain, Monagin, Madaayęą), 109, 206-7, 210, 222, 226, 253, 255, 257, 262, 263, 265, 270, 272, 273
Montney reserve. *See* Su Na chii k'chige (Place Where Happiness Dwells)
Moodie, J.D., 221
Moore, Patrick, xi-xii, 19, 195, 360-61, 363, 371
Moose Creek, 242-43, 286, 323
Mosquito, Billy, 319, 327, 328-29
Muckithay. *See* Makadahay, Felix
Muh-chueh'nalin, 208, 285
muskeg, 3, 54, 68, 72, 85, 256-57, 272, 300
Muskeg people. *See* Ts'ibe Dané? (Muskeg people)
Muskrat (Chehk'aa), 10-11, 20, 24, 33, 45, 67, 112, 295, 372-73

Nááchęą (John Notseta), 189
Naataazhiih, 100
Nachę (Mary Pouce Coupe), 1, 9, 133-34, 141, 206, 209(f), 217, 222, 234-35, 235(f), 244, 252, 265, 283, 287, 294, 295, 309, 315-16; marriages of, 208-10, 362; stories told by, 49-53, 91-95, 167, 210-15
Napoleon, Nora. *See* Apsassin, Nora

Natane (Thunderbird), 178-81
Nedoęslhiine (French/Metis traders), 124-28
Nelson, Gary, 332
Nenan Dane-zaa Deh Zonah, 343-44, 343(f)
New Caledonia, 113, 119-20
North West Company (NWC), 3, 75, 80, 86, 89, 98, 99, 113, 118, 119, 175. *See also* fur trade journals
North West Mounted Police (NWMP), 80, 207, 221. *See also* census (North West Mounted Police)

oil and gas industry, 5, 29, 67, 247, 283, 299-300, 306, 308, 336, 338-39, 344, 346; monitors, 344
Oldman, Juliet (Wanaii), 59, 232
Olla, Margaret, 293
Oker, 185, 208, 210, 216, 223, 284, 287, 288, 319, 352, 378-79
Oker, Alice. *See* Askoty, Alice
Oker, Annie, 208, 284
Oker, Garry (Chief), 13, 44, 195, 208, 343, 345(f), 352, 354, 357, 378
Oker Benson, Madeline, xi, 91, 114, 124, 168, 210, 351, 356, 369
Okimakin. *See* Yehlhézęh
Olah, 208
Ong, Walter, 366-67
oral history, 1, 99, 206, 232, 252, 357, 359
Otter Man's prophesy, 195

Pape, Art, 312-14, 317-20, 322-32
Parsnip River, 75
Peace River, 3, 67-68, 70, 72, 90, 100, 103, 103(f), 110-11, 125, 131-32, 270, 277, 306, 344, 347, 349, 349; country, 97, 99, 102, 104, 133, 197, 220-22, 244, 277-78, 281-82, 306, 344; First Nations, 70, 75, 99, 136, 225, 347, 361; historians, 130, 379; resources, 3, 67-72, 104, 110-11, 119, 122, 215, 238
Peace River, Alberta, 246, 255, 262-63, 282; Peace River Block, 229-30
Peace River Portage, 113

pemmican, 104, 110-11, 240
Petersen's Crossing, 234, 241, 245, 284, 287-92, 294-300, 303-5, 307, 317, 323, 328
Petersen, Ernie, 243, 289, 316, 327
petroleum reserves. *See* oil and gas industry
Pinder, Leslie, 307-8, 310-11, 314-17, 332
Pine River Reserve. *See* Su Na chii k'chige (Place Where Happiness Dwells)
Pink Mountain, 262, 268, 343
Place Where Happiness Dwells. *See* Su Na chii k'chige (Place Where Happiness Dwells)
Pond, Peter, 5, 99
Pouce Coupe, BC, 267, 271
Pouce Coupe, Carl, 346, 352
Pouce Coupe, Jimmy, 298
Pouce Coupe, John, 208
Pouce Coupe, Lena, 292
Pouce Coupe, Mary. *See* Nachę
Pouce Coupe, Thomas (Pouscoopee), 222, 226, 251-52, 256, 275, 285, 294
Pine River. *See* Beatton River
Pine View Reserve. *See* Su Na chii k'chige (Place Where Happiness Dwells)
pioneers. *See* settlers
pronunciation guide, xiii
Prophet River, 11-12, 91, 150, 190, 192, 305, 341, 347
prospectors, 219, 274

Radisson, 97-98
Raft River. *See* Doig River
reincarnation, 152, 360, 363-64
relationship to animals, 45-46, 197-98, 219
reserves: allocation of, 229
Revillon Frères, 132
Ridington Dane-zaa Archive, xi, 8, 9, 11, 341, 346
Ridington, Amber, xi, 6-8, 133, 296, 302, 304, 325, 331, 351, 360, 369
Ridington, Eric, 6
Ridington, Jillian, 7(f), 48, 103, 137, 195, 201, 284-85, 291-92, 298,

342, 345-47, 351-52, 362, 364, 368; genealogies, 142, 206, 223, 231; learning from Dane-zaa, 6-8
Ridington, Robin, 7(f); academic papers of, 362, 364, 366; *Apsassin* case, 310-12, 317, 320-21, 329, 37; dissertation, 364, genealogies, 142, 206, 223, 231; Johnny Beaton interview, 251; learning from Dane-zaa, 2, 6-8, 31, 38, 42, 122-23, 172, 206
Robertson, Donald F., 229
Robinson, Harry, 368
Rocky Mountain Fort, 6, 103, 106-7, 110-13, 118-19, 121, 129, 157
Rocky Mountain Portage House, 113, 119
Rose Prairie, BC (Chimarouche's Prairie), 131, 207, 244, 252, 260-61, 265-66, 268, 279, 289, 292, 299, 316, 379
Rose Prairie School, 288
Rothlesberger, Wes, 344
Rupert's Land, 98(m)

Sagónáá? (Succona, Sakona), Chief, 108(f), 186, 207, 303-5, 323-29, 379
Succona, George, 247, 295, 297
Succona, Madeline. *See* Davis, Madeline Sagónáá?
Sall, Nora, 307
Samaloose. *See* Chimarouche (Jimathush, Samaloose)
seasonal rounds, 3, 69, 197, 230, 234-52, 253, 255, 283, 308
Saulteau, 140, 223, 229, 270
Sawe (Mrs. Jumbie), 12, 187
school, 190, 294-95, 297-300, 307, 337, 350-51; attendance, 6, 245, 287-89, 290-94, 299, 316, 322, 350, 355, 363
Scott, Colin, 361
seismic lines, 6, 247, 281, 295, 344
Sekani, Chief. *See* Makenachę (Bigfoot)
Sekani (Slaves, Tsegenu), 75, 86, 95, 119, 221, 228, 360-61, 366; conflict with Beaver, 77-80, 100, 113; Sekani (Sikanni) Chief River, 163

Seniantha, Alexis, 195, 363
settlers, 6, 3, 181, 207, 229, 233, 277-78, 283, 298, 302-3, 312, 342, 349
Shin kaa, 29, 82, 45-66, 86, 93-94, 146, 214, 218, 365. *See also* vision quests
Silva Ecosystems, 355-56
Site C dam, 103(f), 346-50, 348(m)
Skookum, Mrs. (Amaa), 12, 186(f), 187-90
Sky Keeper. *See* Yaak'ih Sade (Sky Keeper)
Slade, Harry, 300-1
Slavey, 5, 86, 136, 361-62
Slyman, M., 133
Spanish flu, 253, 262, 272-76
Speck, Frank, 361
Spirit River, AB, 251, 253-55, 259, 262-63, 273-74
St. Pierre, Sam, 9, 161, 293
Stoney, Saviour, 298
Storrs, Monica, 278
Su Na chii k'chige (Place Where Happiness Dwells), 1, 180, 183, 185-87, 195, 197, 207, 229-30, 239, 262, 300-1; surrender of 305, 313. See also *Apsassin v. The Queen*
Supreme Court of Canada, 300-1, 306, 331-33, 335, 337
Suzuki, David, 347
Swan (boy). *See* Tsááyaa (culture hero)
swans, 18, 24-27, 29-30, 35, 107, 156-58
Sweeney Creek, AB (McLean Creek, Chuu Degaazhih), 185, 241, 244, 249, 252, 285-86, 291, 299, 250(m)

Tagea (Tachea). *See* Dechezhę (Detchiyay, Tagea, Tachea)
Taylor, BC, 103
tea dance, 245, 280, 284, 319
Tedlock, Dennis, 366
Thomas, Napoleon, 232, 259, 260
Thunderbird. *See* Natane
Tl'ok'ih Náázat (Standing on the Prairie), 19, 208, 210
Tompkins, Bill, 346
trade networks, 69, 98

INDEX

trapping, 3, 106, 120, 133, 135, 144, 183, 216, 220, 223, 225-29, 245-46, 252, 271, 278, 295, 297-98, 318, 320, 325-26, 346, 361
Treaty 8, 143, 197, 206, 212, 219-33, 306, 357, 361; Jumbie's story of treaty, 228; treaty commission, 132, 224, 288; treaty land entitlement, 133, 142; treaty rights, 246, 271, 278, 288, 298, 303, 323, 344, 347, 349, 355; treaty signers, 172, 222-23, 226, 350, 357, 364, 378-80
Treaty 8 Tribal Association, 347, 349, 356(m)
trickster, 42-43
trust funds, 6
Tsááyaa (culture hero), 16, 47, 53, 62-64, 66, 83, 86, 142, 156-57, 167, 219, 306, 352-53
Tseguude (cannibal monster), 172-75
Tse saǫ, 100
Tset'ehkwą̂h (Hudson's Hope), 131
Ts'ibe Dané? (Muskeg people), 5, 95, 114, 202, 206, 210, 258, 265, 274, 283-84
Ts'ibiisaa. *See* Chipesia, George

UBC, 305, 310, 332
Union of BC Indian Chiefs (UBCIC), 309-10
Upper Pine School, 290, 299, 350
Usulets. *See* Big Charlie

Ventress, Cora, 276, 278, 288
veterans, 231, 282, 303, 307-8, 310, 313-14, 332-33, 334-36, 338-39
Veterans' Land Act, 313, 314, 332, 334, 335, 338
Virtual Museum of Canada, 360
vision quests, 34, 140, 144-46, 214, 218, 365. *See also* Shin kaa
voyageurs, 125, 127-28, 136
wagons, 295
Wasage (Crying Man), 175-76
Watson, Johnny. See Johnston-Watson, C.S. (Johnny Watson)
wehch'uuge, 62-66, 172
Weir, Lorraine, 305
weirs, 261
West Moberly First Nation, 347

Wheelock, Angela, 195, 361, 363
Wickwire, Wendy, 368-69
Winchester rifle, 175
wise stories, 1, 9, 46-47, 53, 60, 69, 112, 208, 340, 355, 358, 363, 365
Wokely, Ruby, 188*n*
Wolf, Dan, 273, 285, 298, 328
Wolf, Jack, 293, 320
Wolf, Lana, xi, 1, 50, 169, 317, 321, 330, 350, 369
Wolf, Liza, xi, 51, 86, 187, 189, 274
Wolf, Margaret, 293, 320
Wolf, Marguerite (Margie), 9, 57-59
Wolf, Old. *See* Ch'one?
Wolf, Ralph, 293
Wǫlii Nachii, 27-28, 36-40, 81-86, 92-95, 116, 100
wolverine, 3, 17, 28, 195, 363
Wonla (Douya), 265
World War I, 253
World War II, 233, 253, 282, 336
Worsely, AB, 292
Wuskullie (Wuskula), 223

Yaaetsííghadah (He Who Touches the Sky), 39-40
Yaak'ih Sade (Sky Keeper), 10, 13, 26-30, 33, 43, 67
yaak'ihts'e? atanii (trail to heaven), 1, 143, 146, 147, 189, 197
Yahey, Charlie, 9, 22, 23(f), 46-47, 105 (f), 156, 159(f), 195-96, 199(f), 293, 320, 328; family 11, 59-60, 102, 169, 187, 190-91, 208, 210, 319; Gayęą as teacher, 185-86, 185, 186, 187-95, 199; creation story, 10-24, 196; culture hero story, 25-44; Dreamer's drum, 22, 23(f); knowing through dreaming, 13, 47, 140, 150-52; power and prophecy, 143-44, 161, 166; stories about, 91, 155, 169-71, 274, 286, 187, 190, 193-94; talking about heaven, 191-96
Yahey, John, 208, 210, 320
Yahey, Norman, 210, 390
Yahey singers, 143
Yakatchie, 226, 380
Yatsoose, 226, 380
Yehlhézęh, Atahin, 60, 208

Yehlhézęh, (Muskeg Chief, Okimaken), 80, 95, 128, 172, 207-8, 212, 223, 226, 236, 253, 265-66; family, 50, 60, 80, 95, 128, 172, 207-8, 223; Yehlhézęh band, 210-12, 215, 234, 236, 253, 265-66, 273-75, 284, 362, 381

Yehlhézęh Watchize, 208

Yukon, 302, 349, 365